THE BIG CON

THE BIG CON

GREAT HOAXES, FRAUDS, GRIFTS, AND SWINDLES IN AMERICAN HISTORY

Nate Hendley

ABC-CLIO™

An Imprint of ABC-CLIO, LLC
Santa Barbara, California • Denver, Colorado

Library of Congress Cataloging-in-Publication Data
Names: Hendley, Nate, author.
Title: The big con : great hoaxes, frauds, grifts, and swindles in American
    history / Nate Hendley.
Description: Santa Barbara, California : ABC-CLIO, 2016. | Includes
    bibliographical references and index.
Identifiers: LCCN 2016007741 | ISBN 9781610695855 (hardback) |
    ISBN 9781610695862 (ebook)
Subjects: LCSH: Swindlers and swindling—United States—History. |
    Hoaxes—United States—History. | Fraud—United States—History. | BISAC:
    LAW / General. | TRUE CRIME / General.
Classification: LCC HV6695 .H46 2016 | DDC 364.16/30973—dc23 LC record
available at http://lccn.loc.gov/2016007741

ISBN: 978-1-61069-585-5
EISBN: 978-1-61069-586-2

20 19 18 17 16   1 2 3 4 5

This book is also available as an eBook.

ABC-CLIO
An Imprint of ABC-CLIO, LLC

ABC-CLIO, LLC
130 Cremona Drive, P.O. Box 1911
Santa Barbara, California 93116-1911
www.abc-clio.com

This book is printed on acid-free paper ∞

Manufactured in the United States of America

This book is dedicated to whistleblowers
and skeptics everywhere.

Contents

Section Two
Business Fraud

Section Three
Despicable Scams

Section Four

Great Pretenders

Section Five

Hoaxes, Urban Legends, and Popular Delusions

Section Eleven

Interviews

Acknowledgments

I wish to thank my girlfriend, Jeanne Enright, for her research assistance, patience, love, and support. Also, thanks to ABC-CLIO for asking me to write this book and encouraging me through the whole editorial process.

Introduction

The term "confidence man" allegedly originates from the acts of one William Thompson, an 1840s-era swindler in New York City. Thompson's game was to dress himself in respectable clothes and then saunter up to well-to-do strangers and engage them in conversation. At some point, Thompson would invariably ask his new companions if they had the *confidence* to lend him their watch for a day. If newspaper accounts are to be believed, many people did indeed lend him their watches, out of some sense of misguided Victorian courtesy. Thompson, needless to say, never returned the timepieces.

Upon Thompson's arrest, newspaper reporters referred to him as the "Confidence Man," and soon the terms "con" and "con artist" to denote respectively, a scam and a scammer, entered the popular lexicon.

It is instructive to know that there was a real person named Ponzi—Charles Ponzi to be precise. He was a smooth Boston entrepreneur in the 1920s, who claimed he could generate fabulous returns for investors based on buying and selling international postal coupons. In truth, few coupons were being purchased. All Ponzi did was take money from new investors and give it to old investors. Once the press caught on, new investors stopped investing, and Ponzi's scheme collapsed. His "robbing Peter to pay Paul" scam has been immortalized as "a Ponzi scheme."

Interestingly enough, Ponzi looked like a minnow compared to Leo Koretz, a corrupt Chicago lawyer who stole far more money than Ponzi ever did, at roughly the same time. While Ponzi's empire lasted only a few months, Koretz enticed gullible investors for years with wild talk about oil wells and timber farms in Panama. In truth, he had no holdings but, like Ponzi, merely recirculated investors' cash.

When a group of investors decided to visit Panama to check out Koretz's fabulous business domain, Koretz bade them farewell, then went into hiding. It is only a fluke of history that Ponzi's name became synonymous with financial fraud while Koretz was largely forgotten until recently. Koretz's story is detailed in this book. Also included is an in-depth interview with the author who brought Leo Koretz back from obscurity.

In researching this book, I discovered that some contemporary scams have deep roots. Take, for example, the so-called "Nigerian letter." This is a missive, usually sent in the form of an e-mail, in which a person claims to be both fabulously wealthy and unfairly imprisoned. Because the writer is in jail, he can't access his fortune. He needs someone on the outside to assist him in bribing the proper authorities so he can be released. Once released, the letter writer will gladly share his fortune with whoever was kind enough to help him. The notes always include an e-mail or postal address where the recipient can send money, to defray the necessary costs of bribery.

Many of these notes originate in Nigeria. This is in part because Nigeria has a huge population of well-educated but unemployed people who speak English. As it turns out, however, the Nigerian letter is based on a much older scam called "The Spanish Prisoner," which can be traced back to the Victorian era. The basis of the original scam was almost exactly the same, except the writer was usually being held in a Spanish prison, for unclear reasons.

This book also looks at cases of fraud that aren't business-oriented. Some of these frauds are amusing and relatively harmless—readers will learn of Al Capone's older brother James, who abandoned his family to assume a new name and persona out West as a two-fisted lawman. Other frauds are alarming and potentially dangerous, like the case of Dr. John Brinkley, a medical quack who tried to boost men's virility by transplanting goat testicles into human scrotums. You read that correctly. It's a measure of male vanity and credulity that Brinkley became hugely wealthy from such procedures. Along the way he also became a pioneer in commercial radio and helped popularize country music.

I've tried to explore new angles in much-covered stories and personalities. I discovered, for example, that master showman and huckster P. T. Barnum served as a Connecticut legislator during his career.

The book also looks at contemporary computer-based scourges such as phishing, vishing, spam e-mail, and malware. Included is the strange tale of the wealthy, elderly academic who was duped into being an unwitting drug courier after meeting a voluptuous young lady on an Internet dating site.

The chapter on "Para-Abnormal" examines supernatural fraud, from the Fox sisters (nineteenth-century "rap stars" who used their toe joints to simulate ghostly communications) to government investigations of "remote viewing"— that is, telepathy and clairvoyance. A section on pop culture examines the depiction of con artists and confidence schemes in films such as *The Sting*, *Argo*, and *American Hustle*, among others. I also look at the myth of subliminal messaging.

I've included interviews with four experts on "flimflam," James Randi's term for fraudulent activity. Randi is a celebrated magician and escape artist, turned skeptic of all things paranormal. He is one of the four subjects interviewed in the appendices, offering an insider's view of exposing fake psychics and faith healers. Another interview subject was the legendary Alan Abel, who masterminded some of the most amusing media hoaxes of the past few decades. These included a protest group that wanted to dress animals in clothes and a school that taught lessons on successful begging techniques.

Abel makes an appearance because this book examines hoaxes as well as swindles and cons. Some of the hoaxes covered date back as far as the 1830s (the Great Moon Hoax), while others are of more recent vintage. The entry on "Daycare Devils" discusses the strange panic in the 1980s that daycare centers had been infiltrated by child-abusing Satanists who loved torturing toddlers in highly creative ways. Ridiculous as this may sound today, several daycare operators were accused of serious crimes and spent years behind bars on extremely flimsy evidence. Now, it seems clear there was no demonic activity and that the public had fallen prey to a grand delusion.

Other hoaxes examined look at urban legends about drugs (did a group of LSD-addled hippies really stare at the sun until they went blind?) and evil nonsense like the Protocols of the Learned Elders of Zion. The latter, likely a forgery by Tsarist secret police, accused Jewish people of all manner of calumny. The Protocols have been used by bigots around the world to justify anti-Semitism. Excerpts from the Protocols were published in America by none other than auto mogul Henry Ford.

Whether the confidence artists covered in this book are modern hucksters such as Bernie Madoff, or the slick, fast-talking sharpies described by academic researcher David Maurer, I tried to keep an important fact in mind. Con artists are not the loveable rascals often portrayed by the popular media, but criminal predators who victimize real people.

Some of the historical cons detailed in this book would be difficult to pull off today, largely because of modern technology. It would be almost impossible, for example, for a Leo Koretz-like character to claim he possessed huge tracts of land in Panama, when people can easily check for themselves online.

That said, natural human greed ensures that many scams stay evergreen, while human credulity means many people will continue to embrace nonsensical ideas. Just as the Spanish Prisoner con mutated into the Nigerian Letter scam, Ponzi and pyramid schemes are still with us today. No doubt these schemes will continue to flourish as long as people remain both greedy and credulous.

Nate Hendley
Toronto, January 2016

SECTION ONE
CLASSIC CONS

INTRODUCTION

David Maurer was a professor of linguistics at the University of Louisville who investigated the world of con artists for a fascinating book published in 1940. Maurer's *The Big Con: The Story of the Confidence Man* introduced readers to the peculiar lingo, mannerisms, attitude, and philosophy of so-called "confidence men." The latter are simply people who try to scam other people out of their money in an illegal fashion. "The methods by which I collected my material were not in any way bizarre or unusual ... I simply talked to confidence men, who, little by little, supplied the necessary facts, facts which were not available in libraries or in police records, facts which could come only from the criminals themselves," explained Maurer, in the introduction to his book.

The Big Con took a perceptive look at the activities of con artists across the United States. The focus was on what Maurer referred to as "the golden age" of major cons, a period that ran from the turn of the twentieth century until the Great Depression. This era saw the unprecedented rise in prosperity of the upper middle classes and featured frantic investment in the stock market. It was the perfect environment in which con artists could flourish. The advent of the Depression spelled the end of the "golden age" of the con, as there were fewer wealthy people to scam.

While *The Big Con* might seem like ancient history, the modes and methods of confidence artists haven't changed much over the decades. Any contemporary criminologist reading Maurer's work would certainly find much that would be familiar. The specific rackets and scams might be different, but the modus operandi of the con man—find a dupe, scam the dupe—remains exactly the same.

As Maurer made clear, the con artist was something of a breed apart. "Confidence men are not 'crooks' in the ordinary sense of the word. They are suave, slick and capable. Their depredations are very much on the genteel side," wrote Maurer.

Maurer added, "Although the confidence man is sometimes classed with professional thieves, pickpockets and gamblers, he is not really a thief at all because he does no actual stealing. The trusting victim literally thrusts a fat bank roll into his hands. It is a point of pride with him that he does not have to steal."

According to Maurer, the con man's secret weapon is the inherent dishonesty of his victims. A good con is leveraged on greed: a victim or "mark" thinks he is being introduced to a somewhat shady (or downright criminal) method of making some quick cash. Essentially, con artists make the victim a criminal accomplice to whatever scheme or scam they're pulling. This helps explain why victims of cons are often reluctant to contact authorities.

Strong moral integrity and a refusal to take part in "get rich quick" schemes are two excellent ways to avoid being conned. "You can't cheat an honest man," noted Maurer.

In suitably academic fashion, Maurer broke down the world of the con man into various components. Financial scams can be divided between "short cons" and "big cons," he explained. A short con is a scam that takes a victim for all the money he has on his person. Maurer cites rigged card, dice, or coin tossing games as examples of short cons. These scams are quick in duration and generally don't involve substantial sums of money (unless the victim in question happens to be carrying a briefcase full of cash).

A big con is a much more elaborate play that might take days or even weeks to unfold. Big cons can involve dozens of con artists and their helpers, all playing different roles. The two most important figures in a big con are "the roper," or "outside man," and the "inside man." The roper seeks out victims. At the time Maurer wrote his book, trains and cruise ships were two of the best feeding grounds for ropers on the prowl. Long-distance car and air travel was still rare in the early twentieth century, so rich folks taking long journeys often opted for the train. Luxury cruise ships, of course, also presented a cornucopia of potential victims.

Ropers tended to be cosmopolitan (they travelled a lot and were well versed in the history and geography of cities and towns across the country), good company (all the better to gain the victim's confidence), excellent listeners (a good con artist waits for the victim to express a religious, political, or social viewpoint, then pretends to share that same opinion), and inventive.

A skilled roper has to estimate the wealth of a potential victim in an unobtrusive way. The roper does this through the power of observation and by asking seemingly innocent questions about the dupe's job, neighborhood, hobbies ("Oh, you play golf? Me too. You play at the Ritz Golf Club, huh? Very exclusive"), and vehicles ("So, you're a three-car man? I get by with only one"). The roper pays close attention to how the dupe dresses, speaks, and handles money.

The roper also needs to know whether a dupe is willing to go along with his con. A dupe who seems rigidly puritanical or religious is unlikely to agree to lend his money for a get rich quick scheme.

Once a roper selects an appropriate target, he ingratiates himself with the victim. This can be a very slow process. A smart roper knows better than to appear as though he's hustling someone. The dupe might be stalked and worked on for days or even weeks. Because so much time must be devoted to seeking out and cultivating dupes, an average roper might be involved in only a handful of successful cons in a given year. An inside man, on the other hand, might be involved in dozens of cons. This is because he only sees the mark periodically and usually only for short periods of time.

After gaining the victim's confidence, the roper steers the "mark" to the inside man. Like the roper, the inside man has to be a good actor and adept at adjusting to abrupt changes. The inside man is typically posh and personable.

In a "big con" the inside man might pretend to be a high-rolling gambler or master of the stock market. To make this illusion more realistic, the inside man and associates might set up a fake stock brokerage or gaming house, complete with bustling activity and plenty of rich patrons (in reality, other con artists or their accomplices) apparently making huge bets or stock purchases. Once the victims get a taste of the supposedly well-heeled ambiance of the inside man's world, they are ready to be fleeced. While the particulars of various "big cons" differ, the rule of thumb is to convince a victim that the inside man has figured out a clever way to "rig the system" so he always win on his bets or stock purchases. With a little money from the victim, the inside man promises he can earn the dupe a fortune.

Whether playing the role of a roper or an inside man, a good con artist knows how to dress, act, and speak around rich people. "They are able to fit in unobtrusively on any social level … although their culture is not very deep, it is surprisingly wide and versatile. They must be well-informed in business and financial matters, have a glib knowledge of society gossip and enough of an acquaintance with art, literature and music to give an illusion of culture," wrote Maurer.

Wealthy people make ideal targets, and not just because they have money. Upper-class people tend to have an innate snobbery or sense of superiority. They see themselves as standing above the herd and think they are too clever to be conned. Tycoons tend to see themselves as masters of business and finance, which of course makes them prone to falling for financial scams. Once duped, a person of wealth isn't likely to go to the authorities, because doing so would be an admission that he was fooled.

The con artists Maurer wrote about had strict rules about certain aspects of their work (it was frowned upon to drink with the victim, for example, or to use violence). They also tended to lead somewhat precarious hand-to-mouth existences. Many con artists were addicted to gambling. Earnings were blown quickly, which meant the con artist had to work steadily. Even if the con artist didn't himself gamble, he needed to maintain a seemingly wealthy lifestyle in order to impress rich victims.

It should also be pointed out that the con men of the past and present are entirely cold-blooded and have no hesitation about stealing a victim's last dollars. Ripping off a dupe's hard-earned savings is a point of pride for con artists, who feel no shame.

Maurer's con artists tended to remain in the confidence profession until they died. They stayed youthful in spirit despite their actual age and had a certain pizzazz that other criminals couldn't match. "Confidence men are the elite of the underworld," noted Maurer—an observation that still holds true today.

Further Reading

David Maurer, *The Big Con: The Story of the Confidence Man*, 1940.

SHORT CONS

"The short con games are, theoretically, any confidence games in which the mark is trimmed for only the amount he has with him at the time," explained David Maurer in *The Big Con*.

Here's a look at some timeworn short cons. Some of these cons have largely disappeared, while others have mutated into contemporary scams.

The Gold Brick

This is a very primitive, somewhat ancient scam. Quite literally a brick or rock is painted to resemble a bar of gold. A sucker is induced into purchasing said "gold brick" for whatever cash he happens to have on hand. Generally, this scam only works on rather unintelligent or unobservant people. That said, more refined variations of this scam continue to flourish to this day. Con artists successfully continue to peddle fake jewels and phony gold mines.

Pig in a Poke

The original version of this scam can be traced back to medieval Europe. A salesperson would approach a likely looking "sucker" and ask whether he was interested in acquiring a small pig in a "poke," that is, a bag. If the mark agreed, what he actually received was a bag containing a wild cat—then, as now, not nearly as popular a food item as pork. This con required a certain degree of credulity, which was in no short supply during the Middle Ages.

The concept behind the Pig in a Poke scam (seller offers a valuable item for a steep price, then substitutes an item of far lesser value without the buyer noticing) has endured through the ages. Pig in a Poke–style scams are particularly common among street merchants, hawking goods (legally or not) on sidewalks. For example, an expensive-looking Rolex watch is switched with a cheap model for an unwitting sucker.

In all cases, the seller is counting on the buyers walking away without opening the bag to examine their purchase more closely. Victims of the original version of this scam who opened their sack were said to have let the proverbial "cat out of the bag"—in other words, revealed a secret.

The Fiddle Game

This scam requires two con artists. One con man, dressed in ragged clothes, eats in an expensive restaurant. Upon presentation of the bill, the confidence man claims to have left his wallet at home. The con man promises to retrieve his wallet. As a show of good faith, the con artist promises to leave his only valuable possession, an old violin, as collateral. The restaurant manager or owner agrees.

Con Man #1 exits, while Con Man #2 enters. Con Man #2 spots the old violin and exclaims that it's incredibly valuable. "Why, it's a Stradivarius!" the second con artist might say, pegging the value of the instrument at $50,000.

Con Man #2 can't stick around, however. He only popped by the restaurant to see if a friend was there, but alas he wasn't. Con Man #2 leaves a business card with the restaurant manager/owner, urging him to pass on his phone number to the owner of the violin. At this point, Con Man #2 exits.

Con Man #1 re-enters the restaurant with his retrieved wallet. The restaurant manager or owner gets greedy. Remembering the second con artist's inflated estimate of the violin's worth, the manager or owner offers to buy the violin himself. Con Man #1 acts as if he isn't aware of the real value of his instrument. He is broke, however, and reluctantly agrees to sell the violin for, say, $500. Money in hand, Con Man #1 leaves the premises.

The restaurant manager or owner thinks he has acquired a hugely valuable instrument for a fantastic bargain. The manager or owner tries to phone the number on the business card, only to discover that it's not in service or was selected at random from a phonebook. When the manager or owner takes the violin to a music store to be appraised, he is told the instrument is only worth a few dollars at most.

Dog Store

This con is a variation of the Fiddle Game.

A scruffy-looking con artist with a dog on a leash approaches a store or coffee shop. The dog walker ties his pooch up outside, then enters the shop and asks the manager where the bathroom is. Meanwhile, a second con artist who is already inside steps out to leave. Con Man #2 is well-dressed, with an air of wealth and power. The second con artist spots the dog and appears shocked.

"That's an incredibly rare dog!" Con Man #2 tells the store/café manager. "I've been looking for that breed for years!"

Unfortunately, Con Man #2 is already very late for a pressing engagement and can't wait for the dog owner to re-emerge from the men's room. The second con artist hands the store/coffee shop manager a business card with his phone number and address on it. He begs the manager to pass the card on to the dog owner to see if he's willing to sell his valuable hound.

"I'm willing to pay $10,000!" the second con man might say, before rushing off to his appointment.

Eventually, the dog owner returns from the washroom. The manager engages the dog owner in conversation. The manager tries to determine whether the dog owner is aware of the valuable pedigree of his hound. The dog owner breezily replies that he knows nothing about dog breeds; the dog was just a stray he found on the streets of his neighborhood.

Having established that the dog owner is clueless about the real value of his pet, the store/café manager offers to buy the canine himself. He figures that if he can get the dog for, say, $500, he can then contact the wealthy dog owner and collect $10,000.

The dog owner is reluctant at first but then concedes that, say, he still has huge student loans to pay off, so he's willing to part with his pet. Money changes hands, and the store/café manager is now the owner of a new dog. When the manager tries to contact the rich dog lover, however, he discovers that the phone number doesn't work and no such person lives at the address on the card. The person who does live at the address knows nothing about any dog deals and tells the now distressed store/café manager and his hound to take a hike.

The Glim Dropper

A con artist with only one eye is required to pull off the Glim Dropper scam. The one-eyed con man enters a store and says he's lost a glass eye. The store staff look for the eye in question but can't find it. The one-eyed man is upset and offers a $1,000 reward to whoever can find it. He leaves his address at the store, so anyone who finds the glass eye can return it to him.

The next day, one of the con man's two-eyed accomplices enters the store and "finds" the glass eye (actually hidden up his sleeve and secretly deposited in an appropriate locale). The store clerk remembers the $1,000 reward and offers to take the eye to its owner. Con Man #2 refuses. The store clerk offers him $100 for the eye. Con Man #2 bids the price up as high as possible, then "sells" the eye to the store clerk. The storekeeper tries to return the eye to collect his reward, only to discover that the address doesn't exist or the one-eyed man doesn't live there.

The Pigeon Drop

The Pigeon Drop was depicted in the opening scene of *The Sting*, a classic 1973 film centering on a "big con" originally mentioned in David Maurer's book.

The con involves two fraudsters. One man plays a victim, while the other man plays a friendly stranger. The pair lure a well-dressed passerby with a tale of woe. The "victim" (who pretends to be old, infirm, or injured) explains that he was supposed to meet a man to pay off a debt. But now the victim can't make the meeting because he's too ill or frail. The "friendly stranger" says he can't help because he's on the way to work. Could the passerby possibly help out? The supposed victim pulls an envelope from a pocket, which he opens to reveal a significant amount of cash.

Seeing all this cash, the passerby agrees to help. But before the passerby can accept the envelope, the friendly stranger intervenes. The friendly stranger suggests that the passerby add some money of his own to complement the cash in the envelope, as a sign of trust. It only seems right, considering the victim is entrusting someone he doesn't know with a large amount of cash. The passerby agrees and hands some cash from his wallet to the friendly stranger, who places it inside the envelope. Once this is done, the passerby seals the envelope and gives it to the passerby. The victim reminds the passerby of the name of the man he was supposed to meet and the address of the meeting. Then, everyone goes their own way.

If the passerby is honest and tries to hunt down the address in question, he will soon discover that it doesn't exist. If the passerby is dishonest and decides to keep all the cash in the envelope for himself, he will discover he has been robbed. The friendly stranger has substituted the original envelope for a new envelope, which is filled with tattered strips of newspaper, cut to feel like paper dollars.

Change Raising

Change Raising is a very small-scale con that was depicted in the movies *Paper Moon* and *The Grifters*.

A con artist goes into a store and buys an inexpensive item for $10. The con artist asks the store clerk if he can exchange ten one-dollar bills for a $10 bill. The con man makes sure the clerk gives him the $10 bill first. The con man then inserts the same $10 bill, along with nine one-dollar bills. The clerk assumes the con man has made a mistake and hands the $10 back. At this point, the con artist either leaves or says he will give the clerk a $1 bill if he gives him a $20 bill. The transaction is done.

This con only works in countries such as the United States, where paper bills are all the same color.

The Smack

The Smack is described in detail in Maurer's *The Big Con*.

In this scam, a roper waits in a railway station while an inside man lurks nearby, out of sight. The roper keeps a lookout for a good mark, preferably a merchant waiting for a train. Modern hustlers would probably move the scene from a train station to an airport.

Once the roper finds a mark, he engages the victim in seemingly idle conversation. The roper learns what train the victim is waiting for and says that happens to be the very same train he is waiting for, too. As the train in question isn't leaving for some time, the roper suggests taking a walk around town.

The pair stroll around, eventually encountering the inside man. Speaking in a distinct Southern accent, the inside man asks whether either of the duo knows where the Merchants Bank Building is. The roper is dismissive and sneering. The inside man accuses the roper and his newfound friend of being "cheapskate" Yankees who can't be bothered helping someone from out of town. Conversation ensues. The Southerner calms down and apologizes for "insulting" the two men. The roper accepts the apology and invites the Southern stranger to have a drink with him, to prove he is no cheapskate. The inside man turns him down. The roper offers a cigar, which the Southerner also turns down. The roper offers to "match" the smokes (that is, flip a coin in the air, landing heads or tails). The roper and the mark will take turns calling heads or tails against the Southerner.

The roper quietly whispers instructions to the mark. Always call heads, says the roper. The roper will always call tails. This will increase the odds of one of them winning against the Southerner.

The coin is flipped a number of times. The stakes are raised, to the point where the men are now flipping a coin for all the money in their wallets. The Southerner loses more than he wins and reluctantly hands over his cash. The roper holds onto the winnings, whispering to the mark that they will divide the loot later.

The mark and the roper walk off together and go around a corner. The roper starts dividing the cash when suddenly the Southerner returns in a huff. The inside man accuses the pair of working together to trick him. The roper insists the two men never met before that morning and weren't in cahoots. The Southerner insists that to prove there was no conspiracy, the roper and the mark must go their separate ways onto the train. The roper whispers to the mark, "Meet you on the train" or something to that effect. The mark goes on to the train, expecting the roper to meet him. The roper, meanwhile, departs with the Southerner and divides the mark's cash between them.

The Tat

A tat is a "fixed" die used in rigged games of chance. The fixed die has fives on four sides and sixes on two. The fixed die has an exact match, which looks and feels just like its crooked counterpart. The only difference is that the "straight" die is numbered properly, from one to six.

With the fixed die and legitimate die secured in a pocket, the roper heads to a bar. He avoids groups of men with women, and positions himself near a group consisting solely of males. The roper starts chatting with the men. He acts a bit tipsy, joins the group, and orders drinks for everyone. The roper is generally witty and amusing. At some point, the roper's partner enters the bar. The partner pretends to be surprised to see the roper: "I thought you were going to England on business," the partner might say. "Leaving next week," the roper might reply. The partner joins the merry throng. More drinks are ordered.

The normal die is placed on the floor or somewhere else where it can be noticed. If no one notices the die, the roper or partner picks it up and offers to show the group a game. The roper puts the die in a hat. It is suggested that everyone around the table take the hat, shake it vigorously, and see what score turns up. The process is to be repeated by each person three times in a row. Whoever has the highest overall score wins one dollar from each person and has to buy a round of drinks. The die remains in the hat during this process.

Someone is appointed to keep track of each person's scores. The hat gets shaken, and scores are counted. The roper suggests it might be more interesting to bet some serious cash and not just beer money. Highest score wins. Naturally, the good-natured group agrees.

The roper keeps the tat concealed in his hand at all times, except when it's his partner's turn to shake the hat. At such times, the normal die is surreptitiously removed and replaced with the tat. The tat is never removed from the hat as the partner makes his three shakes.

Once the partner has completed his series of shakes, the tat is replaced with the regular die. Thanks to the tat, the partner runs up the highest score and wins whatever cash has been wagered.

The con men both depart soon after winning (though not at the same time). They make sure to leave the legitimate die behind for the marks to inspect. It may eventually dawn on the marks that they've been had, but they still won't be able to figure out how.

The Money Machine

The Money Machine scam requires nimble fingers and some sleight-of-hand ability.

A con artist finds a mark and tells him that the two of them can make a lot of money—literally. The confidence man happens to possess a nifty little machine, the only one of its kind in the world (the inventor was apparently murdered before he could build any more). The machine contains plates that were stolen from the United States Printing Office and can turn out genuine-looking $10 bills. In order to whip up a batch of money, all the operator needs is some of the official paper used by the government to create currency.

The mark is probably skeptical, so the roper takes him into a room to show off the money machine. He also displays a sample of the official government paper required to print money. The con man cuts the paper, places it in the machine, and produces two new, crisp $10 bills. The bank notes are given to the mark to inspect. The mark confesses they look just like the real thing—not surprising, since the bills are authentic ones that had been hidden in the machine ahead of time.

At this point, the roper confesses that he only has a tiny amount of U.S. Printing Office paper left. However, he knows a crooked government worker who can supply enough paper to print $10,000 worth of bills at a time. But the problem is that this crooked public servant wants $1,500 in advance and the roper is broke.

The con artist suggests that the mark pay the $1,500 fee. Naturally, the victim is suspicious, so the con man sets him at ease. They will rent out a safety deposit box at a bank. The money machine will be placed inside, and the mark will have the only key. This reassures the dupe, who hands over $1,500. Once the money is exchanged, the mark never sees the con man again. When the mark opens the safety deposit box, he discovers that all he owns is a bit of mechanical junk.

Hot Seat

Another scam mentioned in Maurer's *The Big Con* is called the "Hot Seat." This scam is typically done abroad, with well-heeled American tourists as the primary victims. The scam involves a roper, an inside man, and a rosary.

The roper seeks out a mark that he figures can be conned. He engages the mark in pleasant conversation. The roper gives a secret signal to the inside man, who sticks close by. The roper "discovers" a rosary lying on the ground. He examines it with the mark. The rosary is clearly expensive. The inside man blusters in, loudly proclaiming the rosary to be his. The inside man says the rosary is a family heirloom blessed by the Pope and is enormously valuable to him.

The inside man lets it be known he is a rich Irishman. He offers the roper and mark some cash as a reward for finding his lost rosary. The roper refuses the cash, as does the mark. The alleged Irishman says their humbleness is admirable. The Irishman reveals that he was planning to give a considerable amount of money to charity. Unfortunately, the Irishman is a busy man. He suggests that the roper and the mark take his charitable donation and give the money to a needy cause.

The roper says the Irishman is a bit too trusting and has no guarantee that they won't just keep the charitable donation for themselves. As a test of their good faith, the roper suggests that he and the mark put up $5,000 each. The Irishman thinks this is a great idea. He takes the man to his hotel room where he produces a metal box. The Irishman places the money he was intending to give to charity inside the box. The mark is induced to go to a bank and produce $5,000 that can be added to the box. This is done. The roper also adds his $5,000 bond. All the cash is secured in the box.

The Irishman and the roper begin an animated conversation about how much they trust each other. As proof of this trust, the Irishman suggests the mark and roper take the box outside and walk around the block with it then come back to the hotel room. The pair take a stroll, with the mark holding the metal box securely in his grip. To complete the sign of trust, it is suggested the roper and the Irishman take a turn walking the box around the block. The pair leave, and the mark waits for the duo to return to the hotel. They never do. The mark is left on the "hot seat," growing increasingly anxious, which is what gives this con its name.

In a variation of this con done back in the United States, a roper seeks a dupe. The roper informs the mark that he plans to give some money to the church, but for some plausible reason he's too busy to make the donation himself at that time. The roper says he admires the mark's honesty and asks if he can take his cash—say, $500—to the church in question. The mark agrees. The roper hands over $500 and a handkerchief in which to store the money. The mark counts out $500, then places it in the handkerchief, as the roper suggests.

The roper proposes that as an act of faith, the mark place $500 of his own money in the handkerchief. The mark can retrieve this money when he locates the church in question and hands over the donation. The dupe thinks this is fine. He goes to the bank, withdraws a sum, then opens the handkerchief and puts $500 of his own cash inside. The roper tells the mark to head over to the church to drop off the cash. Or he might suggest that the mark hide the money under his mattress until the two reunite to make the donation together. In either case, the mark is told not to open the handkerchief until he is either at the church or when the two men are back together. At some point, curiosity probably gets the best of the mark and he opens the handkerchief. But instead of $1,000, he finds nothing but a bunch of newspaper clippings cut out in the same shape as dollar bills.

Femme Fatale

This con requires an attractive female con artist. The beautiful fraudster dresses up in expensive clothes, puts on elaborate makeup, and then travels to a wealthy residential area. The lady promptly faints in the street, which attracts the attention of passers-by. Inevitably, some hero rushes to her side. The fainting lady groggily comes to and induces the hero to take her inside his home. "I just need to rest for a minute. I don't need to go to the hospital," she might say. Once inside, the femme fatale either steals a few items of value while the hero is fetching a glass of water or "cases" the interior layout. In the latter scenario, the fainting lady later returns to the home to steal the valuables she spotted or tells some accomplices where such items can be found. Either way, a burglary ensues.

Modeling/Talent Agency

An agency claims they are looking for "fresh faces" or "new talent" to round out their modeling and/or talent roster. People are encouraged to contact the agency for work, even if they have no prior acting or modeling experience, or don't fit the typical model profile.

Anyone who contacts the agency is invited to come in for an interview. Inevitably, the interview goes extremely well. The aspiring star is told she has the right "look" and that the agency can almost guarantee her work as a model or actress in films, on TV, on the Internet, etc. Before the aspirant can get work, however, she needs to pay a fee to the agency. She also needs a professional portfolio of photographs and/or video clips. The aspirant might already have a portfolio, but it's never quite up to agency standards. Fortunately, the agency works closely with an excellent photographer/videographer who can do a shoot and put together a top-notch portfolio—for a small fee, of course.

If the aspirant goes through with this and acquires an expensive portfolio, she discovers she will find few actual working gigs. The agency blames the industry: "That's the nature of the business, kid. Sometimes there's just no demand for models and actors." The agency and the photographer split the proceeds from the portfolio.

This con works because it appeals to people's vanity. Who doesn't want to be told she looks like a model or a Hollywood actress?

An interesting variation of this scam actually plays up imperfection. The agency claims they are specifically looking for "non-traditional" or "ordinary"-looking models and/or actors. People who might never consider a modelling or acting career are encouraged to contact the agency. Anyone who signs up with the agency is told, once again, she needs to pay a fee to the agency and acquire a professional portfolio before she can get any work.

In other versions of this con, a victim is induced to send or pose for nude or sexually provocative photos or videos. ("Don't worry. No one will ever see these images except us. The studios just want people who are comfortable with their sexuality," an agent might explain.) Once the agency has the pictures and videos, they can essentially blackmail the victim into paying high "fees" to prevent the images from being released.

The Modeling/Talent Agency scam has been around for decades and continues to flourish. Arguably, this con might be even more common today. Thanks to the Internet, scam agencies don't even require a brick-and-mortar office any more to pull their con. They can simply set up a website and ask people to submit photos, and eventually money, online.

Clip Joint

A clip joint is a bar or other establishment that promises salacious entertainment (typically striptease) but delivers instead watered-down drinks, bad service, and no strippers. If the victim complains or runs out of money, he is tossed out of the club by bouncers. Generally the mark won't go to the authorities, because he's too embarrassed to admit he got ripped off at what he thought was a strip bar.

This scam flourished during Prohibition (1919–1933), when alcohol was banned and anyone wanting a drink had to seek out an illegal "speakeasy."

Fake Auction

This scam requires a con artist with the gift of gab and several assistants.

The con artist claims to represent a famous manufacturer or retail chain. The fraudster displays several appealing items (perhaps high-end cameras or computers) and pitches their virtues. An interested crowd gathers. The con man promises to auction off the array of enticing items at rock-bottom prices. But first, the auctioneer has to follow certain rules and start the bidding on smaller, less expensive goods—perhaps a jar of jam or engraved dinner plates.

The auctioneer sells a series of small items at a very low price, perhaps one dollar apiece. After the assistants hand the items out, the auctioneer asks everyone who received an item to put up his hand. He then instructs his assistants to give back the money the crowd just spent.

This process is repeated, with a series of items that slowly grow in value. Every time the audience purchases a line of goods, they get their money back. The crowd thinks they've hit the retail jackpot.

The bidding ends abruptly, however, before any of the high-end items can be auctioned off. The fraudsters depart halfway through one of the payout/payback rounds, while still holding the crowd's money. Audience members feel slightly cheated because the expensive items were never made available but are generally satisfied with the less pricey goods they purchased.

Street Vendor with a Van

A salesperson, typically in a white van, tries to interest pedestrians in high-quality goods sold at rock-bottom prices. The salesperson claims, for example, to be peddling top-of-the-line speakers or computers. The pitchman insinuates that these items were obtained in not-entirely-legal fashion. Anyone who stops to listen to the salesperson will quickly discover that he's more than willing to haggle. The price of the goods gets lower and lower until the victim thinks he's getting a steal and agrees to a purchase. Needless to say, when the mark gets home and tries out his new purchase, he discovers it's actually a low-quality item that would retail for less than what he just paid for it on the street.

Sleazy Street Vendor

This is a variation on the Street Vendor with a Van scam. A con artist acquires some cheap jewelry or watches. He gathers his loot in a bag or suitcase, then enters an establishment with a mildly seedy air—a dive bar or barbershop would fit the bill. The fraudster acts nervous and anxious, constantly looking around the place. In a low voice, he openly announces that he's got "hot" (i.e., stolen) merchandise that he's willing to part with for a bargain. In this manner the con artist sells a bunch of, say, watches for $20 each. The patrons of the establishment think they've just acquired a real bargain on the sly. The con man leaves before anyone realizes the watches were purchased at a discount store for $5 apiece.

Malcolm X talked about this scam in his autobiography and said it flourished in areas where people might not be familiar with what valuable watches or jewels actually look like.

Mentally Handicapped Person

Acting ability is essential to pull off this con.

A fraudster pretending to be mentally handicapped approaches a stranger on the street. The con artist explains that he found a packet of coins. The packet has a label on it reading, "If lost, please return to A. J. Johnson. Call 416-------. Reward offered."

The con man says that he can't read very well. Could the stranger help him? Glad to be of service, the stranger calls the number labeled on the packet. Mr. A. J. Johnson answers and seems both startled and grateful the packet of coins has been found. The insinuation is that these coins are very valuable. Johnson informs the stranger that the $500 reward is his, provided he can bring the packet of coins to his residence. Oh, and to be fair, could the stranger maybe give the helpful mentally handicapped person $100 of his own money? Mr. Johnson says he will pay this back, along with the reward. It just seems right.

When the stranger tries to return the item, however, he finds that the address he was given doesn't exist, or no one named A. J. Johnson lives there. The packet of coins turns out to be worthless bits of modern currency from foreign locales.

Distressed Car Owner

A stranger knocks on your door and seems incredibly grateful to see you. He claims to be a neighbor from a nearby street and goes into a long, harrowing tale about losing his car. The car was apparently towed and is in a lot, but the owner left his wallet and cell phone inside the vehicle. The man's wife is out of town, and there's no one else who can help him. He desperately needs $20 to pay for cab fare to get to the towing yard. Could you help out?

In a variation of this scheme, the distressed stranger walks up to you on the street and gives the same spiel. He might add a few colorful touches—he's new in this city and didn't know he had parked his car in a tow zone, etc. He too needs money so he can get a taxi to the towing yard.

Further Reading

Herbert Asbury, *The Gangs of New York*, 1927.
Crimes of Persuasion website, http://www.crimes-of-persuasion.com/.
Malcolm X and Alex Haley, *The Autobiography of Malcolm X*, 1965.
David Maurer, *The Big Con: The Story of the Confidence Man*, 1940.

BIG CONS

In a short con, a confidence artist might be lucky to get a few hundred dollars at most. In a big con, dupes are taken for tens of thousands of dollars or more. The timeframe is another key difference. Short cons can be played out in a matter of minutes or hours. A big con might take place over the course of several days or weeks.

Additionally, in a short con, the victims usually realize they've been duped. In a big con, that isn't necessarily the case. According to David Maurer, in his book *The Big Con*, "In the most sophisticated cons … [the dupe] may ever after remain unaware that he has been bilked, merely registering the affair as a gambit that failed."

The large-scale cons outlined by Maurer sometimes include elaborate preparations involving dozens of con men and their associates. Much like a movie or a play in which the mark is the unwitting protagonist, the big con features sets, props, and complex character roles on the part of the swindlers. "Big-time confidence games are in reality only carefully rehearsed plays in which every member of the cast except the mark knows his part perfectly," wrote Maurer.

While big cons differ in various details, they are generally based on the same premise: the con artist claims to have "inside knowledge" that can be used to make a "killing" in stocks, gaming, or sports gambling. This "inside knowledge" is usually obtained in a fraudulent or at least shady fashion. The mark is aware of this, which makes him an accomplice to the scam and therefore unlikely to complain to police.

Here's a look at some of classic big cons cited by Maurer.

The Fight Store

This scam requires a roper or two, an inside man, a "doctor," two boxers, and other sundry folks.

The roper's job is to entice people to witness and bet on a boxing match (or wrestling bout or footrace) taking place in a secret locale. At the time Maurer wrote his book, prizefighting (boxing for money) was illegal across much of the United States. Prize matches were held on the sly, often in the back room of a store or saloon. Anyone witnessing such a match could be pretty sure that he was breaking the law.

With this in mind, the roper would enter a train or some other place where suitable victims could be found. The roper would pretend to be the disgruntled personal secretary of a millionaire sporting figure who had his own personal prizefighter. The roper complains to the victim that his boss is cheap. The roper wants to quit working for the sportsman—but not before making some big money. The roper claims he's "fixed" the next match, so the prizefighter will "take a fall" (that is, pretend to be knocked down) in the tenth round. The millionaire sportsman doesn't know this, of course, and will presumably bet heavily on his own fighter.

Although the fight is fixed, the roper faces a problem. He can't possibly bet against his own employer, lest he arouse suspicion. The roper needs to find someone willing to bet against the fighter. After the bout, the roper can split the proceeds with the third-party bettor.

If the victim takes the bait, the roper steers him to meet the millionaire sportsman (played by another con artist, naturally) and the prizefighter (yet another con man). The sportsman comes off as a wealthy fop. In the presence of the mark, the sportsman makes sure to show off how rich he is, perhaps by counting a roll of $100 bills. The sportsman boasts about how much money he's betting on his own boxer.

"As soon as the victim was convinced that he could win heavily, he was sent home, procured his money, contributed something to the purse and made his bet," wrote Maurer.

Often, the victim was given a satchel supposedly containing all the money bet on the match. This satchel would actually be filled with scrap paper, while the real satchel remained in the possession of the con artists.

The prizefight is held. Since the fight is illegal, the audience is small. The spectators are rowdy and rambunctious, however, and they cheer on their champion. In the sixth round, the boxer who was supposed to "take a fall" hits his opponent heavily in the chest, over the heart. The opponent collapses in the center of the ring, spitting blood (actually a "cackle bladder," or balloon filled with chicken blood). The ringside "doctor" checks the man's vital signs and, in solemn tones, announces that the boxer is dead. The cry is given to run. People start dashing away as the victim is told by the roper to make a fast exit, lest he be dragged into a messy murder investigation. The mark has lost his money but is thankful he won't be arrested.

At this point, the con artists make tracks. The roper has the real satchel filled with the actual bets from the match (including the mark's money). Once the mark had made himself scarce, the con artists reunite and split the profits from the fight.

Once prizefighting was legalized in the United States, this con faded from the scene.

The Wire

This con has its roots in the late nineteenth century. As the use of the telegraph became commonplace, unemployed telegraph operators sometimes carried out a simple scam. Out-of-work operators would find a mark and tell him a tempting story. The operator would claim that he could tap into telegraph wires to get advance horse racing results being transmitted across the country. Naturally, anyone who had these results could make a fortune through illicit betting.

For some plausible reason, however, the telegraph operator was broke and required some financial aid. The mark would be induced to lay out a large sum of money for telegraph equipment. The scammer would operate the telegraph, sometimes actually getting early racing results, other times simply ripping the mark off by selling him overpriced telegraph equipment.

This scam led to the advent of the "wire store." The wire store involves one insider man, who poses as an official with the Western Union telegraph company, and a group of accomplices and ropers. The ropers are charged with seeking dupes for the scam.

Ropers sometimes found victims by running newspaper ads touting "business opportunities." The one cardinal rule: "the mark must not be a resident of the city where is to be trimmed," wrote Maurer. Presumably, this rule was to decrease the risk that the dupe would go to the authorities. Someone conned in his hometown might know a few incorruptible figures of authority to report the scam to. This was less likely to happen if the victim was in a strange city where he knew no one and wasn't sure if the police and courts were in the pocket of the con artist.

Maurer's *The Big Con* described a typical wire store "play." A roper locates the owner of a small department store. The roper pretends to represent a firm buying up small department stores. This gets the victim's attention. The roper and the dupe go over the details of the "deal" for a couple days. At some point, the roper invites the store owner to come to New York City (or some other imposing locale), to consummate the deal with his superiors.

The pair head to the Big Apple, where they meet the roper's "boss" (an accomplice). Once the deal has been sealed, the roper suggests that lunch is in order, to celebrate the occasion. At lunch, the roper tells the store owner he has a cousin who manages an office of Western Union (a prominent telegraph company at the time). The roper pays the bill and suggests the pair pay his cousin a visit. The store owner agrees, delighted at how well things are going.

The roper and store owner meet up with the "cousin" (actually an inside man) at an office, restaurant, or saloon. The cousin asks the roper about his business partner, who is supposedly doing a business deal with him. The roper replies that his partner is out of town. The cousin seems dismayed. Perhaps, suggests the roper, the store owner could take the place of the errant business partner? The cousin pretends to be shocked, but the roper assures him the store owner is a decent man who can be trusted.

Thus reassured, the cousin peddles his story. He says he works for a heartless corporation and has never been promoted. He has cooked up a deal, however, which will make him rich. Once the deal goes through, the cousin plans to retire. The cousin had initially planned to make this deal with the roper's business partner. The cousin explains that he can get advance horse racing results. The cousin plans to relay these results to some assistants, who will then place large bets with bookies operating in an illicit game room at a saloon. Naturally, the cousin can't leave work to make the bets himself.

The store owner seems intrigued. The cousin tells the store owner and the roper to go to a certain pharmacy. The phone will ring at a given time. The cousin will relay the name of the winning horse, then delay the transmission of the results so bets can be made in the saloon/game room.

The store owner and roper go to the saloon in question and are let into the illicit gaming room. The place is packed with men waving money, smoking cigars, and feverishly reading a ticker tape offering horse racing results. There are chalkboards and a cashier behind a counter, handling enormous piles of $100 bills. The store owner watches in amazement as the cashier casually hands out winnings in the tens of thousands of dollars.

The scene impresses the store owner. He has no idea all the men in the gaming room are associates and accomplices of the roper and inside man. The money seen in abundance everywhere belongs to the con artists. The store owner doesn't realize that each pile of cash consists of a hundred-dollar bill on top and a thick load of single dollar notes underneath.

The store owner and the roper go the pharmacy. Sure enough, at a given time, the phone rings, and the cousin gives the name of a horse with 4-to-1 odds against it. The roper and store owner go to the saloon, and each man places a small bet on the horse in question. When the horse wins, the roper and store owner each collect $50.

The store owner is induced to make a larger bet. He and the roper both bet their $50 winnings. Of course, their horse wins again, earning them $250 apiece.

The store owner, caught up in the excitement, wants to bet his full $250 on another horse. The roper pretends he doesn't want to risk it. The phone at the pharmacy rings, and this time the store owner answers and marches off to the saloon with the roper in tow. Unfortunately, there is a very large lineup at the cash window. He gets to the cashier just as the counter closes. He hears a voice announcing, "And they're off!" and the men in the room crowd around the ticker tape. The race the store owner wants to bet on is underway. No more betting is permitted. Of course, the horse wins, and the store owner is frustrated because he thinks he could have cleaned up. This part of the con is called the "shutout" or "prat-out." It's deliberately staged to give a boost to the victim's greed.

As the store owner ponders his fate, another inside man playing the gaming room manager approaches the store owner and the roper. He complains that the men are making petty wagers, that small bets are a nuisance as far as bookkeeping goes. The game room has an image to uphold, says the manager.

In a patronizing tone, the manager urges the pair to go to a nearby pool hall that offers gambling opportunities for working-class men. The store owner is embarrassed and irate. He asks how much the usual bet is in the saloon game room. The manager says $1,000 is the usual minimum but there is no ceiling. Then the manager abruptly turns and dismisses the pair.

The roper and the store owner leave the saloon, and the cousin approaches them on the street. The cousin asks how his con worked. The roper and the store owner say the con worked fine but the manager treated them like small-time pikers. If that's the case, says the cousin, then he has a plan to rip the operation off for a major amount of money—just under a million dollars. The cousin wants to make a huge bet to collect big time. Only he doesn't have sufficient funds on hand to make the bet. This is where the roper's business partner was supposed to come in. The business partner was going to loan the cousin some cash to make the large bet.

By now, the store owner is convinced he's onto a "sure thing." He agrees to take the business partner's place and raise, say, $25,000 (a large sum at the time Maurer was doing his field research). The store owner requires a few days to put this cash together. He is sent home, with strict instructions not to mention a word of the secret deal to anyone. This part of the con is called "the send." In three days, the store owner returns to New York City, with $25,000 in cash. On the appropriate day and time, the store owner and the roper go to the pharmacy, to await the phone call. The call comes in, and the store owner answers. He is clearly told by the cousin to "place it all" on a given horse. The cousin asks to speak with the roper, to whom he repeats these instructions. The roper can be clearly heard repeating the cousin's instructions to "place it all" on the horse in question.

The store owner and the roper go to the saloon and put the bet in. The race goes on. The given horse does not win, but in fact comes second. The store owner is crushed and confused. Outside the saloon, the store owner and roper meet up with the cousin, who is all smiles. The cousin assumes the men have won big on the basis of his tip. The store owner tells the cousin that the roper bet everything on the horse to win. The cousin is enraged.

"Don't you know what the word 'place' means?" he demands.

A furious row between roper and cousin ensues, with the latter loudly berating the former. A few fists might fly, in the roper's direction. The gist of the cousin's rage is the confusion over the betting term "place" (as in, win, place, or show). When a gambler makes a bet to "win," he is counting on his horse to come in first place. If the horse does finish first, the gambler earns a sum based on whatever odds were placed against the horse. Anything other than a first-place finish doesn't earn a payout. A bet to "place" means the gambler gets a payout if the horse finishes first or second. The payout is usually smaller than the payout for a riskier "win" bet. A bet to "show" means a payout is delivered if the chosen horse comes in first, second, or third. Again, this payout would be smaller than a bet to either a "win" or "place." The amount of money to be won decreases down the line.

The store owner is furious with the roper too, who behaves in a sniveling, upset manner. To placate the store owner, the roper agrees to pay his hotel bill and loan him enough cash to get home on the train. The roper assures the store owner that the deal to purchase his business is still a go.

The dazed store owner (who is unknowingly being tailed) returns to his hotel. The roper arrives and makes sure he packs up for the train, with promises to finalize the store purchase deal "within a few days." The mark leaves, and the con men divide up his cash.

The Payoff

This is another big con in which the mark is led to believe that he can make an enormous profit through sports betting, specifically horse racing. In this case, the races in question are allegedly "fixed" in advance so bettors in the know can reap an illicit fortune.

The roper goes onto a steamer or ocean liner. He heads to the ship's bar and leisurely nurses a drink. The roper starts a casual conversation with a well-dressed, prosperous-looking gentleman at the bar. The roper introduces himself under a false name; here, we will call him "James Ryan." The conversation goes so well, the roper orders the dupe—let's say, a real estate agent named William Fink—a drink. If he learns that Fink is from Boston, Ryan will say he himself comes from somewhere like "North Adams, Massachusetts."

The roper always picks a hometown in the same state where the dupe is from. Ropers travel extensively, so they have a vast knowledge of towns and cities across the United States to draw from when making small talk with new acquaintances.

Fink says he is headed to Miami. By coincidence, so is the roper. The roper asks whether Fink knows any good hotels in Miami. Fink offers up the name of such a place. Ryan says he will stay there too.

Throughout the trip, Ryan and Fink see much of each other. The roper lays on the charm. He listens attentively as Fink talks about golf and complains about the tough life of a real estate broker. Ryan claims to be "well fixed" because he received a fortuitous tip to sell his stocks before the stock market crashed in 1929.

Like a good roper, Ryan has determined, roughly, Fink's worth. He figures the man will be good to rip off in the neighborhood of $25,000 or so. Ryan sends a radiogram from the ship to "John," an acquaintance in Miami. The radiogram consists of a coded message along the lines of "Arriving March 10 Miami with Uncle George, coming south for his health," wrote Maurer. This coded message alerts John that a victim has been found.

Ryan and Fink dock in Miami. They go to the hotel recommended by Fink. In his suite, Ryan phones John. The two debate which scam to pull on Fink and when. They agree that "The Payoff" would be ideal. Arrangements are made.

Ryan then contacts Fink and arranges for lunch the next day. After the men have eaten, the roper assumes an embarrassed expression and asks whether he happens to be resting his foot on Fink's shoe. When Fink says no, Ryan looks under the table to investigate. He discovers a fat wallet on the floor. The wallet is opened, and the men discover it's packed with $50 bills. Pieces of identification indicate the wallet belongs to one H. E. Lamster. There's also a membership card for something called the Turf Club, and a slew of telegrams and newspaper clippings. The clippings are all about Mr. Lamster and his phenomenal racetrack winnings.

Ryan and Fink inquire at the front desk and discover that Lamster is staying in that hotel in a suite. They go up to the suite and knock on the door. Lamster is rude and dismissive at first. Ryan asks if Lamster has lost his wallet. Lamster realizes he has and becomes instantly friendlier when he sees that the two strangers at his suite door have it. Lamster correctly identifies the contents of the wallet, so Ryan hands it over.

The two men are invited inside the swanky suite. Lamster apologizes for his initial rudeness. He thought the pair were newspapermen. Lamster is evidently tired of being pestered by journalists because he's so successful at gambling on horse races.

Lamster offers to give Ryan and Fink the money inside the wallet as a reward. They decline. Lamster offers to "place a bet" for the two men. He explains that he works for "a large syndicate" that controls horse race tracks around the country. Lamster says he places bets for the syndicate. He indicates, without directly saying so, that the races are rigged (which explains his astonishing winning streak).

Lamster tells the two that he receives coded instructions from his bosses, usually in the form of a telegram. He urges the two men to stay in his suite and enjoy his cigars and liquor while he goes out and places some bets. Lamster returns after a time and presents the men with $200 as the result of the bet he made for them. A bellboy delivers a telegram with coded instructions for another race. Lamster offers to take the men's $200 and bet it again for them. He does, and returns with $600 for both Ryan and Fink.

The con artists continue to play Fink, but they are careful not to "hook" him too early. Ryan and Fink have dinner, then go to a nightclub. The next day, the roper visits Fink in his hotel room and suggests they met Lamster again. Lamster welcomes the pair to his suite but says the folks at the exclusive Turf Club are starting to suspect him. He wins so much and so often, Turf Club staff figure he must be doing something illegal. So Lamster gives Ryan and Funk a guest card, explaining that he can't go to the Turf Club himself for a while.

Lamster suggests the men combine their winnings, so they now have $1,200. When the time comes to bet, Lamster says they should sign the check for $50,000 (Ryan will put his name to the check). They should add in their $1,200 cash winnings from the previous race, so the total bet comes to $51,200. Lamster tells them to bet on a horse named Dancing Cloud to win in the fifth race. If everything goes as planned, Ryan and Fink stand to make $256,000.

Ryan protests that he doesn't have $50,000 in the bank to cover the check. Lamster tells him not to worry; the entrance card alone will assure their credit. Lamster insists again that the race is a sure thing.

The roper and Fink go to the Turf Club. Sure enough, the guest card gets them through the door and into the exclusive establishment. The club is filled with expensive-looking furniture and well-dressed men, loudly discussing horse races. A chalkboard keeps track of races. Men are betting up to $100,000 at a time. Fink is impressed by the air of casual wealth. He is envious of the gamblers' well-heeled nonchalance.

As in previous big cons, Fink doesn't realize that the whole scene has been created to lure him in. The expensive-looking furniture might have been acquired from a secondhand shop. The supposed rich gentlemen are all con artists or accomplices. The races that the men are supposedly betting on are all bogus.

Ryan and Fink go to the cashier's window and bet $51,200 at 4-to-1 odds to win on Dancing Cloud. The horse wins. Fink is elated. He thinks he's won a fortune. The cashier starts counting out $256,000 in cash. The Turf Club manager suddenly approaches Ryan and Fink. He demands to know how the pair got in the club, which is a private establishment. The roper and the dupe show the manager the private guest card Lamster gave them. The cashier shows the manager the check that Ryan handed over.

The manager tells Ryan and Fink that they have won their bet and are entitled to their money. But first, the club must put the $50,000 check portion of their bet through the bank to make sure there's enough money to cover it. The manager will impound their $256,000 winnings until the bank clears the check. Once cleared, the winnings are all theirs.

Fink complains that $1,200 of the total bet was their own money. He asks for $6,000 in winnings, based on that bet. The manager refuses, however. Fink and Ryan go back to the hotel. The roper seems somewhat perturbed that his name is on the check. Fink asks Lamster for more betting tips, but Lamster doesn't have any more races lined up for the day. He suggests Ryan and Fink go back to the manager and ask him to give them time to cover the check. Lamster says the three of them will figure out a way to cover the $50,000 check.

The roper and the dupe return to the Turf Club. The manager complains that the two entered the club with dubious credentials. He agrees, however, not to put the $50,000 check through right away. Ryan admits he doesn't have enough money in the bank to cover the check.

The manager scolds the men for writing such a large check if they didn't have the means to redeem it. Naturally, Ryan and Fink can't explain that the bet was "sure thing" so they had no fear of paying $50,000. To say so would be to admit they were aware the races were fixed.

The Turf Club manager will give the two men a week to redeem the check. Before it can be redeemed, Ryan needs to deposit $50,000 in cash in the bank used by the club, to prove he could cover the check if he had lost his bet. The manager insists that this be done. In the meantime, he will hold the check.

Ryan and Fink go back to Lamster to explain the situation. Ryan is acting a bit cocky, having made the arrangements with the bank manager. Fink is starting to dislike Ryan and trust Lamster more. This is all deliberate scheming on the con artists' part. Fink is thinking of cutting Ryan out of the deal.

The three men put their heads together to come up with a way to raise $50,000 in a hurry. Lamster is apparently short on funds at the moment (like a lot of gamblers, he tends to burn through any money he makes). Ryan says he has $17,000 in government bonds. He could cash those on short notice. Fink is asked to raise the rest. He says he could cash some bonds himself and get around $25,000. Lamster can pay the remaining $8,000, though he warns that he might get fired by the syndicate if they found out he was making side bets without their knowledge. Lamster promises to arrange his finances at his bank in the morning. Fink's investments are in Boston, and he has to do some arranging himself.

Fink is starting to get annoyed at Ryan. Once the pair collect their $256,000 winnings, Ryan wants to pay Lamster back his $8,000 but not include a share of the big win. Fink thinks this is unfair, given that Lamster provided the hot tip in the first place.

Ryan leaves. Fink and Lamster confer in private. Lamster says that Fink is a fine character, and dependable. He suggests the two of them should continue doing some deals together. Of course, Lamster swears his new friend to secrecy. The conversation turns to Ryan. Fink expresses his dislike of the man. It is agreed that Ryan can't be trusted. Lamster urges Fink to keep a close eye on Ryan and stick near his side. Lamster says he will be busy for a few days but will call once a day to check in.

Fink's loyalties have shifted from Ryan to Lamster. With no idea this is all part of the con, Fink now thinks Lamster is a good friend. Remembering Lamster's warning, Fink urges Ryan to share a room with him. The next morning, Ryan and Fink met Lamster at the bank. The bank president is most accommodating.

The president gets Ryan and Fink each to make out a check for the sum they wish to transfer. Ryan's check comes to $17,000, while Fink's is for $25,000. Lamster puts in a personal check for $8,000. The bank president assures the men that their accounts will be opened as soon as the money for the checks arrives.

Fink continues to "watch" Ryan. Ryan talks about splitting the $256,000 and painting the town red. The two men continue to share a room. Whenever Fink shows signs of nervousness, Lamster comes in and "cools" him down. However, Lamster says he has to lay low in Miami for a spell, because he's being hounded by newspapermen. Lamster assures Fink that the banker will notify him when the money comes in. This waiting period might last for several days or even weeks.

The bank finally sends word that Ryan's money has come in, then Fink's. Lamster suggests they go to the bank to make sure everything is okay. All is well. An account is opened in Ryan's name (as the betting slip and the check were in his name). Fink stays close to Ryan.

All three men go to the Turf Club. Lamster waits outside. Inside, the place is a hive of activity and speculative betting. The manager makes Fink and Ryan wait, but eventually sees them. Ryan says he has money in his account to cover the check. The manager tells them he is too busy to contact the bank to have the money transferred to the club's bank. Instead, he tells the men to bring over $50,000 in cash.

The roper and the dupe go back to the bank. They are given a satchel to carry the $50,000. Fink takes charge of the money (meanwhile, an armed con is following Fink to make sure nothing happens to the money prior to its intended destination). The men take the cash to the Turf Club. Ryan takes charge of the funds. Outside the club, Lamster is waiting with a telegram in his hand. He says a horse named Jitterbug is going to win at 3-to-1 in the fourth race.

Fink starts to contemplate the huge sums they could make if they bet on Jitterbug. They have $50,000 and are about to receive $256,000. Lamster suggests, "Why don't you place it all on Jitterbug?" Ryan seems to think this is a great idea. He enters the club with Fink. Ryan tells the cashier to hold onto their $256,000 in winnings because they want to make a new bet, on Jitterbug. Fink is very anxious but thinks they are doing the right thing. They will win more than a million dollars if all goes to plan.

Ryan picks up the betting ticket. He takes it outside with Fink and proudly shows it to Lamster, who promptly explodes.

"It says you bet the horse to win! But I said 'place'!" he shouts.

Much yelling ensues. Ryan and Fink race back into the club and try to change their bet. Too late; the race is underway. Their horse comes in second place. They have lost their money.

Stunned, Ryan and Fink stagger outside, where Lamster continues to rant and rave. Fink blames Ryan for the loss and starts to hit him. Lamster joins in the beating, then pulls out a gun. He dramatically "shoots" Ryan, who collapses and starts bleeding from the mouth (through the careful placement of a "cackle bladder").

Lamster panics and hustles Fink away from the scene. The two men seek sanctuary in Lamster's hotel suite. Lamster laments how it was his fault Ryan bet on the wrong horse. He is shocked that he might have killed a man. Even worse, Lamster wails, he has made Fink an accomplice to murder. Fink, needless to say, is completely frazzled and convinced he's going to jail. Lamster gathers himself and assures Fink they can beat the rap. Fink is instructed to sneak out of the hotel and go off to a specific hotel in New Orleans. Lamster will join him in a few days. Lamster helps Fink pack. He says he will pay the hotel bill. Fink is overwhelmed with thoughts of going to prison. The fact that he's lost several thousand dollars doesn't register yet.

Fink leaves town as directed. This step of the con is called "blowing the mark off." Fink waits anxiously in New Orleans. A letter arrives at his hotel from Lamster, who says Ryan has died, so he is now a murderer. Lamster urges his friend to travel to St. Louis, to another hotel. This is done. Then Fink gets a letter advising him to meet Lamster in Detroit. This goes on and on. Eventually, Lamster pens a sad letter saying he's going to Europe because the police are after him. Lamster will keep a low profile in the Old World until the situation dies down and he can figure out a way to recoup their losses.

Fink eventually slinks back home. He probably doesn't even realize he's been swindled. He thinks Ryan is an idiot who got what he deserved. Fink worries obsessively that the police will track him down—although, oddly, they never do. Fink hides his financial losses from his family. He misses Lamster, though, and wishes they were together again; maybe Lamster would have some more racing tips for him. A pity that Lamster is now a wanted man and they can't see each other.

A variation of this Golden Age con formed the basis of the main scam in the movie *The Sting*.

The Rag

A roper with connections to a legitimate brokerage office in New York acquires a list of people who purchase stock through the mail. The roper hunts through the list looking for people who tend to make a lot of risky or speculative purchases. He eventually settles on a dupe. The roper contacts the dupe and explains he's a kind of special broker. The roper knows a man in Indianapolis named "Mr. White," who owns 3,000 shares of a gold mine. The mine isn't currently active. However, through certain insider connections, the roper has learned the mine is going to be reopened shortly. There will be good returns for anyone who holds stock in the gold mine.

The roper adds a sad twist to this tale of gold mines and stock: Mr. White suffers from tuberculosis and is dying. He doesn't know his stock will be worth a fortune soon. Since Mr. White might not even live long enough to see the gold mine return to life, it seems right to purchase the stock from him at a low price.

The mark likes the sound of all of this. He meets the roper, and they travel to the hotel where the consumptive Mr. White is staying. Mr. White is staying in a suite, looking deathly sick. The roper gives Mr. White a bogus story about why he needs to buy the dying man's stock. Mr. White agrees to sell. All the roper and the mark have to do is find someone who will purchase the stock once its value dramatically increases.

The roper knows three brokerage houses that may possibly buy the stock. Fake telegrams are sent, and the roper gets an "offer" from a Chicago brokerage house to purchase the stock at $4 per share.

The roper and the dupe return to the hotel and bargain with Mr. White. He finally agrees to sell his stock at $1.50 per share. The mark gives the "dying" Mr. White $4,475 in cash. Mr. White hands over a thick pile of stock certificates. The dupe is looking forward to selling the stock to the Chicago brokers. He envisions a profit of $7,500, split two ways with the roper.

At this point, the roper announces that he's too busy with other business matters to accompany the mark to Chicago. The roper suggests that the dupe take the stock to the Chicago brokerage house by himself. The roper will pay the mark's travel expenses; then the two of them will split the profit from the sale. The roper sees the dupe off at the trains. He admonishes the man to guard the package of stock carefully.

When the mark gets to Chicago, he finds there is no brokerage house at the address supplied by the roper.

Meanwhile, back at the hotel, Mr. White makes a miraculous recovery. He leaves his deathbed, removes his cadaverous makeup, and splits the mark's cash with the roper.

The Bigger Rag

A roper acquaints himself with a sucker on a train headed to Denver. After spotting the potential mark, the roper contacts a fellow con artist in the Mile-High City. The wheels of a scam begin to turn.

The roper befriends the dupe on the train. When the train reaches Denver, the two have breakfast together. While out on a stroll, the roper happens to spot an acquaintance (in fact, an inside man) in a limousine driven by a chauffeur. The limo is parked by the curb. The con artist excitedly notes that he knows the man in the back seat of the limousine: it's a tycoon named "Duff," who does business deals with the roper's uncle. Old Duff is apparently quite the wizard of Wall Street.

The roper approaches the limousine. Duff is standoffish at first, until the roper mentions his uncle. Duff smiles upon hearing the uncle's name. He complains that he is constantly hounded by reporters and had mistaken the pair for two newspapermen. Duff shows a newspaper clipping containing a story about his amazing success on Wall Street.

Anyone familiar with the Payoff will know how this scam proceeds. The roper asks Duff to "invest" $50 for him. The mark is encouraged to hand over a similar sum. If the sucker demurs, the roper says that's fine; they will split any profits made from his $50 investment. Duff promises to catch up with the two men at their hotel the next day.

Back at the hotel, the roper reveals that Duff is actually a notorious stock manipulator. He works for a well-heeled "combine" that is backed by millions of dollars.

A day after the meeting, Duff shows up at the hotel. He says that each man's $50 investment has reaped $150 apiece. Duff offers to "reinvest" the $150 from each man. This goes on throughout the day. Duff keeps returning with larger and larger amounts of cash. Eventually, the mark's share is built up to around $1,500.

Duff must leave town, but the dupe is hooked at this point and wants to keep investing. Duff suggests the two men make their own investments. He tells them the address of a local brokerage, then explains how he receives insider information from New York City via telegram. Duff wants to know if either the roper or the mark has a bank account in Denver. Neither man does. Duff suggests that $1,500 is too trifling a sum to invest. Duff gives the men a blank check and suggests they fill it in for $100,000.

At this point, the roper balks. He doesn't think he can make good on a $100,000 check. The mark is equally nervous. No fear, says Duff; they won't have to redeem the check. If they follow his instructions, they can make a cool $200,000. It's a sure thing. The roper suggests each man add their $1,500 to the pool, so they have a total of $103,000 to invest.

Duff, the roper, and the mark head off to the brokerage. As in previous similar cons, the place is packed with important-looking men making enormous stock trades. A chalkboard shows the latest bargains, while a ticker tape spits out paper. People are smoking and drinking and passing around huge piles of cash. Again, all of this action is staged for the benefit of the dupe.

Duff introduces the roper and the mark to some people at the brokerage. Before he leaves, Duff suggests they watch American Petroleum. As soon as it goes under $3 per share, the roper and the dupe should buy $103,000 worth of the stock. The price will fluctuate but eventually hit $5.75 a share. At that point, the men should sell out.

Duff leaves. The stock for American Petroleum is listed at $3.75. When it hits $2 7/8, the mark and the roper invest their $103,000. They wait for the stock to increase to $5.75, then sell. The jubilant pair head to the cashier window to collect their enormous winnings. The cashier checks their receipt and begins to count out $206,000. The brokerage manager steps in. The manager wants to know who these men are. The roper and the dupe say they were invited to the place by Duff. The cashier confirms this. The roper admits, however, that he doesn't have enough money in his bank account to cover the $100,000 check. The manager is not impressed. He will hold the $100,000 check until the roper and mark can deposit enough money in the bank to redeem it. Once the check clears, the men will get their $206,000.

The mark protests about the $3,000 in cash each man invested on top of the $100,000 check. The manager says the investment was made in one lump total so he can't release any money until the two men can prove they could cover the $100,000 check.

The roper and dupe retreat to their hotel. Duff arrives and says he will help the men raise their $100,000. The mark puts $55,000 in the pot. The mark sends away for his cash at his local bank, while the roper claims to do the same. Duff contributes a personal check. The mark's money arrives in a few days, and he opens a bank account.

The manager insists the pair bring the $100,000 in cash to the brokerage. This is done. The cashier begins handing over $206,000, when suddenly Duff arrives with a telegram containing an order to sell up to 20,000 shares of a company called Gypsum Consolidated at $20.50 per share.

Duff says he "can handle" 11,000 shares. He tells the roper to put up the $206,000 as security and he will cover the rest.

The roper goes to the cashier window. The mark is contemplating the enormous fortune he thinks is within reach. The roper tells the cashier to hold the $206,000. He returns to Duff and the mark, proudly holding a purchase receipt. Duff explodes. He meant for the men to sell the stock short, not make a purchase. A bitter scene ensues as Duff angrily berates the red-faced roper. When Duff said he "could handle" 11,000 shares, the roper assumed he meant for a purchase to be made.

The roper begs the brokerage manager to countermand the Gypsum purchase. This cannot be done. The order has already been phoned in to New York City. Gypsum Consolidated drops like a stone. The men have lost their $206,000 investment.

The mark, the roper, and Duff end up on the street. The roper is now crying and sniveling and begging forgiveness. Duff tears into him. The men retreat to the mark and the roper's hotel to try to figure out how to get their investment back. A telegram arrives for Duff, instructing him to go to Los Angeles. The telegram refers to "trouble in Denver," which Duff interprets to mean that his bosses are angry with him for botching the sale of Gypsum Consolidated.

Duff says he must leave immediately for LA. He tells the mark to meet up with him there at a certain hotel. When the mark travels to Los Angeles, he receives a letter at the hotel, instructing him to move to another city. This game keeps going until the mark receives a letter from Duff explaining that authorities are investigating the syndicate he works for and all has been lost. Duff is heading to South America to hide out.

The mark wearily travels home. He feels bad for Duff and hopes that someday he can help the man out.

In a variation of this scam, two fake detectives enter the brokerage to "arrest" Duff for insider trading. The brokerage manager identifies the roper and the mark as Duff's accomplices. Duff insists the two are innocent and "convinces" the detectives to let the pair go. The mark and the roper leave in a hurry. The roper urges the mark to return to his hometown and lay low. The mark does just that, relieved at not being arrested.

Further Reading

Herbert Asbury, *The Gangs of New York*, 1927.
Crimes of Persuasion website, http://www.crimes-of-persuasion.com/.
David Maurer, *The Big Con: The Story of the Confidence Man*, 1940.

RIGGING THE NUMBERS RACKET

Essentially an illegal lottery, the numbers racket first made its appearance in the U.S. in the late nineteenth century.

For a small fee (often as little as a few pennies), players bought a "policy" slip from a bookie, containing a three-digit number from 000 to 999. Each day or week, depending on who was running the racket, a winning combination would be selected. If your three-digit number "hit," you won a cash prize. Winning numbers were taken from sports scores, stock market prices, or other objective sources.

For the sake of convenience, bookies would sell "policy slips" in workplaces or at home. Policies were then collected at "policy banks." The gangsters controlling the operation were called "bankers." Each banker employed a large stable of "runners" whose task was to transport bets and policy slips to the bank.

Numbers offered a cheap, low-risk way to gamble. Numbers was a widely accepted vice, played by all members of the community, particularly in low-income neighborhoods. For African Americans, numbers represented one of the few rackets they controlled themselves. While white mobsters dominated other rackets, they turned their noses up at numbers.

Dutch Schultz was one of the first white mobsters to recognize the potential of numbers. Schultz (real name, Arthur Flegenheimer) was a vicious Jewish-American gangster who rose to prominence selling low-quality bootleg beer in the 1920s.

By the early 1930s, far-seeing gangsters realized that Prohibition was such a failure that there was a good chance it would be repealed—which is, in fact, exactly what happened in 1933, after the inauguration of President Franklin D. Roosevelt. Some gangsters branched into labor racketeering and prostitution. Schultz, for his part, decided to earn a new fortune with the numbers game.

Using violent means of persuasion, Schultz took over the Harlem numbers racket in the early 1930s. He allowed African American bankers to stay in business, provided they gave him most of their profits and all their decision-making authority.

At his peak, Schultz was making $12 to $14 million a year just from numbers. This wasn't enough to satisfy him, however. Schultz agreed to a complicated scheme to rig the game and make it tougher to win.

The plan was proposed by a professional gambler named Otto Berman. Berman went by the name "Abbadabba" because he was a mathematical genius, able to juggle complex figures in his head. Abbadabba was a highly successful gambler, with a propensity for choosing winning mounts in horse races.

Bankers under Schultz's control determined their winning three-digit combinations from horse racing results. The cash payoffs from a pre-selected series of races would be tallied. Bankers would take the third digit from each payoff and put them together for the winning combination. Say the payoffs were $125.09, $252.75, and $1,681.34. The winning combination would therefore be 521—as in, 12<u>5</u>, 25<u>2</u>, and 1,68<u>1</u>.

Everyone who had purchased a policy slip bearing the number 521 would be a winner. If only a handful of people played the winning number, the policy bank would earn a healthy profit. But if many people played that number, the bank would have to hand out a fortune in winnings. Policy bankers lived in dread of the day when a popular number "hit."

This is where Abbadabba Berman came in. Each day, Berman would go to one of the racetracks where policy numbers were derived. These tracks were located as far afield as Florida or Ohio.

Berman would watch a few races and then phone a Schultz associate in New York to find out what the most popular numbers were that day. After receiving this information, Berman would calculate the odds in various upcoming races, then place a bunch of late-minute bets. His intention was to alter the payoffs so that heavily played numbers didn't hit.

The scheme was mind-bogglingly complex—but it worked. Berman soon increased the Dutchman's profit margin by a healthy share. Abbadabba himself became the beneficiary of a $10,000 a week salary, courtesy of Schultz. Apparently, the mostly poor African Americans who played numbers never caught on to Schultz's fix.

Schultz and Abbadabba Berman were both gunned down together in 1935, but the numbers racket lived on.

The advent of legal lotteries and "scratch and win" cards available in convenience stores has cut into the popularity of numbers, but the game still exists in certain locales. After all, winnings are tax-free, and it still costs relatively little to play.

Further Reading

Rich Cohen, *Tough Jews: Fathers, Sons, and Gangster Dreams*, 1998.
Nate Hendley, *American Gangsters: Then and Now*, 2010.

Nate Hendley, *Dutch Schultz: The Brazen Beer Baron of New York*, 2005.
Paul Sann, *Kill the Dutchman!* 1971.
Burton Turkus and Sid Feder, *Murder, Inc.: The Story of the Syndicate*, 1951.

THE SPANISH PRISONER

The Spanish Prisoner con is the forerunner of the modern-day "419" or "Nigerian e-mail" scam.

A person receives a letter from a foreign city, supposedly written by a Spanish prisoner or on his behalf. The letter explains that the prisoner is a wealthy man who is being held captive on totally unjust charges. Because the man is in jail, he can't access his fortune. The letter asks the dupe to send some money to another address in Spain (or elsewhere). Supposedly, this money will be used to bribe the guards to release the prisoner from his Spanish hell-hole. The mark is promised a huge fortune for being so helpful. Money is sent, but the "wealthy prisoner" never makes good on his promise of a huge payout. The address the dupe sent his money to, of course, is controlled by the con artist who penned the letter in the first place.

This scam has deep roots. An article published in the March 20, 1898, *New York Times* is headlined, "An Old Swindle Revived—The 'Spanish Prisoner' and Buried Treasure Bait Again Being Offered to Unwary Americans."

"One of the oldest and most attractive and probably most successful swindles known to the police authorities has again come to the surface, having been brought to the attention of Anthony Comstock, president of the Society for the Prevention of Crime ... it is known as the 'Spanish Prisoner' and has been in operation more than 30 years," explained the *Times*.

The *Times* detailed several other attributes of the Spanish Prisoner scam, which are worth noting, given the durability of this con. The letter in question is usually neatly written, though with a few grammar mistakes or foreign idioms to indicate the writer doesn't speak English as a first language. The letter writer has been imprisoned on either trumped-up or political charges. Often, the supposed prisoner has a poor, helpless daughter. The writer hopes to recover his fortune to help his daughter. The "helpless daughter" gambit is designed to tug on the dupe's heart strings and make him more likely to put money in the mail. The prisoner says he sent the letter to the dupe after a mutual friend (who goes unnamed) vouched for his integrity and dependability.

Like many classic cons, the Spanish Prisoner letter mutated into a new scam that continues to be carried on today. The scam in question comes in the form of a frantic e-mail message sent by a foreign dignitary or tycoon (often from Nigeria) who is desperate to recover his lost fortune. The e-mail recipient is promised a share of the wealth if only he can help the poor man regain his wealth.

Further Reading

"An Old Swindle Revived," *New York Times*, March 20, 1898.
Crimes of Persuasion website, http://www.crimes-of-persuasion.com/.

CLASSIC CARD SCAMS
Huge Duke

The Huge Duke is another short con cited by David Maurer in *The Big Con*. It requires good card-playing ability and timing. This con flourished in the early part of the twentieth century, when train travel was more common than it is today.

Three con artists, all expert card players, enter a train. They separate, and each man seeks out a mark. Marks in hand, the con men gather in the club car. One of the con artists requests a card table. The three confidence men determine which mark appears to be the biggest sucker, and invite the sucker to play cards. The discarded marks can stick around and watch the action or amble back to their seats.

At first, the group plays euchre. One of the three con men opines that it is a shame the group isn't playing poker, because he's got such a great hand. The men start betting on their hands as if they were playing poker. At first, they bet with cigars. Eventually, it is suggested that the card players ante up real money to make the game more interesting.

At some point, when the mark wins, the con men let him deal the cards for the next round. By now, the men are playing poker. Because he's able to shuffle the deck, the mark thinks the game couldn't possibly be rigged. The mark is wrong. One of the three con artists "cuts" the deck, secretly introducing a duplicate deck featuring cards that have been carefully pre-arranged in a specific order.

The mark deals and is delighted to get four aces. The con men encourage the mark to bet as high as he is willing to go. If the mark has a limited amount of cash on him, he is told he can write a check, which is put into the pot.

Once the betting ends, the mark confidently puts down his four aces. Only one of the con men, thanks to the carefully pre-arranged deck that was substituted into the game, has a straight flush. The con man wins the pot.

If the mark gets huffy, one of the con artists will offer to give the man his money back (this scenario works best when the mark has put a check in the pot). The con artist offers to rip up the check. This is done. As an added flourish, the con artist might burn the check in an ashtray with a match. In reality, the con man hasn't destroyed the mark's check, but instead a blank check of the same size and color. The con man carries a number of blank checks on him, for just such an occasion. The mark thinks his check has been torn up and burned, and relaxes—until some time later, when his bank informs him that the check has been cashed out.

The apparent destruction of the check is called a "tear up," wrote Maurer. The mark's real check is cashed almost as soon as the con men exit the train, usually at a bank that is in collusion with the scam artists in question.

Further Reading

David Maurer, *The Big Con: The Story of the Confidence Man*, 1940.

Bill Kaplan's Card Sharks

In 1977, Bill Kaplan decided to put his advanced education on hold to play cards. More specifically, he planned to play blackjack or "21," which Kaplan excelled at on the card tables of Las Vegas, where he managed a team of players. It was an audacious move, given that Kaplan had been accepted at the prestigious Harvard Business School.

According to a later profile in *Inc.* magazine, "Kaplan started playing blackjack as an intellectual exercise and always enjoyed the theory of the game as much as its application."

Kaplan was also inspired by a book on the arcane art of "card counting" by Edward Thorp, titled *Beat the Dealer*. Published in 1962, the book advocated a system whereby blackjack cards were assigned numerical values. "Aces, face cards and tens are worth -1; two through six are worth +1; and seven, eight and nine are worth zero," explained *Inc.* magazine.

The player kept a running total in his head of the values of cards displayed. This would allow him to keep track of the number of high-scoring cards yet to be dealt so the player could bet accordingly. The system gave players a slight edge, but it took a lot of play to master (up to 1,000 hours) and even then was somewhat hit and miss. Accordingly, there are several variations on the card-counting practices advocated by Thorp.

While card counting is not against the law, casinos regard it as a form of legal cheating and actively discourage the practice. Some casinos were known to get rough with card counters and administer physical beatings whenever one was spotted. In other situations, card counters were merely asked to leave the premises and never return. Casinos kept photographs and records of known card counters and intercepted them when spotted.

Harvard Business School was less than impressed with Kaplan's extracurricular activities and revoked his acceptance. In a panic, Kaplan wrote a long letter by hand, explaining how he was applying his background in math, statistical analysis, and computer science as head of a team of gamblers. Captaining such a team was excellent real-world experience for a business student, Kaplan pointed out. The letter did the trick, and Kaplan was re-accepted at Harvard Business School.

Kaplan attended classes while running his blackjack team on the side. By the time Kaplan graduated from Harvard Business School in 1980, his team was too burned-out to continue. Unsure of his next move, Kaplan was dining in a Chinese restaurant in Cambridge, Massachusetts, when he overhead some students from MIT (Massachusetts Institute of Technology) discussing card counting. Intrigued, Kaplan introduced himself and soon found himself traveling to Atlantic City, New Jersey, to watch these neophyte hustlers in action.

Kaplan noted some deficiencies in the play of the MIT gang. They played as individuals and used card-counting strategies that were unnecessarily complicated, in his view. Back in Cambridge, Kaplan offered to manage the team, but only if they followed his rules. The students agreed, and the MIT Blackjack Team was formed.

While card counting remained at the core of what the team did, Kaplan believed team play was key. Card players were given specific roles and worked together to beat the blackjack tables. Some players would serve as "spotters," who simply kept an eye on the blackjack table and bet small amounts. The spotters' main function was to signal to "big players" when a game looked ripe for the taking (i.e., when "the count" indicated a dealer was poised to deal high cards). Big players, as the name implied, always bet large sums.

During the week, players on the MIT Blackjack Team took classes and studied. On the weekends, they hit casinos. New team members were attracted through campus advertising and word-of-mouth. At its peak around 1984, the team boasted 35 players.

At first, Kaplan would join in the action himself. By the mid-1980s, however, casinos had made it clear he was an unwanted presence. Kaplan found he was recognized in every casino he went to. He faded into the background, happy to manage the Blackjack Team from a distance and work at his "straight" job—a real estate firm he founded, called Linden Properties. By the late 1980s, Kaplan was no longer involved in the MIT Blackjack Team at all but working full-time in real estate.

Kaplan might have remained happily ensconced in the world of buildings and properties but for the opening a casino in Connecticut in the early 1990s. In 1992, Kaplan decided to put together a new team of card counters. This time, he organized the team as a limited partnership called Strategic Investments. The SI team included 75 players over the course of Kaplan's involvement, hitting casinos in Las Vegas, Montreal, Connecticut, and New Orleans.

It was very difficult to get on one of Kaplan's SI teams. He invented a series of staged tests dubbed "checkouts" to test the mettle of new recruits. Using an MIT classroom as a practice space, newcomers (who were usually referred to Kaplan by word of mouth from other players) would be taught basic blackjack strategy. Then came the "checkout," which consisted of two straight hours of play without making any mistakes. Kaplan encouraged the members of team to shout, act rowdy, and project the bustling ambiance of a typical casino in order to distract the novices. If the newcomer passed this stage, they were taught to count cards. This was followed by another two-hour checkout.

"Every few rounds, we'd ask them, 'What's the count?' If they were off more than once or by more than one, they failed," Kaplan later explained to *Inc.* magazine.

If a player made it through the second stage, they faced one final checkout: three sessions, each lasting two hours, in a casino.

In addition to being a brilliant games strategist, Kaplan was a canny manager of human resources. Players who made it through training and onto a blackjack team had to pony up some of their own cash when gambling. The minimum amount anyone had to give would be around $1,000.

"We required our blackjack players to put some money in the bank so that they understood it from the investors' perspective. It was called the MIT Blackjack Team for a reason. It wasn't a club, it was a team and everyone had a significant stake in the outcome," Kaplan later explained in an interview with *USA Today.*

Kaplan was a strict manager. He put together business plans for his teams, which included details on the number of active players, hours played, team strategy, projected return on investment, etc. He would continuously input new information into the equation when it became available. For instance, a casino might introduce a stricter card shuffling routine, or casino investigators might unmask some of his card counters.

Players also faced a daunting amount of homework. They had to surreptitiously carry Excel spreadsheets with them when they hit the casinos. During bathroom breaks, players would fill in over two dozen rows of data on such things as when they started play, how many chips they cashed, how much they either won or lost in a given hour, etc. After a weekend of gaming, players would hand in their spreadsheets to Kaplan, who fed the information into a computer to determine the earnings for each team member.

Keeping such a close eye on all this data also enabled Kaplan to know if a team member was stealing money. Kaplan didn't horde this information. He would share it with team members so they could work on their game.

Other tactics involved a subtle form of espionage. The Blackjack Team kept a very close watch on new casino openings: "We had one person whose job was to monitor casino openings throughout the world and we would hit them in the first week or two when they were still figuring out how to run things," Kaplan told *USA Today.*

In addition to counting cards, Kaplan advocated other winning strategies. His players had to keep cool and focused at all times, tracking cards despite a multitude of distractions around them. He encouraged patient, steady play over wild, "go for broke" long-shot bets.

"If you bet $500,000 a hand, even with a one percent advantage, you're going to get wiped out if you lose one or two hands in the short run," Kaplan told *USA Today*.

For all of Kaplan's efforts, things didn't always go smoothly. Sometimes, the teams would lose. Sometimes players would be caught counting cards and tossed out of casinos or banned from re-entering them.

In 1993, a player left a paper bag filled with $125,000 in cash in an MIT classroom. The player realized their mistake in the middle of the night and raced back to retrieve the bag, only to discover it was missing. It turned out a janitor had discovered the stash and placed it in his locker for safekeeping.

This incident helped convince Kaplan to abandon his blackjack efforts. He also started to feel he had outgrown the somewhat juvenile, clandestine nature of his casino initiatives.

"As Kaplan got older, professional gambling seemed increasingly at odds with his domestic life, which by the time of the limited partnership included a wife and two small children," stated *Inc.* magazine.

In 1993, Kaplan stopped managing the MIT Blackjack Team. Team players kept going on their own speed for a few more years.

Seven years after leaving the Blackjack Team, Kaplan joined an e-mail company called FreshAddress, where he found new success. He might have remained a wealthy, if obscure entrepreneur, except for a series of books and magazine articles that detailed the adventures of the MIT Blackjack Team. One of these books—*Bringing Down the House*, by Ben Mezrich—was turned into a hugely successful 2008 movie with Kevin Spacey, called *21*. Both the book and the movie took considerable liberties with the story.

If card counting is not against the law, some of the ancillary actions of the Blackjack Team certainly were illegal. These included, among other things, smuggling large amounts of money through airports. An article by Mezrich on the MIT Team published in *Wired* magazine in 2002, for example, opens with an account of a player smuggling a store of $100 bills and $100,000 worth of casino chips on a Boston to Vegas flight. Large amounts of cash are supposed to be declared at airports; failing to do so will trigger suspicions that the courier is shipping money for drug traffickers.

In his magazine account, Mezrich expressed no fear that the customs would spot much less confiscate his casino chips. Apparently, they resemble shapeless blobs on an X-ray, and the customs agents wouldn't likely appreciate their true value.

"The $100 bills are another matter. This is an airport; they can drag me to a windowless room in the basement and handcuff me to a chair. They can confiscate my stash, call in the DEA, FBI and IRS. It will be up to me to prove that I'm not a drug dealer. *To customs agents, $100 bills smell like cocaine*," wrote Mezrich.

Today, Kaplan continues to be a highly successful entrepreneur. His approach to his new business ventures is the same as his approach to the MIT Blackjack Team: minimize risk as much as possible, don't spend money recklessly, and keep a cool head.

In his interview with *USA Today*, Kaplan said his blackjack experience offered some good lessons for businesses: "Seeking opportunity and disequilibrium in the marketplace, managing and mitigating risk, generating returns in the long run without being beat by short-term swings. Pooling capital and human resources because it can't be done with one person with a small amount of money," he said.

Further Reading

Leigh Buchanan, "Luck Is for Losers," Inc.com, August 1, 2008, http://www.inc.com /magazine/20080801/luck-is-for-losers.html.

Del Jones, "5 Questions: Interview with Bill Kaplan," *USA Today*, April 11, 2008.

Ben Mezrich, *Bringing Down the House*, 2002.

Ben Mezrich, "Hacking Las Vegas," *Wired*, September 2002 (NOTE: a slightly fictionalized account of the MIT Blackjack Team).

Rick Swogger, "Interview with 'MIT Mike' Aponte," Blackjackinfo.com, https://www .blackjackinfo.com/interviews/mit-mike-aponte/.

Jenny Zhang, "Card Counting Gig Nets Students Millions," *The Tech*, October 25, 2002.

Three-Card Monte

Three-Card Monte is a simple, if devious, con that was popular in the Old West.

A dealer places three cards on a board, face down, and asks people to pick out the queen. A few marks step forward to play. Several rounds of cards are played. Sometimes a queen is selected, most times it isn't.

The dealer, who has been keeping up a continuous, amusing line of patter, introduces a gambling element into the game. Pick out the queen, you win a dollar. If you fail to find the queen, you owe a dollar. Lured by the scent of easy money and the dealer's witty spiel, a small crowd gathers. The dealer keeps shuffling and re-dealing, talking all the while like a circus carny.

An accomplice sources the crowd and finds someone who looks wealthy. The shill chats up the mark and offers to "rig" the game. The accomplice will pretend to "examine" the cards. When a queen comes up, they will slightly bend the corner so the card can be easily detected the next time it is dealt out. If the mark bets big, the two men stand to make some fast cash. The accomplice pleads poverty, which is why they need to work in conjunction with a well-heeled partner.

The mark agrees to the shill's proposal. The shill steps forward and demands to examine the cards. The dealer hands the deck over. The mark moves close to the accomplice as the latter goes through the deck. The shill makes a big show of going through the cards. With the mark looking over his shoulder, he sources a queen and slyly bends the corner of the card. The shill winks at the mark, then hands the "rigged" deck back to the dealer.

The dealer, who has been gabbing all the while, seemingly oblivious to the shill's machinations, deals out three new cards. The mark waits for the card with the slightly bent ear to turn up. When it does, he bets big—maybe $50. The dealer turns the three cards over and—no queen. The mark is astonished but can't say anything because that would be tantamount to admitting he was cheating.

The game goes on. What the dupe doesn't realize is that the dealer surreptitiously bent the corner of another card while distracting everyone with his ongoing spiel.

The Three-Card Monte keeps going until the crowd gets bored or runs out of money.

Further Reading

David Maurer, *The Big Con: The Story of the Confidence Man*, 1940.

SECTION TWO

BUSINESS FRAUD

INTRODUCTION

Business fraud operates on two underlying principles: people are gullible and people are careless. Con artists who run pyramid or "Ponzi" schemes seek victims who fit the first category. Con artists who counterfeit money or arrange ways to divert cash from automatic bank machines seek victims who fit the latter.

Many of the con artists profiled here, such as Leo Koretz and Charles Ponzi, offered "get-rich-quick" investment schemes that promised spectacular returns. In the face of such scams, the U.S. Securities and Exchange Commission website offers some sage advice: "If an investment seems too good to be true, then it probably is."

While some of these business frauds are decades old, they continue to reappear in new guises, as con artists develop new ways to enrich themselves at their victims' expense.

ADVANCE FEE FRAUD

Advance fee frauds frequently show up in spam e-mails. These messages promise that you've won a lottery or qualify for a loan or credit card, even though you have a shaky credit history (or no memory of having bought a lottery ticket, for that matter). All that's necessary to receive this lottery win/loan/ credit card is to pay an "advance fee" to a particular company or individual.

Sometimes, these offers come over the phone. A financial firm you've never heard of calls to give you a spiel about a lottery win or easy loan/credit terms. Once again, all that is required of you is to pay a little fee, in advance.

The "easy loan/credit" scam is particularly tempting, because there are plenty of more or less legitimate financial firms that specialize in loans and credit for low-income clients. Fortunately, it's relatively easy to determine if a financial firm is really on the level.

For one thing, does the lender care about your credit history? Any legitimate lender or credit card company wants to know your financial background. A lack of interest in how the client has handled loans, money, and credit in the past is a definite red flag. Be wary of advertisements that say things such as, "Bad credit? No problem," or promise "no-hassle" loans/credit in spite of an awful financial history. Be doubly wary of a financial institution that doesn't care about your finances but is very eager to get your Social Security number or bank account information.

Does the lender charge mysterious fees that are difficult to decipher in their financial documents? All banks and financial institutions charge fees for their services. The difference, however, is that legitimate institutions clearly indicate how much these fees are and what they are for. Legitimate institutions don't demand payment of these fees in advance of getting your loan or credit card.

Loans offered over the phone are another major red flag. According to the Federal Trade Commission (FTC), it is illegal in the United States for companies to offer a loan or credit card over the phone and demand that you pay an advance fee before receiving it.

Be equally wary of lenders with sound-alike names. A name that sounds very similar to an established, legitimate financial firm is a giveaway that you're dealing with fraud. If approached by a financial firm offering a loan or a credit card, check to see if the company is listed in the phone directory and actually has a physical address. A financial firm that only advertises a post office box instead of a proper address is deeply suspect.

Lenders and loan brokers are required by law to register in the states where they do business. To determine whether they are registered, contact the Attorney General's office or the Department of Banking or Financial Regulation in your state. Checking registration is a quick way to determine whether you're dealing with a legitimate firm or not.

Be wary if the financial institution asks you to pay a fee to one individual or wants you to send cash via a wire transfer service. The FTC strongly advises against making an advance fee payment for a loan or credit card directly to one individual. A legitimate financial institution would not ask you to direct a fee to one person. The FTC also warns against using a wire transfer service or sending money orders for a loan. If there's a problem, it might be difficult to get your money back. Legitimate financial institutions do not pressure clients to wire money.

People should also rely on simple common sense to avoid getting scammed. Just because you've received a slick brochure in the mail or a polished, well-written e-mail offering loans or credit cards, don't assume they're from legitimate firms. Con artists will go to great lengths to create phony websites and promotional material to look legit.

People suffering from debt problems should turn to a legitimate credit or debt-counseling service rather than a shady lender or a mysterious voice on the phone telling you of the fabulous windfall that can be yours, for a fee.

Further Reading

Federal Bureau of Investigation, "Common Fraud Schemes," https://www.fbi.gov/scams-safety/fraud.

Federal Trade Commission, "Consumer Information: Advance Fee Loans," http://www.consumer.ftc.gov/articles/0078-advance-fee-loans.

AFFINITY FRAUD

On October 8, 2014, Ephren Taylor II, an African American entrepreneur, author, conference speaker, and self-described "social capitalist" pled guilty in an Atlanta federal court to conspiracy to commit mail and wire fraud.

"From at least April 2009 through October 2010, Ephren Taylor II, then CEO of City Capital Corporation and his co-defendant, Wendy Connor, the former COO of City Capital Corporation, participated in a conspiracy to defraud investors. In pleading guilty, Taylor acknowledged that he defrauded hundreds of investors of more than $7 million nationwide," stated a press release from the U.S. Attorney's Office, Northern District of Georgia.

Prior to his arrest, Taylor was known as a financial wizard who preached a gospel of self-improvement and upward mobility to primarily black, church-going audiences. In 2006, Taylor spearheaded an "Urban Wealth Tour," in which he and a clutch of bankers and company executives traveled to communities to spread their vision of financial uplift. Speaking engagements were often held in churches. Among other venues, Taylor spoke at mega-churches run by black celebrity minister Eddie Long in Atlanta and white celebrity minister Joel Osteen in Texas.

During this tour, Taylor promoted two schemes that his rapt followers could buy into: promissory notes that could be used to fund worthy small inner-city businesses (including laundries, juice bars, and gas stations) and "sweepstakes" machines (basically, computers loaded with various games that let players win cash prizes). People who bought into either of these initiatives could earn very healthy returns, all the while improving the lot of the black community.

Or that was the theory, at least. In truth, most of the millions these schemes brought in ended up in Taylor's back pocket. By promoting financial skullduggery to a very specific audience, Taylor epitomized a con known as "affinity fraud." Information provided on the U.S. Securities and Exchange Commission website describes affinity fraud as "investment scams that prey upon members of identifiable groups, such as religious or ethnic communities, the elderly or professional groups."

According to the SEC, "fraudsters who promote affinity scams frequently are—or pretend to be—members of the targeted group. They often enlist respected community or religious leaders from within the group to spread the

How to Avoid Affinity Fraud

1. Check out everything: "Never make an investment solely on the recommendation of a member of an organization or religious or ethnic group to which you belong."
2. Do not fall for investments that promise spectacular profits or "guaranteed" returns: "If an investment seems too good to be true, then it probably is."
3. Be skeptical of any investment opportunity that is not in writing: "Fraudsters often avoid putting things in writing, but legitimate investments are usually in writing."
4. Don't be pressured or rushed into buying an investment before you have a chance to think about—or investigate—the "opportunity": "Just because someone you know made money or claims to have made money, doesn't mean you will too."
5. Fraudsters are increasingly using the Internet to target particular groups through e-mail spam: "If you receive an unsolicited e-mail from someone you don't know, containing a 'can't miss' investment, your best move is to pass up the 'opportunity' and forward the spam to the SEC at enforcements@sec.gov."

Source: U.S. Securities and Exchange Commission website, https://www.sec .gov/investor/pubs/affinity.htm

word about the scheme by convincing people that a fraudulent investment is legitimate and worthwhile. Many times, those leaders become unwitting victims of the fraudster's ruse."

Taylor himself was born in Fort Gibson, Mississippi, in 1982. His family moved to Alabama, Georgia, Massachusetts, and Florida before settling down in Kansas City, Kansas, in 1993. Taylor's father worked as an electrical engineer at a nuclear power station and later became a minister in the Church of Christ. Taylor's mother was a homemaker.

At age twelve, Taylor apparently started designing his own video games. Supposedly he picked up a few books, figured out how to program computers, and developed a game, which he sold to schoolmates for $10 a disc. In 1999, Taylor and a high school friend named Michael Stahl launched a job-search website called 4TeensNetwork, which gave high school and college students access to job listings from companies such as Wal-Mart and Target. Renamed GoFerret.Go.com, the website was a success.

The company that ran the site "was eventually dissolved in the 2001 tech bust, but at its height was valued at $3.5 million," reported a March 3, 2009, article posted on Forbes.com.

Taylor's next move was to launch an investment firm called Christian Capital Group to expand upon his interest in socially conscious investing. The group supposedly arranged real estate development deals in inner cities that channeled money toward churches and community organizations.

Taylor formed a company called AmoroCorp in 2000. This later merged with City Capital, where Taylor ended up as CEO. At the time of the appointment, Taylor boasted that he was the youngest African American CEO of a publicly traded company in the United States.

Like the Christian Capital Group, City Capital prided itself on being progressive-minded. Taylor touted himself as a "social capitalist," wrote books, and appeared on many TV shows, including Fox News and CNBC, to expound his cause. He gave financial management seminars and lectures and claimed (falsely, as it turned out) to donate a fifth of City Capital's profits to charity. At one point, Taylor even met with members of the Congressional Black Caucus to share his views on social betterment through investment.

Taylor's key investments continued to be promissory notes and sweepstakes machines. He promised interest rates as high as 20 percent on the promissory notes, which would supposedly be used to fund various worthy causes. He claimed that the sweepstakes machines could generate owners 300 percent investor returns and were 100 percent risk-free, neither of which was actually the case.

Although highly successful at first, some of Taylor's backers soon became concerned about their investments. At one point Taylor locked the doors of the offices he worked out of in North Carolina, because so many panicked investors were showing up in person. Investors tried unsuccessfully to contact him via e-mail or phone about the money they had given him.

Eventually, the authorities had enough. A Securities and Exchange Commission press release from April 12, 2012, accused Taylor and Co. of "running a Ponzi scheme that targeted socially conscious investors in church congregations."

In a Ponzi scheme, money from new investors is used to pay off old investors. Ponzi funds do not back anything tangible that would generate wealth. When new investors stop buying in and old investors en masse start demanding their money, plus interest, the scheme falls apart.

Taylor "preyed upon investors' faith and their desire to help others, convincing them that they could earn healthy returns while also helping their communities," said David Woodcock, director of SEC's Fort Worth Regional Office, in the press release.

The SEC press release went on: "Instead of investor money going to charitable causes and economically disadvantaged businesses as promised, Taylor secretly diverted hundreds of thousands of dollars to publishing and promoting his books, hiring consultants to refine his public image and funding his wife's singing career … City Capital's business ventures were consistently unprofitable and no meaningful amount of investor money was ever sent to charities."

Among other things, Taylor and his wife, Meshelle Johnson, made a music video for a song called, appropriately enough, "Billionaire." In the video, Johnson is seen wearing white fur and diamonds, while the lyrics praise wealth and lavish living.

In June 2014, Taylor and his business partner Wendy Connor were arrested on federal charges of conspiracy to commit mail and wire fraud.

Further Reading

Leslie Collins, "'Youngest African-American CEO' Pleads Guilty to $7M Fraud," *Kansas City Business Journal*, October 9, 2014.

Common Ground Foundation website, Biography, Ephren W. Taylor II, http://www.commongroundfoundation.org/ephren.html.

Melanie Linder, "The First Million: Ephren Taylor II," Forbes.com, March 3, 2009, http://www.forbes.com/2009/03/03/first-million-taylor-entrepreneurs-finance_ephren.htm.

U.S. Securities and Exchange Commission website, "Affinity Fraud—How to Avoid Investment Scams That Target Groups," http://www.sec.gov/investor/pubs/affinity.htm.

ATM SKIMMING

ATM Skimming is the art of ripping off automated teller machines. This has traditionally been done through the use of hidden cameras, to pick up a customer's personal identification number (PIN), or a phony keyboard placed over the real thing to record keystrokes.

According to the FBI, skimming devices are generally only installed for short periods of time—usually just for a few hours. Keeping a camera or phony keyboard on an ATM for longer runs the risk of detection. Often the phony keyboards are held in place by nothing more elaborate than adhesive tape.

Once the cameras or keyboards have been removed, criminals "download the stolen account information and encode it onto blank cards. The cards are used to make withdrawals from victims' accounts at other ATMs," states the FBI.

ATMs aren't the only target; scammers have also hit up automated gas pump machines and point-of-sale devices.

The FBI points out that ATM skimming is far from a petty crime; in fact, the Bureau reports that "ATM skimming is a favorite activity of Eurasian crime groups." Indeed, the FBI helped break an alleged ATM ring that linked bank card thefts in Europe to unauthorized bank machine withdrawals in the United States.

A March 26, 2014, press release from the Chicago division of the FBI stated, "Seventeen defendants are facing federal fraud or related charges for their alleged roles in an international ATM skimming and money laundering scheme involving hundreds of thousands of dollars. Two defendants were arrested in Sofia, Bulgaria, and 13 defendants were arrested yesterday in Chicago and several suburbs by FBI agents following a lengthy international investigation."

The release continued, "The alleged scheme involved using ATM and debit card numbers and the personal identification numbers associated with them, which were fraudulently obtained in Europe, to withdraw money from victims'

Tips from the FBI on How to Avoid Being a Victim of ATM Skimming

- Take a close look at the ATM, gas pump, or credit card reader prior to actually using it. If something looks out of place or suspicious (adhesive tape is a dead giveaway), don't use the machine in question.
- If you enter your PIN, shield the keypad with your free hand so hidden cameras can't record your number.
- Where possible, use ATMs that are indoors (it is more difficult for criminals to install skimming devices on an indoor ATM).
- If the ATM won't return your card after completing the transaction or hitting the "cancel" button, immediately get in touch with the financial institution that issued you the card.

Source: FBI website, https://www.fbi.gov/news/stories/2011/july/atm_071411

accounts using automated teller machines at various locations in the Chicago area. The charges were brought in a 29-count indictment which was returned by a federal grand jury on March 12 and was unsealed following the arrests and made public today.

"The indictment also seeks forfeiture of approximately $200,000 from the fifteen defendants as alleged proceeds of fraud. The federal government also seeks another $50,000 from three defendants as alleged proceeds of money laundering."

According to the FBI, the ring would illicitly obtain bank card information in Europe. The data was allegedly encoded onto the magnetic strip of blank or recycled cards. The cards would then be used in Chicago-area ATMs to withdraw funds.

The defendants are accused of "making ATM withdrawals shortly before and after midnight in the time zone of the issuing bank in an attempt to circumvent the daily withdrawal limits on the victims' accounts. The defendants also coordinated ATM transactions to withdraw money before the issuing banks could detect the fraud and deactivate the ATM and debit card numbers," stated the Chicago division FBI press release.

In the same press release, Robert J. Holley, Special Agent in Charge of the Chicago Office of the Federal Bureau of Investigation, said the indictment was intended to "address a transnational crime problem that can affect virtually anyone with a bank account and carries significant financial consequences."

Some new point-of-sale devices in stores don't require customers to manually enter their PIN. Instead, a customer merely taps the device with their credit or debit card to record a sale. While highly convenient for customers, this technology opens new vistas to ATM scammers always on the lookout for new ways to thieve.

Further Reading

Federal Bureau of Investigation, Chicago Division, "Seventeen Defendants Indicted in Chicago in International ATM Skimming and Money Laundering Scheme, Two Arrested in Bulgaria," March 26, 2014.

Federal Bureau of Investigation, "Taking a Trip to the ATM? Beware of 'Skimmers,'" https://www.fbi.gov/news/stories/2011/july/atm_071411.

U.S. Attorney's Office, Southern District of Florida, "Debit Card Skimming Group Arrested and Charged with Fraud and Identity Theft," May 1, 2009.

U.S. Attorney's Office, Southern District of New York, "Bulgarian Citizen Sentenced in Manhattan Federal Court to 21 Months in Prison for Stealing $1.8 Million from Banks Using ATM 'Skimming' Scheme," July 13, 2011.

U.S. Attorney's Office, Southern District of New York, "Manhattan U.S. Attorney Charges Bulgarian Man with Using Stolen Bank Account Information to Defraud Banks of Over $1 Million," September 23, 2010.

COUNTERFEITING

Counterfeiting has a long, notorious history in the United States. At the outset of the Civil War, it was estimated a third of all currency in circulation was fake. This might have had something to do with the fact that 1,600 state banks at the time printed their own bank notes.

"Each note carried a different design, making it difficult to distinguish the 4,000 varieties of counterfeits from the 7,000 varieties of genuine notes," explains the website of the United States Secret Service.

In 1863, the U.S. government introduced a national paper-based currency. While so-called "greenbacks" were intended to fund the Civil War, it was also hoped that a national currency would cut down on counterfeiting. Alas, that was not the case, and two years after the national paper currency was issued, the U.S. Secret Service was formed, with a mandate to fight counterfeiting. The Secret Service didn't start guarding presidents until decades later.

The Secret Service website states, "Although counterfeiting has been substantially curtailed since the creation of the Secret Service, this crime continues to represent a potential danger to the nation's economy and its citizens. Production methods used in counterfeiting operations have evolved over the years from the traditional method of offset printing to color copiers and more recently, to scanners, computers, and inkjet printers."

The advent of technology has been bad news for enforcers of the law. According to the Secret Service website, "Today's counterfeiter is able to produce counterfeit currency with basic computer training and skills afforded by trial and error and public education. Counterfeiting passing statistics are likely to increase because of several factors: the instruments of production are more readily available, the capabilities of these machines continue to improve, and the techniques are more readily understood by an increasingly large segment of the population, including those with criminal intent."

The U.S. government, of course, is quite interested in outsmarting counterfeiters, which is why on October 8, 2013, the Federal Reserve began supplying newly redesigned $100 bills. These new bills boasted two premium security features: "a blue 3D security ribbon with images of bells and 100s and a color-changing bell in an inkwell," reported the Secret Service. The government is confident such measures will thwart counterfeiters.

Frank Bourassa, the "most prolific counterfeiter in American history" according to *GQ* magazine, might beg to differ. In the 2010s, Bourassa allegedly created over $200 million in fake U.S. currency but never served time in an American prison.

Bourassa's hometown and base of operations was Trois-Rivieres, Quebec. While Bourassa's nationality was Canadian, his counterfeit notes were designed to resemble American dollars.

How to Detect Counterfeit Money

Portrait—The genuine portrait appears lifelike and stands out distinctly from the background. The counterfeit portrait is usually lifeless and flat. Details merge into the background, which is often too dark or mottled.

Federal Reserve and Treasury Seals—On a genuine bill, the saw-tooth points of the Federal Reserve and Treasury seals are clear, distinct, and sharp. The counterfeit seals may have uneven, blunt, or broken saw-tooth points.

Border—The fine lines in the border of a genuine bill are clear and unbroken. On the counterfeit, the lines in the outer margin and scrollwork may be blurred and indistinct.

Serial numbers—Genuine serial numbers have a distinctive style and are evenly spaced. The serial numbers are printed in the same ink color as the Treasury seal. On a counterfeit, the serial numbers may differ in color or shade of ink from the Treasury seal. The numbers may not be uniformly spaced or aligned.

Paper—Genuine currency paper has tiny red and blue fibers embedded throughout. Often counterfeiters try to simulate these fibers by printing tiny red and blue lines on their paper. Close inspection reveals, however, that on the counterfeit note the lines are printed on the surface, not embedded in the paper. It is illegal to reproduce the distinctive paper used in the manufacturing of United States currency.

Source: United States Secret Service website, http://www.secretservice.gov/money _detect.shtml

In an extensive profile published in *GQ* magazine, Bourassa claimed he left school and home at age fifteen and promptly organized scams to enrich himself. He said he ran a car-theft ring that was responsible for 500 vehicle thefts and was involved in the illegal marijuana trade. In 2006, he was charged with and convicted for drug offences after one of his pot suppliers was raided by police. Bourassa was fortunate in that he was in Canada, not in the U.S., home of punitive jail sentences for drug criminals. Bourassa told *GQ* he received a 12-month sentence but only served a quarter of that time, under house arrest.

Following this encounter with the law, Bourassa decided to try his hand at counterfeiting. He visited online chat rooms frequented by counterfeiters and studied the website for the Secret Service, which offers insights on fake currency. Through this self-education process, Bourassa learned that big-time counterfeiters don't try to pass their own currency at local businesses. Instead, large-scale counterfeiters typically sell their phony banknotes in bulk to other criminals, at the going rate of 30 real dollars for every 100 fake. Bourassa also discovered that it was foolhardy to print large denominations: clerks are more suspicious of $100 bills than twenties—which means the $100 bill redesign might be for naught.

Bourassa rented a garage in Trois-Rivieres from a farmer who wasn't concerned about what he did with the space. Using profits from his pot business, Bourassa acquired $300,000 worth of equipment, including a four-color Heidelberg offset printer and a single-color Heidelberg printer. He also secured the services of a print shop employee with a criminal record, who knew how to make fake money.

Counterfeit banknotes not only have to look real, they have to feel like the genuine item as well. American dollars are made with special paper that is a blend of 75 percent cotton, 25 percent linen. Before it leaves the U.S. Mint, this stock is loaded with features such as watermarks, security strips, and miniscule red and blue fibers embedded in the paper itself to make counterfeiting difficult.

Mills that sell blank paper are wary of customers who ask for the special 75/25 cotton/linen blend: such transactions tend to attract the attention of the Secret Service. Bourassa started hitting up paper mills outside of the U.S. in Europe and Asia. He sometimes claimed to be "Thomas Moore," a representative of a Quebec stationery shop. Other times, he pretended to be "Jackson

What to Do If You Receive a Counterfeit Bill

- Do not return it to the passer.
- Delay the passer if possible.
- Observe the passer's description, as well as that of any companions and the license plate numbers of any vehicles used.
- Contact your local police department or United States Secret Service field office.
- Write your initials and the date in the white border areas of the suspect note.
- Limit the handling of the note. Carefully place it in a protective covering such as an envelope.
- Surrender the note or coin only to a properly identified police officer or a U.S. Secret Service special agent.

Source: United States Secret Service website, http://www.secretservice.gov/money _receive.shtml

Maxwell," representing the Keystone Investment and Trading Company, a securities firm.

In January 2009, Bourassa landed a deal with the Artoz paper company, based in Lenzburg, Switzerland. He claimed he was looking for paper with a few security features, on which to print bond certificates. According to *GQ*, Bourassa "tweaked and refined his order over many months, nudging one felonious tidbit after another onto the papermaker's plate." Among other things, Bourassa convinced the paper mill to add a security strip with microscopic numerals and a watermark to his bulk paper order.

Bourassa received his shipment of special paper in late 2009. The hired gun from the print shop used the paper to make millions of dollars in counterfeit banknotes. With some difficulty, buyers willing to purchase Bourassa's phony money were located. One of Bourassa's contacts, a man who sold stolen heavy equipment, was interested in buying some counterfeit cash in order to resell it to a customer of his. Unknown to the equipment vendor, this customer was actually an undercover police officer. Bourassa directly sold the vendor a supply of fake cash, which was passed on in turn to the undercover cop.

On May 23, 2012, police staged an early morning raid on Bourassa's girlfriend's house. Police rousted Bourassa and his girlfriend from bed. In the residence, police found guns, computers, printing plates, and over $1 million in fake currency. As a bonus for police, Bourassa's car was found to contain residue from illegal drugs. Under questioning at police headquarters, Bourassa didn't deny that the money and equipment were his. He chose not to mention, however, that he apparently had an even bigger stash of counterfeit cash, with a face value of over $200 million, at his rented garage.

In addition to counterfeiting, Bourassa faced firearm and drug offences. He was alarmed to discover that police wanted to charge his girlfriend and seize her house. Bourassa insisted she knew nothing and was innocent. He was even more alarmed when a pair of U.S. Secret Service agents dropped by the interrogation. These agents told Bourassa they wanted him extradited to the U.S., where he faced decades of jail time in a federal penitentiary.

Bourassa's lawyer argued that the warrant used to search the girlfriend's home was based on shaky evidence—police had observed Bourassa delivering counterfeit cash to the equipment vendor but didn't actually see him enter the man's house—and therefore the search was illegal. The lawyer threatened to file a motion to dismiss the case. The Crown (the Canadian authorities who prosecute criminal offences) agreed to drop extradition proceedings if the lawyer dropped the motion to dismiss. This was accepted. Bourassa would not serve time in America.

Released from jail, Bourassa took a construction job and avoided the garage containing his printers and stockpile of fake money. He was aware police were almost certainly tailing him, to bolster their case.

In the fall of 2013, the Crown offered Bourassa a three-year jail term. Canadian jail sentences being what they are, Bourassa would only actually serve six months. He turned the offer down, however, and in December the case went to trial. At this juncture, Bourassa mentioned the extra loot he had stashed in his rented garage to his lawyer. The lawyer passed on this information to the Crown. Bourassa offered to give up the fake millions if prosecutors agreed not to seize his girlfriend's house, gave him back his car, and reduced his jail sentence to six weeks, already served.

"After some negotiation, the Crown agreed, more or less, to Frank's offer. If he could indeed produce the bills, he would pay a fine of $1,350 on the drug possession charges and one of the biggest counterfeiters in the history of the trade would slip off the hook after a month and a half behind bars," stated *GQ*. The black-market equipment vendor, by contrast, received 31 months in jail, for selling illegal goods and involvement with counterfeiting.

Canadian authorities arranged for Bourassa to take them to his missing millions in counterfeit banknotes on January 31, 2014. Prior to that date, Bourassa had a friend pick up the stash in a truck, then leave said truck in the parking lot of a hotel where another associate worked. On the day in question, Bourassa led a caravan of police to the parking lot in question, then to the truck and the phony money inside.

Further Reading

Frank Bourassa website, http://www.frankbourassa.com/en/.
Randy James Monday, "The Art of Counterfeiting Money," *TIME*, June 15, 2009.
Wells Tower, "The Great Paper Caper," *GQ*, October 28, 2014.
United States Secret Service, "Criminal Investigations," http://www.secretservice.gov/criminal.shtml.
United States Secret Service, "Know Your Money," http://www.secretservice.gov/know_your_money.shtml.

CHARLES PONZI

Throughout the early summer of 1920, newspapers in Boston regularly regaled their readers with stories about the amazing financial acumen of one Charles Ponzi. "DOUBLES THE MONEY WITHIN THREE MONTHS; 50 Per Cent Interest Paid in 45 Days by Ponzi," read the front of the *Boston Post*, on July 24, 1920. The same article claimed that Ponzi was worth $8.5 million—a staggering sum in an era when an annual salary of a few thousand dollars was considered respectable.

The man at the center of this media adulation was an Italian immigrant who ran a Boston-based financial house called the Securities Exchange Company. Founded in December 1919, the Securities Exchange Company was taking in millions of dollars a week by mid-1920, much of it from low-income Italian immigrants.

"For a few months in 1920, Boston was the site of an astonishing daily ritual. Every morning, hundreds of people, their numbers swelling week after week, lined up in front of Ponzi's office—the Securities Exchange Company he called it—often with their life savings in their pockets. They would hand over their greenbacks to tellers behind old-fashioned caged windows, their bills piling up so fast that when the drawers were filled with them, they would be tossed into wire baskets. In return, each would receive a small, ornate certificate, promising a 50-percent return in 45 days," stated the *New York Times*.

The supposed secret of Ponzi's success was the lowly International Reply Coupon (IRC). These coupons could be redeemed for stamps and were designed to facilitate global correspondence. Someone in Europe who wanted to solicit a reply from a missive sent to a citizen in the United States would include an IRC in their letter. That way, the recipient of the letter wouldn't have to pay for return postage out of their own pocket.

Ponzi claimed he had figured out a clever way to profit from IRCs. According to international treaty, the purchase price of the coupons was set at the cost of postage in their country of origin. Once mailed abroad, however, IRCs could be redeemed for stamps set at the price of postage in the country of receipt. In theory, someone could purchase reply coupons in a country with a weak economy then redeem them for higher value stamps in a country with a strong economy. The stamps could then be sold for cash, earning a tidy profit.

Ponzi said he had an army of agents, backed with U.S. dollars, who purchased enormous amounts of IRCs in war-torn European nations with battered economies. These coupons were then brought to America, redeemed, and sold. Or so Ponzi said. And now, Ponzi was looking for people who wanted to invest in this intriguing venture.

Ponzi saw himself as more than just a clever financier; he thought he was a hero to the downtrodden masses: "With considerable skill, he portrayed himself as a populist champion who would enable small investors to earn their rightful places in the world. He claimed to accept money from investors as a form of altruism and they rewarded him with fanatic loyalty," stated an article on Ponzi and financial fraudsters by noted author Ron Chernow in the March 23, 2009, *New Yorker*.

The problem was that Ponzi wasn't actually buying many IRCs, much less enough to fund the massive returns he promised. He was simply robbing Peter to pay Paul: paying off old investors with money coming in from new investors. As long as new investors kept coming on board, the scheme worked fine. Only Ponzi's luck was about to run out.

Within days of the *Boston Post's* laudatory article, Ponzi's house of cards collapsed, leaving most of his investors broke while attaching his name to a financial scheme that remains common even today.

The man whose name become synonymous with investment fraud was born in northern Italy in 1882. Originally named Carlo Ponzi, he would later tell reporters he came from a rich family and had studied at the University of Rome. Whatever the truth was, Ponzi arrived in Boston Harbor on November 15, 1903. The 21-year-old immigrant had $2.50 in cash on him. Ponzi would have had more, but he had indulged himself by purchasing a second-class ticket, so he didn't have to travel in steerage.

"In style, breeding and aspiration, he was less one of those huddled masses yearning to breathe free than he was a hustler yearning to be rich," noted an April 10, 2005, article in the *New York Times*.

Like most new immigrants, Ponzi did a series of menial jobs, from waiting tables in New York City, to sign painting in Florida. He wound up in Montreal, where he worked for a bank. In 1908, he was placed in a Canadian prison for check forgery. Upon his release in 1910, Ponzi went back to the United States, where he was slapped with a two-year term for trying to smuggle Italian immigrants from Canada to the U.S. He served his time in the federal penitentiary in Atlanta.

In 1917, lured by a newspaper ad from one J. R. Poole, a merchandise broker looking for a clerk, Ponzi returned to Boston. Shortly after his return, he spotted a lovely young lady on a streetcar; her name was Rose Gnecco. They became romantically involved and were married in February 1918. By this point Ponzi was no longer working for Poole. For a while, Ponzi ran his father-in-law's grocery business. By all accounts, he was not a success at the grocery trade.

Somewhat at loose ends, Ponzi decided to start an international trade journal. He asked a bank called the Hanover Trust Company for a $2,000 loan to launch his publication but was haughtily turned down.

In August 1919, Ponzi received a life-changing piece of correspondence from Spain. A Spanish correspondent had somehow found out about Ponzi's proposed international trade journal, and contacted him for further information. Included in the Spaniard's letter was an International Reply Coupon. The letter writer hoped that Ponzi would use this coupon to buy return postage and write him back. Ponzi, however, had other ideas.

"Purchased in a Spanish post office for 30 centavos, [the IRC] could be exchanged for a U.S. postage stamp worth five cents, a redemption rate that was fixed by international treaty. But the Spanish peseta, as Ponzi knew, had fallen recently in relation to the dollar. Theoretically, someone who bought a postal reply coupon in Spain could redeem it in the United States for about a 10 percent profit," reported the *Smithsonian* magazine.

Many European countries were in situations similar to Spain, with struggling currencies. Knowing this, Ponzi smelled opportunity. In December 1919, he launched the Securities Exchange Company, promising investors a 50 percent return on their money in 90 days (later halved to 45 days). The money to pay for such staggering returns was supposedly derived from sales of IRCs.

Business was slow at first: in February 1920, the Securities Exchange Company took in a mere $5,290. Word soon spread of the miracle financial man, however. By April, Ponzi's company brought in $140,000. This leapt to $440,000 by May, and $2.5 million in June 1920. In July, at the peak of business, the Securities Exchange Company generated nearly $6.5 million in investments.

Ponzi was living it up. He had a 12-room mansion in a posh Boston suburb, servants, cars, and lovely clothes. He purchased commercial and rental properties in Boston and even bought out the Hanover Trust Bank (the same institution that spurned him months before). The worm soon turned, however.

U.S. postal authorities pointed out that there weren't enough IRCs in circulation to generate millions of dollars in profit. Indeed, to bring in the kind of earnings claimed by Ponzi, his agents would have to be purchasing and transporting shiploads of postal coupons. Making the situation worse, authorities in Italy, France, and Romania temporarily stopped selling IRCs.

When questioned about such matters, Ponzi would demur. He claimed he had figured out a secret formula that he was loath to reveal, that allowed him to earn massive postal coupon profits despite certain setbacks.

Needless to say, government officials became interested in Ponzi and wanted to take a closer look at his books.

On July 26, 1920, Ponzi announced he would no longer take any new investors until the U.S. District Attorney had completed an audit of his business. This news caused a run at the Securities Exchange Company, as fearful investors demanded their money back. Strangely enough, Ponzi obliged. Instead of taking his profits and running, Ponzi stayed in Boston and paid out investors as best he could. In one day, he gave out over $1 million. Ponzi sent out sandwiches and coffee to be distributed free to the lines of people snaking outside the building that housed his office.

Such magnanimity didn't stop the bleeding. Investors continued to besiege Ponzi, and he was rapidly running out of money.

At month's end, financier Clarence Barron spoke to reporters, casting scorn on Ponzi's investment methods. In remarks printed in the July 30, 1920, *Wall Street Journal*, Barron said he doubted a recent, penniless Italian immigrant could have discovered "a hole in international postal arrangements by which he can pull out practically from government treasuries millions a month."

Barron said there was a shortage of paper in Europe, making it highly unlikely that any country was printing millions of dollars' worth of postal coupons. He also pointed out the obvious: "no government, rich or poor, carries any stock of postage stamps or post cards in any post office beyond the legitimate weekly or monthly requirements of the local community." Post offices kept such a limited supply of IRCs on hand, there was no way anyone could purchase them in bulk, as Ponzi claimed his agents were doing.

On August 2, 1920, Ponzi's former publicity manager, William McMasters told the *Boston Post* that his ex-boss was "hopelessly insolvent."

More revelations were to come. On August 11, 1920, the *Boston Post* reported on Ponzi's criminal past, complete with mug shots from his stint in a Canadian prison. By this point, a government auditor had determined that Ponzi had $3 million worth of debt (a figure that later jumped to $7 million) and almost no assets. The same day, the Massachusetts Commissioner of Banks closed the Hanover Trust Co. Half a dozen other banks would soon crash in the wake of this closure.

Ponzi was arrested, charged by federal authorities of using the mails to defraud. He surrendered himself to the Federal Building in Boston and was held on $25,000 bail.

"It turned out that Ponzi had never actually got around to buying many postal coupons and that [his business] was all a colossal fraud," stated the *New Yorker*. By one estimate, Ponzi had purchased a little more than $60 worth of IRCs, hardly enough to fuel a powerhouse investment company.

It remains unclear if Ponzi was a cold-blooded conman or was simply deluded. "Ponzi's investors, it turned out, were not the only dreamers; so too, was Ponzi himself. Never did he think he was doing anything wrong. Always he thought he would find a way out of his fix, a way to make everyone whole," reported the April 10, 2005, article in the *New York Times*.

Indeed, some investors refused to believe that Ponzi was a crook. They held onto their investment certificates, convinced their man would triumph at trial and pay them their promised returns.

Authorities took another view. Ponzi was convicted on federal charges of using the mails to defraud. He was given a five-year sentence. He served 3.5 years, in Plymouth, Massachusetts, then was paroled. More legal troubles followed, involving fraud. Ponzi tried to hide out as a seaman working on an Italian freighter. Authorities tracked him down in New Orleans and sent him back to Massachusetts, where he spent time in state prison in Charlestown.

Ponzi was released from jail in 1934. He was promptly deported to Italy on October 7, 1934, never having taken out U.S. citizenship. His wife divorced him two years later.

At the time, Italy was dominated by Fascist dictator Benito Mussolini. Ponzi did well for himself, at first. He got a job with an Italian airline that did business between Italy and Brazil. This new career failed, however, after the United States entered World War II in December 1941. The Brazilian government had discovered the airline was covertly shipping strategic supplies to Italy. This was not something the U.S. government—now at war with Italy, Germany, and Japan—would approve of. Brazil backed out of their airline deal, and Ponzi lost his position.

Ponzi took up menial jobs, teaching English and French. He also worked as an interpreter. He died on January 18, 1949, in a Rio de Janeiro charity hospital. Although Ponzi was broke when he died, he did achieve a curious kind of immortality. His name is now a byword for a particular kind of financial fraud.

The website of the U.S. Securities and Exchange Commission states, "A Ponzi scheme is an investment fraud that involves the payment of purported returns to existing investors from funds contributed by new investors. Ponzi scheme organizers often solicit new investors by promising to invest funds in opportunities claimed to generate high returns with little or no risk. With little or no legitimate earnings, Ponzi schemes require a constant flow of money from new investors to continue. Ponzi schemes inevitably collapse, most often when it becomes difficult to recruit new investors or when a large number of investors ask for their funds to be returned."

Ponzi schemes still exist, to this day. In 2009 New York City financier Bernie Madoff was convicted of essentially running a Ponzi scheme with investors' money. Just as Ponzi had his supporters, people who invested with Madoff thought he was a financial wizard. As it turned out, Madoff's financial kingdom was built on foundations as shaky as the rickety structure Ponzi built around postal coupons.

Further Reading

"Big Run on Ponzi Company," *Wall Street Journal*, August 4, 1920.

Ralph Blumenthal, "Lost Manuscript Unmasks Details of Original Ponzi," *New York Times*, May 5, 2009.

Ron Chernow, "Madoff and His Models," *New Yorker*, March 23, 2009.

"C. W. Barron Skeptical About 'Exchange Wizard,'" *Wall Street Journal*, July 30, 1920.

Mary Darby, "In Ponzi We Trust," *Smithsonian Magazine*, December 1998.

Federal Bureau of Investigation, "Another Ponzi Case and a Warning for Investors," 2010, https://www.fbi.gov/news/stories/2010/may/ponzi_050310.

Federal Bureau of Investigation, "Common Fraud Schemes," https://www.fbi.gov/scams -safety/fraud.

Stephen Greenspan, "Fooled by Ponzi," *Skeptic*, Vol. 14, No. 4, 2009.

David Margolick, "His Last Name Is Scheme," *New York Times*, April 10, 2005.

"Ponzi Arrested by Federal Authorities," *Wall Street Journal*, August 13, 1920.

"Ponzi Creditors Get Final Payment," *Wall Street Journal*, December 24, 1930.

Catherine Rampell, "A Scheme with No Off Button," *New York Times*, December 21, 2008.

U.S. Attorney's Office, District of New Jersey, "CEO of Capitol Investments USA Charged in $880 Million Ponzi Scheme Based on Phony Grocery Business," April 21, 2010.

U.S. Securities and Exchange Commission, "SEC Enforcement Actions Against Ponzi Schemes," http://www.sec.gov/spotlight/enf-actions-ponzi.shtml.

PYRAMID SCHEMES

A pyramid scheme is a financial scam that's a close cousin to the Ponzi scheme. In a Ponzi scheme, money from new investors is used to pay off old investors. Nothing is actually invested in anything material. Pyramid schemes operate in a similar manner, except that participants are expected to recruit new members.

Pyramid schemes are typically built around a product or service, real or imagined. Individuals are offered a franchise or distribution rights to market this product or service in a given area. They usually have to pay a fee for these franchise or distribution rights. Participants are strongly encouraged to bring in new members. Each new member brought in earns the recruiter a commission, creating a strong incentive to lure as many people as possible into the scheme. New members in turn are also encouraged to bring in fresh members; thus the program expands like a pyramid, getting broader with each descending level. A very small number of people at the apex of the pyramid will actually earn money from recruitment commissions. Most members won't earn anything and will, in fact, lose money.

According to the FBI website, "At the heart of each pyramid scheme is typically a representation that new participants can recoup their original investments by inducing two or more prospects to make the same investment. Promoters fail to tell prospective participants that this is mathematically impossible for everyone to do, since some participants drop out, while others recoup their original investments and then drop out."

The U.S. Securities and Exchange Commission adds, "In the classic 'pyramid' scheme, participants attempt to make money solely by recruiting new participants into the program. The hallmark of these schemes is the promise of sky-high returns in a short period of time for doing nothing other than handing over your money and getting others to do the same."

The U.S. Securities and Exchange Commission offered some stark math outlining the daunting odds facing participants in a pyramid scheme. Say that at level 1, you have six members. Each of these members is expected to bring in six new members themselves. So level 2 will feature 36 members. Level 3 will feature 216 members. The required number of new members keeps expanding exponentially. By level 11, some 362,797,056 members will be required to keep the scheme going (more than the entire population of the United States). Level 13 requires participation by over 13 billion members—which is higher than the globe's current population.

Sometimes pyramid schemes are disguised as "Multi-Level Marketing" programs.

The U.S. Securities and Exchange Commission website explains, "In an MLM program, you typically get paid for products or services that you and the distributors in your 'downline' (i.e., participants you recruit and their recruits)

Ways to Tell If a Multi-Level Marketing Program Is Really a Pyramid Scheme

1. No real product or service. Genuine MLM programs involve selling real products or services to people who are not in the program. Be cautious if there doesn't appear to be an underlying product or service being sold to others, or if the product/service being offered is speculative or seems inappropriately priced.
2. Promises of high returns in a short period of time. Be cautious when faced with pitches that promise huge returns in "get-rich-quick" fashion. High returns and fast cash in an MLM program could suggest that commissions are actually being paid out of money from new recruits instead of revenue generated by product sales.
3. Easy money or passive income. Being promised compensation for minimal effort (namely, doing nothing more than making payments, recruiting others, and placing advertisements) is a major red flag.
4. No demonstrated revenue from retail sales. Ask to see financial statements and other documents, audited by a certified public accountant (CPA), showing that the MLM program generates revenue from selling its products or services to people outside the program. Lack of such documentation is a major red flag.
5. Buy-in required. At the heart of an MLM program, the goal is to sell products. Be cautious if you are required to pay a buy-in to participate in the program, even if the buy-in or recurring fee is relatively low.
6. Complicated commission structure. Be wary if commissions are based on products and services you or your recruits sell to people outside the program. If the commission structure is unusually murky and difficult to comprehend, walk away.
7. Emphasis on recruitment. If the program seems mostly focused on recruiting other people to join the program for a fee, you are almost certainly looking at a pyramid scheme. Be cautious if you receive more money for recruiting new members than for selling products or services.

Source: U.S. Securities and Exchange Commission website, https://www.sec.gov /investor/alerts/ia_pyramid.htm

sell to others. However, some MLM programs are actually pyramid schemes—a type of fraud in which participants profit almost exclusively through recruiting other people to participate in the program."

Pyramid schemes pretending to be MLM programs often violate federal laws on securities that prohibit fraud and require registration of securities offerings and any brokers or dealers involved.

Further Reading

Federal Bureau of Investigation, "Common Fraud Schemes," https://www.fbi.gov/scams -safety/fraud.

U.S. Securities and Exchange Commission, "Investor Alert: Beware of Pyramid Schemes Posing as Multi-Level Marketing Programs," http://www.sec.gov/investor/alerts/ia _pyramid.htm.

U.S. Securities and Exchange Commission, "Pyramid Schemes," http://www.sec.gov /answers/pyramid.htm.

PUMP AND DUMP

On April 4, 2013, charges were announced against seven individuals for "conspiring to commit securities fraud and extortion" according to a press release from the New York office of the FBI.

The press release explained, "The defendants worked to fraudulently inflate the prices and trading volumes of publicly traded stock of small companies, also known as 'penny stocks' and then to sell shares of the stock at the fraudulently inflated prices to the investing public for a profit."

The alleged offence centered on a scam known colloquially as a "Pump and Dump" scheme. Here's how the scheme works: a group of scammers start off by hyping a company and spreading word about how the firm's stock is set to skyrocket. The con artists might make these claims on social media, in online chat rooms, and through fawning press releases. With luck, the scammers' message is picked up by financial newsletters and analysts who supposedly offer unbiased market predictions.

Anyone who can read financial results can see the stock is being purchased by lots of people. In the early stages, most of the people buying the stock are the con artists themselves, eager to start a buying stampede. Encouraged by glowing media accounts of the stock and the feeding frenzy around it, deluded investors begin purchasing shares en masse, driving the price up. When the stock hits peak value, the scammers sell off their shares.

The U.S. Securities and Exchange Commission website explains, "Once these fraudsters 'dump' their shares and stop hyping the stock, the price typically falls and investors lose their money."

"Fraudsters frequently use this ploy with small, thinly traded companies because it's easier to manipulate a stock when there's little or no information available about the company. To steer clear of potential scams, always investigate before you invest," added the FBI's website.

One other piece of simple advice: don't believe the hype, as rap group Public Enemy so eloquently put it. Be suspicious of high-pressure sales pitches for stock and deals on "sure things" that seem too good to be true.

The seven scammers arrested in New York focused on a block of shares of the Face Up Entertainment Group Inc. (FUEG). This was a real company that was "purportedly involved in the reality gaming social network market with its principal place of business located in Valley Stream, New York," stated the press release from the New York FBI office.

Once the con artists acquired a large amount of FUEG shares, they allegedly went about touting the stock through phony press releases posted on the Internet. Interestingly enough, for all their efforts, the Face Up scammers' financial shenanigans failed miserably.

As Manhattan U.S. Attorney Preet Bharara stated in the New York FBI press release, "As alleged, these defendants preyed on unsuspecting investors by manipulating the share price of a publicly traded stock in a classic 'pump and dump' scheme that they thought would reap big dividends. But when their pot of gold failed to materialized, they allegedly turned on a co-conspirator with threats and extortion, showing that their greed was strong enough to make them turn to violence."

While the seven arrested in New York City might have been incompetent con artists, Pump and Dump scams remain rampant in financial circles.

Further Reading

Greg Farrell, "$50M 'Pump-and-Dump' Scam Nets 20 Arrests," *USA Today*, March 3, 2001.

Federal Bureau of Investigation, New York Office, "Manhattan U.S. Attorney and FBI Assistant Director in Charge Announce Charges Against Seven Individuals for Conspiring to Commit Securities Fraud and Extortion: Defendants' 'Pump and Dump' Scheme Targeted 'Penny' Stocks," April 4, 2013.

U.S. Attorney's Office, District of New Jersey, "Florida Man Pleads Guilty in Stock Scheme That Swindled Millions from Investors," January 21, 2010.

U.S. Securities and Exchange Commission website, "Pump-and-Dumps and Market Manipulations," http://www.sec.gov/answers/pumpdump.htm.

LEO KORETZ

Leo Koretz was a hugely successful Chicago swindler who earned millions from bogus business operations in Central America and almost got away with it—but for one sharp-eyed tailor.

In 1887, eight-year-old Koretz and his family emigrated from what is now the Czech Republic to Chicago. Koretz was a bright young man who took night classes and earned a law degree. He clerked at a leading Chicago firm and hung out his shingle as a lawyer in 1905. He yearned for better things, however. To feed an insatiable appetite for money, Koretz "drew up a fake mortgage, sold it to a client as an investment and pocketed the proceeds. When he needed more money, he forged more mortgages," stated an article in *The Walrus* magazine by author Dean Jobb, who wrote a book about Koretz.

Koretz soon realized that fake mortgages could only get him so far. In 1911, he came up with a new scam. He claimed he controlled five million acres of timberland in a remote part of Panama. According to Koretz, Panamanian workers grew mahogany and other valuable timber on the property. Enticed by visions of massive profits, investors flocked to buy into Koretz's newfound Bayano River Syndicate (the Bayano was a river in Panama).

In reality, Koretz didn't have land in Panama or any other investments. Instead, he ran what we would recognize today as a classic Ponzi scheme: money from new investors went to pay off old investors. As long as new cash kept coming in, the scam flourished.

Koretz skimmed off a considerable share of investment monies to pay for a mansion, a pair of Rolls Royce limousines, and pricey hotel suites. He also entertained frequently and was chummy with members of Chicago's upper crust. Koretz had a wife and two children but led a dissolute private life, complete with a series of mistresses.

In mid-1920, Boston financier Charles Ponzi was revealed to be a con man running a fraudulent investment operation. Oddly, this revelation didn't dampen enthusiasm for Koretz's growing empire. His supporters dubbed him "our Ponzi" in a weird show of affection.

Koretz was highly popular with women, even though he was middle-aged and dumpy, with a round, pasty face highlighted by thick glasses. His money and charm, however, guaranteed him a steady supply of female friends.

A year after Ponzi was exposed, Koretz put his scam into overdrive. He claimed oil had been found on his Panama land. He now offered investors spectacular annual returns of 60 percent. He claimed that Standard Oil, the biggest petroleum company in the world at the time, was clamoring to invest $25 million (the modern-day equivalent of $300 million) with the Bayano River Syndicate.

In December 1923, a group of investors decided to go south to check out Koretz's Panamanian property for themselves. The group assumed his land would be dotted with oil rigs. Koretz saw the investors off on a steamer, gathered as much loot as he could, then vanished.

Needless to say, the investors were shocked when they got to Panama and quickly discovered that everything they had been told was a lie. Koretz didn't own any property in Panama, and no one in the country had a clue who he was.

The collapse of the Bayano River Syndicate made headlines around North America. It was the 1920s' equivalent of the shocking collapse of Bernie Madoff's equally fraudulent business operations. Investors' losses have been estimated at around $400 million in today's currency.

Koretz hid out in New York City. He grew a beard, changed his name to "Lou Keyte," and pretended to be a businessman turned literary critic. He purchased a bookstore on the Upper East Side at Madison Avenue and 73rd Street. Soon, however, he decided New York was too hot for him. There was an international effort to track down Koretz, so he decided to find a more obscure locale to hide in.

Koretz had heard about a hunting lodge named Pinehurst that was for sale in Nova Scotia. The lodge was situated on an isolated lake near the town of Liverpool. Koretz—still calling himself "Lou Keyte"—moved to Nova Scotia in the spring of 1924 and took up residence at Pinehurst.

From the start, Koretz/Keyte violated basic rules of being a fugitive. He lived large and made little effort to keep a low profile. He wore tailored suits, threw money around town, and hosted lavish parties.

In May 1924, Koretz arranged for a grand soiree at a swanky hotel in the neighboring town of Bridgewater. He paid for a long line of taxis to escort his guests from Liverpool, then presented them with gifts of chocolate and cigarettes at the hotel. A band played live music, while illegal alcohol flowed. Guests were offered a three-course meal and could choose between fried salmon or roasted chicken for their entrée.

At the same time, Koretz turned the Pinehurst lodge into a country estate. The newly renovated lodge had 15 rooms, including separate rooms for music and billiards. It boasted an outdoor tennis court and its own power plant, to guarantee that Pinehurst always had heat and electricity.

Koretz's extravagant behavior would have drawn attention anywhere. In Nova Scotia, which was already gripped by an economic downturn even before the Great Depression, he stood out like a beacon.

Koretz was happy to chat with reporters, whom he regaled with stories of his literary ambitions. He claimed he had written plays (none actually performed, however). He also claimed to have discovered and popularized Zane Gray, a best-selling author of adventure books set in the Old West.

As he had done in Chicago, Koretz hung out with the province's elite. He spent time at the tony Royal Nova Scotia Yacht Squadron and, in August 1924, hosted a huge housewarming bash at Pinehurst. He had 100 guests, including important politicians and business people. There was dancing and liquor and a definite Jay Gatsby–like ambiance.

Everything came to an end in November 1924, when police arrested Koretz in a Halifax hotel room. Koretz had been discovered after dropping off a suit jacket at a Halifax tailor for some repairs. In looking the jacket over, the tailor discovered a label with Koretz's real name in the lining. The tailor recognized the name from newspaper headlines and contacted authorities.

Koretz's arrest drew a mixed response from his new Maritime friends: "In Nova Scotia, where he had fooled almost as many people as he had in Chicago, reaction ranged from bemusement to disbelief," stated *The Walrus*.

Koretz was extradited back to Illinois and placed in state prison, where he died in January 1925, at age 45. Acutely diabetic, it has been suggested he committed suicide by deliberately wolfing down smuggled chocolates.

It remains unclear why Koretz maintained such a high profile in Nova Scotia instead of keeping out of sight. Perhaps being praised as a financial genius in Chicago for so many years had given him a taste for attention and adoration that he couldn't let go of, even in hiding.

Further Reading

Dean Jobb, *Empire of Deception*, 2015.
Dean Jobb, "The Jolly Millionaire," *The Walrus*, May 27, 2015.
Dean Jobb, "The Scam Artist Who Turned to a Life of Literary Lies," *Toronto Star*, May 23, 2015.

SECTION THREE

DESPICABLE SCAMS

INTRODUCTION

While any con can be described as "despicable," some frauds seem particularly sordid. These include adoption and surrogacy scams (in which prospective parents desperate for babies are taken advantage of), people who pretend to have cancer (for sympathy and money), and frauds that victimize senior citizens. Disaster fraud, which takes the form of fake charities and fake ailments among first responders, is also seen as extremely loathsome.

All of these scams have one thing in common: they play on people's emotions. In the face of such frauds, it pays to be wary, even when confronted with seemingly tragic or joyful circumstances.

DISASTER SCAMS
Natural Disasters

Natural disasters can bring out the best in some people. They can also bring out cold-hearted scam artists looking to make a quick profit from widespread misery.

After a series of wildfires in Southern California in 2014, for example, the San Diego division of the FBI issued a warning about what it called "disaster fraud": "There are five main forms of disaster fraud. They include charitable solicitations, price gouging, contractor and vendor fraud, property insurance fraud, and forgery," according to the FBI.

Fraudulent charitable solicitation involves "people posing as both legitimate (e.g., Red Cross) and non-existent organization workers collecting money to assist with disaster relief," explains the Bureau.

Price gouging refers to businesses drastically increasing the price of goods or services in high demand after a disaster. Contractor or vendor fraud centers on individuals posing as contractors or repair services, who solicit fees for work they have no intention of actually doing. Insurance fraud happens when people or businesses inflate losses or seek claims for fake repairs or lost services.

"Finally, forgery comes into play when dealing with disaster fraud. Commonly forged documents include insurance checks and building permits and receipts for claims submitted to insurance companies," stated the FBI.

The Bureau press release urged members of the public to report wildfire-related fraud to their offices or the National Center for Disaster Fraud. The Center grew out of a Hurricane Katrina Fraud Task Force established by the Department of Justice in 2005. The Task Force was set up to ensure that the billions in federal disaster relief funding that poured into the Gulf Coast region in the wake of Hurricane Katrina were lawfully spent. The Task Force involved a long list of players, including the U.S. Attorneys' Offices, the FBI, the Postal Inspection Service, the U.S. Secret Service, the Federal Trade Commission, the Securities and Exchange Commission, and various representatives from state and local government.

How to Avoid Being a Victim of Disaster Fraud

Advice from the Federal Emergency Management Agency (FEMA):

- If someone shows up at the doorstep to your residence or small business, claiming to be a housing inspector from FEMA or the U.S. Small Business Administration, ask to see the person's identification badge. Real federal employees and contractors have official, laminated photo

ID. Don't give out any banking information. "It is important to note that FEMA housing inspectors verify damage but do not hire or endorse specific contractors to fix homes or recommend repairs. They do not determine your eligibility for assistance," added FEMA.

- If you hire a contractor after a disaster, only use a licensed, local contractor with good references. Insist the contractor carry general liability insurance and worker's compensation.
- If someone solicits disaster relief funds from you, ask for the name and contact information (street address, phone number, website URL) of the charity they claim to represent. Phone the charity and ask if the solicitor is an official employee or volunteer with the charity. Don't pay in cash, and insist on a proper receipt that includes the name, address, phone number, and website URL of the charity.
- If someone contacts you with an offer of federal or state aid, do not divulge your Social Security, banking, or credit card information. If the person suggests they can secure you a large government grant if you pay a deposit or advance fee, they are almost certainly conning you. Real federal or state workers do not ask for or accept money and do not charge applicants for disaster assistance. If you are suspicious, report the person to police.

Advice from the San Diego Division of the FBI:

- Don't respond to spam e-mails asking for disaster relief donations. Do not click on links in these messages, because they might put your computer at risk of getting a virus. Do not open any attachments allegedly containing photographs of the disaster scene.
- Be wary of an organization with a name that's quite similar to, but not exactly the same as, a real, established charity.
- Be wary of giving money to a charity that offers no other contact information beyond a post office box.
- Websites for established charities usually end in .org, not .com.
- To avoid identify theft, contact your creditors as soon as possible to report lost credit cards. Do the same thing with your bank if you've lost your bank card or bank checks. Get a copy of your credit report a few weeks after the disaster to determine if anyone is using your banking/credit information.

Sources: FEMA website, http://www.fema.gov/news-release/2014/10/10/beware-scams-and-fraudulent-phone-calls; FBI website, https://www.fbi.gov/sandiego/press-releases/2014/fbi-alerts-public-to-be-aware-of-disaster-fraud-in-aftermath-of-recent-wildfires

In the three years after Hurricane Katrina made landfall, the Task Force's efforts led to federal charges against 907 individuals in 43 federal judicial districts nationwide. A sampling of charges included the following:

- Charity Fraud: Barely a week after Hurricane Katrina struck, two brothers fraudulently claiming to represent the Salvation Army registered a website at www.salvationarmyonline.org to solicit donations for relief efforts. Needless to say, donations ended up in the hands of the two sibling scammers, not the drenched souls of New Orleans. The fake site generated nearly $50,000 in donations before authorities caught on and froze all accounts connected to the phony charity. For their efforts, the two brothers were received sentences of, respectively, 111 months and 105 months in prison, on November 28, 2007, in the U.S. District Court for the Southern District of Texas.
- Contract Fraud/Corruption: On May 15, 2008, a onetime contract employee with the U.S. Army Corps of Engineers and a dirt, sand, and gravel subcontractor were indicted by a federal grand jury in the Eastern District of Louisiana. The pair had worked on a $16 million hurricane protection project involving the reconstruction of the Lake Cataouatche Levee south of New Orleans. Both were charged with one count of conspiring to commit bribery. One defendant was also charged with two counts of offering a bribe to a public official, while the other defendant was charged with one count of demanding and agreeing to receive a bribe as a public official.
- Individual Assistance Fraud: Eight defendants were sentenced on June 9, 2008, by the U.S. District Court for the Southern District of Texas, for their involvement in a conspiracy to defraud the Federal Emergency Management Agency (FEMA), the government division responsible for providing assistance following disasters. The eight defendants made over 70 applications for Hurricane Katrina and Hurricane Rita benefits for residents who hadn't actually been victimized by these disasters. The leader of the eight defendants received a sentence of 33 months in jail and had to pay $92,958 in restitution and forfeit an SUV she had purchased with funds garnered by the scheme.

The Hurricane Katrina Task Force eventually transformed into the National Center for Disaster Fraud. In addition to the name change, the Center's mandate expanded, to investigate fraud stemming from "any domestic natural or manmade disaster," in the words of the FBI.

Man-Made Disasters

Hundreds of police and fire personnel died during the 9/11 terror attack in New York City, in which a pair of hijacked jets were deliberately rammed into the twin towers of the World Trade Center, causing them to collapse. Other first responders grew sick from exposure to the toxic dust and debris churned up at Ground Zero, and/or suffered from posttraumatic stress disorder (PTSD).

Unfortunately, not all the police and firemen who claimed illness as a result of the September 11, 2001, attack were telling the truth. On January 7, 2014, authorities arrested 72 former members of the New York Police Department (NYPD) and 8 former members of the Fire Department of New York (FDNY). They were accused of faking mental distress to collect Social Security disability benefits. Over half of those accused blamed their turmoil on time spent at Ground Zero during 9/11.

This firefighter and police officers' fakery was allegedly part of a bigger scam involving more than 100 people and $400 million worth of fraudulent Social Security disability payments. The accused NYPD and FDNY retirees were allegedly recruited and coached by a group of ringleaders who specialized in Social Security fraud.

According to a January 7, 2014, article in the *New York Post*, these ringleaders included former police officer and union official John Minerva, who served as the main recruiter, and ex-cop Joseph Esposito, who allegedly coached scammers on how to play at being mentally ill. The other ringleaders were Raymond Lavallee, a lawyer and former FBI agent who ran a company that guided people through the Social Security application process, and Thomas Hale, a disability consultant. According to authorities, the quartet had, since the late 1980s, helped hundreds of people—not all of them ex-cops or firefighters—make fraudulent disability claims. In exchange, the ringleaders received a cut of any ill-gained Social Security payments.

Former NYPD and FDNY officers recruited by this foursome were given tips on how to score poorly on memory tests in a believable manner and appear sufficiently distraught during medical examinations. They were also coached on what to wear and how to act in front of doctors and government officials. A majority of the ex-cops and firefighters claimed that their mental trauma stemmed from 9/11. Some first responders claimed to be so depressed and/or anxious they were unable to work, drive, use a computer, or even leave their homes. These stories were believed, and many ex-cops and firefighters started receiving disability benefits in the neighborhood of $20,000 to $50,000 a year.

Investigators began taking a closer look at these claims and at social media accounts run by first responders receiving disability payments. Authorities found posts on Twitter, Facebook, and YouTube, of supposedly house-bound and incapacitated victims jet-skiing, teaching karate, deep-sea fishing, running marathons, and engaging in other energetic activities. Also uncovered were receipts for car rentals, airplane flights, and shopping excursions. As it turned out, some of the retirees citing 9/11-related PTSD hadn't actually served at Ground Zero.

The four ringleaders at the center of the scam were charged with first- and second-degree grand larceny and attempted second-degree grand larceny. The 80 retired members of the NYPD and FDNY were charged with second-degree grand larceny and attempted second-degree grand larceny. Hale and Laval- lee each posted $1 million bail after their arrests and were released. Esposito posted half a million dollars' bail, while Minerva posted $250,000.

While the scam organized by the ringleaders possibly involved hundreds of people, it was the presence of former police officers and firemen invoking 9/11 that drew the loudest scorn. The *New York Post* quoted Police Commissioner Bill Bratton as saying, "As a New Yorker and as a U.S. citizen, I can only express disgust at the actions of the individuals involved in this scheme, particularly the 72 former members of the New York City Police Department who have certainly disgraced themselves, embarrassed their families with their abuse of the system."

Further Reading

Department of Justice, "Justice Department Officials Raise Awareness of Disaster Fraud Hotline Following Typhoon Haiyan," November 14, 2013.

Federal Bureau of Investigation, "Fighting Fraud in the Wake of Natural Disasters," https://www.fbi.gov/news/stories/2008/october/disasterfraud_100808.

Federal Bureau of Investigation, National Press Office, "More Than 900 Defendants Charged with Disaster-Related Fraud by Hurricane Katrina Fraud Task Force Dur- ing Three Years in Operation," October 1, 2008.

Federal Bureau of Investigation, San Diego Office, "FBI Alerts Public to Be Aware of Disaster Fraud in Aftermath of Recent Wildfires," May 16, 2014.

Federal Emergency Management Agency, "Beware of Scams and Fraudulent Phone Calls," October 10, 2014.

Aaron Katersky, "New York Cops, Firefighters in Massive 9/11 Fraud, Indictment Says," ABC News, January 7, 2014, http://abcnews.go.com/US/york-cops-firefighters -massive-911-fraud-indictment/story?id=21445783.

Rebecca Rosenberg, Jamie Schram, and Daniel Prendergast, "FDNY, NYPD Retirees Who 'Faked 9/11 Illness in Scam' Not Too Sick to Have Fun," *New York Post*, Janu- ary 7, 2014.

Ray Sanchez, Susan Candiotti, and Lorenzo Ferrigno, "Prosecutor: More Than 100 NYC Police and Firefighters Indicted in PTSD Scam," *CNN.com*, January 7, 2014, http:// www.cnn.com/2014/01/07/justice/new-york-ptsd-9-11-scam/index.html.

FAKING CANCER

Some people pretend to have cancer, for sympathy and money. Dina Leone, for one, was very up-front about soliciting funds for her alleged treatment. As reported in a February 1, 2009, story on the ABC News website, Leone, a Balti- more mother of two, began reaching out to friends on the Internet in late 2004. Leone claimed she had stage-four stomach cancer, lacked insurance, and was desperate to pay her medical bills. Friends obliged, and money came pouring in. Some friends took to visiting Leone or calling or e-mailing to cheer her up.

Through a stream of Internet posts and text messages, Leone repeatedly asked for funds and offered details about her medical condition. She spoke of being laid up in a hospital bed for months at a time, due to complications from surgery. She sent colleagues and contacts a photograph of herself with a bald head, the hair loss supposedly stemming from chemotherapy treatment.

Leone's dramatic hair loss proved her undoing, in part. Real chemotherapy patients tend to lose their hair in clumps over a period of time. Leone, however, went from having a full head of hair to being bald overnight. What's more, 5′ 3″ Leone, who tipped the scale at nearly 200 pounds, never seemed to lose weight, even though chemotherapy treatment usually causes intense nausea. Far from looking emaciated and ill, she seemed to be in fine health to her friends. Leone was also unable to answer medical specifics about the nature of her treatment. Friends took note and grew suspicious.

Leone's reaction to a potential donor was another red flag. This would-be donor offered to write a check for Leone's care, but wanted to make it out directly to her doctor. Leone, however, angrily insisted the check be made out to "cash" instead.

Finally, one of Leone's friends got in touch with police. An investigation was launched in the summer of 2008. Authorities checked in at various hospitals and medical centers where Leone claimed she was receiving treatment. These facilities denied she was a patient. A search warrant was issued for Leone's home. Police investigated and couldn't find any evidence that would indicate Leone was suffering from cancer. No pill bottles, no oncologist reports, no sick bed, no prescriptions. There was simply no evidence of the medication or paperwork that a typical cancer patient would have lying around.

Authorities also took a look at Leone's checking account. There were no payments to cover medical fees or visits to doctors. Instead, Leone was using the money she was bringing in to pay school fees for her kids and to buy a dog, among other things.

In November 2008, a grand jury indicted Leone on theft and conspiracy charges. She was released in January 2009 on $25,000 bail.

In an interview with Baltimore's WJZ-TV news, Leone admitted she had faked having cancer. She claimed, however, that she put on an act under orders from her abusive husband. Leone's spouse denied both the abuse charges and her claims that he forced her to fake illness. In other interviews with authorities, Leone said she had bipolar disorder or was suffering from posttraumatic stress disorder (PTSD).

Eventually, in June 2010, Leone pled guilty to a felony theft charge.

Sadly, Leone wasn't the first person to make a name for themselves as a phony cancer patient. The ABC website article cited two other cases: in

2006, a Boston-area special education high school teacher named Heather Faris pled guilty to larceny and fraud charges after telling friends and family she had stomach cancer. Faris used the phony diagnosis to squeeze $31,000 in donations for medical expenses out of friends, family, colleagues, and students.

In September 2009, a Napa, California, police dispatcher named Danielle Vanderpool was convicted on charges of grand theft after bilking individuals and groups out of $50,000. Vanderpool claimed to have ovarian cancer and that the money was paying for her treatment.

Another brazen case of alleged cancer fakery was detailed in a May 25, 2013, article in the *Toronto Star*. In spring 2013, prosecutors accused a young woman named Brittany Ozarowski in Medford, New York, of pretending to have cancer. She made the claim in order to raise funds to pay for heroin, to which she was addicted, said authorities. The heroin addiction actually aided Ozarowski's deception, giving her a drawn, gaunt appearance. Ozarowski was also severely underweight (80 pounds) and hobbled about on a cane, making her look even more like a cancer victim. She convinced 25 business owners to put donation jars in their locales. She told different people at various times that she suffered from brain, ovarian, bone, and stomach cancer.

People became suspicious when Ozarowski didn't lose any hair and failed to show up for a free appointment with a doctor. She was arrested in April 2013. In December of the same year, Ozarowski entered a guilty plea to two dozen counts of fraud in Suffolk County Court, New York, reported the *Examiner*, an online news website.

Even some celebrities have faked having cancer.

In the summer of 2005, Victoria Gotti (daughter of notorious New York City crime boss John Gotti), announced she had been diagnosed with breast cancer. Her timing was suspect, coming as it did shortly before the launch of the third season of the reality show, *Growing Up Gotti*, in which she starred.

Victoria Gotti quickly retracted her statement. In an August 24, 2005, article posted to the Fox News website, Gotti said she didn't have breast cancer but had suffered from pre-cancerous cells. Fortunately, she stated, she had received treatment that prevented these cells from mutating into full-blown cancer.

The sheer ubiquity of cancer is one reason people pretend to have it. According to the American Cancer Society, there will be an estimated 1,685,210 new cancer cases in the U.S. in 2016 (the gender skew is 841,390 men and 843,820 women). A large percentage of these cases will be terminal. Along with predictions about new cases, the Cancer Society estimates that cancer will kill 595,690 Americans in 2016, a death toll that breaks down to 314,290 men and 281,400 women.

While sympathy is always warranted in real cancer cases, it helps to be skeptical before offering money to individuals who claim to have the disease or organizations that claim to fight it. Basic online research might indicate whether a charity is a sham. Real cancer patients, meanwhile, tend to lose weight and their hair, thanks to chemotherapy treatments. Be wary of cancer patients who ask for money but appear to be in perfect health, even after months of supposed treatment. Cancer patients who refuse offers of free medical help or insist on receiving donations in cash, rather than a donation in kind to a hospital or health-care facility, also justify suspicion.

Further Reading

American Cancer Society, "Cancer Facts and Figures 2016."

Kim Carollo, "Are Cancer Fraudsters Desperate or Psychopathic?" ABCNews.com, August 12, 2010, http://abcnews.go.com/Health/MindMoodNews/ashley-kirilow -cancer-charity-fraudsters/story?id=11369697.

Russell Goldman, "Maryland Woman Allegedly Lies About Cancer, Bilks Friends for Thousands of Dollars," ABCNews.com, February 1, 2009, http://abcnews. go.com/Business/dina-leone-maryland-woman-accused-fraud-lying-cancer/story? id=9703436.

"Heroin Addict Pleads Guilty to Cancer Scam," Examiner.com, December 12, 2013, http://www.examiner.com/article/heroin-addict-pleads-guilty-to-cancer-scam.

Joni E. Johnston, "Cancer Fraud: People Who Fake Illness to Scam Others, Gain Sympathy, Get Rich and Avoid Other Problems," Psychologytoday.com blog, January 28, 2010, https://www.psychologytoday.com/blog/the-human-equation/201001/cancer -fraud-people-who-fake-illness-scam-others-gain-sympathy-get.

Nick Madigan, "Baltimore County Woman Who Bilked Friends for Fake Cancer Treatments to Be Sentenced," *The Baltimore Sun*, October 27, 2010.

"Report: Gotti Breast Cancer a Sham," FoxNews.com, August 24, 2005, http://www .foxnews.com/story/2005/08/24/report-gotti-breast-cancer-sham.html.

Scambusters.org, "What Everyone Ought to Know About Cancer Fraud," http://www .scambusters.org/cancerfraud.html.

"She Played on the Heartstrings," *Toronto Star*, May 25, 2013.

FAKING CAR ACCIDENTS

You're driving along a busy highway, minding your own business. A car ahead cuts off the vehicle directly in front of you, forcing that driver to hit the brakes. You hit the brakes too, but there's not enough time or road to stop your car before it slams into the vehicle in front of you. As you sit, dazed, in the driver's seat, you notice with horror that the car you just rear-ended is packed with passengers. Many of those passengers appear grievously injured, crying out in pain and dramatically flailing their limbs.

An unfortunate accident? Maybe not. The whole incident might have been staged, in an effort to rip off insurance companies.

This particular incident is called a "Swoop and Squat": "the first car 'swoops' in while the second car 'squats' in front of you," states an auto fraud advisory on the FBI website. The car you rear-end is almost always crammed with passengers, all of whom file fake injury claims with your insurer. Chief among these injuries is whiplash and other soft-tissue wounds that are difficult to medically verify.

Similar scams cited by the FBI include the following:

- The Drive Down—On a busy road, a driver waves his arm out the window, indicating he wants you to pass. When you move forward, however, he doesn't get out of the way. Your car smashes into their vehicle. Police arrive, and the driver insists he didn't wave you forward or indicate in any way he wanted you to pass him.
- The Sideswipe—The setting for this scam is a busy intersection boasting multiple turn lanes. As you drive around a corner, your vehicle drifts a bit into the lane next to you. A car driving in that lane deliberately sideswipes you.
- The T-Bone—Once again, the action takes place at an intersection. You're crossing the intersection in your car when a driver on a side street hits the gas and crashes into your vehicle. Police are called to the scene. The driver and some "eye witnesses" (actually planted stooges milling about on the sidewalk) claim you ran a red light or stop sign.

Sometimes fake automobile accident scams involve more than just a deliberate crash. Those passengers complaining of vague neck injuries might be treated by doctors or physiotherapists who are in on the con. The role of these conniving physicians and healers is to bolster fake insurance claims about terrible injuries. The "injured parties" might also be represented by crooked lawyers who are also out to make some money. And finally, auto mechanics and technicians might be brought into the con to exaggerate the extent of vehicular damage resulting from the crash.

Some fake accident scams are considerably less elaborate, however, and merely involve one reckless individual operating on their own. Such was the case with Briana Nguyen, a serial insurance fraudster in Colorado who made more than two dozen suspicious claims for car crashes over a period of two decades, beginning in 1995.

Nguyen "typically slammed on her brakes, forcing drivers to rear-end her car. The damage usually was minor and the impact slight. Even so, Nguyen lied to auto insurers that she had painful injuries to her back neck, shoulders and other areas of her body," stated a January 2015 news release from the Washington DC–based Coalition Against Insurance Fraud.

Nguyen became so blasé about her fakery, she claimed the exact same injuries to herself and exact same damage to her car in a series of different crashes. Sometimes, she even drove with her young daughter in her car, claiming the poor girl suffered terrible injuries. Nguyen typically exaggerated the extent of any injuries she allegedly endured. She also operated under a series of aliases in an effort to hoodwink insurers and authorities.

In the end, Nguyen was convicted of 21 felonies and received a sentence of three months in jail plus restitution costs.

Phony collisions can be costly, even to drivers with clean records. "Staged accidents cost the insurance industry about $20 billion a year. Those losses get passed on to all of us in the form of higher insurance rates—an average of $100–300 extra per car per year," states the FBI auto fraud advisory.

Besides being detrimental to insurers, fake car accidents can be life-threatening for all involved, especially on a highway, where the margin for error is slim. What was intended by fraudsters to be a simple fender-bender can easily turn into a major road incident, causing death and widespread destruction, particularly if the vehicles in question were driving at high speed.

Technology is increasingly being used as an effective tool against staged automobile accidents. Some jurisdictions have installed red-light cameras, for example, which automatically photograph cars that zoom through red lights without stopping. Evidence from such cameras can work against con artists trying to pull a T-Bone scam, claiming you caused an accident by running a red light when, in fact, you did no such thing.

Likewise, the growing popularity of dashboard cams that record all sound and action in front of them might put a dent, so to speak, in the staged accident industry. Roadside claims from con artists that they didn't wave you forward can be easily disputed thanks to these miniature cams. This is also why it's a good idea to carry a smart phone when driving, to take photographic evidence from accident scenes you're involved with.

Other tips from the FBI: if you're in a collision, always call police to investigate. Always report each accident to your insurance company. Be wary if the "victims" involved in your accident suggest a cash payout on the spot. If you have a smart phone or digital camera with you, take photographs of your vehicle, plus any other vehicles involved in an accident, as well as the passengers and drivers. Make sure you get the names, addresses, and phone numbers of everyone involved in the accident. Don't rely on doctors, lawyers, or auto mechanics suggested by the "victims." And of course, drive carefully and be aware that some unscrupulous gangs and/or individuals might be eager to stage an accident for insurance money.

Further Reading

Danielle Alvarez and Julie Patel, "Florida Officials, Insurers Demonstrate Staged Car Crash," *Sun Sentinel*, September 15, 2011.

Jeff Atwater, Chief Financial Officer, Florida Department of Financial Services, "CFO Jeff Atwater Announces Nine Miami PIP Fraud Arrests," January 27, 2015.

Coalition Against Insurance Fraud, "Crashing—A Serial Staged-Crash Artist Earns Colorado Attorney's Prosecutor of the Year Award," January 5, 2015.

Coalition Against Insurance Fraud website, "The Impact of Insurance Fraud," http://www.insurancefraud.org/the-impact-of-insurance-fraud.htm#.VZBfFNFRHIU.

Coalition Against Insurance Fraud website, "Impact of Insurance Fraud Statement by John Sargent at the Sentencing of Joseph Haddad," July 10, 2014, http://www.insurancefraud.org/IFNS-detail.htm?key=18967#.VZBgR9FRHIU.

Federal Bureau of Investigation, "A Cautionary Tale—Staged Auto Accident Fraud: Don't Let It Happen to You," February 18, 2005, https://www.fbi.gov/news/stories/2005/february/staged_auto021805.

FUNERAL FRAUD
Faked Funerals

It takes a certain degree of gall to fake funerals to collect insurance money, but that's exactly what four female con artists did in California. The quartet of funeral fraudsters ripped off insurance companies for $1.2 million in total.

The scam centered on a Lynwood, California, mortuary owned and operated by Lydia Pearce, one of the four swindlers. Pearce was aided by mortuary employee Jean Crump and two other partners, who worked, respectively, as a phlebotomist (someone who draws blood for medical purposes) and a notary.

On its website, the FBI cited a specific case to show how the scam worked. In this case, one of the foursome purchased a life insurance policy for a "Jim Davis." The policy was made out to the man's alleged niece and nephew. The subject of this life insurance policy never actually existed, except in the minds of the conspirators. Shortly after they created him, the funeral fraudsters killed Jim Davis off.

The FBI website states, "Mr. Davis conveniently had an untimely demise and the conspirators created false documents, including a death certificate with a doctor's forged signature, to collect his life insurance. They also prepared grossly inflated bills for different amounts from a mortuary to cover the man's funeral and burial costs and wired the bills to two different assignment companies."

Assignment companies are "often used by funeral homes and mortuaries to advance cash for funeral expenses in exchange for a portion of the deceased's life insurance policies," explains the FBI.

The assignment companies dutifully paid up (the first bill was for almost $30,000, while the second bill came to over $16,000), with the money going right to the conspirators. An insurance company, meanwhile, paid out over $230,000 to Davis's alleged nephew.

To make the scam seem more real, the female conspirators went so far as to buy a funeral plot and bury Davis in it. A funeral was held, attended by fake family members who did their best to look sad for the occasion.

A pair of insurance companies became suspicious and began to probe the death of Mr. Davis a little more closely. The funeral fraudsters panicked and had the coffin that allegedly contained Davis dug up. Into this empty coffin they packed a mannequin and assorted cow parts to give it the proper heft of a real, occupied coffin. Thus packed, this coffin was shipped off to a crematorium. Fake paperwork was filed indicating that Mr. Davis had been cremated. His ashes couldn't be examined, because they had supposedly been sprinkled in the Pacific Ocean.

The Los Angeles office of the FBI got involved with the case, and the fake funeral ring quickly unraveled. "Upon closer inspection of the life insurance policies, death certificates, funeral bills, and financial information of the ring members, our investigators gathered the evidence needed to charge the four women—whose scheme ultimately met its own demise," stated the FBI.

The funeral fraudsters were tried in federal court. The quartet were all convicted, with Crump receiving the final conviction in August 2010, on two counts of wire fraud and one count of mail fraud.

Prepaid Ponzi

On November 14, 2013, before a U.S. District Judge in the Eastern District of Missouri, six defendants were sentenced on over 40 counts of fraud, money laundering, and other related offences. The charges related to a particularly pernicious brand of funeral fraud, involving prearranged funeral contracts. The six received a total of 36 years and one month of incarceration. The stiffest sentence was handed down to James Douglas Cassity, who previously entered a guilty plea after admitting he had organized and led the scam.

Cassity ran a Missouri company called National Prearranged Services (NPS) Inc., which sold prearranged funeral contracts. Such contracts aren't particularly unusual. A person enters into such a contract in order to arrange their funeral in advance and pay off some of the forthcoming funeral expenses, so their family and loved ones aren't stuck with the bill.

Working with the Lincoln Memorial Life Insurance Company and other affiliated firms, NPS sold prearranged funeral contracts in Missouri, Illinois, Ohio, and other states from 1992 to 2008.

A press release from the Office of the U.S. Attorney, Eastern District of Missouri explained, "During that time, insurance companies affiliated with NPS issued life insurance policies related to those prearranged funeral contracts. As part of the contracts, the total price for funeral services and merchandise for a funeral was agreed upon, and that price would remain constant regardless of when the funeral services and merchandise would be needed."

Customers who took out a prearranged funeral contract with NPS would generally pay a single sum up front. This fee would either go directly to NPS or be routed through a funeral home involved in the contract. NPS assured customers, funeral homes, and state regulators that money paid by customers under the terms of the prearranged funeral contracts would be kept safe in a secure trust or insurance policy, as stipulated under state law.

As it turned out, NPS made ample use of funds that were supposed to be kept safe. Customer fees were used for unauthorized investments or the personal benefit of NPS officers and accomplices. According to authorities, NPS officials changed deposit amounts on customer contracts and performed other feats of financial skullduggery.

NPS business practices devolved into a Ponzi-like arrangement, in which funds from new customers covered funerals paid in advance by old customers. Victims of NPS scamming included individual customers, funeral homes, and state insurance guarantee associations.

In 2008, the Department of Justice began sniffing around NPS's books, after being informed of the firm's dodgy business practices. The result was a trial in which NPS boss Cassity and five others were found guilty.

Authorities determined that the defendants defrauded nearly 100,000 customers in over 16 states. In the process, the six also ripped off hundreds of funeral homes and numerous financial institutions. Total losses were estimated at over $450 million.

"This case affects us all because part of the life insurance premium we pay goes to cover such loss from fraud," stated Dean C. Bryant, special agent in charge of the FBI St. Louis division, as quoted in a press release from the U.S. Attorney's Office, Eastern District of Missouri.

Further Reading

Federal Bureau of Investigation, "Fake Funerals, Empty Caskets—A Different Kind of Scam," https://www.fbi.gov/news/stories/2010/september/funeral-scams/financial -fraud-and-funeral-scams.

Federal Bureau of Investigation, "Prepaid Funeral Scam—Fitting End to Multi-State Fraud Scheme," January 17, 2014.

"Mortuary Employee Convicted for Role in Fake Funeral Scam," The Associated Press, August 2, 2010.

U.S. Attorney's Office, Central District of California, "Woman Who Staged Fake Funerals as Part of Life Insurance Scam Found Guilty of Federal Fraud Charges," August 2, 2010.

U.S. Attorney's Office, Eastern District of Missouri, "Six Defendants Sentenced to a Total of 36 Years in Prison in National Prearranged Services Case," November 14, 2013.

SCAMMING SENIOR CITIZENS

On March 23, 2010, President Barack Obama signed the Elder Justice Act into law. Part of the Patient Protection and Affordable Care Act (better known as "Obamacare"), the Elder Justice Act provides federal resources to combat the neglect, abuse, and exploitation of older Americans. Among other things, the Department of Justice set up an Elder Justice website, which collects statistics and data on scams involving seniors.

"Studies estimate that, each year, over five percent of older Americans will be financially exploited by a family member and over eight percent will be the victims of consumer fraud," stated the Elder Justice website.

According to the Department of Justice, elderly Americans are financially exploited out of nearly $3 billion every year. Unfortunately, seniors make excellent targets for con artists.

The Elder Justice website states, "Older adults tend to have more wealth [than younger adults]. Persons 65 and older deposit 70 percent of all funds in financial institutions and collectively control over $7 trillion in invested assets. The complexity of financial instruments makes financial management challenging and with modern mobility, many older adults are separated from friends and family who might assist them. Over five million Americans have been diagnosed with Alzheimer's disease and many more have other forms of dementia."

In addition to the Department of Justice, the AARP—a nonprofit advocacy group for seniors, based in Washington DC—also promotes elder fraud awareness. Formerly known as the American Association of Retired Persons, the AARP offers bulletins and blog posts warning members about cons and scams.

Such awareness is vital, given demographic trends: "When the Elder Justice Act was enacted in 2010, 13 percent of the U.S. population was 65 years or older. By 2030, that percentage is expected to grow to almost 20 percent," noted the Elder Justice website.

The following are some common frauds involving seniors.

The Grandparents Scam

A senior citizen is sleeping peacefully, when suddenly the phone rings. Groggily, she picks up the telephone only to discover it's one of her grandchildren on the line—or someone at least claiming to be her grandchild. The alleged grandchild relates a sad tale: he's been arrested on spurious grounds while traveling in a foreign country. He needs bail money, fast. The caller explains that he got in touch with his grandparent, rather than his mom and dad, because he's embarrassed to let his parents know.

The concerned grandparent follows instructions and arranges for a money transfer to the number provided. And then she waits … and waits some more. Strangely, the grandchild never calls back to say if the wire transfer has arrived and bail has been paid.

This well-known con is called the "Grandparents Scam." It's not new, but modern technology has enabled con artists to make it seem more convincing. A scammer might study Internet postings and online social media sites to garner pointers about the person he's pretending to be. For example, a young person might mention online that he plays the piano and that his favorite foreign country is Italy. With this information in mind, the scammer tells a grandparent he's been incarcerated by authorities on trumped-up charges while on a performance tour in Italy.

If the scammer is using the phone, rather than e-mail, he will usually call late at night or early in the morning, when most people are still asleep or muddle-headed. Sometimes, instead of getting a call from a phony grandchild, seniors are contacted by a phony police officer, lawyer, or doctor, claiming to be speaking on behalf of a grandson or granddaughter.

Scammers have also been known to send out fake distress e-mails, supposedly from foreign countries, begging grandparents for quick cash. In general, however, the Grandparent Scam works best when a phone call is the mode of communication. An e-mail gives seniors too much time to ponder. A desperate phone call in the middle of the night, by contrast, will almost certainly catch an elderly person off-guard, making them more susceptible to sending money on dubious grounds.

Tips on Avoiding Being Duped by the Grandparents Scam

- If a mystery caller wakes you in the middle of the night claiming to be your grandchild, ask them "Which one?" Insist that the caller gave their name. If it isn't the name of one of your grandkids, hang up.
- If the mystery caller does have the correct name of one of your grandchildren, still be wary. The scammer might have gleaned the name from Facebook, other social media, an obituary, or an ancestry website. Ask the caller to identify a recent Christmas present you sent them. Even if they provide the correct answer (it might be a lucky guess), tell the person on the line you will return their call on your grandchild's land line or cell phone.
- Be immediately suspicious of any request made for funds to be sent via wire transfer. Fraudsters pulling the grandparents scam will insist you send them hefty payments for bail or legal fees for their grandchild via Western Union or MoneyGram. Such a request is a glaring red flag.
- Once the mystery caller is off the line, contact your grandchild or their parents, just to confirm your family member's safety.

Source: AARP, "Inside the Grandparents Scam: A Con Artist Reveals All," http://blog .aarp.org/2014/04/21/inside-the-grandparents-scam-a-con-artist-reveals-all/

"Few emotions are as powerful as love. So when a phone call comes, claiming a grandchild was hurt or arrested and your help—your money—is needed, you listen," stated an April 21, 2014, post on the AARP blog.

The FBI has some simple tips on their website for seniors looking to avoid being scammed: "resist the pressure to act quickly; try to contact your grandchild or another family member to determine whether or not the call is legitimate; never wire money based on a request made over the phone or in an e-mail; wiring money is like giving cash—once you send it, you can't get it back."

Many seniors are too embarrassed to report being conned, stated the FBI. And if they do report a scam, seniors often have difficulty remembering all the details of the con. What's more, seniors grew up in a more trusting era. Older people in general tend to be overly polite when dealing with scammers and naïve about their intentions.

No matter how old you are, it's always a good strategy to react skeptically to phone calls or e-mails asking for money, even if the message is supposedly from a grandchild in need.

Phony Phone Numbers

Some unscrupulous con artists acquire toll-free phone numbers that are very close to actual toll-free numbers for institutions frequently contacted by seniors. The latter might include the Social Security Administration, the Department of Veterans Affairs, the IRS, etc.

When callers connect with these phony numbers after misdialing, "they are told they have won a prize or are eligible for a survey and are promised complimentary or low-cost medical alert systems, magazine renewals, vacations, even dental plans," stated an AARP bulletin from September 2015.

Callers are asked to provide bank and credit card information or their Social Security number to "verify" their win or to pay "taxes" or "shipping costs" on their prize. Needless to say, the prizes never materialize.

The colloquial term for this scam is "Fat Finger Dialing," reported the AARP. Con artists purchase phone numbers that share the same seven-digit number as a real institution but with a different toll-free area code. So while the real institution might use an 800 toll-free area code, the fraudster's number might have an 888 or 866 toll-free area code.

The AARP September 2015 bulletin listed warning signs for seniors to know when they've misdialed a number and have been connected to a con artist. Being greeted by a live operator or recorded message that doesn't name the institution the caller was trying to reach is one sign. Being offered a prize that requires bank or credit card payments on the part of the caller is another red flag, as is being asked for your Social Security number. In all cases, the AARP recommended hanging up on all suspicious connections.

Veteran Scams

Many seniors are military veterans or are married to military veterans. Scammers know this and fashion their cons accordingly.

In one such scam, fraud artists "call widows of military veterans, saying the deceased had a hefty life insurance policy but payments are in arrears—and a few thousand dollars will bring the life insurance policy up to date," reported a June 11, 2015, AARP bulletin.

A variation of the above con involves scam artists impersonating officials from the Department of Veterans Affairs. These phony reps will contact seniors by phone, e-mail, or door-to-door solicitation, claiming that the VA has changed its policy regarding veteran benefits. The victim is asked to provide credit card or bank information, or their Social Security number, in order to "straighten out" the situation. The means of communication is a hint that a con is underway: the VA usually sends official information by surface mail. If approached by an alleged Department of Veterans Affairs representative, contact a VA office to confirm they are legitimate before handing over any money.

Another con involves e-mails or phone calls on behalf of fake military charities. This scam typically "targets patriotic older donors" who strongly support the military and any organization claiming to help active-duty soldiers or veterans, stated the June 11, 2015, AARP bulletin. The bulletin continued: "Veterans Day (along with Memorial Day) is prime time for swindles in the name of service personnel. Scammers often use sound-alike names (if not inventing authentic organizations) to solicit funds."

Any senior who receives a pitch for a military charity should first check the organization out with the Better Business Bureau or the agency in their state that regulates charities. Websites such as Charity Navigator and GuideStar also provide details about the legitimacy of charitable organizations.

A variation of the Grandparents Scam sees fraudsters contacting seniors who have a grandchild on active duty in the armed forces. The scammer claims be an army official reporting bad news about a grandchild in uniform. The grandchild has been discovered absent without leave (AWOL) or has been hospitalized. Medical or legal bills need to be immediately paid, or the grandchild will face serious repercussions. Con men who conduct this scam frequently glean names of actual soldiers from media accounts about troop deployments, to add authenticity to their fraudulent phone calls. In all cases, the elderly are urged to send money via wire transfer to help their grandchild.

Additional Scams Involving Senior Citizens

Seniors have also been victimized by medical equipment fraud (a medical equipment supplier offers "free" products to the elderly, then bills their insurance company even if the products are never delivered), lab scams ("Unnecessary and sometimes fake tests are given to individuals at health clubs, retirement homes or shopping malls and billed to insurance companies or Medicare," according to the FBI), and services-not-rendered scams (seniors agree to home repair or other services, pay an advance fee, and never get any service).

Further Reading

AARP blog, "Eight Scams That Take Aim at Veterans," June 11, 2015, http://blog.aarp .org/2015/11/06/veteransdayscams/.

AARP blog, "Inside the Grandparents Scam: A Con Artist Reveals All," April 21, 2014, http:// blog.aarp.org/2014/04/21/inside-the-grandparents-scam-a-con-artist-reveals-all/.

AARP Bulletin, "Phony Phone Numbers Can Cost You Money," September 2015, http:// www.aarp.org/money/scams-fraud/info-2015/avoid-scam-800-numbers.html

Department of Justice, Elder Justice website, http://www.justice.gov/elderjustice/.

Federal Bureau of Investigation, "Senior Citizen Fraud," https://www.fbi.gov/news/stories /2008/april/seniofraud_041008.

Federal Bureau of Investigation, "The Grandparent Scam—Don't Let It Happen to You," https://www.fbi.gov/news/stories/2012/april/grandparent_040212.

SURROGACY/ADOPTION FRAUD
Deceiving Prospective Parents

To prospective parents in Indiana, Victoria Farahan seemed like a godsend. She claimed she had connections with a hospital in Moscow and could provide healthy newborns for childless couples in the Midwest. As proof, she offered photographs of cooing babies. She also frequently went on trips to Russia, to check on potential adoptees. She sent encouraging e-mails to prospective parents, updating them on her Russian activities.

As it turned out, however, Farahan was a fake. According to a report on the FBI website, the photos she showed potential moms and dads were of her own kids. She never made any trips to Russia to visit maternity hospitals. The e-mails she sent to prospective parents while supposedly in Russia were flat-out lies.

Farahan swindled at least half a dozen Indiana couples out of just under $100,000. On July 17, 2006, she pled guilty to mail fraud (two counts) and wire fraud (five counts). The judge sentenced her to house arrest and probation.

Interestingly enough, Farahan had apparently been involved in a similar case a decade prior. In 1995, it was alleged she victimized some 30 families with an adoption scam. For some reason, charges were never laid in that case.

The FBI's website has advice for adoptive parents on how to avoid being scammed. Among other things, the FBI urged prospective moms and dads to do some research and find out whether the adoption agency or facilitator they are dealing with is properly licensed. Don't do all of your research online, however. Ask for a face-to-face meeting with the adoption agency or facilitator.

Be suspicious if the agency or individual refuses to meet in person. During the face-to-face meeting, ask to see documents and references from other parents for whom they have successfully arranged adoptions. Be suspicious of any agency or facilitator who claims they have found a "shortcut" that allows them to fast-track the adoption process.

Other red flags: adoption agencies that force prospective parents to make snap decisions, without giving them a proper amount of time to ponder an adoption. A website that doesn't offer the names of any agency staff or a brick-and-mortar address is also grounds for suspicion. Agencies that won't provide proof of pregnancy to adoptive moms and dads (ultrasound scans, photographs, doctor's notes) are also fishy.

If the prospective parents are trying to arrange an international adoption, the FBI urges them to first check in with the U.S. Department of State for information to adoption procedures in foreign countries.

People scammed by international adoption agencies should contact the U.S. embassy or consulate in the country of the child's origin, states the Bureau of Consular Affairs for the U.S. State Department. If a U.S.-based agency was arranging the international adoption, ripped-off moms and dads should register a complaint with the licensing authority in the state in which the agency is based. A complaint to the state's Better Business Bureau is also a good idea, adds the Bureau of Consular Affairs.

Selling Babies

"Baby selling"—like grave robbing—is one of those crimes that seems too lurid to be real. But real it was for three women who all pled guilty in 2011 for their involvement in a "baby-selling ring," as the FBI put it.

The ring consisted of Theresa Erickson (a respected California lawyer who specialized in reproductive law), Hilary Neiman (a lawyer who ran a Maryland adoption/surrogacy agency), and Carla Chambers of Nevada. In pleading guilty, the trio admitted to "taking part in a scheme to illegally create an inventory of babies to sell to unwitting would-be parents for fees of between $100,000 [to] 150,000 each," according to the FBI.

The scheme cooked up by these three women centered on surrogacy. "A surrogacy is an arrangement, which sometimes involves payment, between intended parents and a surrogate who agrees to carry an embryo to term. A traditional surrogacy is when the surrogate and her egg is fertilized through artificial insemination with the sperm of the intended father. In gestational surrogacy, the carrier has no biological connection to the child," explained FBI agent Mollie Halpern, in a podcast released after the case broke.

Chambers was in charge of the first part of the scam. She trolled adoption and surrogacy online chat rooms and forums hunting for young women willing to be mothers for hire. Surrogates recruited by Chambers were told they could earn between $35,000 and $38,000 for being "gestational carriers" of other people's embryos. They were also informed that they would be matched with prospective parents in their twelfth week of pregnancy. That this was a violation of California law didn't seem particularly to concern Chambers.

Under California statutes, for-pay surrogacy arrangements are legal, but only if the surrogate and the intended parents sign a contract prior to the former's pregnancy. Once a surrogate is pregnant, parental rights for the unborn child cannot be sold. Parental rights can still be transferred, but only through a formal adoption process. But no matter; Chambers assured her charges that everything was above-board and legal.

To earn their fee, surrogates in the baby-selling scheme had to travel to Ukraine to be implanted with embryos from anonymous sources. All travel arrangements were made by Chambers. Surrogates were told there was a long waiting list of prospective moms and dads, eager to acquire their infants. In reality, no such waiting list existed. Some surrogates would enter the thirty-third week of pregnancy without being matched with parents. The surrogate mothers would start to get panicky, thinking they might be responsible for raising the child they were carrying.

At this stage, Neiman entered the picture. She was in charge of connecting pregnant surrogates with eager parents. To source the latter, Neiman scoured adoption websites, looking for prospective couples desperate for a baby. Once a suitable couple had been located, Neiman would approach them with a sad story.

Neiman explained that she ran a surrogacy/adoption agency. Unfortunately, one of her surrogacy arrangements had fallen through. The intended parents had dropped out of the deal, leaving a pregnant surrogate mother to her own devices. It would be possible, explained Neiman, to connect this unfortunate mom-to-be with a new set of prospective parents. Now, of course, there would be some expenses involved. Any new prospective parents would have to pay Neiman a hefty fee, around $100,000–150,000. While the arrangement was definitely unorthodox, Neiman told couples everything was legal. Once a contract had been inked, the surrogates would be flown to San Diego, in order to give birth in the state of California.

The stage was now set for lawyer Erickson. Erickson was in charge of acquiring paperwork that would put a legal stamp on the dodgy proceedings. More specifically, she would ask the San Diego Superior Court to issue what's called a pre-birth order, which transfers parental rights from surrogate mothers to the intended parents. Such orders are only supposed to be issued upon proof of a contract signed by surrogate and prospective parents before the former gets pregnant.

The filings Erickson issued were filled with lies but convincing enough to fool a series of judges. The latter were led to believe that pre-pregnancy contracts existed between surrogates and would-be parents. Erickson was a much-respected lawyer, so judges had no reason to suspect her. In many cases, the San Diego Superior Court issued pre-birth orders without holding hearings or having all parties involved present.

A press release from the FBI's San Diego division explained, "With these fraudulently obtained pre-birth orders, the [intended parents'] names would be placed on the babies' birth certificates through a surrogacy and the conspirators would be able to profit from their sale of parent rights."

The scam began to unravel in mid-2010, when a surrogate who was seven months pregnant became concerned that she hadn't yet been matched with a set of parents. The surrogate contacted a lawyer who specialized in reproductive law, who, in turn, got in touch with the FBI.

Supervisory Special Agent Jeffrey Veltri of the FBI's San Diego division took on the case. The FBI was fortunate, in that the trio of conspirators treated their surrogates with cavalier disdain. In addition to not being matched up with parents early in their pregnancies, the surrogates didn't receive all the payments they had been promised, forcing them to shoulder medical bills on their own.

In the FBI podcast, Veltri explained, "One of the surrogates came into town; she was due to deliver. And we approached her. And we asked her if she'd be willing to assist us in our investigation. Throughout the course of the surrogacy, she felt like she was getting the run-around, so she was very willing to help us."

The FBI secured a second witness and built a case. When the case closed in December 2010, Erickson, Neiman, and Chambers all faced serious allegations. Erickson and Neiman were both charged with conspiracy to commit wire fraud, while Chambers was charged with conspiracy to engage in monetary transactions in property derived from specified unlawful activity.

Neiman pled guilty on July 28, 2011. Chambers followed with a guilty plea one week later. Then, on August 9, 2011, Erickson pled guilty as well. In making her plea, Erickson "admitted to being part of a baby-selling ring that deceived the Superior Court of California and prospective parents for unborn babies," stated a press release from the FBI's San Diego division.

On February 24, 2012, Erickson was sentenced to five months in prison and nine months of house arrest. Erickson was also slapped with a $70,000 fine and three years of supervised release.

In an FBI press release from the San Diego division, United States Attorney Laura Duffy stated, "Out of sheer greed, Erickson preyed upon people's most basic need: to raise a child. We cannot and will not allow individuals like Erickson to profit by taking advantage of vulnerable people who have a sincere desire to lawfully adopt and parent children."

The same judge who sentenced Erickson gave her co-conspirator Chambers a five-month jail sentence, seven months of house arrest, $180,020.20 in forfeiture, and three years of supervised release.

Neiman had already been sentenced, on December 1, 2011, to 12 months' custody (five months in prison, seven months of house arrest), a $20,000 fine, $133,000 in forfeiture, and three years of supervised release.

Authorities were in agreement about the special offensiveness of the trio's crimes. As FBI Special Agent in charge, Keith Slotter, stated in an FBI press release, "Though the FBI investigates many different types of fraud, it is particularly disturbing when victims have been taken advantage of because of their desire to create a family. In this case, the victims were exploited at a time in their lives when they were in a most vulnerable situation and trusting in legal counsel to abide by the laws of this country to provide them with legitimate services."

Scamming Donors, Surrogates, and Prospective Parents

The website for SurroGenesis, a surrogate and egg donation agency based in Modesto, California, seemed so inviting.

"We are dedicated to assisting infertile couples to have a baby through third-party assisted reproduction. In most cases, by the time people decide to look into surrogacy or egg donation, they have been through a lot emotionally and financially. Our goal at SurroGenesis USA INC is to help guide you through each step of this delicate process, making each step as simple as possible, and making this journey to parenthood an enjoyable experience," stated the company's archived website.

SurroGenesis was run by director/president Tonya Collins. The company existed to serve two different sectors: infertile couples who wanted children and healthy young women willing to donate eggs or serve as surrogates. The company promised that all egg donors and surrogates had been medically vetted. Egg donor compensation was pegged at roughly $5,000. Surrogates could expect a much more substantial fee, in the range of $18,000–30,000.

Egg donation sounded pretty good to Amanda Cram, a Fresno State student. In 2008, Cram spotted the SurroGenesis website and approached them with a view to selling her eggs. Cram passed a medical exam, then signed a contract with SurroGenesis. Under the terms of the contract, SurroGenesis was supposed to cover any medical expenses arising from complications in the egg donation.

Cram's first donation went off without a hitch. Her eggs were used to create triplets in a happy new mom. The student received $6,000 in total for her efforts and didn't have to pay a single medical bill.

A few months went by, and SurroGenesis contacted Cram again. Would she be interested in donating eggs again? Cram was interested, but things didn't go as smoothly the second time around. Her ovaries became inflamed as a result of the egg donation, and Cram was hospitalized for over a month. She assumed that her lengthy stay would be covered by SurroGenesis, but she was wrong.

After Cram was released, bills from the hospital began pouring in to her mailbox. In total, Cram was told she owed $40,000.

Cram's tale of woe was reported by the media in mid-2009. Reporters discovered that SurroGenesis owed money to dozens of clients—egg donors, surrogates, and prospective parents alike. When reporters investigated further, they revealed that Collins had disappeared, owing more than $2 million to various sources.

The FBI got involved, and on April 19, 2012, a federal grand jury returned an indictment against Collins. The indictment cited seven counts of wire fraud, four counts of mail fraud, nine counts of bank fraud, and ten counts of money laundering in connection with a scam to defraud. According to the indictment, Collins's company actively defrauded clients from November 2006 to March 2009.

Collins claimed that fees from clients and payments to egg donors and surrogates would be handled by an independent personal property escrow company called the Michael Charles Independent Financial Holding Group. As it turned out, this escrow company was actually set up by Collins herself, who went to great lengths to portray the firm as independent and fully staffed, when it was neither.

A day after the federal indictment was handed down, Collins was arrested at her residence in Antelope, California. Collins was accused of repeatedly dipping into the bank accounts for SurroGenesis and the Michael Charles Independent Financial Holding Group escrow company to make "unauthorized personal purchases, without the clients' knowledge or authorization. Those personal expenditures included automobiles, homes, jewelry, clothing and vacations for herself and others. Collins at times directly used client funds in the Michael Charles accounts to pay for her personal purchases and at times transferred client funds from the Michael Charles accounts to other bank accounts that she controlled before spending the funds," stated a press release from the Sacramento, California, office of the FBI.

Thanks to Collins's reckless spending, SurroGenesis and the Michael Charles Independent Financial escrow company experienced regular cash flow problems. Fees to surrogates or egg donors such as Cram went unpaid, while services to prospective parents were not fulfilled.

The FBI press release continued: "Collins nonetheless allegedly continued to solicit new surrogate parent clients and funds. The indictment also alleges that, in an effort to conceal and forestall the collapse of the scheme, Collins kited checks and wired amounts between banks, which resulted in losses to financial institutions. Eventually, the scheme collapsed in 2009. As a result of Collins' conduct, SurroGenesis and Michael Charles clients, surrogates and financial institutions suffered losses of more than $2 million."

Collins pleaded guilty on February 19, 2013, to four counts of wire fraud. As part of her plea, she admitted that she steered clients to the Michael Charles fund, all the while concealing her ownership and control of the escrow company. On May 13, 2013, Collins received a five-year sentence. A few months later, she was also ordered by a judge to pay $1.760 million to people she had conned.

An FBI press release from the Sacramento division, issued after her guilty plea, stated that "Tonya Collins cruelly took advantage of clients who sought nothing more than to bring children into the world. Her greed left a trail of devastation, both financial and emotional, in its wake."

Further Reading

Sandra Chapman, "Woman Sentenced in Adoption Scheme," WTHR.com, http://www.wthr.com/story/5453762/woman-sentenced-in-adoption-scheme.

Federal Bureau of Investigation, "Adoption Scams Bilk Victims, Break Hearts," August 28, 2006, https://www.fbi.gov/news/stories/2006/august/adoptscams_082806.

Federal Bureau of Investigation, podcast, "Baby Selling Ring," https://www.fbi.gov/news/podcasts/inside/baby-selling-ring.mp3/view.

Federal Bureau of Investigation, Sacramento Division, "Modesto Surrogate Parenting Agency Owner Indicted for $2 Million Fraud Scheme," April 20, 2012.

Federal Bureau of Investigation, Sacramento Division, "Modesto Surrogate Parenting Agency Owner Pleads Guilty in $2 Million Fraud Scheme," February 19, 2013.

Federal Bureau of Investigation, Sacramento Division, "Surrogate Parenting Agency Owner Ordered to Pay $1.7 Million to Victims," September 10, 2013.

Federal Bureau of Investigation, San Diego Division, "Baby-Selling Ring Busted," August 9, 2011.

Federal Bureau of Investigation, San Diego Division, "Prominent Surrogacy Attorney Sentenced to Prison for Her Role in Baby-Selling Case," February 24, 2012.

Federal Bureau of Investigation, "Surrogacy Scam Played on Emotions of Vulnerable Victims," September 13, 2011, https://www.fbi.gov/news/stories/2011/september/surrogacy_091311/surrogacy_091311.

Margot Kim, "Surrogacy Scam," ABC30.com, May 1, 2009, http://abc30.com/archive/6790514/.

SurroGenesis archived website, http://www.otheroom.com/archive/surrogenesis/index.html.

U.S. Department of State, Bureau of Consular Affairs, "Alert—Adoption Scams and Frauds," April 7, 2014, http://travel.state.gov/content/adoptionsabroad/en/about-us/newsroom/alert-adoption-scams-and-fraud.html.

SECTION FOUR

GREAT PRETENDERS

INTRODUCTION

What makes a person pretend be someone else, for years on end?

For Frank Abagnale, who claimed to have successfully passed himself off as an airplane pilot, university instructor, lawyer, and doctor, the answer was simple. Being an imposter was a good way to earn an easy living, meet women, and gratify his ego.

The cases of James Capone (older brother of the infamous Al Capone) and Espera DeCorti are more mysterious. Both men were of Italian heritage. Both abandoned their families to go out West and invent frontier personas for themselves. Capone became a tough, well-respected lawman known as Richard Joseph "Two-Gun" Hart, while DeCorti became Iron Eyes Cody, a wise American Indian who appeared in movies and a famous anti-littering commercial on TV.

"Emperor Norton" of San Francisco, meanwhile, was a once-wealthy businessman who assumed a regal guise after going bankrupt in the mid-1800s. He became a much-loved eccentric treated with royal courtesy by bemused citizens and merchants of that city.

Joseph Pistone was an FBI agent with an aptitude for play-acting. He successfully passed himself off to the New York Mafia as a young criminal on the rise. So successful was his masquerade that Pistone was on the verge of becoming the first FBI agent ever inducted into the Mafia's official ranks, when his superiors shut his investigation down.

As disparate as these cases are, they all point to an underlying question: how well do you ever really know a person?

FRANK ABAGNALE

Frank Abagnale traveled around the world as a fake Pan Am pilot, supervised hospital interns, taught a college sociology course, and practiced law before turning 22, all without proper training or ID. He served time in French, Swedish, and American prisons and made two daring escapes from custody. Abagnale's exploits were detailed in a best-selling book called *Catch Me If You Can* and a Steven Spielberg movie of the same title, staring Leonardo DiCaprio.

Abagnale was a born scammer. His biggest con, however, might be his public image as a master impersonator and forger. Elements of his much-publicized but hard-to-verify life story have been questioned by investigative journalists. What is known is that he was arrested by the FBI in 1970 for passing bad checks and served four years in a U.S. prison. Abagnale was paroled in 1974 and started a new life as a fraud prevention expert, sharing his insider's wisdom during seminars in front of police, banks, corporations, and the FBI.

Abagnale was born in 1948 and grew up in Bronxville, New York. His parents broke up when he was 12 years old and divorced two years later.

The first person Abagnale scammed was apparently his own father. The latter had given his son a gasoline credit card and a truck, so he could commute to a part-time job. Eager to make himself seem impressive to girls, Abagnale conjured up a scheme involving the gasoline credit card. He used the card to get cash from gas stations while supposedly purchasing car tires, batteries, etc. The illicit funds were largely spent on extravagant dates with various girls. Women, he would later claim, were his only real vice, not counting forgery and faking identities. The gasoline scam eventually came to light when Abagnale's father was billed $3,400 from the company that supplied the card.

Inspired by this first feat of thievery, Abagnale started writing bad checks and cashing them. He left home at age 16, in June 1964, traveling to New York City. There, he took a series of low-end but legitimate jobs, none of which paid well. In an effort to boost his earnings, Abagnale decided to "age" himself. The young man stood six feet tall and already had gray in his hair; people were often surprised to discover that Abagnale was still a teenager. So Abagnale altered his driver's license, changing the birthdate from 1948 to 1938, and sought out work as an adult. His grown-up jobs didn't pay much better than his previous gigs, so he resorted once again to "paperhanging"—that is, writing and cashing bad checks.

In his autobiography, Abagnale claimed he was walking near a hotel on 42nd Street in Manhattan when he had a life-altering epiphany. He spotted the crew of an Eastern Airlines plane leaving a hotel. The pack consisted of a captain, the co-pilot, a flight engineer, and a quartet of stewardesses.

Abagnale recalled, "They were all laughing and animated, caught up in a joie de vivre of their own. The men were all lean and handsome and their gold-piped uniforms lent them a buccaneerish air. The girls were all trim and lovely, as graceful and colorful as butterflies aboard in a meadow."

Abagnale decided on the spot that this was the kind of life he wanted to lead. He wasn't interested in actually flying a plane, but just wearing a pilot's uniform and earning respect as he cashed bad checks and pulled other scams.

Abagnale plotted and schemed. After spotting a Pan American World Airways Building, he contacted the airline, claiming to be a co-pilot named "Robert Black." Mr. Black said his uniform was stolen and he needed a new one. Pan Am arranged for him to get a new set of clothes from a uniform supplier. He acquired further hardware—Pan Am "wings" and an emblem—from a Pan Am supplier at an airport.

Uniform and trim in hand, Abagnale proceeded to call Pan Am, pretending to be an inquisitive high school student writing an article for his student newspaper. Pan Am put Abagnale in touch with a pilot who cheerfully responded to the boy's telephone queries. Abagnale's purpose was to acquire information to make his planned charade more believable. Among other insider details, Abagnale learned about the concept of "deadheading" (extra flight crew tagging along in the cockpit, to get a free ride) during this chat.

Abagnale illicitly acquired an ID card and an FAA pilot's license. He dressed in his ill-gotten uniform and started making the rounds in airports, garnering respect from all he encountered. Abagnale used the uniform to cash bad checks and gratify his ego. (No one ever questioned a pilot, and his checks were always readily accepted.)

"During the next five years, the uniform was my alter ego," wrote Abagnale. "I used it in the same manner a junkie shoots up on heroin. Whenever I felt lonely, depressed, rejected or doubtful of my own worth, I'd dress up in my pilot's uniform and seek out a crowd. The uniform brought me respect and dignity. Without it on, at times, I felt useless and dejected."

Abagnale continued cashing checks at bank branches and airport shops. He also continued to closely observe how real pilots spoke and acted. He started dating stewardesses, using them for sex and insider information. He called various airports and airlines, looking for more details that would enhance his pilot act. Once he felt confident enough, Abagnale began deadheading. Most planes contained a jump seat in the cockpit, for extra crew. The crew members who used these extra seats for flights were rarely asked to take the controls. Abagnale had acquired enough lingo and knowledge to make small-talk with the real crew, about flying conditions, planes, or other pilots.

Once he landed in other cities, Abagnale was usually put up at hotels where Pan Am crew were billeted, with all expenses paid by the airline. He started extensively paperhanging in all the cities he visited.

Abagnale got away with his pilot scam for several years. He attributed his success to a number of factors. He was always careful to cash checks for only relatively small amounts so as not to arouse suspicion. More important, the National Crime Information Center (NCIC—an initiative computerizing police and crime databases around the country) hadn't been established yet. Finally, there was the fact that his scam was so extreme, people couldn't conceive he was faking.

In total, Abagnale claimed he made around 200 "duplicitous flights." While deadheading on a flight from New Orleans to Miami, he was nearly caught. The pilot and co-pilot received information over their headphones that led them to scrutinize his phony ID and pilot's license. Two sheriffs came on board after the plane landed and escorted him to a police station. The FBI then became involved, and Abagnale was interrogated. The FBI agent asked for references, and Abagnale obliged, providing some names and numbers of stewardesses and flight crew he was on friendly terms with. These contacts apparently vouched for him, and the FBI let Abagnale go.

Frightened by this close call, Abagnale stopped pretending to be a pilot. He ended up in Atlanta, applying for an apartment at a singles residence. On the application form, Abagnale claimed to be a doctor, specifically a pediatrician. While this was apparently a spur-of-the-moment decision, his application was accepted. One of his apartment neighbors turned out to be a real doctor, and Abagnale found himself working at a local hospital supervising interns and nurses. He obtained the job with a forged medical certificate and kept it by maintaining a laissez-faire attitude. As a supervisor, Abagnale simply let the interns do all the work while he pretended to "observe." He also studied on the side about medical terms and doctors' slang, to pass himself off as the real thing.

This charade ended after a close call involving a baby suffering from oxygen deprivation. A nurse called in an emergency about a "blue baby." Unfamiliar with the term, Abagnale made a joke instead of rushing to help. Fortunately, the nurse got someone else to assist, and Abagnale decided he'd had enough playing doctor.

After being a fake physician, Abagnale's next logical move was to be a pretend lawyer. He faked a Harvard Law School degree and a university transcript, then brushed up on his knowledge of the law. He passed the Louisiana state bar exam (after failing twice) and found himself working in the Louisiana State Attorney General's Office. This scam ended when one of his co-workers—who had actually attended Harvard Law School—kept peppering Abagnale with questions about his time in the Ivy League.

Abagnale next found himself in Utah, where he forged credentials and taught a sociology course at Brigham Young University for a summer semester. By his own account, the experience was rewarding and the class lively and instructive.

More criminal adventures followed, including a period in which Abagnale graduated from writing bad checks to forging checks. Eventually Abagnale's luck ran out. He was arrested in 1969 in Montpellier, France, after an Air France flight attendant he once dated recognized him and alerted police. European authorities, like their American counterparts, were eager to punish him for passing bad checks.

Abagnale served half a year in a French prison before being released, only to be taken into custody by Swedish authorities. Abagnale was placed on trial in Sweden for various check fraud–related offences in that country. He was found guilty and began serving time. At this point, Abagnale discovered that a long list of countries were eager to try him for check fraud. The list included, among others, Italy, Germany, Spain, Turkey, Egypt, Greece, and Denmark. Italy was the first to request extradition, so it was decided he would be sent there after finishing his Swedish sentence.

The Swedes took pity on Abagnale and devised a plan whereby his U.S. passport was revoked, making him an alien in their country. He was sent back to the United States to stand trial for scores of American-based offences. Upon landing at John F. Kennedy International Airport with a police escort awaiting him, Abagnale escaped through the airplane bathroom. It was nighttime, and Abagnale apparently scurried across the runway and made good his escape. He traveled from the airport into New York City proper, where he phoned his parents.

Despite their tearful entreaties, Abagnale did not visit his mother and father in person, fearing that their residences were under surveillance. Instead, he contacted a girl he knew in the Bronx, with whom he had supposedly stashed clothes, money, and a key to a bank safe deposit box in Montreal. He took a train to Montreal, retrieved the $20,000 he had previously stashed in the safe deposit box, and made plans to journey to Brazil, which had no extradition treaty with the United States at the time.

While waiting in line at a Montreal airport to buy a ticket, Abagnale was arrested by the Royal Canadian Mounted Police (RCMP). He was turned over to U.S. authorities and locked away in a secure federal detention center in New York City. Abagnale was eventually transferred to a Federal Detention Center in Atlanta to await trial. "It was from this prison that I perpetrated what has to be one of the most hilarious escapes in the annals of criminal history," he modestly proclaimed, in his memoir.

According to Abagnale, the U.S. marshals who took him to the detention center in Atlanta forgot his detention commitment papers. The prison officials mistook him for an undercover prison inspector. Through the connivance of a girlfriend, Abagnale acquired business cards from real officials with the FBI and the U.S. Bureau of Prisons. He used these cards to convince Atlanta authorities that he really was an undercover prison inspector who had to be let out early to provide information to the FBI. He left the prison and made his way back to New York City on a bus. Once again, his plan was to escape to Brazil. This was not to be, as he was recognized and arrested by New York police officers.

Abagnale claimed that authorities in all fifty states wanted to try him for various check-related swindles. In April 1971, he ended up pleading guilty before a federal judge in Atlanta. His plea condensed all the state and federal charges against him (which apparently numbered in the hundreds) to a handful of accounts. He received a sentence of 12 years in jail, to be served at the Federal Correction Institution in Petersburg, Virginia.

Abagnale did not serve his full sentence. He was paroled after four years to the city of Houston, Texas. The former federal prisoner tried his hand at a few menial jobs, all of which he hated. Abagnale decided he was made for better things. He approached a bank, told them exactly who he was, and offered to put on a seminar to employees about check fraud and forgery. His appearance was a hit, and Abagnale was soon giving the same lecture to a series of banks. In this manner, he transformed himself into a "white collar crime specialist." Abagnale eventually founded a very successful consulting firm, Abagnale & Associates, which is currently headquartered in Washington DC.

Along the way, Abagnale appeared as a guest on *The Tonight Show* in the late 1970s and co-wrote a book about his life, *Catch Me If You Can*, that was published in 1980. This book was turned into a hit movie of the same title in 2002. Today, Abagnale is a popular author (his other books include titles such as *Stealing Your Life* and *The Art of the Steal*) and much in-demand speaker with an impressive client list.

As of early 2015, Abagnale's website stated, "Mr. Abagnale has been associated with the FBI for over 35 years. He lectures extensively at the FBI Academy and for the field offices of the Federal Bureau of Investigation ... more than 14,000 financial institutions, corporations, and law enforcement agencies use his fraud prevention programs ... today the majority of Mr. Abagnale's work is for the U.S. government."

The post-prison Abagnale has given insightful interviews to journalists on the subject of fraud, forgery and other skullduggery: "When I forged checks 40 years ago, I needed a Heidelberg printing press. The press was $1 million. It was 90 feet long; it was 18 feet high ... there were color separations, negatives, plates, type settings ... now, because of technology, all someone does today is basically sit in their hotel and look out the window and look for a victim. If they see, for example, *U.S. News & World Report*'s building, they can basically just go to their laptop [and] in a matter of minutes, they [can create] a beautiful, four-color check from that company," stated Abagnale in an interview with *U.S. News & World Report*, published in 2008.

To the same media outlet, he explained how a contemporary paperhanger might scam cashiers. He cited Tulsa, Oklahoma, a state where thousands of people work for American Airlines. A forger could make a check allegedly from

American Airlines and take it to a grocery store with a check-cashing service. In all likelihood, as soon as the cashier sees the "American Airlines" logo and imprint, he will assume the check is good, explained Abagnale.

While Abagnale has been successful in posing as a redeemed scoundrel, questions have been raised about the veracity of his criminal tales. In 1978, a *San Francisco Chronicle* reporter checked into Abagnale's claims after he spoke at an anti-crime seminar in the city. The *Chronicle* reporter made queries to banks, hospitals, schools, and a variety of other institutions cited by Abagnale, none of whom were familiar with any of his cons or the aliases under which he worked.

An article in the *Deseret News* on December 26, 2002, noted that there was no record of Frank Abagnale or anyone with the aliases he used teaching a summer semester on sociology at Brigham Young University. The article contained an astute observation from Michael Smart, a BYU spokesperson: "It's important to remember we are dealing with someone who is famous for being a liar. You get the feeling he could tell a good story," the article quoted Smart as saying. Indeed, Abagnale's own website describes him as "one of the world's most famous confidence men."

When confronted with such discrepancies, Abagnale has said he doubted anyone would confirm his tales because of the embarrassment involved in admitting to being conned. He has, however, admitted that certain elements of his story have been exaggerated. The media, for example, often said he wrote a total of $10 million worth of bad checks over his criminal career. Nonsense, said Abagnale. The actual figure was $2.5 million. The book and movie *Catch Me If You Can* also fictionalized elements of his past. The movie presented him as an only child (when he actually had three siblings) and portrayed his straight-arrow father as something of a slick hustler. The movie also invented a dogged FBI agent (played by Tom Hanks) who spends years pursuing Abagnale.

Interestingly enough, Abagnale's own website tries to put some distance between himself and his past: "I consider my past immoral, unethical and illegal. It is something I am not proud of. I am proud that I have been able to turn my life around and in the past 25 years, helped my government, my clients, thousands of corporations and consumers deal with the problems of white collar crime and fraud," he stated on the site.

As for the film about his life, "I know that Hollywood has made a number of changes to the story, but I am honored that Steven Spielberg, Leonardo DiCaprio, and Tom Hanks participated in the making of a movie inspired by my life. It is important to understand that it is just a movie … not a biographical documentary," added Abagnale.

Further Reading

Frank W. Abagnale and Stan Redding, *Catch Me If You Can*, 1980.
Frank Abagnale website, http://www.abagnale.com/.

Bob Baker, "The Truth? Just Catch It If You Can," *Los Angeles Times*, December 28, 2002, http://articles.latimes.com/2002/dec/28/entertainment/et-baker28.

Jeffrey P. Haney, "Did Con Man Teach at BYU?" *Deseret News*, December 26, 2002, http://www.deseretnews.com/article/956024/Did-con-man-teach-at-BYU.html?pg=all.

Luke Mullins, "How Frank Abagnale Would Swindle You," *U.S. News and World Report*, May 19, 2008, http://money.usnews.com/money/blogs/the-collar/2008/05/19/how-frank-abagnale-would-swindle-you.

Jeremy Scott-Joynt, "Fighting Back on ID Theft," *BBC News*, May 9, 2006, http://news.bbc.co.uk/2/hi/business/4754733.stm.

JAMES CAPONE (AKA RICHARD JOSEPH "TWO-GUN" HART)

America's most notorious gangster had an older brother who fashioned a public persona as a tough, no-nonsense lawman of the Wild West.

The gangster was Al Capone, and his brother was named Vincenzo Capone. At the tender age of two, Vincenzo traveled with his parents Gabriele and Teresina (or Teresa) Capone from Naples, Italy, to New York City. The year was 1894. The young Capone clan was part of a huge wave of people fleeing from southern Italy and Sicily to the New World. These immigrants were eager to escape the poverty and lack of opportunity in their homeland for the bounty of America.

Gabriele Capone was a barber by trade. He could also read and write, which put him ahead of many of his immigrant peers. He settled his family in a Brooklyn slum and then acquired a job at a grocery store patronized by Italian immigrants. More children were born to the Capones, including son Alphonse, who entered the world in 1899. Shortly after Alphonse was born, the Capones moved up a notch on the social ladder. The Capone family moved to better quarters in Brooklyn. They resided above a barber shop run by Gabriele.

The Capone children quickly adapted to their newfound country. As soon as they were old enough, the Capone siblings anglicized their names: Vincenzo became James, Raffaele became Ralph, Alphonse became Al, etc.

James Capone proved to be a strong-willed boy with big dreams. Bored with life in Brooklyn and looking for adventure, James left his family at age 16, in 1908. He ended up in the Midwest, where he worked for a circus for a while. James was muscular and tough and enjoyed living outdoors and away from the squalor of Brooklyn. He drifted around the American West, never revealing to anyone that he was Italian-born. In fact, he worked hard to lose his Italian accent. If asked about his dark hair and olive complexion, James claimed he was part Mexican or Native American Indian.

In 1917, the United States entered the First World War. James Capone joined the army, serving in an infantry unit. He rose to the rank of Lieutenant and was well-regarded for his shooting skills. He received a medal from General John Pershing, commander of the American Expeditionary Force.

James returned to the U.S. in 1919, winding up in Homer, Nebraska. He was 27 at the time and decided to dramatically change his life. He cut ties with his family in New York City (he would remain out of touch with them for years) and changed his name to Richard Joseph Hart. He modeled himself after silent movie cowboy William S. Hart—and borrowed his last name.

James Capone/Richard Hart did odd jobs, such as painting houses, to earn his keep. He also became known around town as a sharpshooting former soldier with a medal. In May 1919, severe flooding hit the area where he lived. "Richard" helped rescue some locals, one of whom—a young lady named Kathleen Winch—he fell in love with. The pair got married on September 1, 1919. Within a few years, the union produced four boys.

By 1920, Prohibition had become national law. It was a crime to manufacture, sell, transport, or traffic alcohol. In the summer of 1920, Richard Joseph Hart got a commission to be a Prohibition Agent from the Governor of Nebraska. Richard soon began raiding stills and confiscating moonshine (illegal backwoods liquor). He earned publicity in local papers and affected a flamboyant air, just like his namesake Hollywood cowboy idol.

It's unclear how much Richard was influenced in his career choices by the criminal actions of his family. By the early 1920s, younger brothers Al and Ralph were rising in the Chicago underworld. Al Capone would become the most famous gangster in America, a defiant, publicity-loving mob boss who openly flouted the law.

In his comprehensive book, *Capone: The Man and the Era*, which chronicled Al Capone's rise and fall, author Laurence Bergreen stated, "Richard was determined to differentiate himself from [his family] and not merely by changing his name. If they found themselves on the wrong side of the law, he would make certain to be on the right side."

In October 1920, Richard went undercover in an investigation in Randolph, Nebraska. In this capacity, he helped break up a major moonshine operation. For another undercover mission, he posed as a wounded veteran with plenty of money and a taste for illicit liquor.

Richard impressed his superiors and ended up getting a job with the Federal Bureau of Indian Affairs. His new mission was stamping out moonshining on Indian reservations. Richard earned a reputation as a tough, effective agent who often traveled to crime scenes on horseback. It was around this time that he acquired the nickname "Two-Gun" because of his habit of wearing holstered pistols on each hip. The people with whom Richard worked and lived, of course, knew nothing about his connection to the Capone clan.

In the autumn of 1923, while on a mission, Richard accidentally shot and killed an innocent man. The man happened to be white rather than Indian, which in the racist milieu of the day spelled more trouble for Richard. Richard was charged with manslaughter. A coroner's jury found him not guilty on the grounds that the killing was justifiable. Still, the shooting damaged his reputation.

Richard continued to work as a special agent for the Bureau of Indian Affairs. This meant he traveled around quite a bit with his family. He spent much of his time rounding up intoxicated Indians. Despite the bad press he had received from the shooting incident, he was still largely respected as a tough lawman.

Richard decided to rekindle ties with his clan. He visited the Capone family in 1924, after lying low for some time. In many ways, Richard was a lot like his younger, more notorious brother, Al: they were both strong-willed, and they both liked guns. "Each brother personified one aspect of a duality deep in the Capone family's collective psyche, one choosing to become an outlaw, the other a lawman, each a mirror of the other," stated Bergreen. By this point, Gabriele was dead, so Richard was unable to talk to his father about life as a lawman.

The initial family visit was a success, and Richard began coming to Chicago once a year to see his family. When reporters figured out who he was, they pushed him to make a statement. If it came down to it, would Richard "Two-Gun" Hart choose family or the law? Richard said he would arrest any of his clan if they bootlegged in Nebraska, but as long as the Capone clan remained in Chicago, he would turn a blind eye to their misdeeds. After an initial flurry of newspaper stories about his true identity, the press largely forgot about Richard for decades.

In the summer of 1927, Richard served as a bodyguard to President Calvin Coolidge, when the latter visited the Black Hills of South Dakota. President Coolidge used the visit to reflect on his career and ponder whether or not to run for re-election. In the end, the president decided not to try for a second term, allowing Herbert Hoover to assume the presidency.

After his bodyguard duties ended, Richard spent four years wandering around the West, going from Indian reservation to Indian reservation. He chased bootleggers and once again found himself on trial for killing a man—an Indian fugitive, this time. Once again, Richard was acquitted.

By the early 1930s, Richard was pushing middle age, and Prohibition was clearly on the way out. Richard began struggling to make ends meet. None of his law enforcement gigs paid particularly well. He worked as a peace officer in Homer, Nebraska, for a while but found that the income was too low to adequately support his family. Richard started doing odd jobs, anything to pay the bills.

Ironically, as Richard struggled, Al Capone and other male members of his family had become fabulously wealthy selling illegal liquor. In 1933, Richard went to Chicago to see his family and ask for money. Ralph Capone provided cash. Richard was soon making periodic visits to Chicago, cap in hand, to secure cash to help his family out in Homer.

By 1940, Richard was broke. He requested cash from his brother Ralph again, but the latter had another idea. Ralph Capone invited his straight-edge sibling to visit a summer retreat in Mercer, Wisconsin. The place was run by Ralph, who was happy to help out his floundering sibling.

Richard continued to visit Mercer, Wisconsin, in the summertime and beg his family for cash. The former two-gun lawman met Al Capone during a visit, after the latter was released from jail where he was serving time on income tax evasion charges. Al apparently befriended Richard's three sons. While pleased to receive support from his family, Richard never expressed remorse for abandoning the Capone clan for so many years.

Richard's true identity came to light once again, after the Internal Revenue Service (IRS) began investigating Ralph Capone's finances in the early 1950s. Richard's real name and relation to the Capone family were revealed, which caused a media sensation. The press seemed to forget that they had already exposed Richard during previous family visits to Chicago, decades before.

James Capone/Richard Hart was subpoenaed to appear before a grand jury in Chicago. By this point, Richard was overweight, had diabetes, and walked with a cane. Richard testified but died shortly thereafter of a heart attack, on October 1, 1952. James/Richard was 60 years old when he passed away. He had outlived his younger, better-known brother Al by five years; Al Capone died at age 48 in 1947, from a stroke.

Further Reading

Laurence Bergreen, *Capone: The Man and the Era*, 1994.
Nate Hendley, *Al Capone: Chicago's King of Crime*, 2010.
John Kobler, *Capone: The Life and World of Al Capone*, 1971.

EMPEROR NORTON OF SAN FRANCISCO

One day in September 17, 1859, a nondescript middle-aged man made his way into the offices of the *San Francisco Bulletin* newspaper. The man was Joshua Norton, formerly a well-known businessman who had fallen on hard times. Norton was in the office to hand-deliver a proclamation that he had written and wanted published in the newspaper.

The proclamation read, "At the peremptory request of a large majority of citizens of these United States, I, Joshua Norton, formerly of Algoa Bay, Cape of Good Hope, and now for the past nine years and ten months of San Francisco, California, declare and proclaim myself Emperor of these U.S."

The *Bulletin* ran the announcement the following day under the headline, "Have We an Emperor Among Us?" In a follow-up proclamation published the next month, Norton abolished Congress on the grounds that it was rife with corruption and fraud. In January 1860, peeved to discover that Congress was sitting in Washington, in clear violation of his declaration, Norton issued a proclamation demanding that "Major-General Scott, the Command-in-Chief of our Armies, immediately upon receipt of this, our Decree, to proceed with a suitable force and clear the halls of Congress."

In other proclamations coming soon after, Norton abolished "the republican form of government" in the United States and established "in its stead, an Absolute Monarchy," with himself as Absolute Monarch, of course.

Thus began the strange reign of Emperor Norton, self-declared Monarch of America. For two decades, the self-proclaimed Emperor "ruled" San Francisco, making regal inspections, eating for free at restaurants, riding free on public transit, and issuing taxes and imperial promissory notes. While Norton carried himself with dignity in public, wearing an old military coat, he lived in a boarding house that was a far cry from a royal palace.

The real Norton was born to Jewish parents in England. The date of his birth is uncertain, with some accounts saying he was born in 1811 and others pointing to 1818 or 1819. In 1820, Norton and his parents emigrated to Algoa Bay in what is now South Africa, with a few thousand other British families. In 1841, the Norton family moved to Cape Town, South Africa.

Joshua Norton began working as a clerk in a ship chandlery (a candle business) owned by his father. By 1848, both of Norton's parents had died, along with his two brothers. Norton inherited his father's estate, which came to around $40,000—not an inconsiderable sum in those days.

The Gold Rush hit California in 1849. Norton joined thousands of young, ambitious men heading west to make their fortune. Norton crossed the Atlantic Ocean and made his way to San Francisco. He didn't actually pan for gold but turned to the more genteel professions of real estate and commerce. He founded a business called Joshua Norton & Company, General Merchants, and purchased an anchored ship to store goods (a common practice in San Francisco at the time).

Norton did well for himself: "He was occupied in extensive transactions in real estate and many tremendous operations in importation commissions ... his intelligence was wonderfully clear and his business judgment was remarkably accurate ... some of his commissions involved transactions to the extent of several hundreds of thousands of dollars weekly, and Joshua Norton rapidly became wealthy," stated a 1923 write-up in *Quarterly of the California Historical Society*.

Norton acquired parcels of land and opened a cigar factory, an office building, and a rice mill. By 1852, his assets were estimated at around $250,000 (the equivalent of roughly $5 million today). Norton appeared destined for a life of wealth—until he got ripped off in a rice deal. At the time, China was the main exporter of rice to California. In the early 1850s, a famine in China cut off shipments to San Francisco. Because there wasn't much rice to be had, its price rose exponentially, going from 4 cents a pound to 36 cents.

Commodities at the time were bought, sold, and traded at the Merchant's Exchange in San Francisco. A mercantile bank called Goddefroy and Sillem represented the owners of a ship called the *Glyde*, which was docked in the city and packed with some 200,000 pounds of rice from Peru. Willy Sillem, from the bank, conferred with Norton. Norton was shown a sample of high-end rice, supposedly from the *Glyde*. Norton was told he could purchase the entire shipment for $25,000, which worked out to 12.5 cents a pound. He could then turn around and sell the shipment at 36 cents a pound, making more than $70,000 in the process.

On December 22, 1852, Norton put down $2,000 for the shipment of rice. He signed a contract agreeing to pay the entire price within 30 days. To Norton's fury, one day after he inked the contract, another ship arrived in San Francisco harbor bearing more rice from Peru. Then more ships arrived, also laden with rice. Suddenly, the city had a rice glut. The price collapsed, to three cents a pound. Making matters worse, the rice in the *Glyde* was of a lower quality than the rice contained in new shipments.

Double-crossed, Norton attempted to nullify his contract, on the grounds that the rice sample he had been shown wasn't representative of the low quality of the rest of the *Glyde* shipment. The owners of the *Glyde* sued Norton for the $23,000 outstanding in his contact. This led to years of court battles and huge legal fees for all the players involved. In 1855, the court ruled in favor of the *Glyde*'s owners.

The ruling came at a particularly bad time for Norton. The Gold Rush was over. San Francisco entered into an economic downturn. Prices dropped, the real estate market lost value, and many businesses closed.

Banks began foreclosing on some of Norton's properties. He had to sell off businesses and real estate at huge losses. A client accused him of embezzling money. Invitations to high-society parties dried up. He was thrown out of the Freemasons because he couldn't afford his dues. His living quarters went from high-end hotels to low-rent boarding houses.

On August 25, 1856, the *Bulletin* newspaper announced Norton's bankruptcy. The notice listed his liabilities at $55,811 and assets at around $15,000.

The bankruptcy shattered Norton's psyche. Three years after his insolvency was announced, he declared himself Emperor of the United States. By this point, the nation was coming apart at the seams, riven by regional factions divided over the issue of slavery. Norton, who had long admired the stability of the British monarchy, felt that a firm hand was needed to unite the nation. In 1863, with the country now embroiled in the Civil War, Napoleon III (a nephew of his more famous namesake) invaded Mexico. Norton added a new title to his regal name: "Protector of Mexico."

The Emperor of the United States and Protector of Mexico did not live large. In 1863, Norton took up residence at a decrepit boarding house called the Eureka Lodging. He paid 50 cents each day for some 17 years to maintain his residency. This fee paid for a small room with an iron cot, a beat-up couch, and no closet. Appropriately enough, Norton decorated his grimy walls with lithographs of Queen Victoria in England, Queen Emma of the Sandwich Islands (now Hawaii), Empress Carlotta of Mexico, and Empress Eugenie, the wife of Napoleon III.

Emperor Norton became a well-known man about town. He began visiting local businesses and imposing "taxes," which were often dutifully handed over. He wore a series of uniforms, primarily military coats and hats. For formal occasions, he garbed himself in a coat with gold epaulets that had belonged to an officer in the Union Army during the Civil War. Along with this coat, Emperor Norton would wear a tall beaver hat with an ostrich plume. He kept a cavalry sword by his side and was usually seen with a wooden walking stick, complete with a silver plate engraved with his name and "Emperor U.S."

By all accounts, Norton was a lucid, affable man with a regal air and the gift of gab. He could converse on all manner of erudite subjects and generally charmed everyone he met.

At lunchtime, the emperor would head to a bar named Marin & Horton's for a free lunch. The establishment served this lunch for anyone who bought a drink. Norton didn't touch alcohol, but management figured he was good for business, so they let him be.

In the afternoons, Emperor Norton hung out in libraries at the Bohemian Club Mercantile Institute and Mechanic's Institute. There, he would read books, play chess (apparently, he was quite good), and use the Institute's stationery to write new proclamations.

During the evening, Norton would attend debates or take in the theatre or a lecture. The president of the Central Pacific Railroad gave Norton a free pass good for anywhere in California. Norton used the pass to ride the city's ferries and streetcars, and to venture to Sacramento to watch the state legislature. Norton also reviewed cadets in the Bay Area, visited schools, and attended church on Sundays. He divided his spiritual attendance among numerous churches, so as not to appear biased in favor of any particular denomination.

In 1867, a policeman made the mistake of arresting Norton for vagrancy. At the station, the desk sergeant protested that the emperor had $4.75 on him and a key to his boarding house room, and thus was no homeless vagrant. The sheepish arresting office realized his error and charged Norton instead with "lunacy." This infuriated the burghers of San Francisco and led to outraged newspaper accounts of the insult against His Majesty. The chief of police wisely ordered Norton freed.

To a visitor who knew Norton in his pre-emperor days, he explained the logic behind his imperial claim. Norton told the visitor that John and Sarah Norton were not his real parents, that his genuine mother and father were members of the Bourbon family. The Bourbons were a line of kings who reigned in France from 1589 to the French Revolution in 1793. During the Revolution, many members of the royal family left France to avoid being jailed or executed.

Often, these regal figures took refuge in the houses of commoners. When the French monarchy was restored in 1814, countless individuals stepped forward claiming to be Gallic royalty in exile. Norton insisted he was part of this regal flock.

In 1869, the Transcontinental Railroad linked the United States from the Atlantic Ocean to the Pacific. People could now travel from the east coast to the west coast in a matter of days; previously, the journey took months and involved either an uncomfortable cross-country wagon ride or an endless trip by ship, underneath the tip of South America. With more tourists coming to town, Emperor Norton became a popular attraction. Some of Norton's old business instincts remained intact, and he began selling Imperial Treasury Bond Certificates to tourists and locals. These promissory notes were priced from 50 cents to 10 dollars. Norton promised that the bonds would be repaid at seven percent interest in 1880. No one actually believed they would be repaid or particularly cared. People bought the Bond Certificates to keep as unusual souvenirs of San Francisco, complete with Emperor Norton's signature.

Stores in the city began displaying signs that claimed Emperor Norton patronized their premises. Merchants sold picture postcards and lithographs of the emperor. There was an Emperor Norton doll (complete with plumed hat) and Emperor Norton cigars. Newspapers followed his antics avidly. Media outlets would occasionally print phony proclamations that were usually far more ridiculous than anything the real Norton wrote. When the papers criticized Emperor Norton for his increasingly shabby wardrobe, the San Francisco Board of Supervisors decided to provide him with a new beaver hat and officer's coat.

To his delight, Emperor Norton attracted regal visitors. In 1876, the emperor of Brazil, Dom Pedro II, visited San Francisco. Among other requests, the Emperor of Brazil wanted to meet the Emperor of the United States. Norton and Dom Pedro II did indeed have a meeting, appropriately enough in the royal suite at the Palace Hotel. The two men chatted for more than an hour. To newspapermen, Pedro II did not indicate whether he saw through the charade and realized there was no actual monarchy in the United States, much less an emperor.

Emperor Norton continued making proclamations, many of which were published in local newspapers. Occasionally, he actually came up with some good ideas. In the early 1870s, for example, he issued a proclamation calling for a suspension bridge to be built from Oakland Point over Goat Island and then to Telegraph Hill. Some six decades after he made this announcement, the city opened the San Francisco Oakland Bay Bridge. This suspension bridge followed a similar path to that outlined by Norton, passing through what used to be called Goat Island but was now known as Yerba Buena Island.

Sadly, the emperor was unable to attract a royal consort during his reign to produce heirs to the throne. At one point, Emperor Norton became smitten with a teenage schoolgirl named Minnie Wakeman. Norton sent her a note asking for her hand in marriage. She politely turned him down, on the grounds that she was already engaged to be married.

The evening of January 8, 1880, was cold and rainy. Emperor Norton was strolling up California Street towards Nob Hill. He wanted to attend a monthly debate held by the Hastings Society of the Academy of Natural Sciences. The emperor approached Old St. Mary's Church, then collapsed and died on the spot. Police quickly moved his body to the morgue. When they searched him, they discovered the emperor was carrying a jumble of currency. He had a gold piece, some silver, a French franc coin from 1828, and a bunch of imperial treasury notes (priced at 50 cents). These promissory notes now promised repayment in 1890. Norton was hoping to exchange the old promissory notes for these new notes, to avoid repaying the original bonds.

Emperor Norton lay in state in the morgue. Thousands of people came to view him and pay their respects. The *San Francisco Chronicle* reported, "These visitors included all classes from capitalists to the pauper, the clergyman to the pickpocket, well-dressed ladies and those whose garb and bearing hinted of the social outcast, however, the garb of the working man predominated."

Some prominent citizens were concerned that Emperor Norton might be consigned to a pauper's grave. James Eastland, president of the Pacific Club and a former Freemason with Norton, back when he was a successful businessman, started a fundraising drive. The drive was successful, and Norton was put to rest in a fancy funeral at the Masonic Cemetery. The funeral boasted a cortege two miles long. In 1934, Emperor Norton's remains were moved to Woodlawn Memorial Park and reinterred with honors.

Norton's funeral was held January 10, 1880. A day after it took place, a major article in the *San Francisco Chronicle* covered the event, under the headline "Le Roi Est Mort" (the king is dead). Papers across the country ran banner headlines marking Emperor Norton's passing.

There were rumors that the emperor was secretly wealthy and had been living the life of a miser. His boarding house and possessions were searched, but no fortune was found.

Emperor Norton lived on in pop culture consciousness. Mark Twain based a character called "the king" after Norton, in his book *The Adventures of Huckleberry Finn*. Robert Louis Stevenson included Norton as a character in an 1892 novel called *The Wrecker*.

Norton's popularity was a reflection of the open-mindedness of San Francisco denizens. The emperor had the very good fortune to live in a city that celebrated its bohemian characters. If he had lived elsewhere, he might have been seen as a madman and a nuisance rather than the valiant, self-declared Emperor of the United States and Protector of Mexico.

Further Reading

"Emperor Norton, Zaniest S.F. Street Character," *San Francisco Chronicle*, September 17, 2009.

Joel Gazis-Sax, An Almanac of California, Emperor Norton's Archives, http://www .notfrisco.com/nortoniana/.

"Le Roi Est Mort," *San Francisco Chronicle*, January 11, 1880.

"Norton I—Emperor of the United States and Protector of Mexico," *Quarterly of the California Historical Society,* October, 1923.

"Who Is Emperor Norton? Fans in San Francisco Want to Remember," *Wall Street Journal*, August 12, 2015.

IRON EYES CODY

It is one of the best-known Public Service Announcements (PSAs) of all time. Broadcast on TV in 1971, the PSA features a grim-faced American Indian with long black braids and a buckskin jacket canoeing up a filthy, polluted river. The Indian passes by smokestacks on shore and various pieces of flotsam in the water. He beaches the canoe on a trash-strewn shore, then walks to a nearby highway. As a car zips by, one of its occupants causally tosses a bag of garbage out the window. The garbage lands at the feet of the astonished Indian. A close up of the Indian's otherwise immobile face reveals a single tear sliding down his cheek. A narrator intones, "People start pollution; people can stop it."

The PSA was created by the nonprofit group Keep America Beautiful. The star of what became known as the "Crying Indian" ad was one "Iron Eyes" Cody, an actor in Hollywood films. Cody had long black hair, angular facial features, and the proud, stoic manner commonly attributed to Indians in pop culture accounts. He claimed Cherokee/Cree background and had been playing Indians in films since the silent movie era.

The only problem was, Iron Eyes was a complete fake. His real name was Espera DeCorti, and his parents hailed from Sicily. DeCorti was born in small-town Louisiana in 1904. When DeCorti was five years old, his father abandoned his family and headed to Texas. As a teenager, DeCorti and his two brothers joined their father in Texas. In 1924, DeCorti's father died. The three brothers relocated to Hollywood to work in the fledgling movie business.

DeCorti adapted his last name to the more Native-sounding "Cody" and began presenting himself as a genuine Indian. It was a good career move. There were few Indian film actors at the time, so directors were apt to hire extras who looked "Indian" even if they weren't Native American. Sicilians and Italians apparently fit the bill, and DeCorti began getting regular work. His two brothers also did some films but eventually moved into other occupations.

To bolster his Indian bona fides, DeCorti claimed to be an expert in Native American customs, sign language, mores, and habits. Naïve filmmakers ate this act up. DeCorti almost always dressed in a buckskin jacket and beaded moccasins, both on and off-screen. He took great interest in Indian causes and married a woman of Native American background (Bertha Parker). DeCorti and his wife adopted two boys of Indian descent.

DeCorti appeared in dozens of films and TV shows. He portrayed renowned Chief Crazy Horse in two different movies (*Sitting Bull* from 1954 and *The Great Sioux Massacre* from 1965). He starred in well-regarded TV shows such as *Rawhide* and *Daniel Boone*, and critically acclaimed movies like Richard Harris's *A Man Called Horse* (from 1970). And of course, in 1971, DeCorti took the main role in the TV PSA that has ensured his cinematic fame.

Throughout his career, DeCorti had to face rumors that he wasn't a real American Indian. He dismissed such stories, insisting he was the genuine article. Even after DeCorti's half-sister went public in 1996 with family documents proving his Sicilian heritage, DeCorti refused to back down. He died in 1999, at age 94.

DeCorti got away with his scam for as long as he did because he fit the popular image of a Native American, in both looks and temperament. Although he was a fake, DeCorti has been praised for helping propel environmental issues into mainstream consciousness. All for a commercial that played up Native stereotypes (a proud and noble but technologically primitive Indian disgusted with modern Western civilization) to highlight the ill effects of littering and pollution.

Further Reading

"The Crying Indian," Public Service Television Announcement, Keep America Beautiful, 1971, https://www.youtube.com/watch?v=j7OHG7tHrNM.

"Iron Eyes Cody," *Los Angeles Times*, January 5, 1999, http://projects.latimes.com /hollywood/star-walk/iron-eyes-cody/.

"Iron Eyes Cody," *New York Times*, 2010, http://www.nytimes.com/movies/person /13889/Iron-Eyes-Cody/biography.

"Native Son," *Times-Picayune*, May 26, 1996.

JOSEPH PISTONE (AKA "DONNIE BRASCO")

During the late 1970s and early 1980s, FBI agent Joseph Pistone fooled the Mafia into believing he was an ambitious young criminal named Donnie Brasco who wanted to join their ranks. Pistone's dangerous masquerade was so successful, he was on the verge of being officially inducted into the Mafia brotherhood when the FBI shut his undercover mission down.

The man who conned the underworld was born in 1939 to an Italian-American family. Pistone was raised in Pennsylvania, then in Paterson, New Jersey. Pistone played high school sports and went to college on a basketball scholarship. He dropped out at age 20 to get married, then spent a year doing construction work.

Pistone wanted to become an FBI agent. He spent a few years with Naval Intelligence, assisting with military investigations before joining the Bureau. He was sworn in as a special agent July 7, 1969, and underwent training. After graduation, he was assigned to an FBI office in Florida.

By 1974, Pistone was working in New York City, on a squad that investigated truck hijackings. The FBI wanted to crack a ring of thieves who stole 18-wheel trucks, bulldozers, and luxury cars along the east coast. Thanks to the year he spent in construction, Pistone knew how to drive 18-wheelers and bulldozers. The FBI decided he would be the perfect man to infiltrate the ring.

With help from his fellow agents, Pistone settled on a cover name ("Donnie Brasco") and a fake identity. As Donnie Brasco, Pistone easily penetrated the theft ring and won the trust of the thieves. Thanks to Pistone's efforts, 30 members of the ring were arrested in February 1976.

When the mission ended, Pistone went back to the truck and hijack squad in New York City. At the time, the city was plagued by a rash of truck hijackings, sometimes as many as five to six a day. It was thought that the Mafia might be involved. The FBI decided to initiate a long-term undercover operation to determine whether the Mafia were behind the truck hijackings. Pistone was the obvious choice for the mission. He had undercover experience, a Sicilian background, spoke Italian, and was cool under pressure.

Pistone spent months preparing for his new role. It was decided that Pistone would use his previous pseudonym, Donnie Brasco. Brasco would be a jewel thief and burglar who worked alone and traveled between New York City, Miami, and California. If anyone asked personal questions, "Brasco" would say he was a bachelor and an orphan.

In September 1976, Pistone went undercover. Pistone couldn't tell anyone about his mission. His own wife and children (by this point, Pistone had three daughters) knew only the barest details of his new assignment.

The FBI set up "hello phones"—that is, numbers Mafia members could call for character references. The people answering the phones were either FBI agents or informants. Pistone opened a checking account, leased a car, and rented a Manhattan apartment.

Pistone began patronizing bars, nightclubs, and restaurants that were known Mafia hangouts. Pistone would eat or drink by himself, then leave without saying much. The point was to get his face known in underworld circles. Pistone frequented a Manhattan restaurant called Carmello's that was owned by members of the Genovese Mafia family.

Pistone noticed that the gangsters at Carmello's played backgammon for money. One day, Pistone challenged the winner of a backgammon match to a new game. For the first time, the FBI agent introduced himself (as "Don") and chatted with patrons.

Pistone also befriended Carmello's barkeep, who seemed to know quite a few Mafia members. To build criminal credibility, Pistone showed the bartender diamond rings and wristwatches he implied were stolen.

In early 1977, Pistone was introduced to members of the Colombo family. One of the men was named "Jilly," and he ran a "crew" (i.e., a squad) of Mafiosi in Brooklyn. Jilly's crew used a store in Bensonhurst as their headquarters. Pistone began spending time there.

FBI protocol meant Pistone couldn't take part in any actual crimes while undercover. He made himself useful in other ways, such as unloading trucks for Jilly's crew, filled with stolen food, liquor, clothes, and TVs. Sometimes, Pistone brought in "swag" (stolen jewels or other items taken from FBI storage) to impress his peers.

At one point during this period, a gangster challenged Pistone about his identity. Pretending to be upset, Pistone gave the name and number of a contact who would vouch for him (in reality, an FBI plant). Pistone waited for hours as one of Jilly's crew tracked down the contact. Once reached on the phone, the contact gave a resounding reference for Donnie Brasco.

In March 1977, Pistone met Anthony Mirra, a "made" (i.e., formal) member of the Mafia. Through Mirra, Pistone was introduced to a hitman named Benjamin "Lefty Guns" Ruggiero. Both men were members of the Bonanno Mafia family. Ruggiero ran a Little Italy social club for Bonanno family members and "associates"—criminals who worked for the Mafia but didn't officially belong to the organization as sworn-in members.

Pistone began to follow a routine. Around 10 am, he would go to Ruggiero's club, drink coffee, read the papers, and listen in on conversations. In the afternoon, Pistone would go to Brooklyn and hang out at Jilly's store. In the evening, he would connect with Mirra.

Ruggiero handled bookmaking operations for Nicky Marangello, underboss of the Bonanno family. In this capacity, Ruggiero was bringing in $20,000 to $25,000 every weekend. Pistone discovered that the New York Mafia made most of its money from gambling. Ironically, many Mafiosi also loved to gamble and were frequently broke as a result. Illegal drugs and thievery were also major money-makers for the mob.

Ruggiero "schooled" Pistone in the way of the mob. Ruggiero instructed Pistone to dress sharply and always show deference to made men. Never argue with a made man. Always take a made man's side, even when they're wrong, said Ruggiero. As a Mafia associate, Pistone was expected to do Ruggiero's bidding.

Ruggiero was divorced, with four grown children. When Ruggiero remarried, he asked Pistone to be his best man.

By mid-summer 1977, Pistone was making solid inroads in the underworld. He had a fleeting encounter with Bonanno family leader Carmine Galante, helping guard a restaurant where the boss was having a meeting.

Every few days, Pistone phoned his FBI contact agent to give him an update of his activities. Once or twice a month, he met the agent in person to receive money for living expenses. Pistone only got to see his family every two or three weeks, if that.

The undercover operation took on a new dimension. Instead of investigating truck hijackings, Pistone was told to simply gather as much evidence as he could against the New York Mafia in general. His mission was extended far beyond the initial six-month time frame.

Pistone's acting skills were put to the test. He had to pay close attention to Mafia conversations without appearing to be nosy. To put himself above suspicion, Pistone sometimes feigned disinterest in mob talk, walking away from conversations or changing the topic when his peers were discussing illegal activities.

Pistone accompanied Ruggiero on various operations. He journeyed to Milwaukee, where he met local Mafia boss Frank Balistrieri. In Florida, Pistone was introduced to Santo Trafficante, a major Mafia player.

By mid-1981, Pistone was close to becoming a "made" man. Dominick "Sonny Black" Napolitano, a Bonanno family captain, was willing to vouch for Pistone's induction into the formal ranks of the Mafia. No FBI agent had ever been "made" before. It would be a tremendous coup for law enforcement. There was one catch: in order to be "made," Napolitano wanted Pistone to murder a mobster named Anthony "Bruno" Indelicato.

Pistone was eager to stay undercover and try to get "made" without murdering anyone. The FBI thought it was too risky. Donnie Brasco would be put under tremendous pressure to carry out Indelicato's assassination. To Pistone's disappointment, the six-year undercover operation was terminated on July 26, 1981.

Shortly thereafter, FBI agents approached Napolitano to inform him he had been fooled by an imposter. Pistone's mob peers tried, unsuccessfully, to track him down. Pistone had withdrawn completely from the underworld and was busy giving information to the FBI and getting reacquainted with his family.

When the Mafia bosses realized they'd been conned, the New York underworld exploded in violence. Several of Pistone's mob peers were killed by Mafia gunmen, as punishment for allowing an FBI agent into their midst. Napolitano was ordered to attend a Mafia meeting in New Jersey. He left for the meeting and was never seen alive again. His lifeless body was eventually recovered from a creek on Staten Island. Anthony Mirra was shot dead in a Manhattan parking garage. Ruggiero was also targeted, but FBI agents arrested him before he could be killed. Pistone and his family were put under 24-hour FBI protection.

On August 2, 1982, Pistone began testifying against his former colleagues in federal court. He testified at 10 trials and before countless grand juries during the 1980s. Pistone's statements led to 200 indictments and 100 convictions of Mafia members, including Ruggiero.

Pistone didn't feel much guilt in "betraying" his comrades: "I felt close to Sonny Black. I felt a kind of kinship with him. But I didn't feel any guilt of betrayal because I'd always maintained in my own mind and heart the separation of our worlds … I knew that both Lefty and Sonny loved me in their own ways. Either would have killed me in a minute," he would later write in an autobiographical account of his undercover mission.

Indeed, the FBI heard that a $500,000 "open contract" had been put on Pistone's life. While the Mafia usually avoids murdering lawmen (for fear of massive retaliation), they were willing to make an exception for Pistone.

Pistone left the FBI in 1986. One year later, his book, *Donnie Brasco: My Undercover Life in the Mafia*, was released. This was turned into a successful movie in 1997, with Johnny Depp as Pistone and Al Pacino as Ruggiero. Pistone lent his expertise to other police forces and helped Scotland Yard in the UK with an investigation into Asian Triad crime gangs.

In testimony before the U.S. Senate in 1988, Pistone discussed steps that the Mafia had taken to prevent future infiltration: "I understand that the New York families have instituted new rules to thwart further undercover penetrations. They have reinstituted the requirement that before someone is made a soldier, he will have to 'make his bones'; that is, he will have to kill someone. In addition, they are now requiring two [Mafiosi] to vouch with their own lives for the new member, rather than as before, when only one did so."

As for any residual personal feelings he might have had about his six-year mission, Pistone offering the following rationalization: "I knew that no matter what I did, I was not going to reform anybody, they were going to lie, steal, cheat, murder and kill, whether Joe Pistone (or) Donnie Brasco was there or not. So my main goal was to gather information for later prosecutions. I was not a reformist or a social worker nor a reformer, and that is the mindset I had, and I also maintained that if they found out who I was, they would kill me just as soon as they have killed their best friends."

Further Reading

Federal Bureau of Investigation, "Organized Crime: Italian Organized Crime—Overview," http://www.fbi.gov/hq/cid/orgcrime/lcnindex.htm.

Nate Hendley, *American Gangsters: Then and Now*, 2010.

Nate Hendley, *The Mafia: A Guide to American Subculture*, 2013.

Joseph Pistone, *The Way of the Wiseguy*, 2004.

Joseph Pistone with Richard Woodley, *Donnie Brasco: My Undercover Life in the Mafia*, 1987.

Joseph Pistone, Testimony before the U.S. Senate Permanent Subcommittee on Investigations of the Committee on Governmental Affairs, 1988.

SECTION FIVE

HOAXES, URBAN LEGENDS, AND POPULAR DELUSIONS

INTRODUCTION

A "hoax" can be defined as a deliberate falsehood designed to mislead. Hoaxes can be amusing, as in the case of nineteenth-century newspaper accounts of "man-bats on the moon" and wild animals causing mayhem in Manhattan after escaping from the Central Park Zoo. Or they can be malicious, as with *The Protocols of the Elders of Zion*, an infamous anti-Semitic forgery designed to stir up hatred against Jews. The notorious *War of the Worlds* radio broadcast, meanwhile, is an example of a hoax about a hoax.

If a hoax involves the deliberate telling of lies, urban legends are stories created and passed on by people who genuinely believe them to be true. One of the main urban legends examined in this section (on "Blackout Babies") continues to be repeated today in various forms by credulous media outlets.

A popular delusion can best be described as a ridiculous notion embraced en masse by the public despite a complete lack of evidence. During the 1980s, for example, the public became inflamed by the notion that devil-worshipping daycare staff were torturing small children under their care. In the ensuing hysteria, innocent individuals were jailed on preposterous charges, sometimes for decades.

ALAN ABEL, MASTER HOAXER

Master prankster Alan Abel has been hoaxing the press and public alike for decades with ridiculous stunts masquerading as serious ventures. These stunts include a school for professional panhandling and activist groups against breastfeeding and naked animals.

Abel was born in 1924. One of his first (and arguably best-known) stunts concerned a pressure group called The Society for Indecency to Naked Animals (SINA) The group demanded that dogs, horses, cows, cats, and other creatures wear pants. Driven by the slogan, "a nude horse is a rude horse," SINA was launched in 1958. Abel and his wife Jeanne picketed together, waving signs deriding the sight of unclothed animals.

A friend of Abel's named Buck Henry (later to become a famous comic actor, director, and writer) did a series of deadpan interviews, pretending to be SINA president G. Clifford Prout. In this manner, the organization received media coverage on *The Tonight Show*, *The Today Show*, and *CBS Evening News* with Walter Cronkite.

Abel revealed his inspiration for the stunt to *Esquire* magazine: "I saw a cow and bull stopping traffic down in Texas, having sex on the highway. There were two ladies hiding their faces and another couple was angry. It was about 15 or 20 minutes of delay on the highway and I thought up the idea of clothing all these naked animals," he recalled.

The amount of media attention the prank attracted planted a seed in Abel's mind. He realized that with only a limited budget and a handful of props, he could successfully fool the American public. SINA was the first in a long series of straight-faced hoaxes masterminded by Abel. According to Abel's website, his goal has always been to give people "a kick in the intellect."

In 1964, Abel organized a fake presidential campaign for "Yetta Bronstein," supposedly a Jewish grandmother from the Bronx. Yetta's catchy campaign slogan was, "Vote for Yetta, and things will get betta!" Yetta promised to install a White House lie detector, put truth serum in water fountains in the Senate, and pay members of Congress on a commission basis. "Yetta" was portrayed by Abel's wife, Jeanne, to perfection. In her Yetta guise, Jeanne did hundreds of newspaper and radio interviews. When reporters demanded to see a photograph of Yetta, Abel gave them a picture of his mother, Ida.

Three years after the Yetta campaign, Abel put together a "Topless String Quartet," supposedly featuring four beautiful young women playing music sans shirts. Apparently, Frank Sinatra was so intrigued by the concept he wanted to record them. "I would say they were in Europe or Australia. They were never available," said Abel to *Esquire*. During this period, Abel also wrote a humor column for the *San Francisco Chronicle* and other papers.

In 1970, after being audited by the Internal Revenue Service (IRS), Abel formed a fake pressure group called Taxpayers Anonymous. The group sued the U.S. government, demanding, among other things, to see the government's accounting books and records. Abel also insisted that federal authorities deliver all cancelled government checks to his house. The prank was featured in the second issue of *National Lampoon* magazine, which came out in May 1970.

In 1972, Abel pretended to be reclusive millionaire Howard Hughes. He showed up at a press conference at the St. Regis Hotel in New York City, swathed in bandages. Abel/Hughes explained to reporters that he wanted to be frozen via cryogenic technology, then thawed and returned to life when the stock market hit a peak. At a second press conference held shortly thereafter, Abel revealed it was really him and not Howard Hughes beneath all the bandages.

Two years after imitating Hughes, Abel pretended to be a White House staffer who had somehow acquired tapes containing the missing minutes of the Watergate recordings. These were tapes President Richard Nixon had made, of conversations in the Oval Office, some of which discussed the attempted cover-up of the Watergate scandal. When the recordings were made public, it was revealed there was an 18-and-a-half-minute gap in the tapes.

At the press conference, Abel feigned shock when he discovered that the tape containing the lengthy gap had also been erased. This gag was held to promote an Abel mockumentary called *The Faking of the President*.

One of Abel's most enduring pranks was launched in 1975, but lasted right up to the late 1980s. The prank centered on "Omar's School for Beggars"—an institution offering tips on successful panhandling. Abel did a series of media appearances and interviews connected with Omar's school. The prank was launched with an interview on NBC's *Tomorrow Show with Tom Snyder*. Abel's motivation was to highlight poverty and homelessness in the United States. Despite Omar being repeatedly "outed" as a fake, the media continued to run stories on the School for Beggars for years.

In 1976, Abel turned once again to the Watergate scandal for prank fodder. He arranged for an actor to pretend to be "Deep Throat," the mysterious source of many of reporter Bob Woodward's Watergate-related scoops. A press conference was held in New York City, with an estimated 150 reporters in attendance. At the conference, the actor playing Deep Throat pretended to get into an argument with his spouse and fainted. He was taken away by ambulance before reporters could cotton on to the scam.

Three years later, Abel arranged an ambitious stunt at the Plaza Hotel in New York. A fake wedding was staged between an African American man who resembled Ugandan dictator Idi Amin and an actress playing a Long Island WASP (White Anglo-Saxon Protestant). The wedding was allegedly being held so Amin could get a green card and move to the United States. Once again, droves of reporters turned up to cover the elaborate fake nuptials. All the characters at the charade, including bride, priest, and bodyguards, were actors hired by Abel. The man playing Idi Amin was apparently someone Abel had found riding the NYC subway system.

Abel hit a crowning peak of prankster brilliance in early 1980, when he got the *New York Times* to publish his obituary. According to the obituary, Abel had died of a heart attack in Utah, while skiing. When the truth was discovered, the chagrined *Times* was forced to retract the obituary, something the paper had never had to do before.

To *Esquire* magazine, Abel explained how he pulled off this impressive feat: "It was on a Sunday and I did it an hour before press time, so everybody was home and the second-stringers were on duty. They didn't dig too deeply. I told a friend of mine who lived in a house trailer and couldn't afford a telephone that I'd pay for his phone to be installed if he listed it as Wellington Funeral Home. So [that] was the listing for where they found my body in Orem, Utah. I put a down payment on a wake at All Soul's Church on the Upper East Side. It all checked out when they made their basic phone calls."

Another spectacular prank occurred three years later. Abel arranged for a phony official to get onto the field during the Super Bowl between the Miami Dolphins and Washington Redskins. The official called four plays, then was chased down the sideline by a police officer. The game was temporarily halted, as the crowd watched in amazement. Unknown to them, both the cop and the fake official had been hired by Abel.

In January 1985, *The Phil Donahue Show* was televised live for the first time. Abel planted several women in the studio audience who fainted during the broadcast, to Donahue's great consternation. The entire audience was evacuated halfway through the show, which left Donahue speaking to empty seats. Donahue initially blamed the mass fainting on hot studio lights and the anxiety of being on live TV. Abel then revealed he was behind the stunt. He claimed the fainting was part of an effort to protest sensationalist TV fare.

Abel changed media four years later, to prank the book world. During the furor over writer Salman Rushdie—condemned to death by Muslim authorities for supposedly "insulting Islam" with his book *The Satanic Verses*—Abel arranged for a Rushdie lookalike to show up at a Washington DC book convention. The fake Rushdie began merrily signing copies of his controversial tome, to the astonishment of all in attendance. The phony Rushdie's appearance caused a stampede of reporters, who had been at a different event, featuring Nancy Reagan signing books.

The early 1990s saw the risible rise of David Duke, a former Ku Klux Klan member and Nazi sympathizer, who tried to break into mainstream Louisiana politics. After being elected to the Louisiana state legislature, Duke ran for governor in 1991. This prompted Abel to organize something he called the "Ku Klux Klan Symphony."

Abel told *Esquire* magazine, "I had a few musicians record 'The William Tell Overture' out of tune, and I sent it to radio stations in Louisiana. It was supposedly a rehearsal of the KKK Symphony with David Duke as guest conductor."

This wasn't the last time Abel chose a topical subject for his unique brand of humor. In 1993, "Dr. Death" Jack Kevorkian and the issue of assisted suicide (euthanasia) were much in the news. Accordingly, Abel invented a firm called Euthanasia Cruises Ltd., complete with Florida office, 1-800 number, and press releases on realistic company stationery. The cruise line advertised one-way trips for suicidal guests. After partying on board for a few days, the guests could jump over the side of the ship and drown in the ocean.

The following year, Abel formed a pressure group called Citizens against Breastfeeding: "Abel claimed that breastfeeding was incestuous and that it led to oral addiction. He also stated that the 'naughty nipple' was responsible for many of society's ills," stated Abel's website.

Abel picketed both the Democratic and Republican National Conventions in 2000, and did more than 200 interviews. When speaking to the press, he claimed that breastfeeding led to crack-smoking, among other evils. The prank wasn't revealed until four years later, when Abel told all in an article he penned for *U.S. News & World Report*.

Six years later, Abel was at it again, playing an activist named Irwin Leba, who promoted a national fat tax. As part of the hoax, Abel created a legitimate-looking website (www.fattaxfacts.org) to outline Leba's plan. Leba wanted to abolish income tax and put a body fat tax in its place. All taxpayers and their pets would be weighed at a post office on or near April 15. Citizens would pay $5 for every pound of flesh on their bodies and their pets. The hoax was revealed in the *Washington Post* as an April Fool's prank.

In 2007, Abel and a comrade-in-arms picketed the White House on behalf of color-blind citizens. Abel said he was protesting Homeland Security's use of a color code (green, yellow, red) to indicate the level of potential terrorist danger against the United States. This scheme clearly discriminated against color-blind citizens, he claimed, who wouldn't be adequately warned in case of danger.

A year later, Abel assisted with a prank to establish a graffiti art museum in downtown Toronto. The museum—which would be the first of its kind—was all part of a promotional stunt for a double-showing of the films *Abel Raises Cain* and *Is There Sex After Death?* (another "mockumentary," released by Abel in the early 1970s) at Toronto's Bloor Cinema. *Abel Raises Cain* was a legitimate documentary, made by Abel, his daughter Jenny, and her partner Jeff Hockett, that examined the career of the legendary prankster. It was released in 2005.

In 2009, an Abel confederate going by the name Lena Potapova claimed to be spokesperson for a group protesting bird watching. According to Potapova, bird watchers were actually voyeurs, deriving sexual satisfaction from watching birds mate. Potapova was quite convincing in interviews with the media and received much coverage for her mission.

To *Esquire* magazine, Abel explained how he pulled off some of his hoaxes: "For the big, costly stunts, I had a backer, Maxwell Sackheim, a founder of the Book of the Month Club. He would call me and complain about something in the news that pissed him off. My job was to poke satirical fun at the unholy situation," he said.

Even Abel's most outlandish pranks, such as the Citizens against Breast-feeding group, were taken seriously in some quarters. "There were people who actually believed that 'the naughty nipple' as I called it, was addictive and that mothers and babies were getting too, shall we say, close to one another. Even with clothed naked animals there were people who wanted to send in money. A woman in Santa Barbara, California, sent in a $40,000 check. I fondled it for about five minutes then I sent it back. I told her I couldn't accept money from strangers," Abel said to *Esquire*.

Esquire inquired whether it was harder to pull off a hoax in the twenty-first century than it had been decades earlier. "Yes and no," Abel replied. "With the Internet, it can take just seconds for the truth fairies to play party pooper. On the other hand, the Internet allows for more spectacular hoaxes. But I need another backer with deep pockets and a sense of humor. Hello out there," he added.

Abel has also provided glimpses into his mindset through his writings. In *Confessions of a Hoaxer*, published in 1970, Abel described his pranks as an adventure in absurdity that engaged the public on an emotional and intellectual level. Mocking the media, by demonstrating the gullibility of the press, has been another major motivating factor for Abel.

Some media outlets have come to recognize and appreciate Abel's twisted talents. In 2000, *Life* magazine listed Abel as a cultural icon of the twentieth century. Now well into his senior years, Abel continues to mock and shock with nonsensical campaigns and nutty ideas, presented with a straight face.

Further Reading

Alan Abel, E-mail interview with author, April 25, 2015. Phone interview with author, April 30, 2015.

Alan Abel website, http://www.alanabel.com/.

Jenny Abel, Producer, Director, *Abel Raises Cain*, 2005.

Esquire.com, "Q&A with Alan Abel, Hoax Master," February 7, 2007, http://www.esquire.com/entertainment/interviews/a1960/esq0406-esq04006news-76-1/.

Esquire.com, "Ten Questions for the Best Prankster Ever," March 30, 2011, http://www.esquire.com/entertainment/interviews/a5816/alan-abel-hoaxes-033109/.

THE BERMUDA TRIANGLE

The Bermuda Triangle is a large section of ocean shaped roughly like a triangle, with the cities of Miami, Florida, and San Juan, Puerto Rico, and the island of

Bermuda at its points. It has gained a reputation as a place where ships and planes mysteriously vanish.

When examined closely, it turns out that most of the famous disappearances in the Triangle are easily explainable. Take, for example, the case of a tanker ship, the *V. A. Fogg*. The tanker was supposedly found adrift in the Triangle and abandoned by its crew in 1972. A search of the vessel turned up no crew members beyond the captain, allegedly found sitting at his desk, very dead.

The truth is no less dramatic but considerably less mysterious. The *V. A. Fogg* had delivered a cargo of benzene to the Phillips Petroleum Depot in Freeport, Texas. It was traveling through the Gulf of Mexico with a skeleton crew when it blew up. The blast resulted in a 10,000-foot plume of smoke. The U.S. Coast Guard investigated and discovered the ship, 100 feet below the surface of the water and split in two. The explosion might have been inadvertently caused by the crew, attempting to clean the fuel tanks. Whatever the cause, the truth of the matter was that the tanker exploded and sank, taking all of its crew with it. The accident didn't even occur in the Bermuda Triangle. In other words, no weird drifting without crew, no petrified captain sitting dead at his desk.

More than fifty years earlier, on March 9, 1918, the U.S.S. *Cyclops* disappeared in the Triangle while en route from Barbados to Baltimore. The ship's cargo consisted of 10,800 tons of manganese. The most likely explanation is that the cargo shifted weight and sent the ship to the bottom.

Likewise, the 1963 disappearance of the S.S. *Marine Sulphur Queen*, traveling from Norfolk, Virginia, to Belmont, Texas, can be easily explained. The ship vanished on February 3, 1963, near Key West, Florida. The ship was carrying molten sulphur in big tanks. It is speculated that the sulphur might have leaked fumes, which overwhelmed the crew. A spark might have triggered a huge explosion. Equally plausible, the crew detected the leaking sulphur and abandoned ship in lifeboats, which proceeded to sink along with the *Sulphur Queen*.

In total, roughly 50 ships have disappeared in the Bermuda Triangle over the past century. This is not a huge number, given the fact that the Triangle covers roughly 500,000 square miles. Bearing in mind the substantial amount of shipping that goes on in the Triangle, the loss of 50 vessels over 100 years isn't statistically significant. The Naval History and Heritage Command (NHHC) website explained, "Since the days of early civilization, many thousands of ships have been sunk and/or disappeared in waters around the world due to navigational and other human errors, storms, piracy, fires and structural/mechanical failures."

Located in the Washington Navy Yard in the nation's capital, the NHHC is responsible for maintaining a navy library, historic ships such as the U.S.S. *Constitution*, and roughly a dozen museums and heritage centers. The NHHC's website urges Bermuda Triangle buffs to understand "how common accidents are at sea."

The Naval History and Heritage Command website also pointed out that planes are frequently lost over water too. Indeed, one of the most famous cases of Bermuda Triangle lore involves aircraft, not ships.

In mid-afternoon on December 5, 1945, five United States Navy Avenger torpedo bombers left the naval air station at Fort Lauderdale, Florida. The five planes were supposed to be going on a routine two-hour training mission. The planes would fly out to sea, some 66 miles due east from their original air base. Once they reached this point, the torpedo bombers would be put through practice bombing runs, then head north for another 70 miles. This achieved, the planes would turn again and go back home. The planes were led by Lieutenant Charles Taylor, who served as flight commander. The pilots in the other four planes were trainees.

Within minutes of taking off, Lieutenant Taylor radioed in to say his compass wasn't working properly. It's unclear how well the compasses on the other four planes were working: some accounts say they too were malfunctioning, while others say they were operable. In any case, Flight Commander Taylor tried to navigate via landmarks, which was difficult as he wasn't familiar with the area. At some point in the flight, Taylor spotted a group of islands, which he took for the Florida Keys. He radioed this in and was told by Flight Command to head north, which should have taken them back to their base in Florida. Unfortunately, the planes weren't actually over the Keys, but rather, the islands of Bermuda.

The planes continued to head north—into the open Atlantic Ocean. One of the trainee pilots (whose compass might have been working) suggested diverting to the west, but Flight Commander Taylor wouldn't hear of it. The pilots did not try to overrule their leader and change course. The weather became stormy, which reduced visibility, meaning the pilots couldn't use the sun as a directional guide.

At some point, after flying over open water, Fight Commander Taylor apparently decided he was in the Gulf of Mexico. He ordered the planes to turn east, which would have taken them back to Florida, if they indeed were in the Gulf. As it was, the maneuver pushed the planes even further over the Atlantic Ocean. Radio contact was lost. The planes disappeared, into history.

All sorts of stories have tried to explain the fate of the five torpedo bombers. The pilots were even featured in the movie *Close Encounters of the Third Kind*. In that film, aliens were blamed for absconding with the planes and pilots.

The truth is more matter-of-fact. According to the book *Loch Ness Monsters and Raining Frogs*, which debunks supposedly mysterious or supernatural events, Flight Commander Taylor was badly hung-over. This being the military, however, the pilots of the four planes under his command would be very unlikely to challenge their leader even if his judgment was a bit foggy. Quite simply, Commander Taylor got disoriented and lost over open water. In a pre-GPS era, when radar was still in its infancy, such pilot error was not unusual. Almost certainly, the planes ran out of gas and ditched in the ocean.

While disappearances in the Bermuda Triangle are largely explainable, the sector is not without navigational challenges. The area features very strong currents from the Gulf of Mexico, which can definitely impact shipping, particularly if a captain isn't paying attention. These same strong currents also have the effect of scattering wreckage far and wide—which helps explain why some ships seem to vanish without a trace.

As noted in *Loch Ness Monsters and Raining Frogs*, the Bermuda Triangle is reported to have some strange magnetic anomalies that could affect compass readings, which might explain the problems faced by Flight Commander Taylor. But none of these factors makes the Triangle unusually dangerous.

The U.S. Coast Guard dismisses the Triangle a "mythical geographic area." A notice on the Coast Guard website states, "The Coast Guard does not recognize the existence of the so-called Bermuda Triangle as a geographic area of specific hazards to ships or planes. In a review of many aircraft and vessel losses in the area over the years, there has been nothing discovered that would indicate that casualties were the result of anything other than physical causes. No extraordinary factors have ever been identified."

Further Reading

Bermuda Triangle, Naval History & Heritage Command website, Frequently Asked Questions, www.history.navy.mil/faqs/faq8-1.htm (webpage no longer operable).

Albert Jack, *Loch Ness Monsters and Raining Frogs*, 2007.

Joe Nickell, "The Bermuda Triangle and the 'Hutchinson Effect,'" *Skeptical Inquirer*, September 2007.

Howard Rosenberg, Naval History & Heritage Command website, "Exorcizing the Devil's Triangle," http://www.history.navy.mil/research/library/online-reading-room/title-list-alphabetically/e/exorcizing-the-devils-triangle.html.

U.S. Department of Homeland Security, United States Coast Guard website, Frequently Asked Questions, "Does the Bermuda Triangle Really Exist?" http://www.uscg.mil/history/faqs/triangle.asp.

THE BLACK HAND EXTORTION RACKET

The Black Hand racket was a simple scam that was extremely common in Italian-American communities from the late nineteenth century to the early twentieth century. An anonymous note would arrive at the home of an Italian immigrant, threatening all manner of torture and violence unless a large fee was paid. The extortionist sending the letter would typically "sign" it by dipping his hand in black ink and pressing the palm against the paper. This would leave the impression of a black hand, which is how the scam got its name.

The Black Hand racket was prevalent in any city with a large Italian population. Many new Italian immigrants were poorly educated, deeply superstitious, and profoundly mistrustful of police, who tended to be very corrupt in their homeland. Italians were unlikely to report Black Hand intimidation to authorities. All of these factors allowed the racket to flourish.

Italian-Americans ascribed all manner of quasi-mystical powers to the Black Hand "organization," which was viewed as all-knowing and all-powerful. In reality, there was no Black Hand organization, only a few solo operators who counted on their countrymen's ignorance to propagate the scam.

It wasn't only poor immigrants who were victimized. The famous singer Enrico Caruso was once the target of Black Hand intimidation. Unlike most victims, Caruso reported the intimidation to police, who set a trap and arrested his would-be extortionists.

Strangely enough, some Black Handers tried the scam on fellow criminals. Big Jim Colosimo, crime boss of Chicago in the early twentieth century, was on the receiving end of countless Black Hand threats. Annoyed, Colosimo brought his wife's nephew, Johnny Torrio, from New York City, to deal with the problem. Torrio's solution was to organize hit squads to murder the Black Handers who were bothering his uncle. With the problem resolved, Torrio elected to stay in Chicago and introduce a fledgling mobster named Al Capone to the city.

Some brave Italians fought back against the Black Handers. In one famous case in 1909, New Orleans mobster Paul Di Cristina was rebuffed by a grocer named Pietro Pepitone, who refused to pay Black Hand tribute. Di Cristina decided a personal visit was in order. When he arrived at Pepitone's store, the plucky grocer pulled out a shotgun and blasted the gangster at point-blank range. Pepitone was sentenced to twenty years in jail for his act of defiance but served only six.

Several dedicated policemen also fought against the Black Hand scam. One of the most notable was Italian-born police lieutenant Joseph Petrosino. Petrosino headed up a squad in New York City that dealt specifically with crime in the Italian immigrant community. Fearless, Petrosino made hundreds of Black Hand related arrests, in spite of death threats from mobsters. He also didn't hesitate to apply a little rough street justice, beating Black Handers up in public to lower their status in the eyes of their victims.

In early 1909, Petrosino made a brave but foolhardy solo mission to Sicily, to gather more information about criminals who had left the island to plague New York. Petrosino was set up and murdered in Palermo on March 12, 1909. His body was brought back to the United States, and Italian immigrants mourned the loss of a very courageous officer. An estimated 250,000 people viewed his coffin as it passed by on the street. Petrosino remains the only New York City police officer to be killed while on assignment in a foreign country.

The Black Hand scam eventually petered out in the early 1920s, due to a combination of factors. For one, the Italian community had become more acclimatized to their new surroundings and less likely to fall for blatantly obvious extortion scams. Also, the federal government began cracking down on Black Hand extortionists, charging them with using the mails to defraud. What really killed the Black Hand racket, however, was Prohibition. Italian gangsters realized there was more money to be had selling illegal alcohol than extorting cash from their countrymen.

Although the Black Hand racket disappeared, extortion hasn't. Threatening merchants or local businesspeople with murder and dismemberment (or threatening the same to their families) remains a tried-and-true gangster racket. The only difference is that today extortionists generally don't send their victims notes containing inky palm prints and dire warnings of violence.

Further Reading

Pierre de Champlain, *Mobsters: Gangsters and Men of Honour*, 2004.

Nate Hendley, *American Gangsters: Then and Now*, 2010.

Officer Down Memorial Page—Joseph Petrosino, http://www.odmp.org/officer/10600 -lieutenant-joseph-petrosino.

Thomas Repetto, *American Mafia: A History of Its Rise to Power*, 2004.

David Southwell, *The History of Organized Crime: The True Story and Secrets of Global Gangland,* 2006.

BLACKOUT BABIES

Did you know that nine months after the massive blackout in New York City of November 1965, the number of births exploded in area hospitals?

An article published August 10, 1966, in the *New York Times* stated, "A sharp increase in births has been reported by several large hospitals here, nine months after the 1965 blackout. Mount Sinai Hospital, which averages 11 births daily, had 28 births on Monday. This was a record for the hospital; its previous one-day high was 18 … at Bellevue, there were 29 new babies in the nursery yesterday, compared with 11 a week ago and an average of 20. Columbia-Presbyterian averages 11 births daily and had 15 Monday; St. Vincent's averages 7 and had 10; Brookdale averages 10 and had 13 and Coney Island averages 5 and had 8. However, New York and Brooklyn Jewish Hospitals reported that their number of births was normal."

"Asked to comment on the increase in births, Paul Siegel, a sociologist, said: 'The lights went out and people were left to interact with each other.'" continued the *Times*.

The only problem with this story is that its conclusions were completely off-base. The story is a good example of what happens when we mix wishful thinking with statistical illiteracy.

Unlike the reporters at the *New York Times*, J. Richard Udry, of the School of Public Health at University of North Carolina at Chapel Hill, actually bothered to compare meaningful data. In an article published in the August 1970 edition of the *Demography* journal, Udry explained how he went about his research.

"The effect of the blackout on birth rates is a relatively easy matter to determine," wrote Udry. "I obtained the number of births for each calendar day for the years 1961 through 1966. I took November 10, 1965, as the date of conception for the blackout babies ... it was estimated that more than 90 percent of the births conceived on November 10, would have been born between June 27 and August 14, 1966. I reasoned that if there were an unusual number of conceptions on November 10, then the period between June 27 and August 14, 1966, would contain a greater percentage of the year's births than that contained by the same period in other years."

Udry compared the number of births in New York City from June 27 to August 14 for the years 1961 to 1966. In 1961, for example, there were 478.7 mean births per day in the period cited, or 3,350.6 mean births per week. In total, 13.9 percent of babies born in New York City hospitals in 1961 emerged between June 27 and August 14.

In 1966, by comparison, there were 434.5 mean births per day for the period of June 27 to August 14, and 3,041.6 mean births per week. The total number of births in this period, as a percentage of the year's total was ... 13.9 percent.

"For no week is the 1966 value significantly above average for the previous five weeks. We therefore cannot conclude from the data presented here that the great blackout of 1965 produced any significant increase (or decrease) in the number of conceptions," wrote Udry.

He also noted that nine months after a huge blizzard in Chicago in 1967, area hospitals were preparing for a huge spike in births. None happened.

So, what about the big baby boom reported in the *New York Times*? Take a closer look at the figures stated in the article.

The numbers of supposed "blackout babies" born nine months after the 1965 blackout are not particularly impressive. Only one hospital (Mr. Sinai) in the article reported a large increase (28 babies on the day in question, versus an average of 11 births daily). Bellevue cited 29 new babies on the day the reporter checked in, versus an average of 20. Other hospitals reported very small increases, on the order of three or four more births than normal. Two hospitals (New York and Brooklyn Jewish Hospitals) didn't report any increase.

These numbers are well within the regular monthly fluctuations in the number of deliveries. To be truly statistically significant, the number of births nine months after the blackout would have to double or triple across the board.

The notion that "mini baby-booms" routinely occur nine months after natural disasters or crises has been disproven again and again but remains a hugely popular urban legend perpetuated by a gullible media. The enduring legacy of this legend can be explained by faulty reasoning: reporters approach a story with predetermined conclusions, then try to make the data fit. It also helps that the mini baby-boom myth is an appealing cultural concept, as is the notion of something good—such as babies—coming out of something bad, such as a blizzard, hurricane, or blackout.

Further Reading

Marty Tolchin, "Births Up 9 Months After the Blackout," *New York Times*, August 10, 1966.

J. Richard Udry, School of Public Health, University of North Carolina, Chapel Hill, "The Effect of the Great Blackout of 1965 on Births in New York City," *Demography*, August 1970.

THE CARDIFF GIANT

On October 16, 1869, workers digging a well on a property near Cardiff, New York, came across a 10-foot stone figure of a man in the earth. The figure was naked, and it was unclear whether it was a statue or the petrified remains of a real-life giant.

Word spread quickly about the weird stone man. William C. "Stub" Newell—who owned the property where the figure was found—began charging admission (50 cents a head) to see the stone man.

Biblical authority was cited to back up claims that the figure was a petrified giant. After all, Genesis 6:4 states, "there were giants in the earth in those days."

Some critics believed the figure was just a large statue, but even these speculations came wrapped in a religious cloak. Dr. John F. Boynton, for example, theorized that the figure was a statue that had been carved by Jesuit missionaries in the 1600s, presumably to amaze the Indians into accepting the white man's God.

The Cardiff Giant (as the figure became known) was actually created by one George Hull, a New York tobacconist. The concept for the statue apparently was born out of an argument Hull had with a Methodist minister about Bible inerrancy. Was the Bible intended to be taken as the literal truth or as a series of metaphors and legends? The Reverend took the former position, arguing that everything in the Bible was true, even Genesis 6:4. Hull took the opposite position. The debate was never settled, but it did plant a seed in Hull's mind. Why not make a big statue of a man and pretend it was a petrified giant? It would be a fun way to tweak the noses of Biblical literalists and generate revenue from curiosity seekers.

Hull invested some $2,600 in the project. He arranged for workmen to cut out a giant block of gypsum, which is a soft rock. The giant block was wrapped in canvas, then painstakingly moved 40 miles to a railhead. The block found its way into a barn on property owned by Newell (who happened to be one of

Hull's relatives). There, a stonecutter and two assistants carved a giant statue of a man. Apparently, they used Hull's face for the likeness of the giant. They used special hammers to make it look as though the figure had pores and gave it a good rubdown with acid, sand, and water to age its appearance.

Newell (who was in on the scheme, in exchange for a share of the profits) agreed to have the statue buried on his property. The nearly 3,000-pound statue was placed in a hole near his barn, and the hole was then filled in. Newell waited a year before hiring some neighbors to dig a well and conveniently "discover" the stone figure.

Hull sold the Cardiff Giant for $37,500 to some businessmen, who moved it to Syracuse for exhibition. It was in Syracuse that experts began taking a closer look at the stone giant. A Yale paleontologist examined it and pronounced it a fake—and clumsily made, at that. The paleontologist pointed out where chisels had left visible marks on the figure. If the giant had actually been in the earth for two millennia, all chisel marks would have been worn away.

Hull eventually confessed to the hoax, but oddly enough, the Cardiff Giant remained a popular tourist attraction.

At this stage, master showman P. T. Barnum offered to rent the Giant for three months, for a fee of $60,000. The figure's new owners turned him down. Chagrined, Barnum had his own giant man statue built out of plaster. Barnum's creation was pretty much a double of the Cardiff Giant. This facsimile of a fake went on display in New York City. People flocked to see the "new" giant, which became an even more popular attraction than the original.

The owners of the "real" Cardiff Giant were not amused and filed a lawsuit against Barnum. The judge refused to hear the case until the authenticity of the original figure could be proven. In other words, was the Giant a custom-made statue—as Hull admitted—or a petrified giant from the era of the Old Testament? The owners of the Cardiff Giant shied away from this judicial challenge and dropped their lawsuit.

The Cardiff Giant can still be seen today, on display at the Farmer's Museum in Cooperstown, New York (near the Baseball Hall of Fame), a monument to the perennial allure of hoaxes.

Further Reading

"The Cardiff Giant," The Farmer's Museum website, http://www.farmersmuseum.org/node /2482.

"The Cardiff Giant," The Museum of Hoaxes website, http://hoaxes.org/archive/permalink /the_cardiff_giant/.

DAYCARE DEVILS

The 1980s saw one of the more curious moral panics of the age: the widespread fear that little children were being abused, tortured, murdered, and filmed by devil-worshipping staff at daycare centers. While the charges sound ridiculous today, this hoax proved to be anything but amusing for the dozens of people charged with Satanic-related child abuse.

The best-known case of alleged Satanic ritual abuse (as it became called) centered on the Virginia McMartin Preschool in Manhattan Beach, California. Staff at the preschool were accused of a series of demonic crimes against kids, resulting in a very long-running criminal trial. Some of the defendants spent years behind bars. In the end, virtually no evidence was found that the McMartin staff had abused any children, much less engaged in human sacrifices, child rape, or animal murders.

The McMartin case began in August 1983, when Judy Johnson, mother of a child in the McMartin Preschool contacted police. She complained that her son had been molested, by both her estranged husband and Raymond Buckey, the youthful grandson of the McMartin Preschool founder.

As the weeks went by, the accusations against Raymond Buckey became weirder and more lurid, while accusations against Johnson's husband appear to have receded. Johnson claimed that the young man had worn a cape and mask while torturing her son.

On September 8, 1983, Manhattan Beach police sent an incendiary letter to 200 parents who either had children in the McMartin Preschool or whose children had once attended the facility. The letter cited possible abusive behavior on the part of Raymond Buckey, then asked parents to quiz their children as to whether they ever saw Buckey leave the classroom alone with a child during naptime. Parents were also requested to ask their children whether they had ever seen Buckey tie any kids up.

Soon, hundreds of parents were beseeching Manhattan Beach police for information. Police interviewed several children but drew a rebuke from concerned mothers and fathers, who felt the interrogations were too harsh. In response to these concerns, the local prosecutor's office began referring parents to a therapeutic center called Children's Institute International. Children there were interviewed by a woman named Kee MacFarlane.

At first, the vast majority of children denied that they had been molested. Under pressure from MacFarlane, however, boys and girls began revealing fantastical tales. Of the 400 or so children interviewed, more than 350 claimed abuse. Kids told tales of being molested by staff, of being photographed and filmed nude (during a game called "Naked Movie Star"), of animals killed in their presence and hidden passageways beneath the preschool. According to the children, McMartin staff had supernatural abilities, including levitation and flying in the air. Kids who made disclosures were praised, while their less forthcoming peers were mocked during interviews.

On February 2, 1984, KABC-TV, the local ABC station, issued a widely seen broadcast about child pornography, animal sacrifices, and torture at the

McMartin Preschool. A month later, on March 22, 1984, a grand jury indicted McMartin staff. Police arrested Raymond Buckey and his mother Peggy Buckey, his grandmother, Virginia McMartin, who founded the school that bore her name, his sister Peggy Ann Buckey, and three teachers, Betty Raidor, Babette Spitler, and Mary Ann Jackson. These defendants were slapped with 115 counts, later expanded to over 320 counts involving nearly 50 kids.

The McMartin case did not happen in a vacuum. The roots of the panic over Satanic child abuse can be traced in part to a 1980 book called *Michelle Remembers*. Penned by psychiatrist Dr. Lawrence Pazder and his patient and later wife, Michelle Smith Pazder, the book cited horrific abuse by a cabal of Satanists in the unlikely locale of genteel Victoria, British Columbia. The book claimed that Michelle had been sexually abused with candles, locked in a room with snakes, and other horrors. She apparently repressed all these memories of demonic abuse until she began therapy with Dr. Pazder.

Throughout the 1980s, countless other allegations of bizarre Satanic child abuse emerged. "From 1984 to 1989, some 100 people nationwide were charged with ritual sex abuse; of those, 50 or so were tried and about half convicted, with no evidence except testimony from children, parents, 'experts' expounding on how the children acted traumatized and doctors talking about … 'signs of abuse' that later research would show on non-abused children," wrote journalist Debbie Nathan in the January 12, 1990, *Village Voice*.

Nathan, one of the first reporters to thoroughly investigate Satanic ritual abuse, now sits on the board of directors of the National Center for Reason and Justice. The latter is a Roxbury, Massachusetts, organization devoted to fighting wrongful convictions and draconian punishments meted out to teens and adults in the name of protecting children.

While reporters such as Nathan took the time to carefully investigate claims of Satanic child abuse, much of the mainstream media offered shallow, sensationalized coverage. Such coverage implied that the United States was in the grip of a Satanic conspiracy to molest and torture children. Daycare staff in particular were accused of all manner of horrifying, devil-inspired abuse.

The prosecution in the McMartin case believed that the motivation behind all the abuse was simple. It was claimed that McMartin staff were making child pornography, which could be sold on the black market for huge profits. The FBI and Interpol, however, were unable to track down a single frame, video, or film clip of any of the McMartin children being sexually abused, despite a worldwide hunt for such evidence. Nor did authorities find any animal bones or secret passageways beneath the school, during archeological investigations. Likewise, innocent items belonging to McMartin staff were seized as evidence of Satanic abuse. A black graduation gown that belonged to Peggy Buckey was seen as evidence that she was a cape-wearing Satanist, as the children had claimed.

The prosecutors were unable, however, to explain how parents and neighbors of the McMartin Preschool could have failed to notice any diabolical doings at the center, even though such events had allegedly been going on for years. One of the more colorful charges against the McMartin staff involved the ritualistic murder of a horse, supposedly to intimidate children into silence. The horse was supposedly slaughtered in the middle of the day, despite the fact that parents constantly entered and exited the McMartin Preschool during daylight hours.

A preliminary hearing to determine whether there was sufficient evidence for a criminal trial began in July 1984. The hearing lasted a grueling 18 months and was exceedingly complicated, in part because seven different sets of lawyers represented the seven defendants. Finally, on January 9, 1986, the judge ordered all seven defendants to go to trial, on 135 counts.

DA Ira Reiner seemed unimpressed by the judge's decision. One week after the preliminary hearing ended, the DA dropped charges against five defendants, leaving only Raymond Buckey and his mother, Peggy Buckey, on trial. Reiner told the media that evidence against the other five staff members was "incredibly weak." In another bad sign for those pressing the case forward, a staffer from the prosecutor's office, Glenn Stevens, switched sides and began to assist the defense team.

In January 1990, after what had become the longest criminal trial in U.S. history up to that point, all charges against Peggy Buckey and most charges against Raymond Buckey were dropped. Jurors were deadlocked on 13 charges against Raymond. Raymond Buckey was released from jail on bail, after serving five years in prison, marked as a child sex predator. Raymond Buckey was put on trial for some of the deadlocked charges, and again a hung jury couldn't agree on a conviction. Prosecutors gave up and closed the case, dismissing all charges against Raymond Buckey.

The case had cost an estimated $15 million and shattered countless lives. Judy Johnson, whose accusations sparked the trial, was later revealed to be suffering from paranoid schizophrenia. She died of alcoholism-related symptoms in 1986.

The collapse of the McMartin trial and ensuing investigations did much to tamp down hysteria around Satanic ritual abuse at American daycare centers. In 1992, the Federal Bureau of Investigation issued a report entitled, "Satanic Ritual Abuse." The report dismissed some of the more outlandish claims being made: "Until hard evidence is obtained and corroborated, the public should not be frightened into believing that babies are being bred and eaten, that 50,000 missing children are being murdered in human sacrifices, or that Satanists are taking over America's daycare centers or institutions ... there is little or no evidence for [allegations] that deal with large-scale baby breeding, human sacrifice or organized Satanic conspiracies."

Two years later, the National Center on Child Abuse and Neglect (NCCN) issued the results of an exhaustive investigation into 12,264 accusations of ritual child abuse. In conducting their investigation, the Center surveyed 6,910 mental health professionals and 4,655 law enforcement and social service agencies. The NCCN had been unable to come up with a single substantiated case of ritual child abuse.

Project director Dr. Gail Goodman was quoted in the October 31, 1994, *New York Times*: "After scouring the country, we have found no evidence for large-scale cults that sexually abuse children."

The moral panic over demonic daycare centers stemmed from many factors, including concerns about working women. "Our willingness to believe in ritual abuse was grounded in anxiety about putting children in daycare at a time when mothers were entering the workforce in unprecedented numbers," stated the *New York Times Magazine*, January 7, 2001.

A confluence of additional factors helped fuelled the panic: the 1980s marked the rise of fundamentalist Christianity in the United States. Conservative Christians combined a literal belief in the devil with a profound mistrust of secular institutions such as daycare centers. Young children, they believed, should be at home with their mothers.

The Satanic Panic also underlined a rather naïve attitude in dealing with the testimony of very young children. Bizarre stories about flying Satanists and child murders were taken at face value, despite later evidence that preschool-age children have difficulty separating fantasy from reality. Aggressive investigations by police, therapists, and self-described "Satanic abuse" experts, some of it well-meaning, also led to wild speculation by little children. Sensational media coverage did much to stir up fear as well. Daytime talk show host Geraldo Rivera memorably aired a special on Satanism in America that gave the impression that demonic crime was out of control.

Besides ruining the lives of the McMartin families, accusations of rampant Satanic abuse at daycare centers diverted attention from the very real tragedy of child abuse. The sexual, physical, and mental abuse of children is an unfortunate, not uncommon reality. Typically, however, such abuse happens in the home at the hands of family members, not in daycare centers and certainly not by people espousing a faith in Satanism.

Further Reading

Tom Dart, "Texas Pair Released After Serving 21 Years for 'Satanic Abuse,'" *The Guardian*, December 5, 2013.

Daniel Goleman, "Proof Lacking for Ritual Abuse by Satanists," *New York Times*, October 31, 1994.

Kenneth V. Lanning, "Investigator's Guide to Allegations of 'Ritual' Child Abuse," Behavioral Science Unit, National Center for the Analysis of Violent Crime, Federal Bureau of Investigation, 1992, http://www.religioustolerance.org/ra_rep03.htm.

Patrick Moore, "Their Satanic Majesty's Release: Child Sex Abuse Day Care Owner Released After 20 Years," Allthingscrimeblog.com, December 8, 2013 (article no longer online).

Debbie Nathan, "The Ritual Sex Abuse Hoax," *The Village Voice*, January 12, 1990.

Robert Reinhold, "The Longest Trial—A Post-Mortem; Collapse of a Child-Abuse Case: So Much Agony for So Little," *New York Times*, January 24, 1990.

Linda Rodriguez McRobbie, "The Real Victims of Satanic Ritual Abuse," Slate.com, January 7, 2014, http://www.slate.com/articles/health_and_science/medical_examiner/2014/01/fran_and_dan_keller_freed_two_of_the_last_victims_of_satanic_ritual_abuse.single.html.

Elaine Showalter, *Hystories: Hysterical Epidemics and Modern Media*, 1997.

Margaret Talbot, "The Lives They Lived: 01-07-01: Peggy McMartin Buckey, b. 1926; The Devil in the Nursery," *New York Times* magazine, January 7, 2001.

EXTRATERRESTRIALS
Alien Abduction

The first well-known contemporary case of alleged alien abduction took place in 1961 and involved an interracial couple named Barney and Betty Hill. The Hills apparently had been abducted by aliens while driving in the White Mountains area of New Hampshire. The Hills forgot about the experience until a series of unsettling dreams led them to seek psychological counselling. Under hypnosis, the Hills said that aliens had taken them aboard their craft. These extraterrestrials gave Betty Hill a pregnancy test and removed sperm from Barney.

Benjamin Simon, the Boston-area psychiatrist who treated the couple, had his own theories about what really happened in the White Mountains. "Simon maintained that the story was a folie à deux or shared fantasy, possibly having to do with the repressed tensions of maintaining an interracial marriage," wrote Elaine Showalter, in her book *Hystories*.

Nonetheless, the Hill case laid the groundwork for subsequent alien visitations upon other people. These visitations, note observers, share some common traits. The aliens

- primarily kidnap people at night, generally while the victim is sleeping
- tend to kidnap people from their home or, like Barney and Betty Hill, from their car
- never kidnap anyone in front of witnesses, much less anyone with a camera
- almost always perform some kind of medical experiment on the victims, usually of a sexual nature
- frequently insert some kind of "implant" in the victims, often in their nose, to monitor their behavior and control thinking

Extraterrestrial visitations aside, there are some much more down-to-earth explanations for such occurrences. It has been suggested by publications such as *Skeptical Inquirer* that "UFO abductees" might be experiencing sleep paralysis, a discomfiting but by no means rare phenomenon.

Sleep paralysis refers to a state "in which a person is apparently able to hear and see and feels perfectly awake but cannot move … in a typical sleep paralysis episode, a person wakes up paralyzed, senses a presence in the room, feels fear or even terror and may hear buzzing or humming noises or see strange lights. A visible or invisible entity may even sit on their chest, shaking, strangling or prodding them. Attempts to fight the paralysis are usually unsuccessful," stated a story in the May/June 1998 issue of *Skeptical Inquirer*.

Sleep paralysis is a widespread phenomenon, and there are folk legends about it around the world. Many of these legends describe demons or monsters sitting on people's chests, making it difficult to breathe and impossible to move. This demonic figure is sometimes referred to as the Old Hag in parts of the English-speaking world.

Author Joe Nickell further elaborated on sleep paralysis in a piece published in the November/December 2012 issue of *Skeptical Inquirer*. He suggested that the notion of being visited by aliens might be part of a "hypnagogic experience"—which is to say, a "waking dream." Such dreams take place when a person is on the borderline between sleep and wakefulness. Hypnagogic experiences often involve hallucinations, strange sensations, and sometimes sleep paralysis.

What's more, most "abductees" can only recall their experiences under hypnosis. This immediately raises red flags, including the question of whether the subject is recalling real memories or just parroting suggestions from the hypnotist.

Nickell referred to hypnotism as "an invitation to fantasize … being easily hypnotized is even one of the indicators, though not diagnostic in itself, of a personality type that is characterized by proneness to fantasy." Fantasy-prone people may be the type to have imaginary friends, even as adults, claim unusual psychic powers or connection with spirits, fairies, or God. To such people, ordinary events or objects can be easily misconstrued as evidence of paranormal encounters.

Roswell

Was there a cover-up by government authorities regarding the nature of a mysterious object that fell from the sky onto a ranch near Roswell, New Mexico in July 1947?

Probably.

Was the cover-up intended to hide the fact that the object in question was a UFO?

Almost certainly not.

The notorious incident at Roswell, New Mexico, has been cited for decades by UFO buffs as an example of government machinations in obscuring proof of extraterrestrial life. The actual truth of the matter is probably quite mundane. The object recovered was most likely a secret spy balloon. At the time, however, military investigators either deliberately or mistakenly claimed it was a weather balloon. This story helped fuel the massive conspiracy theory surrounding the Roswell case.

The events at Roswell began on the holiday weekend of July 4, 1947. A rancher near Roswell named William "Mac" Brazel informed the local sheriff, one George Wilcox that a strange object had crashed on his ranch. Brazel told the sheriff he had recovered debris from the crash site and had taken it home.

Wilcox dutifully contacted authorities at Roswell Army Air Field, which was situated close by. A Major Jesse Marcel and two Counter Intelligence Corps agents, Sheridan Cavitt and Lewis Rickett, drove out to Brazel's ranch. At the rancher's house, the men sifted through debris gathered from the crash site. Brazel is believed to have suggested that the wreckage might have come from a UFO.

A few days later, on July 8, 1947, a public information officer at the Roswell AAF issued an eye-popping press release that claimed the military had recovered an extraterrestrial craft. This resulted in a famous front-page headline in the local newspaper, the *Roswell Daily Record*, reading, "RAAF Captures Flying Saucer on Ranch in Roswell Region." "No details of flying disk are revealed," added the sub-head.

According to the paper, Brazel observed a debris field littered with tinfoil, strips of rubber, wooden stick-like objects, and other debris. Brazel admitted he hadn't actually seen the mystery object crash-land on his property, much less fly through the air. The paucity of the debris was also noted. When all the tinfoil, paper, sticks, tape, and rubber found at the site were put together, the small team at Brazel's house estimated the total weight at around five pounds, according to the *Record*.

Within one day, the military changed its tune about the findings. Brigadier General Roger Ramey, who had ordered the debris sent to him at nearby Carswell Air Force Base, held a press conference. He denied that a "flying disk" had been recovered and said the debris was from a weather balloon. Some of the debris was displayed at the press conference for the benefit of photographers.

Following the press conference, the Roswell incident largely receded from public memory, except in the overheated imaginations of ufologists and conspiracy buffs.

In 1978, a UFO researcher named Stanton Friedman met Major Marcel, who related the tale of the "flying disk" at Roswell. It's unclear whether Major Marcel also mentioned that he was present at Brigadier General Ramey's press conference debunking the flying saucer story.

Following this interview, a series of books emerged that claimed to document "the truth" about Roswell. While details varied, the basic outlines of the story were the same: the U.S. military had recovered a crashed UFO and hidden it away for observation. In some accounts, dead aliens were also found with the flying saucer.

The Roswell Incident, by Bill Moore and Charles Berlitz, published in 1980, was one of the more prominent books in this field. The authors of this book claimed to have interviewed over 70 witnesses to the Roswell crash. While that might be true, Moore and Berlitz only saw fit to cite 25 actual testimonies, most of them second-hand accounts. In fact, *The Roswell Incident* only contains seven accounts from people claiming first-hand knowledge of the crash site debris. Of this total, five people told the authors they personally handled wreckage from the crash. One member of this quintet, however, refused to believe the wreckage was from outer space and made his objections known.

Some Roswell accounts cite a neighbor of Brazel named Loretta Proctor who allegedly handled flying disk debris. Proctor's story has changed over the years, however. At first, she merely claimed to have seen debris from the crash site. Tales of holding the wreckage only emerged after her husband Floyd died. While alive, Floyd stoutly denied in interviews that he or his wife ever saw or touched UFO debris.

Another "eyewitness" never claimed to have witnessed anything—to reporters or military authorities, at least. The witness was Sergeant Melvin Brown. Following his death in 1986, his daughter, Beverly Bean, announced that her father had told her about handling alien bodies at the Roswell crash site. The rest of the Brown family firmly denied ever hearing their father claim first-hand knowledge of dead aliens. When Brown's military file was examined, it was determined that he had served as a cook, had no security clearance, and never did guard duty, making it highly unlikely that he took part in any top-secret government operations involving alien corpses.

Key witness Major Marcel has also been proven to be a deeply unreliable source. Writing in the July/August 1997 *Skeptical Inquirer*, UFO debunker Kal Korff noted how Marcel told reporters he was a pilot who shot down five enemy planes. Marcel's military record, however, makes no mention of piloting skills, much less any status as an "ace." Marcel also claimed he had a BA in physics from a specific educational institution, which was untrue.

"In short, no credible evidence from any witness has turned out to present a compelling case that the object was extraterrestrial in origin," wrote Korff in the July/August 1997 *Skeptical Inquirer*.

There is one germ of truth in the Roswell story: the military probably did lie when they said the mystery object from the sky was a weather balloon. In fact, the balloon almost certainly came from Project Mogul, a secret government program in which balloons were rigged with electronic equipment and released into the atmosphere. These balloon arrays were designed to pick up sonic emissions from possible Soviet nuclear bomb tests. In the late 1940s, the United States was very interested in gathering information on Soviet nuclear capabilities.

Launched by the U.S. government after World War II, Project Mogul was an extremely secret operation. It had the same national security rating as the original Manhattan Project, to design the first atomic bomb. In other words, there was good reason the military would be skittish about admitting the true nature of the crashed object at Roswell, but it didn't have anything to do with extraterrestrial spacecraft.

Debris recovered from the crash site also point to a spy balloon: "the best evidence now indicates that the device was really a balloon array (the sticks and foiled paper being components of dangling box-kite like radar reflectors) that had gone missing in flight from Project Mogul," noted the May/June 2012 *Skeptical Inquirer.*

In his investigation, Korff interviewed people from the Project Mogul team, including one Professor Charles Moore. Professor Moore apparently launched the very balloon array that ended up on rancher Brazel's property. Moore said he had previously taken his story to UFO researchers, only to be dismissed as part of a government cover-up. In similar fashion, Roswell witnesses interviewed by Korff complained about being badly misquoted in UFO "exposés." Korff also noted that scientific testing of fragments from the crash didn't turn up anything indicating outer space origins.

In the 1980s, UFO buffs released allegedly secret documents concerning "Operation Majestic-12," a clandestine initiative supposedly launched by President Harry Truman to investigate the Roswell crash. The Federal Bureau of Investigation has looked into the so-called MJ-12 documents and rejected them as phony.

A notice on the FBI website stated, "In 1988, two FBI offices received similar versions of a memo titled, "Operation Majestic-12…" claiming to be a highly classified government document. The memo appeared to be a briefing for newly elected President Eisenhower on a secret committee created to exploit a recovery of an extraterrestrial aircraft or cover-up this work from public examination. An Air Force investigation determined the documents to be a fake."

Equally fraudulent is an "alien autopsy" film, highly popular on the Internet, allegedly depicting doctors conducting a physical examination of a deceased Roswell alien. The crudely shot film consists of nothing more than "the dissection of a rubbery extraterrestrial who appeared to be from the distant Planet Latex," stated the May/June 2012 *Skeptical Inquirer.*

It's worth noting that the Roswell incident occurred at the exact moment in American history when the country was gripped with UFO-mania. In mid-1947, private pilot Kenneth Arnold experienced what had been described as the first modern-day UFO encounter. He reported seeing flying saucers in the sky—in truth, maybe little more than a mirage triggered by a temperature inversion.

Mix this UFO-mania with Cold War paranoia, government secrecy, and highly unreliable witness testimony, and the end-result is endless conspiracy mongering about a crashed balloon.

Further Reading

Susan Blackmore, "Abduction by Aliens or Sleep Paralysis?" *Skeptical Inquirer*, May/June 1998.

Federal Bureau of Investigation, FBI Record, The Vault, "Majestic 12," https://vault.fbi .gov/Majestic%2012.

Kal Korff, "What Really Happened at Roswell," *Skeptical Inquirer*, July/August 1997.

National Archives, "Unidentified Flying Objects—Project Blue Book," http://www .archives.gov/research/military/air-force/ufos.html#mj12.

Joe Nickell, "Return to Roswell," *Skeptical Inquirer*, January/February 2009.

Joe Nickell, "States of Mind: Some Perceived ET Encounters," *Skeptical Inquirer*, November/December 2012.

Joe Nickell and James McGaha, "The Roswellian Syndrome: How Some UFO Myths Develop," *Skeptical Inquirer*, May/June 2012.

Elaine Showalter, *Hystories: Hysterical Epidemics and Modern* Media, 1997.

THE GREAT CHESS AUTOMATON

The Great Chess Automaton was a supposedly mechanical device consisting of a wooden figure decked out in Middle Eastern clothes, whose upper torso extended from a large wooden box. The figure was usually referred to as "the Turk." The wooden box was apparently filled with gears, wires, and other complicated machinery.

The Great Chess Automaton would be trundled out on stage and pitted against a flesh-and-blood chess opponent. To the amazement of eighteenth-century audiences in Europe, the Turk almost always won his matches. The Chess Automaton didn't just make mechanical movements; it seemed to be able to plot strategy and anticipate moves by other players. In other words, the "Turk" seemed capable of independent thought.

The automaton was built by one Baron Wolfgang von Kempelen, a Hungarian nobleman, around 1769. He took his device on tour, often displaying it to upper-crust audiences consisting of royal figures and the very wealthy. Before each show, von Kempelen would typically open sliding doors on the side of the wooden box to display the mechanical interior, "proving" that no one was hidden inside. In a similar fashion, when the "Turk" made a move, audiences could clearly hear gears working.

It was still whispered that von Kempelen was a fraud, that his Great Chess Automaton was a fake controlled by a person, not gears and wires. No one, however, could figure out how this fakery was done. After all, von Kempelen had no problem displaying the inside of his machine, which seemed to rule out the possibility of a hidden human.

Von Kempelen eventually tired of the chess circuit and took his machine apart and put it into storage, around 1790. Roughly fifteen years later, von Kempelen's family sold the device to a German university student named Johann Nepomuk Maelzel. The Great Chess Automaton was reconfigured, then taken out on tour again, dazzling audiences and defeating almost all challengers. Maelzel toured Europe and America with the Chess Automaton.

There was still widespread speculation that Maelzel was pulling a fast one on audiences. Finally, in February 1837, these suspicions were confirmed after an exposé appeared in a periodical called the *Philadelphia National Gazette Literary Register*. According to the article, a man indeed hid inside the wooden box, occupying a portion of the cabinet out of which the wooden "Turk" appeared. Usually, the hidden person was a chess master.

The presence of the man was concealed through sliding panels and a rolling chair. Think of a magician doing the "cutting a person in half" routine with a volunteer in a wooden box. The magician uses concealment and trickery to make it look like the volunteer's torso has been sliced in two. The same kind of trickery was used to conceal the real interior of the Great Chess Automaton.

The chess master inside the box used a 'pantograph' device (that is, a mechanism controlled by a person that copies their hand movements) to move the "Turk's" arm. The chess master followed the progress on the game through the use of magnetic chess pieces.

Sadly, the Great Chess Automaton was destroyed in 1854, during a fire in the warehouse where the device had been confined since its true nature was revealed. The spirit of this hoax lives on, however, in carnival devices with mechanical figures that play cards or tell fortunes. Often, the figure is painted and dressed to look like a "Turk"—a reminder of the Great Chess Automaton that amazed audiences centuries ago.

Further Reading

"The Great Chess Automaton," The Museum of Hoaxes website, http://hoaxes.org
 /archive/permalink/the_great_chess_automaton.

KENTUCKY FRIED LIES

Sometimes, a hoax can break your heart. Such was the case with Victoria Wilcher, a three-year-old girl who became the subject of a media storm after it was claimed she was asked to leave a restaurant because her facial scars were upsetting other customers. The restaurant in question was a KFC in Jackson, Mississippi.

Victoria and her grandmother, Kelly Mullins, allegedly visited this KFC on May 15, 2014. A month prior, Victoria had been badly mauled by three pit bulls belonging to her grandfather, resulting in multiple broken bones, the loss of an eye, and a cruelly scarred visage. The girl's injuries were so severe that she was forced to eat through a feeding tube.

On June 12, a Facebook support page called Victoria's Victories, run by Wilcher's aunt, Teri Rials Bates, posted details of what supposedly took place in Jackson. The page (which urged people to visit a site to donate cash to help pay Wilcher's considerable medical bills) explained how the little girl and her grandmother popped into a KFC following a visit to the Blair E. Batson Children's Hospital in Jackson. After Mullins placed her order, management supposedly asked the pair to leave.

This post and follow-up interviews by Wilcher's family members caused a sensation. The story was picked up by media outlets around the world, resulting in an outpouring of support and shock.

"I ordered a sweet tea and mashed potatoes and gravy. I sat down at the table and started feeding her, and the lady came over and said that we would have to leave because we were disturbing other customers, that Victoria's face was disturbing other customers," Mullins told Jackson news channel WAPT.

After the story broke, KFC staff in Jackson experienced harassment at the hands of furious customers. Restaurant employees said they received death threats, verbal abuse, and drinks tossed in their direction.

Contributions and offers of help poured in to Wilcher's family. Prior to the June 12 post, Wilcher's account had received a total of $595. After the Victoria's Victories post went viral, the account received an outpouring of support. A total of $135,000 was raised in a few days, $30,000 of which came from a very contrite KFC. Plastic surgeons offered their services for free, and people sent gifts to comfort the little girl who had been so cruelly treated.

The story, however, quickly began to unravel.

The Victoria's Victories Facebook page initially listed a KFC at State and High streets in Jackson as the site of the incident. As it turned out, that particular KFC had been closed for years. Bates said it was a simple mistake. She had really meant to say that Wilcher and her grandmother had gone to a KFC on Woodrow Wilson Drive in Jackson.

There was indeed a functioning KFC on that street, but careful analysis of surveillance video indicated that no one who matched Mullins' and Wilcher's descriptions had entered the store on May 15. Further, the store had no record of an order from that day which included sweet tea and mashed potatoes and gravy.

KFC staff noted that patients from the Blair E. Batson's Children's Hospital frequented the Woodrow Wilson Drive store all the time. No one had ever been turned away because of their upsetting appearance. In fact, the hospital itself contained a plaque thanking KFC founder Colonel Harland Sanders for making a multi-million-dollar donation.

It was further pointed out that prior to June 12, the Victoria's Victories page had posted details of the hardship felt by Wilcher's family in dealing with her medical bills and an intransigent insurance company. The evidence pointed to a deliberate hoax, perpetuated to boost fundraising for a little girl's medical expenses.

The family stuck by their story, though they did turn down the $30,000 pledged by KFC (which was still willing to donate the cash despite the probability of having been hoaxed). In July, 2014, it was reported that Wilcher and family members had flown to Florida for plastic surgery, to be performed at no cost by surgeons If nothing else, at least the little girl at the center of the hoax might be able to regain a normal appearance.

Further Reading

"Report: Story of Girl Getting Tossed from KFC Hoax," *The Clarion Ledger*, June 23, 2014.

"KFC 'Hoax' Girl Victoria Wilcher Arrives for Surgery in Florida," News.com.au website, July 8, 2014.

LEARNED NONSENSE

In 1996, a New York University physics professor named Alan Sokal set out to make a point. Sokal was concerned with what he perceived as intellectual laziness and deliberate obtuseness in post-secondary thought. This laziness was exemplified, in his view, by the influence of "postmodernism" on cultural studies and other academic fields.

A 2012 article in *Skeptic* magazine explained, "Postmodernism is an intellectual approach used in fields such as literary theory, sociology and architecture. Although the term describes a broad class of viewpoints, in general postmodernism rejects the ideas of absolute truth and objective reality. Rather, it emphasizes how we construct our apparent realities by describing them, particularly through language."

With this in mind, Sokal cobbled together an essay consisting of complete gibberish and sent it to an academic journal called *Social Text*. The piece was entitled, "Transgressing the Boundaries: Towards a Transformative Hermeneutics of Quantum Gravity." It contained real quotes from real figures to back up a completely nonsensical point of view.

Sure enough, the article was published in the summer 1996 issue of *Social Text*. Evidently, the editors found it worthy of inclusion, even though it was all a joke.

A sample of Sokal's piece: "...the postmodern sciences overthrow the static ontological categories and hierarchies characteristic of modernist science. In place of atomism and reductionism, the new sciences stress the dynamic web of relationships between the whole and the part; in place of fixed individual essences (e.g. Newtonian particles), they conceptualize interactions and flows (e.g. quantum fields). Intriguingly, these homologous features arise in numerous seemingly disparate areas of science, from quantum gravity to chaos theory to the biophysics of self-organizing systems."

Sokal owned up to his hoax in an article published in the academic journal *Lingua Franca*: "For some years, I've been troubled by an apparent decline in the standards of intellectual rigor in certain precincts of the American academic humanities … so, to test the prevailing intellectual standards, I decided to try a modest (though admittedly uncontrolled) experiment: Would a leading North American journal of cultural studies … publish an article liberally salted with nonsense if (a) it sounded good and (b) it flattered the editors' ideological preconceptions?" wrote Sokal.

"I intentionally wrote the article so that any competent physicist or mathematician (or undergraduate physics or math major) would realize that it is a spoof. Evidently the editors of *Social Text* felt comfortable publishing an article on quantum physics without bothering to consult anyone knowledgeable in the field," he added.

Indeed, a closer look at Sokal's article would have revealed evidence that the author was only kidding. In his essay, Sokal made the claim that the speculative science of quantum physics somehow had strong political implications. His jabberwocky passed editorial muster because it was indistinguishable from other articles published in *Social Text*.

Sokal's purpose entailed more than just making pompous academic editors look foolish, however. "While my method was satirical, my motivation is utterly serious. What concerns me is the proliferation, not just of nonsense and sloppy thinking per se, but of a particular kind of nonsense and sloppy thinking: one that denies the existence of objective realities, or (when challenged) admits their existence but downplays their practical relevance," wrote Sokal in *Lingua Franca*.

Sokal was keen to make the point that there are objective realities that no amount of theorizing can change. In *Lingua Franca*, Sokal challenged anyone who denied the laws of physics, for example, to test their belief system by stepping out the window of his twenty-first-story apartment.

More important, Sokal believed that trendy postmodern dialogue subverted pragmatic conversation about real-world issues. "Theorizing about 'the social construction of reality' won't help us find an effective treatment for AIDS or devise strategies for preventing global warming. Nor can we combat false ideas in history, sociology, economics and politics if we reject the notions of truth and falsity," wrote Sokal.

Further Reading

Jim Davies, "Academic Obfuscations," *Skeptic Magazine*, volume 17, number 4, 2012.

Alan Sokal, Department of Physics, New York University, "A Physicist Experiments With Cultural Studies," *Lingua Franca*, May/June 1996.

Alan Sokal, Department of Physics, New York University, "Transgressing the Boundaries: Towards a Transformative Hermeneutics of Quantum Gravity," *Social Text*, spring /summer 1996, http://www.physics.nyu.edu/faculty/sokal/transgress_v2/transgress _v2.html.

THE LURID CONFESSIONS OF MARIA MONK

In early 1835, a young woman was found wandering dazed and distraught in New York City. She was pregnant and clearly in distress. When some good Samaritans arranged shelter for her, she told them an amazing story.

The woman identified herself as "Maria Monk" and claimed she had escaped a convent, located at the Hotel-Dieu in Montreal in what was then called Lower Canada (i.e., Quebec). Ms. Monk offered lurid tales of debauched priests and violated nuns. Among other things, she claimed there was a secret tunnel between the Seminaire de Saint-Sulpice and the Hotel-Dieu, through which perverted priests regularly traveled to force their attentions on the nuns. If any children resulted from these unholy unions, they were birthed, baptized, and then strangled, their little corpses tossed into a lime pit in the basement of the Hotel-Dieu. Monk also claimed to have witnessed the brutal murder of a nun who had rebuffed the advances of the lecherous priests. Monk said of herself that a priest had made her pregnant, and she had fled the convent to prevent her child from being murdered.

Monk's strange confessions were first published in a New York newspaper. Inevitably, a book followed. Published in early 1836, the tome was titled, *Awful Disclosures of Maria Monk*. Although supposedly based on Monk's revelations, the actual writing was done by a Presbyterian minister named Reverend John Jay Slocum, with input from two other Protestant worthies, Reverend William K. Hoyt and Reverend George Bourne. It was claimed the story was based on Ms. Monk's oral account.

Reporters soon found gaping holes in Monk's tale. An American journalist named William Leete Stone went to Montreal and secured permission to investigate the Hotel-Dieu himself. He looked around and soon realized Monk's description of the place didn't match the actual surroundings. Further exposes followed. Needless to say, the Catholic Church in Montreal protested that the book was a lie from start to finish.

No matter: the book was a huge hit, selling an estimated 300,000 copies in pre-Civil War America. The book cleverly packaged lurid sexual escapades with anti-clerical prejudice, feeding into the worst Protestant nightmares about decadent Catholic clergy.

The actual writing was dense and turgid, not something you would expect from a young, barely educated nun speaking aloud. The text leaned toward purple prose and the kind of "fate-worse-than-death" plot developments commonly found in gothic novels of the era.

Sales of the book were helped by the fact that it fed into the virulent anti-Catholic sentiment of the times. This anti-Catholic environment was fuelled by widespread immigration in the early 1800s from Ireland and Germany into the United States. There had been a major riot in Charlestown (Boston) in August 1834, in which a mob burned down an Ursuline convent. Many of the founding New England states had a long, unhealthy history of anti-Catholic legislation, barring Catholics from voting in some cases.

As for Maria Monk, it's doubtful whether she actually spent any time as a nun. Monk was born on June 27, 1816, in Dorchester (Saint-Jean-sur-Richelieu), Lower Canada. Her mother claimed the girl had suffered a serious injury as a child, after she rammed a slate pencil into her ear. Brain damage ensued. Brain damage or not, Monk was a willful child and allegedly became a prostitute. Her mother had her confined to a facility called the Charitable Institution for Female Penitents. Monk was expelled from the Institution in March 1835, by which time she was pregnant.

There have been suppositions that Monk was extremely suggestible and had difficulty sorting fact from fiction. After being kicked out of the Charitable Institution, she wandered into New York City and was taken up by a group of Protestant figures. It is believed the latter encouraged her to embellish her life story and fed her tales of Catholic debauchery that she accepted as her own personal experience.

In August 1837, Monk left New York and showed up in Philadelphia. She had a new tale to tell, claiming that she had been kidnapped by Catholic priests who wanted to put an end to her startling disclosures. One year later, she gave birth to a child, father unknown.

In 1849, Monk was arrested for stealing money and placed in prison on Blackwell's Island (now Roosevelt Island) in New York City. She died there, in the summer of 1849.

Unfortunately, Monk's death didn't spell the end of anti-Catholic prejudice in the United States. The 1840s and 1850s saw the rise of the "Know Nothing" movement, which was opposed to Irish Catholic immigration. The movement was powerful enough to attract a former U.S. president, Millard Fillmore, to run for president on its behalf in 1856.

As for the *Awful Disclosures of Maria Monk*, it eventually became something of a historical curiosity, which even the most ardent anti-Catholic bigot had to admit bore the unmistakable odor of a hoax.

Further Reading

Maria Monk, *Awful Disclosures of Maria Monk*, 1836, http://www.gutenberg.org/ebooks/8095.

"Maria Monk," *Dictionary of Canadian Biography*, 1966.

Joe Nickell, "Old Anti-Catholic Hoax Continues," Center for Inquiry blog, November 14, 2012, http://www.centerforinquiry.net/blogs/entry/old_anti-catholic_hoax_continues/.

NEW YORK NEWSPAPER HOAXES
Man-Bats on the Moon

In the last week of August 1835, a series of astonishing articles published in the *New York Sun* claimed that life had been found on the moon. According to the *Sun*, astronomers had spotted lunar bison, blue-colored goats, beavers that walked on two legs, and a race of man-bat humanoids.

These amazing sightings had allegedly been made by Dr. John Herschel, a renowned astronomer, using a special telescope in South Africa. While Herschel was a real person, the telescope and the alleged discoveries were not. It was all a hoax on the part of the *Sun*: "To this day, the moon hoax is remembered as one of the most sensational media hoaxes of all time," reports an article at the Museum of Hoaxes website.

The hoax was officially launched on Friday, August 21, 1835. On that day, the *Sun* ran a small article on page two, stating that Dr. Herschel had "made some astronomical discoveries of the most wonderful description, by means of an immense telescope of an entirely new principle."

The hoax was spun out over the course of six stories, totaling 17,000 words. The prose was very dense, as was typical of the times. The articles amounted to a long travelogue of sorts, of the intriguing flora and fauna on the moon. The lunar observations allegedly took place in January of that year.

The initial story in the series introduced one Dr. Andrew Grant—supposedly a pupil of Sir William Herschel (father of Dr. Herschel) and author of the *Sun* articles. The paper explained that Dr. Herschel was writing a scholarly article on his lunar investigations, while Dr. Grant had penned "a popular account" for the *Edinburgh Journal of Science*. It was from this "popular account" that the *Sun* supposedly based its articles.

The first article didn't offer much information about lunar life but was devoted to setting the stage for the hoax. The story went into great detail about the mammoth telescope utilized by Dr. Herschel in his observations. Supposedly, the mighty telescope was 24 feet in diameter and contained a special second lens that worked as "a hydro-oxygen microscope," in the *Sun*'s words. Said microscope "further magnified, illuminated and projected the telescopic image onto a canvas screen," explained the *Sun*. In other words, astronomers could magnify distant objects with much greater clarity than any other tele-scope allowed.

Having whetted the public's appetite, the second story announced that Dr. Herschel had discovered life on the moon in the form of "a dark red flower" covering what appeared to be basaltic rock. The presence of flowers meant the moon had a similar atmosphere to earth, which suggested it might support some kind of animal life, explained Dr. Grant.

Sure enough, after spotting flowers, Dr. Herschel allegedly discovered groups of brown quadrupeds that resembled bison. He also spotted goat-like beings of a "bluish lead color." The male goat-beings had horns and beards, while their female counterparts didn't.

The discoveries kept on coming. On the third day, Dr. Herschel located a "biped beaver." Said beaver "resembles the beaver of the earth in every other respect than its destitution of a tail and its invariable habit of walking upon only two feet. It carries its young in its arms like a human being and moves with an easy gliding motion. Its huts are constructed better and higher than those of many tribes of human savages and from the appearance of smoke in nearly all of them, there is no doubt of its being acquainted with the use of fire," read the *Sun*.

Day four revealed humanoid beings that looked a bit like bats: "They aver-aged four feet in height, were covered, except on the face with short and glossy copper-colored hair and had wings composed of a thin membrane, without hair, lying snugly on their backs and from the top of their shoulders to the calves of their legs. The face, which was of a yellowish flesh color, was a slight improvement upon that of the large orang outang, being more open and intelli-gent in its expression and having a much greater expansion of forehead," stated Dr. Grant. Dr. Herschel supposedly dubbed these creatures "Vespertilio-homo or man-bat" and was impressed by the fact that they seemed to carry on con-versations with each other, suggesting intelligence.

The fifth day of articles in the series focused on what appeared to be an abandoned temple made from polished sapphire. The next article revealed that the astronomers had spotted a population of superior man-bats living near the mystery temple found the day before. These new humanoids were "of a larger stature than the former specimens, less dark in color, and in every respect an improved variety of the race," reported the *Sun*. These elite man-bats appar-ently spent most of their time eating fruit, flying about, chatting, and bathing.

Sadly, at this point in the narrative, the observatory containing the tele-scope suffered an accident. The mighty telescope was positioned improperly and magnified the sun's rays, causing a fire. The observatory was partly burned down as a result, and repairs consumed a few days.

At the tail end of the hoax articles, Dr. Grant claimed that a month after the telescope was fixed, Dr. Herschel spotted an even more elite version of the man-bats: "we found the very superior species of the Vespertilio-homo. In stature they did not exceed those last described but they were of infinitely greater personal beauty and appeared in our eyes scarcely less lovely than the general impression of angels by the more imaginative schools of painters," read the *Sun*.

It was at this juncture that Dr. Grant brought his lunar travelogue to a close. Dr. Grant stated that Dr. Herschel was writing an academic account of the super-elite man-bats, and Grant didn't want to steal his thunder.

Needless to say, the six articles in the *Sun* caused a great deal of speculation. Several papers in the city reprinted the story. Newspapers in other eastern cities soon did the same.

Contrary to later accounts, the *Sun's* circulation did not drastically spike during the hoax. Two weeks before the moon articles, the *Sun* hit a peak circulation of 26,000 copies sold in a day. This peak probably had something to do with the fact that the *Sun's* rival, the *New York Herald*, was temporarily out of commission due to a fire. Until the *Herald* reappeared, its readers satisfied themselves with the *Sun*. During the hoax, the *Sun's* circulation stood around 19,000 to 20,000 copies a day. One of the reasons circulation didn't increase was the fact that other newspapers jumped on the story and reprinted it. The *Sun* couldn't complain; after all, they were supposedly reprinting stories that originated in the *Edinburgh Journal of Science*.

The *Sun* did cash in, in another way. The six moon stories were combined in a special-edition pamphlet for sale. The *Sun* also sold prints that supposedly depicted the fabulous moon creatures and humanoids. But did people actually believe the story?

At the time, there was no set standard for "objective" media coverage. Many newspapers of the day received funding from political parties and were openly partisan. Newspaper readers accepted that some of the stories they perused were exaggerations. The notion of just printing basic facts about a real-life event or person hadn't taken hold yet.

That said, there were plenty of skeptics, right from the beginning. The *Herald*, under James Gordon Bennett Sr., dismissed the stories as nonsense. Among other details, the *Herald* pointed out that the *Edinburgh Journal of Science* had ceased publication in 1833.

Then there's the background of the *Sun* itself. The *Sun* was a "penny paper"— that is, a newspaper that cost one cent. High-brow papers of the day cost six cents and were read by a more discerning audience. Penny papers reached a far wider audience and generally printed far more sensationalized stories than their pricier counterparts. So a wild story about man-bats on the moon didn't seem out of place for the *Sun*.

It is important to remember that the nineteenth century was an era of technological advancement. Steamboats, canals, railroads, the cotton gin, and improved printing presses all made their appearance in the early 1800s. A giant telescope with special lenses wasn't beyond the realm of possibility for many readers. "Although the lunar narrative may not have been met with credulity as widespread as most accounts of the hoax suggest, it certainly wasn't dismissed as a fraud out of hand. It was plausible enough to give most people pause," wrote the Museum of Hoaxes.

There were elements of truth in the story as well: Dr. Herschel was indeed working in South Africa at the time the stories ran, examining the skies of the Southern Hemisphere. His arrival in South Africa had been extensively covered by the media.

As for authorship, it is believed that English-born writer Richard Adams Locke was responsible for the moon hoax stories. Locke was born in Somerset, England, in 1800 to a wealthy family. After his father disowned him because of his radical political views, Locke decided to earn his keep as a writer. He worked for literary journals and a newspaper called *The Republican*, then later took a job with a small Somerset paper. The latter was as unimpressed with Locke's politics as his father had been and promptly fired him.

In terms of personal life, Locke married in 1826. Four years later, his wife had a baby girl. The new father found himself unemployable in his home country because of his radical political views. He decided to move to America. On January 13, 1832, Locke and his family set foot in New York City.

In New York, Locke worked as a legal reporter and stenographer. He lied about his background, claiming to be a graduate of the University of Cambridge. He also claimed to be directly descended from famous seventeenth-century philosopher John Locke. In fact, "he was a collateral descendant. His great-great-great-grandfather was John Locke's uncle," reports the Museum of Hoaxes.

In 1834, Locke started working as a metropolitan reporter for the *Courier and Enquirer* newspaper in New York. A year later, he took on a freelance job, writing articles about a sensational murder trial involving a cult leader named Matthias the Prophet, accused of killing one of his followers. Locke was paid to cover the trial by publisher Benjamin Day of the *Sun*. Not wanting his boss to know he was working under the table for a rival, Locke insisted his trial coverage be published anonymously.

Locke's pieces on the Matthias trial proved widely popular. Day put the articles together in a pamphlet that went on to sell 10,000 copies. Day was eager to repeat this success, with another sensational story that could be serialized then turned into a pamphlet. He urged Locke to pen more features for the *Sun*. It is believed that Day was the one who urged Locke to write an account of life on the moon.

In June 1835, Locke changed jobs and became co-editor of the *Sun*. Shortly thereafter, the lunar hoax stories appeared.

The *Herald* "outed" Locke as the author of the moon stories. Publisher Bennett Sr. recalled chatting with Locke at the Matthias trial about astronomy.

At first, Locke denied that he had penned the pieces. He didn't maintain his silence for long, however. In the fall of 1836, Locke left the *Sun* and began working for a penny paper called the *New Era*. In an article for the *New Era* he added the tag "Author of the Moon Hoax" to his byline.

In fall 1839, Locke left the *New Era* and began freelancing. He wrote a piece for the *New World* newspaper, in which he admitted to writing the moon hoax articles. According to Locke, the articles were actually supposed to be a satire on the influence of religion on science.

In 1842, Locke decided a career change was in order. He left journalism and began working for the Customs Service in New York. When he died on February 16, 1871, the *Sun* ran a front-page obituary that identified Locke as "the author of the Moon Hoax."

The obituary described the hoax as "the most successful scientific joke ever published … the story was told with a minuteness of detail and dexterous use of technical phrases that not only imposed upon the ordinary reader but deceived and puzzled men of science to an astonishing degree."

The actual man of science at the center of the hoax, Dr. John Herschel, was initially amused by the story. In years to follow, however, he grumbled about being constantly asked questions about the Moon Hoax, a tale that continued to delight and amuse the public for decades.

Wild Cats in Manhattan

It sounds like the plot to a bad science-fiction movie: wild carnivorous animals escape from the Central Park Zoo and go on the prowl. Lions, tigers, and panthers tear into pedestrians and eat them alive. A polar bear, hyenas, and a rhinoceros join in the human-killing rampage. The mayor urges calm and a curfew, as police try to track the animals down and dispatch them with bullets.

Such was the situation in the fall of 1874, when denizens of New York opened their copies of the *New York Herald*—one the world's leading papers at the time.

The headlines to the story were grim enough: "A Shocking Sabbath Carnival of Death – Savage Brutes at Large – Awful Combats Between the Beasts and Citizens – How the Catastrophe was Brought About – Affrighting Incidents."

According to the *Herald*, a rhinoceros had escaped from its cage at Central Park Zoo the day before. The rhino went berserk and killed a zookeeper. This mayhem took place just as the other zookeepers were feeding their charges. When the zookeepers abandoned their posts to help their comrade, a group of dangerous carnivores somehow joined the rhino in escape. These man-eaters included a polar bear, panther, a lioness, hyenas, and a tiger. These carnivores started attacking humans who had the misfortune to be present nearby in Central Park.

Lurid as this story was, the account was a deliberate hoax, aided and abetted by the *Herald's* flamboyant owner, James Gordon Bennett Jr. His father, James Gordon Bennett Sr., founded the *Herald* in the 1830s then passed the paper to his son. While Bennett Sr. had blasted the *Sun* for hoaxing the public, Bennett Jr. was of a different stripe. Wealthy and eccentric, Bennett Jr. dressed in expensive clothes and took an obsessive interest in the *Herald*—a paper for which he also served as editor-in-chief and publisher.

"The *Herald* had a reputation for being as entertaining as it was informative, its pages suffused with the owner's sly sense of humor," stated a July 24, 2014, article posted on Slate.com.

That said, Bennett Jr. did take newsgathering seriously. He paid large sums to get the latest bulletins via telegraph and trans-Atlantic cable. He also paid considerable fees to get long features from prominent writers such as Mark Twain, Stephen Crane, and Walt Whitman.

While devoted to his newspaper, Bennett Jr. was hardly an all-work, no-play type. He was a sportsman who won the first trans-Atlantic yacht race. He helped to introduce the game of polo to the United States and was made a commodore in the New York Yacht Club at the age of 29, in 1871. Nicknamed "the Commodore," Bennett Jr. also liked to race a horse carriage around Manhattan at night when the mood struck him. On such occasions, he was usually drunk and often nude. Such a dashing character could hardly be expected to run a sober-minded paper.

"Gordon Bennett's most original contribution to modern journalism could be found in his notion that a newspaper should not merely report stories; it should *create* them. Editors should not only cover the news, he felt, they should orchestrate large-scale public dramas that stirred emotions and got people talking," reported Slate.com.

To this end, it was Bennett Jr. who sent Henry Stanley to "find" missionary/ explorer David Livingstone in Africa. Livingstone wasn't exactly lost, but simply wasn't in contact with the outside world. Stanley wrote about encountering Livingstone in a series of widely popular dispatches, published in the *Herald* in 1871.

Critics of Bennett Jr. accused the publisher of organizing stunts just to drive up circulation, which wasn't too far off the mark. Eager to top the Livingstone scoop, Bennett Jr. endorsed the "wild animals on the loose" story, which was published on the morning of November 9, 1874.

The *Herald* went into great detail about the zoo animals' rampage. The panther was said to have been spotted "gnawing horribly" on a man's head. The lioness killed several people, only to be shot dead by a group of armed immigrants from Sweden who happened by. The rhinoceros killed a girl, then fell into an excavation pit for a sewer system and died. The polar bear attacked a pair of men, then sauntered off to the upper reservoir in Central Park. Bellevue Hospital was said to be packed with victims of the animals' onslaught, with doctors feverishly amputating mangled limbs. New York City mayor William Havemeyer urged a rigid curfew until police managed to track down all the animals and kill them, reported the *Herald*.

The *Herald* article did state, admittedly at the end of the story, that the tale was all a fantasy. The paper then went on to explain how the city had no emergency evacuation plan.

"With Bennett's enthusiastic encouragement, the editors had concocted the tale to illustrate that the city had no evacuation plan in the event of a large-scale emergency—and also to point out that, in fact, many of the cages at the Zoo were flimsy and in bad need of repair," stated Slate.com.

Indeed, Central Park Zoo was shabby at the time compared to zoos in other parts of the world, such as Paris. Bennett felt New York deserved a world-class zoo for itself.

Most readers didn't get to the end disclaimer, however. They were too panicked at the headlines and descriptions of mayhem. People headed to New York piers to escape the city by boat. Many people obeyed the mayor's alleged call for a curfew by staying inside. Some intrepid New Yorkers armed themselves and went into Central Park to track down rogue animals themselves.

The *Herald* spun the story out through several editions. Later articles reported that John Adams Dix, the governor of New York and a Civil War hero, had personally shot dead the rampaging tiger. Other animals from the zoo kept joining their carnivore cousins on the prowl. Somehow, a tapir, an anaconda, a gazelle, monkeys, a porcupine, and some sheep also managed to escape. A grizzly bear even made it into a church on Fifth Street, where it "sprang upon the shoulders of an aged lady and buried his fangs in her neck," reported the *Herald*.

Other newspapers in town were mystified at how the Herald had scooped them on such a momentous story. Once they determined they had been hoaxed, these critics complained about Bennett Jr.'s shoddy ethics. Real people could have been killed in the panic the story caused, they pointed out.

The tale became known as "The Wild Animal Hoax." Apparently, Bennett Jr. was delighted at the reaction the story generated. He was even more pleased when the story led Central Park Zoo staff to repair the shabby cages of their charges, to prevent any real-life animal breakouts.

Further Reading

The Museum of Hoaxes website, "The Central Park Zoo Escape," http://hoaxes.org/archive/permalink/the_central_park_zoo_escape/.

The Museum of Hoaxes website, "The Great Moon Hoax of 1835," http://hoaxes.org/archive/permalink/the_great_moon_hoax.

Hampton Sides, Slate.com, "A Shocking Sabbath Carnival of Death," July 24, 2014, http://www.slate.com/articles/news_and_politics/history/2014/07/james_gordon_bennett_jr_s_new_york_herald_the_central_park_zoo_wild_animal.html.

THE PROTOCOLS OF THE LEARNED ELDERS OF ZION

Some hoaxes are harmless. Others are amusing. And some are incredibly vile. The book *The Protocols of the Learned Elders of Zion* falls in the latter category. A collection of insidious commentary on world domination by supposed Jewish insiders, *Protocols* has been repeatedly exposed as a fake. No matter: *Protocols* has enjoyed a lengthy shelf-life and continues to be disseminated today.

Described as "a classic in paranoid, racist literature" by the Anti-Defamation League (ADL), the book has 24 sections or "protocols" on how the Jews plan to take over the world (fomenting revolution, controlling international finance, dominating the media, undermining Christianity, etc., etc., etc.). The text is allegedly based on a secret meeting of high-ranking Jews in Prague's Jewish cemetery.

The *Protocols* were first published in 1903 in a newspaper called *Znamya* (The Banner) in St. Petersburg, Russia. The *Protocols* made another appearance two years later, as the appendix to a book called *The Great in the Small: The Coming of the Anti-Christ and the Rule of Satan on Earth*. The latter was penned by a Russian mystic and writer named Sergei Nilus.

The *Protocols* remained fairly obscure, however, until Russian refugees fleeing the Revolution of 1917 brought the book with them to Western Europe and North America. To these bewildered émigrés, the *Protocols* offered a handy, if entirely spurious, explanation as to how their Imperial world had fallen apart so quickly: it was all a Jewish conspiracy, led by Bolsheviks.

In 1920, *The Dearborn Independent*, a newspaper published by U.S. auto titan Henry Ford, brought the *Protocols* to an American audience. The paper ran a series of articles about the *Protocols*, then gathered the pieces together in a book called *The International Jew: The World's Foremost Problem*. The book sold half a million copies.

In 1921, the *London Times* revealed that *Protocols* was actually a second-rate forgery. The *Times* noted that most of the material in the book was lifted from a French satirical novel called *Dialogue in Hell between Machiavelli and Montesquieu*. In the course of this dialogue, Machiavelli advocates tyranny, while Montesquieu advocates justice. Written by Maurice Joly and published in 1864, the novel was intended to be a poke at Napoleon III, not an international Jewish cabal.

Other elements of the *Protocols* were lifted from an 1868 novel called *Biarritz*. Written by German author Hermann Goedsche, the novel contained a chapter describing a secret meeting by the Twelve Tribes of Israel in the Jewish cemetery in Prague.

It is widely believed, but has never been conclusively proven, that *Protocols* was cobbled together by the Okhrana, the Russian secret police. The figure who organized the literary forgery was said to be Pyotr Rachkovsky, head of the foreign branch of the Okhrana in Paris. He evidently hoped to use the book to channel citizens' anger away from the Tsarist government and onto the Jews, traditional Russian scapegoats and frequent victims of vicious pogroms.

The same year the *London Times* ran their exposé, Herman Bernstein, a reporter for the *New York Herald* published a book called *The History of a Lie: The Protocols of the Wise Men of Zion*. Bernstein's book revealed the truth about the *Protocols* for an American audience.

These exposés did have some impact. In 1927, Henry Ford apologized for publishing the *Protocols*. He admitted the book was a forgery and gave instructions to burn remaining copies of *The International Jew*. He also told overseas publishers to stop printing the book.

Needless to say, anti-Semites weren't troubled by the *Protocols'* fraudulent origins. The book was well received by the fledgling Nazi movement in Germany. In fact, between 1920 and 1939, the Nazis published almost two dozen editions of the *Protocols*. Adolf Hitler cited the *Protocols* approvingly in his turgid memoir *Mein Kampf*. Nazi "philosopher" Alfred Rosenberg penned a scurrilous tome called *The Protocols of the Elders of Zion and Jewish World Policy*.

Not everyone was as enamored with the book as the Nazis, however. In Berne, Switzerland, in 1935, two Nazi activists were taken to court for distributing a German-language version of the *Protocols*. According to the United States Holocaust Memorial Museum, Judge Walter Meyer dismissed the *Protocols* as "obvious forgeries" and "ridiculous nonsense." He also fined the two Nazis for good measure.

Nonsensical as it might be, the book continued to reach a wide audience. In 1938, Father Charles E. Coughlin, the anti-Semitic U.S. "radio priest," published the *Protocols* in his newspaper, *Social Justice*.

Shortly after the turn of the millennium, the *Protocols* showed up on TV. In 2002, the government of Egypt sponsored a 41-part televised mini-series based on the *Protocols*, called *Horseman Without a Horse*. A year later, a 30-part mini-series called *Al Shatat* (The Diaspora) aired in Syria, warning viewers of the kind of Jewish global takeover plan outlined in the *Protocols*. In 2004, *Protocols* was published in Japan, and in 2005, an edition published in Syria blamed the Jews for the terror attacks of 9/11.

Given the hundred-year persistence of the hoax, it seems highly likely that the *Protocols* will remain in circulation, continuing to inspire bigots everywhere with fanciful tales of graveyard meetings and nefarious plots by sinister Jews to control the world.

Further Reading

Anti-Defamation League, "A Hoax of Hate: The Protocols of the Learned Elders of Zion," October 23, 2012.
Walter Laqueur, *Fascism: Past, Present, Future*, 1996.

Martin A. Lee, *The Beast Reawakens*, 1997.

The Museum of Hoaxes, "The Protocols of the Elders of Zion, 1903," http://hoaxes.org /archive/permalink/the_protocols_of_the_elders_of_zion.

"The 'Protocols' at 100: A Hoax of Hate Lives On," *New York Sun*, November 18, 2005.

United States Holocaust Memorial Museum, "Protocols of the Elders of Zion," last updated June 10, 2013, http://www.ushmm.org/wlc/en/article.php?ModuleId=10007058.

THE *WAR OF THE WORLDS* BROADCAST

On October 30, 1938, CBS radio hosted an adaptation of H. G. Wells' science-fiction novel *The War of the Worlds* that was so realistic, the entire nation was supposedly thrown into panic. According to newspaper accounts, millions of people fled their homes to escape the marauding Martians, who were supposedly tearing up the eastern seaboard with "death rays" and poison gas. The broadcast was produced and narrated by Orson Welles, in grim "you are there" fashion.

Even today, decades after the broadcast, the memory of mass hysteria lingers. An October 28, 2013, article in online journal Slate pointed to a PBS *American Experience* episode and a National Public Radio broadcast that both cited the widespread panic stirred up by the broadcast.

"There's only one problem," the Slate article continued: "the supposed panic was so tiny as to be practically immeasurable on the night of the broadcast. Despite repeated assertions to the contrary in the PBS and NPR programs, almost nobody was fooled by Welles's broadcast."

The novel *The War of the Worlds* is set in late Victorian-era England. Creatures from Mars land on Earth and go on a genocidal rampage that ends only when they succumb to common terrestrial germs. It's a great story and one of the first prominent science-fiction novels ever published.

The Mercury Theatre on Air, a group of radio actors led by Welles, decided to update the story and transplant it to the United States. A clever decision was made to introduce the show in the form of breathless "newsflashes." These "flashes" interrupted regular broadcasting, informing listeners that a giant meteor had slammed into the earth near New Jersey. The flashes became more frequent and agitated as the radio reporter realized the meteor was actually a spaceship containing mayhem-minded aliens. Various Mercury actors pretended to be terrified civilians, being interviewed about the horror unveiling in New Jersey. To heighten the sense of realism, *The War of the Worlds* was broadcast without commercials or announcements that what listeners were hearing was make-believe.

If newspaper accounts are anything to go by, the broadcast panicked a nation. The *Daily News* ran a huge October 31, 1938, front-page headline: "Fake Radio 'War' Stirs Terror Through U.S." That same day, the *New York Times* ran a piece headlined, "Radio Listeners in Panic, Taking War Drama as Fact—Many Flee Homes to Escape 'Gas Raid from Mars.'"

The *Times* article stated, "A wave of hysteria seized thousands of radio listeners between 8:15 and 9:30 o'clock last night when a broadcast of a dramatization of H. G. Wells's fantasy, *The War of the Worlds*, led thousands to believe that an interplanetary conflict had started with invading Martians spreading wide death and destruction in New Jersey and New York ... the broadcast, which disrupted households, interrupted religious services, created traffic jams and clogged communications systems, was made by Orson Welles, who as the radio character, 'The Shadow' used to give 'the creeps' to countless child listeners. This time at least a score of adults required medical treatment for shock and hysteria."

Listener statistics, however, simply don't bear out the claims of mass hysteria. For a start, far fewer people actually heard the broadcast than is popularly thought; the play didn't air in Boston, for example. The C. E. Hooper ratings service called 5,000 households on October 30, 1938, to find out what radio programs people were listening to. A mere two percent of respondents said they were tuned into a radio play or the Orson Welles broadcast. In other words, the radio play had very low ratings.

No matter: the newspapers insisted that millions had listened and the nation was on the edge of hysteria. As Slate.com reported, "From these initial newspaper items on October 31, 1938, the apocryphal apocalypse only grew in the retelling. A curious (but predictable) phenomenon occurred: as the show receded in time and became more infamous, more and more people claimed to have heard it. As weeks, months and years passed, the audience's size swelled to such an extent that you might actually believe most of America was tuned into CBS that night. But that was hardly the case."

A couple of years after the broadcast, researcher Hadley Cantril of Princeton University's Office of Radio Research released a book containing many distortions and misleading facts about the broadcast. Cantril derived much of his information from a dubious report put together six weeks after the Welles broadcast by the American Institute of Public Opinion. The latter claimed that roughly a million people had been "frightened" by the broadcast. In Cantril's work and subsequent retellings of the story, vague descriptors such as "frightened" were conflated with more grabbing terms like "mass panic" and hysteria.

One of the pieces of folklore repeated by the newspaper press was the notion that New York City hospitals were packed with panicked patients seeking treatment for shock after the broadcast. Researchers under Cantril's auspices investigated, and couldn't turn up a single case of anyone admitted to hospital in New York City for hysteria related specifically to the broadcast. In a similar manner, newspaper coverage referred to (unnamed) individuals who almost committed suicide because of the radio play but were saved at the last minute by friends or family. Not a single suicide, however, was ever connected directly to the broadcast.

In retrospect, something else should have alerted the public that the "panic" was largely fictitious. If millions of people had indeed gone temporarily insane with fear over a radio broadcast, you might expect the media to cover the issue for weeks or months. Nothing of the kind happened. *The War of the Worlds* "panic" story played out for a couple days in the newspapers then was dropped.

According to Slate.com, the whole notion of mass hysteria was created out of whole cloth by newspaper bosses, as a way to slam their media rival, radio. As Slate.com observes, "Radio had siphoned off advertising revenue from print during the Depression, badly damaging the newspaper industry. So the papers seized the opportunity presented by Welles' program to discredit radio as a source of news. The newspaper industry sensationalized the panic to prove to advertisers and regulators that radio management was irresponsible and not to be trusted."

In fact, Welles wasn't disciplined in any serious sense for creating the broadcast—whereas if real hysteria had reigned, his employers would have fired him. The only real development from the broadcast was an informal agreement between the Federal Communications Commission and radio networks not to use fake "newsflashes" to dramatize future radio plays.

Other factors have arguably contributed to the longevity of the "mass panic" legend. It helped that the story suited the tenor of the times. In late 1938, Nazi Germany was saber-rattling in Europe, threatening war over Czechoslovakia, so the public was allegedly on edge already and ripe for a panic. And, as Slate noted, the alleged listenership for the show ballooned over the years, as people recalled the lurid newspaper stories and falsely remembered hearing the actual broadcast.

The great Martian invasion panic also fits in neatly with the notion that mass media is duplicitous and not to be trusted. Citing the book *Haunted Media* by Jeffrey Sconce, Slate.com noted, "To Sconce, the panic plays a 'symbolic function' for American culture—we retell the story because we need a cautionary tale about the power of the media."

Further Reading

Donna Halper, "How to Be a Skeptical News Consumer," *Skeptic Magazine*, volume 14, number 4, 2012.

Sharon Hill, "Of Martians and Media," *Skeptic Magazine*, volume 18, number 3, 2013.

Alison Hudson, Skeptoid.com podcast, Skeptoid # 438, "The War of the Worlds Panic Broadcast," October 28, 2014, http://skeptoid.com/episodes/4438.

Jefferson Pooley and Michael Socolow, Slate.com, "The Myth of the War of the Worlds Panic," October 28, 2013, http://www.slate.com/articles/arts/history/2013/10/orson_welles_war_of_the_worlds_panic_myth_the_infamous_radio_broadcast_did.html.

"Radio Listeners in Panic, Taking War Drama as Fact," *New York Times*, October 31, 1938.

SECTION SIX

DUBIOUS REMEDIES

INTRODUCTION

There are two different kinds of people who promote dubious medical remedies. There are confidence artists for whom selling "snake oil" medicine is just another scam. Such scammers will knowingly sell useless treatments to dying patients for profit. Then, there are the off-beat would-be medical authorities who genuinely think they've come up with a fantastic breakthrough in the treatment of disease or injury. People in the second category often claim that their miracle medicine is being suppressed by a cabal of mainstream doctors, politicians, and pharmaceutical giants. Sadly, what both types of promoters have in common is the ability to convince seriously ill patients to switch from conventional treatment to remedies of questionable curative value.

DRUGS

Patent Medicines

Back in the late nineteenth century, "patent medicines"—compounds of dubious medical merit, sold as cure-alls for vague ailments—abounded. Some of these medicines were "soothing syrups" designed to quiet crying babies. Other concoctions promised relief from stomach ache, diarrhea, "female problems," and bad coughs.

These patent medicines had cheerful names, such as Ayer's Cherry Pectoral, Mrs. Winslow's Soothing Syrup, Darby's Carminative, Godfrey's Cordial, Dover's Powder, etc. Many of these concoctions contained a heavy dose of alcohol, opium, or cocaine. Ingredients were not listed on the labels, so consumers had no idea what they were taking. Godfrey's Cordial, for example, contained molasses, sassafras, and opium.

Patent medicines were heavily advertised in newspapers, in magazines, and on billboards. They were as common as drugs such as aspirin and cough syrup are today. "Medicine shows"—carnival-like events that were part circus, part medical demonstration—were popular, especially in the rugged West. These shows alternated musical acts, magicians, and dancers with pitchmen for various patent medicines.

In some ways, the popularity of patent medicines was simply a reflection of the times. In the decades immediately following the Civil War, the medical and pharmaceutical industries were largely unregulated. Drugs that are illegal today could be legally purchased in pharmacies, at grocery outlets and general stores, and by mail. Opium poppies, used to make morphine, were grown openly in the United States, and doctors freely prescribed opiate-based drugs, such as laudanum, which consisted of opium in an alcohol solution.

According to the *Consumers Union Report on Licit and Illicit Drugs*, "A survey of 10,000 prescriptions filled by 35 Boston drugstores in 1888 revealed that 1,481 of them contained opiates. Among prescriptions refilled three or more times, 78 percent contained opiates."

Physicians referred to morphine as "GOM"—"God's own medicine." At the time, opiate drugs in particular did seem somewhat miraculous. While the primitive medical systems of the day could do little to treat or cure ailments like cancer, tuberculosis, diabetes, Cholera, etc., opiate-based drugs could at least keep a patient pain-free and happy. Laudanum in particular was hailed as a wonder drug for its ability to ease the intense pain of childbirth.

Cocaine-laced products were also fashionable in the late 1800s. A popular beverage called Vin Mariani (named after the chemist who made it) consisted of a mixture of wine and cocaine. This so-called "tonic wine" was popular with Pope Leo VIII and Queen Victoria. The success of this wine influenced the launch of Coca-Cola, a soft drink that originally contained coca leaves, according to the *Consumers Union Report on Licit and Illicit Drugs*.

The problem with patent medicines, however, was that they were unlabeled. People who would never consider purchasing opium, laudanum, or cocaine for recreational purposes were often imbibing these very drugs in their "medicines." Worse, some drug-laden patent medicines were pitched as soothing elixirs for teething infants or children with colic. As a result, many people became inadvertently addicted. By the turn of the twentieth century, about three people in 1,000 in the U.S. were drug addicts, according to the book *Drug Crazy* by Mike Gray. The medical profession and media became increasingly alarmed by the dangers posed by drugs, particularly in the form of unlabeled patent medicines.

In 1905, *Collier's* magazine ran a famous exposé on patent medicines, pointing out the harmful and addictive nature of many of these products. The U.S. Congress responded one year later with the Pure Food and Drug Act. The Act required medicine manufacturers to clearly label their products when they contained opiates and other powerful drugs. Needless to say, patent medicine interests strongly opposed the Pure Food and Drug Act of 1906. They had good reason to: sales of patent medicines crashed when consumers realized what was actually in them.

Some of the drugs used in patent medicines had legitimate medical uses. Opiates especially are still widely used today to provide relief from pain. The issue surrounding patent medicines wasn't about medical efficacy, however, but rather about lack of disclosure of ingredients, some of which were dangerously addictive. In this manner, the fight against patent medicines was a clear victory for consumer rights. Under the Pure Food and Drug Act, manufacturers and purveyors of patent medicines could no longer simply shrug when asked what their magic elixirs were made of.

Reefer Madness

Following the successful battle against patent medicine, politicians and activists turned their attention to recreational drugs, largely legal at the turn of the twentieth century. This anti-drug movement was motivated by health concerns and base racism—namely, the fear that certain substances drove people of color insane.

Newspaper headlines tell the story: "Drug Crazed Negroes Start a Reign of Terror and Defy Whole Mississippi Town," read a September 29, 1913, piece in the *New York Times*. Another story, from February 8, 1914, was tagged, "Negro Cocaine 'Fiends' Are a New Southern Menace." An April 30, 1905, *Times* article, with the headline "Cocaine Habit's Horrors," claimed that, "In the south, some of the worst crimes committed by the negroes result from the use of cocaine."

Needless to say, many of these accounts were highly exaggerated or outright hoaxes. Underlying all of these tales was the terrifying notion of "uppity" blacks standing up to white people. Similar stories abounded about sinister Asians and their fondness for opium. A March 15, 1906, article in the *New York Times* headlined, "Patent Medicine Bill to Curb Drug Users" stated, "of the 250 white girls, some no more than 14 years old, now living in Chinatown, New York, 60 percent were cocaine and opium fiends."

Blacks and Asians alike were accused of using hard drugs to seduce unwitting white girls. Society began to swing from having a laissez-faire attitude toward narcotics to extreme abhorrence.

Racist fears—combined with international treaty obligations—propelled the U.S. Congress to approve the Harrison Narcotics Tax Act on December 17, 1914. The Act came into force on March 1, 1915. While ostensibly a revenue bill, the Act had the effect of banning non-medical use of opiate drugs and cocaine.

In 1924, it became illegal to import heroin (essentially a stronger version of morphine), even for medical reasons. The law was passed following hysterical media accounts about evil "pushers" spiking ice cream cones with heroin in an effort to get children addicted. This was almost certainly another hoax, given the lack of verifiable cases, but people at the time believed such stories.

Similarly lurid accounts about the dangers of marijuana were standard fare in newspapers throughout the 1920s and 1930s. Marijuana was said to be the intoxicant of choice among Mexican migrants, who lost their minds when they smoked it and terrorized white people. Caucasians who used pot were depicted as degenerate bohemians.

By the mid-1930s, most U.S. states had banned the sale and possession of pot. Marijuana was still technically legal under federal law, however. Harry Anslinger, Commissioner of the Federal Bureau of Narcotics, was determined to rectify this situation. Anslinger helped pen a wildly inaccurate article called "Marijuana: Assassin of Youth" for *American Magazine*, published in July 1937.

One choice paragraph from the article recounted how "An entire family was murdered by a youthful [marijuana] addict in Florida. When officers arrived at the home, they found the youth staggering about in a human slaughterhouse. With an ax, he had killed his father, mother, two brothers and a sister."

Anslinger repeated this tale during testimony before a U.S. Congressional committee. He neglected to mention that the young man in question, one Victor Licata, had been diagnosed as severely mentally ill before he'd ever tried marijuana. For good measure, Anslinger also cited a case where two Chicago boys allegedly murdered a policeman while stoned on pot. The accounts might have been based on real cases, but the role played by marijuana was grossly exaggerated.

The result of such lobbying was the passage of the federal Marijuana Tax Act of 1937. Modeled after the Harrison Narcotics Tax Act, this federal legislation imposed a tax for medical use of pot and banned non-medical, non-taxed use of the drug. While theoretically permitting medical use, the Tax Act was actually used as a bludgeon against all marijuana consumption.

Thanks to harsh laws and societal disapproval, illegal drug use remained uncommon until the mid-1960s, when young people began experimenting with marijuana and LSD en masse. The explosion in youthful drug use also caused an ancillary birth of bizarre drug fables, couched as warnings.

In 1967, for example, newspapers began running cautionary tales about four college students in California who took the powerful hallucinogen LSD, then stared at the sun until they had inflicted permanent damage on their eyes. "The students, all males, suffered damage to the retina, the sensory membrane which receives the image formed by the lens," read an account in the May 18, 1967, *Los Angeles Times*.

While the *Times* report cited the source of this horrific account (supposedly the Santa Barbara Ophthalmological Society), it failed to offer the names of any of the supposed victims. Likewise, no doctors are named, and even the journalist who wrote the piece wasn't identified. (In place of a byline, the story is tagged, rather vaguely, as "exclusive to the *Times* from a staff writer.") The article was reprinted widely by the Associated Press, even though it was almost certainly a hoax.

Another AP dispatch, published by the *Los Angeles Times* on January 13, 1968, moved the action to a western Pennsylvania college, boosted the number of sun-dazzled students to six, and named a source. The source was Norman Yoder, commissioner of the Office of the Blind in the Pennsylvania State Welfare Department. Yoder apparently made the whole story up, to scare kids away from LSD. The February 19, 1968, *New York Times* reported that Yoder was removed from his position when his lie was revealed.

1971 marked the publication of *Go Ask Alice*, one of the most famous anti-drug books ever published. The hard-hitting book was allegedly based on the true-life story of a confused and rebellious teenage girl (who goes unnamed in the book). The title of the book referenced the song "White Rabbit" by the Jefferson Airplane—an ode to altered consciousness.

Go Ask Alice supposedly detailed events taking place from 1968 to 1970, in various U.S. states. At the start of the book, the anonymous diarist claims to be 15 years old. The teenage narrator is initiated into youth drug culture by unwittingly sampling a glass of soda at a party that has been spiked with LSD. The troubled girl goes on to try other drugs and is soon selling illegal narcotics for a college-age boyfriend. The diarist goes to San Francisco, where she works in a jewelry store and gets stoned in her spare time. In due course, the teenage girl at the center of the book is given heroin and raped. The girl returns to her family and tries to stay clean but is scorned by her former friends, who are all still happily taking drugs. The diarist falls off the wagon and starts consuming drugs again herself, becomes a homeless prostitute at one point, and is committed to an asylum. While the book ends on a chipper note, with the narrator returning to school and trying to avoid drugs, a postscript sadly notes that she overdosed and died within weeks of her final diary entry.

Over the years, many critics have doubted the legitimacy of *Go Ask Alice*. A November 15, 1998, *New York Times* essay on anti-drug novels aimed at young people criticized *Alice*'s pseudo-teenage tone. The author had "a tin ear for adolescent dialogue," stated the essay, which also described the book as "poorly written" and laughable. Nonetheless, *Go Ask Alice* was a huge hit, selling millions of copies and inspiring a TV movie-of-the-week.

In a 1979 essay published in the *School Library Journal*, writer Alleen Pace Nilsen revealed that *Go Ask Alice* had actually been penned by a grown woman named Beatrice Sparks. Sparks had apparently moved from southern California to Utah in the late 1960s and was horrified at how ignorant most parents were about drugs at the time. Sparks had apparently worked in a California drug treatment clinic, though "she was vague about specifics," wrote Nilsen. Sparks took it upon herself to educate her peers, becoming a drug expert and frequent lecturer.

During her lectures, Sparks cited the need for communication between adults and young people, and promised to offer a sympathetic ear to youths with drug habits. After giving a talk at a youth conference, Sparks would later claim she was awoken in the middle of the night by a drug counselor. The counselor had been at the convention and was trying to deal with a high, hysterical girl who refused to go home and insisted on speaking to Sparks. The girl was named Alice, and her family lived in California. Sparks met with the girl and calmed her down. The pair soon became friends. Alice's parents encouraged the friendship because they were concerned about their daughter's illicit drug use.

During a visit, Alice revealed she kept a diary. She presented Sparks with two written diaries and various scraps of paper detailing her recent experiences with illegal drugs. Alice didn't want to leave her diaries and notes at home, for fear her parents might find and read them. Instead of destroying the documents, Alice gave them to Sparks, to give her adult friend a first-person account of addiction. Half a year after receiving the diaries, Sparks was informed that Alice had died. Sparks says she decided to use the girl's memoirs as the basis of a book warning kids about drugs.

"The question of how much of *Go Ask Alice* was written by the real Alice and how much by Beatrice Sparks can only be conjectured," wrote the *School Library Journal*. The real diaries at the center of the book were being kept under lock and key by Sparks' publisher, noted the *Journal*. On top of this, Sparks claimed to have foolishly discarded the musings Alice put down on scrap paper after transcribing their contents.

Sparks herself admitted to changing names, locations, and any other details that mighty identify the true author. The real Alice, for example, didn't actually die of a drug overdose. (Her actual cause of death goes unmentioned in the *School Library Journal* essay.)

Sparks went on to pen other similar cautionary tales for young people, including *Jay's Journal*, another allegedly true account of a boy who became involved in the occult and committed suicide. Sparks died in 2012.

Today, *Go Ask Alice* remains widely popular. It was published in a reprint edition by Simon Pulse, an imprint of prestigious book publisher Simon & Schuster, in 2005. As of October 2015, this reprint edition was ranked as a number-one best seller on Amazon.com in the category of books on drug and alcohol abuse for teens. Tellingly, both Simon Pulse and Amazon.com list the book as a work of fiction.

The 1980s saw a drug panic about "crack babies"—the offspring of mothers addicted to crack cocaine, a highly potent, cheap, smokeable form of the drug. In March 1986, for example, *Newsweek* magazine ran a cover story on "Kids and Cocaine: An Epidemic Strikes Middle America." On July 30, 1989, conservative columnist Charles Krauthammer published a column in the *Washington Post* in which he described crack babies as "a bio-underclass whose biological inferiority is stamped at birth."

Like fears of "cocaine-crazed negroes," the crack baby epidemic was focused on black people. While powder cocaine tended to be the expensive preserve of wealthy white people, inexpensive crack was mostly consumed and sold by African Americans.

Objective researchers soon realized that the low-income mothers who birthed "crack babies" also tended to have terrible eating habits, inadequate healthcare, non-existent pre-natal care, and a predilection for cigarettes, alcohol, and other drugs beyond cocaine. In other words, taking crack was just one of a series of pathologies among lower-income women that were potentially damaging to infants.

Krauthammer's ominous prediction never bore fruit: while toxic, the crack cocaine epidemic of the 1980s did not produce an entire generation of brain-dead children. More than anything, it pointed to the need for adequate, affordable drug treatment options for addicted mothers. Needless to say, the crack baby hoax—like earlier media accounts of "cocaine-crazed negroes"—did little to improve race relations in the United States.

While there's wide agreement on the dangers drugs pose to children, repeating unfounded anecdotes and inaccurate sources diminishes credibility. Anti-drug education is best served when supported by facts, not myths, hoaxes, and lies.

Further Reading

Samuel Hopkins Adams, *The Great American Fraud* (collected articles reprinted from *Collier's Weekly*), 1906.

Dan Baum, *Smoke and Mirrors*, 1996.

Edward Brecher and the Editors of Consumer Reports Magazine, *Consumer Reports Magazine*, "The Consumers Union Report—Licit and Illicit Drugs," 1972.

"Cocaine Habit's Horrors," *New York Times*, April 30, 1905.

"A Fortnight Under the Pure Food Law," *New York Times*, January 13, 1907.

"Four LSD Users Suffer Serious Eye Damage," May 18, 1967, *Los Angeles Times*.

Mike Gray, *Drug Crazy*, 1998.

Nate Hendley, *American Gangsters, Then and Now*, 2010.

Nate Hendley, *The Mafia: A Guide to an American Subculture,* 2013.

Charles Krauthammer, "Children of Cocaine," *Washington Post*, July 30, 1989.

Suzette Laboy, "Man Who Chewed on Other's Face Not on 'Bath Salts,'" Yahoo.com, June 28, 2012, https://nz.finance.yahoo.com/news/man-chewed-others-face-not-bath-salts-084801314.html.

Joe Nickell, Center for Inquiry blog, "'Dr.' McLean's Nostrums," February 8, 2013, http://www.centerforinquiry.net/blogs/entry/dr._mcleans_nostrums/.

Joe Nickell, Center for Inquiry blog, "Dr. Porter and His Healing Oil," August 12, 2013, http://www.centerforinquiry.net/blogs/entry/dr._porter_and_his_healing_oil/.

Joe Nickell, "Snake Oil: A Guide for Connoisseurs," *Skeptical Inquirer*, September 2006.

Alleen Pace Nilsen, "*Go Ask Alice* Lit Crit—The House That Alice Built," *School Library Journal*, October 1979.

"Official Will Be Removed for LSD Blindness Hoax," *New York Times*, February 19, 1968.

Mark Oppenheimer, "Just Say 'Uh-Oh,'" *New York Times*, November 15, 1998.

"Patent Medicine Bill to Curb Drug Users," *New York Times*, March 15, 1906.

"Six College Men Take LSD, Blinded by Sun," *Los Angeles Times*, January 13, 1968.

"Slaves to the Cocaine Habit," *New York Times*, May 26, 1886.

"10 Dead, 20 Hurt in a Race Riot—Drug-Crazed Negroes Start a Reign of Terror and Defy Whole Mississippi Town," *New York Times*, September 29, 1913.

Edward Huntington Williams, "Negro Cocaine 'Fiends' Are a New Southern Menace," *New York Times*, February 8, 1914.

CURIOUS CANCER CURES

The lethal nature of cancer has inspired countless "cures" and remedies of dubious value—understandable, given that until recently a diagnosis of cancer was tantamount to a death sentence. While many forms of cancers are treatable today, the therapies and medicines used to combat cancer are often excruciatingly unpleasant.

"Cancer patients are a uniquely vulnerable group. When patients are diagnosed with pneumonia or appendicitis, they expect to recover and they readily accept conventional treatment with antibiotics or surgery. They are not particularly vulnerable to false claims for other treatments. But when patients are diagnosed with cancer, they fear dying; and they fear it will be a slow, painful death. They fear that the treatment itself will add to their suffering—the so-called 'cutting, burning and poisoning' of surgery, radiation and chemotherapy," according to a 2012 article in *Skeptic Magazine*.

Sham cancer "cures" over the decades have included Gerson Therapy, the Hoxsey Treatment, Laetrile, and shark cartilage. A century ago, a fake cancer treatment led to the first federal laws prohibiting false medical claims about new drugs. The cure in question was called Dr. Johnson's Mild Combination Treatment for Cancer. Dr. Johnson's Treatment was promoted through a 125-page book of patient testimonials, all claiming miraculous recoveries from cancer.

Regarding Dr. Johnson's Treatment, an article in the July/August 1977 issue of the *FDA Consumer* explained, "In 1910, the Bureau of Chemistry (now the Food and Drug Administration) attempted to prosecute this product's promoter. At the time everyone thought that the new Food and Drugs Act of 1906 would do away with the thousands of worthless and dangerous 'patent medicines' then on the market. Millions of people were harmed as well as swindled, but the Supreme Court ruled in the Johnson case that the law did not prohibit false 'therapeutic' claims on drug labels but only false statements about the identify or composition of drugs."

President William Howard Taft was outraged and requested action from the U.S. Congress. The latter replied by passing the Sherley Amendment of 1912, which "made it a crime to label drugs with false and fraudulent claims of therapeutic effectiveness," according to the *FDA Consumer.*

This didn't prove to be the end of things, however; thanks to inclusion of the term "and fraudulent," federal authorities found it difficult to prosecute quack medicine promoters. Under the terms of the law, authorities had to prove that the promoters deliberately intended to con the people who purchased these medicines.

As a result, in 1938, Congress passed another law, which stipulated that new drugs had to be accompanied by scientific proof of safety before they could be sold. Even stronger controls were imposed in 1962, stating that drug-makers also had to provide proof of effectiveness before releasing new products.

In spite of these laws, unconventional health advocates continued to promote quack cancer treatments. Some of these advocates genuinely believed their treatments cured cancer. Other promoters were simply old-fashioned "snake oil" salesmen working a new scam.

In the 1930s and 1940s, Gerson Therapy became popular. This was a supposed cancer treatment based on diet and nutrients. The therapy was named after Max Gerson, a German physician who emigrated to the United States in 1938. After passing the New York State Medical Board examinations, Dr. Gerson opened a medical practice in New York City.

Back in his homeland, Dr. Gerson had suffered from migraine headaches. To treat these headaches, he switched to a vegetarian diet. This apparently healed the physician of what ailed him. Dr. Gerson became intrigued by the potential posed by healthy diet and vitamins in the treatment of disease.

As developed by the doctor, Gerson Therapy involved eating an organic vegetarian diet, plus nutritional supplements and pancreatic enzymes. Patients also had to endure regular coffee enemas. The concept was intended to "detox-ify" the body of bad elements while strengthening the immune system and boosting potassium levels in cells.

Information from the National Cancer Institute (NCI), part of the Depart-ment of Health and Human Services, stated, "The Gerson therapy is rooted in the belief that cancer is a disease of the whole organism, the tumor being only a symptom of a diseased body. Gerson considered cancer to be an accumula-tion of several damaging factors that combine to cause the deterioration of the entire metabolic system. The goal of the Gerson therapy is to bring the body back to its normal metabolic state or as near to this state as possible and to keep the metabolism in natural equilibrium."

"Total control of everything that enters and leaves the body is the governing principle of the Gerson regimen. Its three main components are strict diet, nutritional supplements and regular enemas," added NCI.

For six weeks, persons undergoing Gerson Therapy ate nothing but raw or stewed vegetables or fruits, and drank fruit and/or vegetable juice every hour for 13 hours while awake. Any food consumed could only be made in cast-iron pots and pans. Aluminum cookware was specifically prohibited. If possible, all food had to be organically grown—that is, produced from soil that bore no pesticides or chemical fertilizer. Patients also needed to take lots of vitamins and supplements, including Vitamins A, C, and B3 (niacin), along with flax seed oil, pepsin, and others.

Coffee enemas were possibly the most bizarre element of Gerson Therapy. "Coffee enemas supposedly dilate the bile duct in the liver, thereby allowing the liver to release the breakdown products more easily and speed their removal to the intestine. At the beginning of therapy, a patient may take four or more coffee enemas a day," explained NCI information.

Gerson Therapy raised eyebrows—and concerns—in mainstream medical circles. In 1946, and then again in 1949, articles appeared in the *Journal of the American Medical Association* stating that Gerson Therapy was useless as a can-cer treatment. Around the same time, the NCI reviewed data derived from the histories of patients treated by Gerson Therapy. The NCI concluded that the histories didn't provide enough data for adequate evaluation of clinical benefits (a major red flag, as far as medical treatments go). In 1972, the American Can-cer Society (ACS) issued a statement citing negative aspects of Gerson Therapy.

The man at the center of these treatments didn't escape criticism either. Dr. Gerson's malpractice insurance was cancelled in 1953. In 1958, he was sus-pended from practicing for two years by the New York County Medical Society. The suspension outlived him, as Dr. Gerson died in 1959.

NCI information stated, "Because no prospective, controlled study of the use of the Gerson Therapy in cancer patients has been reported in a peer-reviewed scientific study, no level of evidence analysis is possible for this approach. The data that are available are not sufficient to warrant claims that the Gerson Therapy is effective as an adjuvant to other cancer therapies or as a cure." The term "adjuvant" refers to the use of drugs or medical treatments following cancer surgery.

The 1940s saw the rise of another dubious cancer treatment, touted by Dr. William F. Koch of Detroit. The doctor headed an organization called the Christian Medical Research League and claimed to have created a medicine of incredible potency. When analyzed, it was determined that the medicine was mostly distilled water, containing a hint of the chemical glyoxylide. Dr. Koch charged medical practitioners $25 for an ampule of his medicine, and they in turn marketed the medicine for as much as $300 for a single injection.

In 1943, Dr. Koch was taken to court by the FDA, who accused him of making false claims for his medicines and improperly labelling the ingredients. As far as the FDA was concerned, Dr. Koch was making medical claims for what amounted to distilled water. Over 40 expert witnesses testified that the doctor's medicine was useless for treating cancer or anything else. The prosecution was outgunned, however, by the defense, who called more than 100 witnesses of their own. These witnesses insisted that Dr. Koch's products could treat cancer and other ailments, including tuberculosis and coronary thrombosis. The jury deliberated for eight days but couldn't render a verdict.

Dr. Koch was put on trial again in 1946. This trial lasted for five months, but ended in a mistrial after a juror became ill. The doctor sensed the prevailing winds and retired to South America. Medical products based on his original "medicines" continued to be solid in Mexico long after they disappeared in the United States.

The "Hoxsey Treatment" was also the subject of U.S. government investigation and intervention. There were actually two different Hoxsey Treatments, one for internal use, the other for external.

"The herbal tonic for internal use contains a combination of supplements and herbs that may include pokeweed, burdock root, licorice, barberry, buckthorn bark, stillingia root, red clover, prickly ash bark, potassium iodide and cascara … the pastes or salves for external use may contain antimony trisulfide, zinc chloride and blood root and the powder consists of arsenic sulfide, sulphur and talc," stated the American Cancer Society. The external formula was highly caustic; it was supposed to be applied directly to tumors, with the idea of basically burning them off.

Harry Hoxsey, the man responsible for promoting the Hoxsey Treatment, claimed that his great-grandfather had developed the formula after observing a horse in a pasture. The horse apparently was cured of leg cancer after romping through the plants and bushes growing in the pasture. Hoxsey Sr. took note of the flora involved and supposedly created a cancer-cure medicine from their essences.

The formula was passed down from father to son but remained obscure until Harry Hoxsey decided to market the drug in a major way in the early 1920s. Hoxsey first opened a clinic in Taylorville, Illinois. In 1936, he set up a clinic in Dallas, Texas, that quickly grew to become one of the largest privately owned cancer treatment facilities in the world. At the height of his career, Hoxsey oversaw clinics in 17 states.

The July/August 1977 *FDA Consumer* article included a scathing account of how the Dallas clinic operated: "The Hoxsey Clinic offered a package deal consisting of a perfunctory examination by an osteopath and some routine blood and urine tests after which the patients were told they had cancer and the Hoxsey treatment was prescribed. This cost $400 and included a lifetime supply of the two medicines."

Through his clinics and some oil leases, Hoxsey became a wealthy man. Hoxsey attracted the wrath of Morris Fishbein, editor of the *Journal of the American Medical Association*. Fishbein, who famously hated quacks promoting dangerous or unproven treatments, went after Hoxsey. Hoxsey sued the *Journal* for libel and slander after the publication called him a fake. Hoxsey won his case but was awarded a total of one dollar in damages.

In 1956, the FDA issued public warnings about the Hoxsey Treatment that were displayed in U.S. post offices and substations. One year later, faculty members from the University of British Columbia reviewed the Hoxsey Treatment and the facilities selling it. Staff working for Hoxsey provided these researchers with 78 patient records. "The committee was able to follow-up on 71 of these patients, using British Columba's cancer registry, death registry and physician records," stated a report by the Office of Technology Assessment (OTA), a government body which existed from the early 1970s through the mid-1990s.

The UBC committee discovered that half the patients in the study group had either died or gotten considerably sicker following the Hoxsey Treatment. A quarter of patients showed no evidence of ever having cancer. The committee only found one case of someone with external cancer who might have benefited from the Hoxsey Treatment.

In 1960, after years of litigation by health authorities, sales of the Hoxsey Treatment were banned by a federal court injunction. The FDA estimated the public had spent over $50 million for worthless Hoxsey drugs.

The federal court injunction only applied to the United States, however. Starting in 1963, one of Hoxsey's longtime nurses, Mildred Nelson, began offering Hoxsey Treatment in a clinic based in Tijuana, Mexico. The clinic was called the Bio-Medical Center, one of countless facilities set up just across the Mexican border, offering banned treatments to American patients. Hoxsey himself developed prostate cancer in 1967.

"Available scientific evidence does not support claims that the Hoxsey herbal treatment is effective in treating cancer, and there have been no clinical trials of the treatment published in conventional medical journals," noted the American Cancer Society.

The 1950s saw the advent of Krebiozen, "an alleged investigational drug said to have been manufactured from the blood serum of horses inoculated with a mold that causes a disease known to veterinarians as 'lumpy jaw' ... unlike Hoxsey's backwoods herb remedy, Krebiozen had an aura of high scientific prestige. It was sponsored by Dr. Andrew C. Ivy of the University of Chicago, who had joined forces with Stephan and Marko Durovic, Yugoslav immigrants who said they discovered Krebiozen in Argentina," explained the *FDA Consumer*.

Dr. Ivy announced the drug at a press conference in 1951. His endorsement was severely criticized by fellow mainstream doctors but embraced by the public. A number of physicians did accept the drug—or sold it, at least, for $9 per ampule. In 1963, chemists for the FDA analyzed Krebiozen and discovered it was simply creatine monohydrate, an amino acid with zero cancer-fighting potential. Samples of injectable Krebiozen turned out to be nothing more than mineral oil.

Dr. Ivy, the Durovics, and the Krebiozen Research Foundation were indicted by a federal grand jury on 49 counts of fraud and conspiracy. A nine-month

Signs of Health Fraud

All consumers seeking information about any health product or medical treatment should be familiar with the following signs of health fraud:

- Statements that the product is a quick and effective cure-all or a diagnostic tool for a wide variety of ailments
- Suggestions that a product can treat or cure serious or incurable diseases
- Claims such as "scientific breakthrough," "miraculous cure," "secret ingredient," and "ancient remedy."
- Impressive-sounding terms, such as "hunger stimulation point" and "thermogenesis" for a weight-loss product
- Claims that the product is safe because it is "natural"
- Undocumented case histories or personal testimonials by consumers or doctors claiming amazing results
- Claims of limited availability and advance payment requirements
- Promises of no-risk, money-back guarantees
- Promises of an "easy" fix for problems like excess weight, hair loss, or impotency

Source: FDA Consumer Health Information, Beware of Online Cancer Fraud, http://www.fda.gov/ForConsumers/ConsumerUpdates/ucm048383.htm

jury trial ensued in federal court in Chicago. In the end, the defendants were found not guilty. The verdict didn't vindicate Krebiozen but, rather, was a reflection of the fact that the government couldn't prove deliberate fraud. Krebiozen remained unapproved and illegal to distribute.

Even if Dr. Ivy and the Durovics couldn't be successfully prosecuted, the federal trial took the bloom off the popularity of Krebiozen. Stephan Durovic went to Switzerland, where he had banked some of his share of Krebiozen profits. It was a good move, given that Marko Durovic found himself battling the Internal Revenue Service (IRS). Dr. Ivy continued to sell Krebiozen from his Chicago office, under the new brand name, Carcalon.

A committee consisting of two dozen cancer specialists, working for the NCI, reviewed 504 case histories provided by Dr. Ivy of patients treated with Krebiozen. Their unanimous conclusion was that the drug was an ineffectual cancer treatment.

Other quack cancer products that briefly flourished as popular treatments include Millrue, "a herbal extract with iron and vitamins, prescribed and dispensed by Roy Paxton, an Illinois healer who diagnosed all diseases by feeling the patient's feet. After serving a three-year sentence for violating the federal Food, Drug and Cosmetic Act, he became a director of the National Health Federation, which [advocated] quackery as 'freedom of choice' in health matters," reported the *FDA Consumer*.

The Rand Vaccine was also touted as a cancer cure. The drug was supplied for free by its manufacturer (largely in an attempt to boost the stock price of the company making the stuff). As it turned out, the "vaccine" was made from the blood of animals that had been dosed with medical gunk from human cancers gathered in hospital operating rooms. The Rand Vaccine was both toxic and prone to bacterial contamination. On February 7, 1967, at the behest of the FDA, a federal court ordered the vaccine makers to stop making and selling the substance.

"Laetrile," a supposed cancer cure derived from apricot pits, was both hugely popular and hugely controversial during its brief heyday in the 1970s. As an article in the March/April 1981 edition of *CA: A Cancer Journal for Clinicians* stated, "All prior forms of cancer quackery ... pale in comparison with the Laetrile crusade, unquestionably the slickest, most sophisticated, and certainly the most remunerative cancer quack promotion in medical history."

The alleged cancer-fighting agent in Laetrile is the chemical amygdalin, which is found in the pits of apricots and other fruits and nuts. In the 1920s, a San Francisco medical practitioner named Dr. Ernst Krebs Sr. somehow deduced that amygdalin could reduce tumors in rodents. It's unclear, however, how scientific his tests were. *CA* described Dr. Krebs Sr. as "an obscure general practitioner ... working in a home laboratory to find a method for improving the taste of bootleg whisky."

Dr. Krebs Sr. didn't try to capitalize on his apparent discovery. He concluded that in its initial pill form, amygdalin was too dangerous and unpredictable to be given to humans. Enter Ernst Krebs Jr. In the 1950s, Krebs Jr. claimed he had come up with a non-toxic, partly synthetic version of amygdalin, which he patented under the name "Laetrile."

Laetrile might have remained an obscure alternative medicine but for some astute promotion and marketing. "In 1970, Ernst Krebs Jr. announced that he had discovered the etiology of all forms of cancer. Cancer, he concluded, was a vitamin deficiency disease … according to Krebs Jr., the missing vitamin in cancer was Laetrile, which he called 'Vitamin B17,'" stated *CA*.

There was some clever thinking going on here. If Laetrile was considered a vitamin (i.e., a food), not a drug, it wouldn't have to pass through the strict testing protocols demanded by the U.S. government for new drugs on the market.

Proponents of the substance claimed that Laetrile, unlike traditional anti-cancer treatments such as chemotherapy, was universally safe. This was patently untrue: "Amygdalin contains six percent cyanide by weight. If all the cyanide of a single 500 mg dose of Laetrile were released, it would be a potentially lethal amount," wrote *CA*.

Fortunately, for various chemical reasons, the full load of cyanide is not released when Laetrile is consumed by humans. There remains some risk of cyanide poisoning, however, especially for people who take huge amounts of the stuff. Side-effects of Laetrile are similar to the symptoms of cyanide poisoning and can include nausea and vomiting, headache, dizziness, liver damage, abnormally low blood pressure, difficulty walking, fever, mental confusion, coma, and death, according to the NCI.

Because the FDA wouldn't approve Laetrile as a treatment for cancer in the United States, the drug was made primarily in Mexico. Quality and purity of the Laetrile doses varied enormously, with some samples containing dangerous bacteria, noted the NCI.

However, lack of FDA approval didn't slow the momentum of Laetrile supporters. "When it became apparent that Laetrile could not meet the federal standards of the Food and Drug Act, supporters developed an 'end-run' approach by promoting legalizing statutes within the states," stated *CA*. Alaska legalized Laetrile in the 1976–77 session. Thirteen more states legalized it in the 1977–78 session, followed by seven additional states a year later.

Laetrile supporters viewed the use of the substance as a matter of freedom of medical choice. The far-right John Birch Society took up the cause of Laetrile, as did natural health advocates. Laetrile supporters tapped into the distrustful, skeptical public mood of the 1970s, following the Watergate scandal and the debacle of the Vietnam War. Proponents couched their arguments for Laetrile in political terms, accusing "big government" of trying to stifle innovative health research.

Meanwhile, some Laetrile advocates became rich. Laetrile was cheaply manufactured, then sold for a dollar a tablet or $10 an ampule, in the 1970s. The *FDA Consumer* notes that "court records show that Dr. John A. Richardson, a California physician who was convicted of conspiring to smuggle Laetrile, charged $50 for a single injection of Laetrile and deposited more than $2.5 million in a single bank account between 1973 and 1976."

By 1978, the NCI estimated that over 70,000 Americans had tried Laetrile. But no scientific studies could find any evidence of cancer-fighting properties in Laetrile. *CA* reported, "In 23 different animal tumor models, Laetrile has consistently failed to demonstrate any reproducible benefit … where it has been feasible for independent analysts to study reports of nearly 200 human cases of Laetrile treatment, it has not been possible in a single instance to demonstrate any unequivocal anti-cancer benefit."

For its part, the NCI stated, "Although many anecdotal reports (incomplete descriptions of the medical/treatment history of one or more patients) and case studies (detailed reports of the diagnosis, treatment and follow-up of individual patients) are available, they provide little evidence to support Laetrile as a treatment for cancer."

Scientific studies blunted Laetrile's appeal. After its initial round of popularity, it largely receded from public view. It is still being promoted in some circles, however, as a cancer-fighting cure. On June 18, 2004, Jason Vale, president of Christian Brothers Contracting Corp., based in New York, was sentenced to 63 months in prison for selling Laetrile. Vale's sentence also included three years of parole.

"There is no scientific evidence that Laetrile offers anything but false hopes to cancer patients, some of whom have used it instead of conventional treatment until it was too late for that treatment to be effective. This sentence sends a strong message that we will not tolerate marketing of bogus medicines," stated Dr. Lester M. Crawford, Acting FDA Commissioner, in a June 23, 2004, FDA press release.

A well-known contemporary cancer treatment involves shark cartilage, cartilage being "the tough, flexible connective tissue that forms part of the skeleton in many animals," as the NCI explains. Popular belief has it that sharks, whose skeletal systems primarily consist of cartilage, do not suffer from cancer. The fact this is actually a myth (sharks do indeed get cancer, and more rarely, malignant tumors) hasn't diminished the popularity of shark cartilage in alternative medical circles.

"Cartilage does not contain blood vessels, so cancer cannot easily grow in it. It is suggested that a cancer treatment using cartilage may keep blood vessels from forming in a tumor, causing the tumor to stop growing or shrink," explained the NCI. Shark cartilage products can be eaten, injected into a vein, or applied to the skin.

As of mid-2013, there has only been one randomized clinical trial of cartilage as a cancer treatment that has been published in a peer-reviewed scientific journal, stated the NCI. The trial in question compared treatment with shark cartilage to treatment with a placebo.

"In 83 patients having either advanced breast or advanced colon cancer, there was no difference in the quality of life or survival rate between the group that received the shark cartilage product and the group that received the placebo," reported the NCI.

The FDA has not approved shark cartilage as a cancer treatment. As a result, shark cartilage products are often marketed as dietary supplements, which are considered food, not drugs, under U.S. regulatory law. Companies don't require FDA approval to sell dietary supplements, provided they don't make medical claims.

As the current popularity of shark cartilage proves, questionable cancer treatments continue to flourish today, much to the detriment of those with cancer. "What has been learned from the long fight against ineffective cancer treatments? … first and most important, no matter how harmless their ingredients, all such products are death traps for those whose cancers are curable by effective means," stated the *FDA Consumer*.

Further Reading

American Cancer Society, Hoxsey Treatment, http://documents.cancer.org/acs/groups/cid/documents/webcontent/002420-pdf.pdf.

Violante E. Currie, J. Paul Davignon, Thomas R. Fleming, Stephen E. Jones, Robert Koch, Larry K. Kvols, Charles G. Moertel, Joseph Rubin, Gregory Sarna, Charles W. Young, "A Clinical Trial of Amygdalin (Laetrile) in the Treatment of Human Cancer," *The New England Journal of Medicine,* January 28, 1982.

Food and Drug Administration website, "Beware of Online Cancer Fraud," June 17, 2008, http://www.fda.gov/ForConsumers/ConsumerUpdates/ucm048383.htm.

Food and Drug Administration, "New York Man Sentenced to 63 Months for Selling Fake Cancer Cure," June 23, 2004.

Food and Drug Administration poster, "Public Beware! Warning Against the Hoxsey Cancer Treatment," April 1956.

Harriett Hall, "CAM for Cancer—Preying on Desperate People," *Skeptic Magazine*, Volume 17, Number 4, 2012.

Wallace F. Janssen, "Cancer Quackery: Past and Present," *FDA Consumer*, July/August 1977.

Dr. Irving J. Lerner, "Laetrile: A Lesson in Cancer Quackery," *CA—A Cancer Journal for Clinicians*, March/April 1981.

Douglas Main, "Sharks Do Get Cancer: Tumor Found in Great White," Yahoo.com, December 5, 2013, https://ca.news.yahoo.com/sharks-cancer-tumor-found-great-white-142906847.html.

National Cancer Institute, Cartilage (Bovine and Shark) (PDQ), http://www.cancer.gov/about-cancer/treatment/cam/hp/cartilage-pdq.

National Cancer Institute, Complementary and Alternative Medicine (CAM), http://www.cancer.gov/about-cancer/treatment/cam.

National Cancer Institute, Gerson Therapy (PDQ), http://www.cancer.gov/about-cancer/treatment/cam/patient/gerson-pdq.

National Cancer Institute, Laetrile/Amygdalin (PDQ)—Patient Version, Last modified February 20, 2013, http://www.cancer.gov/about-cancer/treatment/cam/patient /laetrile-pdq/.

United States Congress, Office of Technology Assessment, "Unconventional Cancer Treatments," 1990, http://www.quackwatch.org/01QuackeryRelatedTopics/OTA/ota00 .html.

GOAT GONAD THERAPY

For a period of several years, "Doctor" John Brinkley grew rich and famous transplanting goat testicles into men's scrotums. The operations were designed to boost male virility and came with a hefty price tag that thousands of desperate men were happy to pay.

The surgeon doing the goat gonad transplants was one of the most astonishing characters in American medical history. In addition to growing wealthy performing operations of dubious merit, Dr. Brinkley helped develop the nascent radio industry and propel country music into the mainstream. He also ran for governor of Kansas three times and fought a decades-long battle with the *Journal of the American Medical Association*.

Dr. Brinkley was born on July 8, 1885, in Beta, North Carolina. At the time, Appalachia was very rural and very isolated. Brinkley's father, John Richard Brinkley, was a "country physician"—meaning he had little or no formal medical training. Brinkley was orphaned at age ten and raised by an aunt.

As a young man, Dr. Brinkley did a variety of jobs. He worked in a railroad telegraph office, then entered Bennett Medical College in Chicago. He failed to complete his studies at this unaccredited institution. No matter; Brinkley purchased a medical degree for $500 from the oddly named Eclectic Medical College in Kansas City, Missouri.

In 1918, Dr. Brinkley set up a practice in Milford, Kansas. That same year, he had a fortuitous visit from an area farmer. The man's name was Stittsworth, and he complained to Brinkley that his sex life was lacking. According to later accounts, Dr. Brinkley's mind flashed to billy goats, notoriously randy creatures. The doctor suggested facetiously that he give Swittsworth some goat gonads. The farmer apparently took the suggestion seriously and asked for a transplant. Dr. Brinkley took the man up on this offer. He found a suitable goat, removed its testicles, then transplanted pieces of these gonads into the farmer's scrotum.

Fortunately for Dr. Brinkley, the farmer didn't develop an infection and die. In fact, Stittsworth said the transplant revitalized his sex drive. As proof positive, his wife soon became pregnant after her husband's unorthodox surgery. A boy was born and given the name "Billy" for obvious reasons.

This initial successful operation led a parade of other men into the Brinkley clinic, seeking the same treatment. Dr. Brinkley charged $750 for a procedure (a hefty sum at the time) but had no shortage of takers. He began performing upwards of 100 surgeries a week, despite his rather shaky operating skills.

The notion of transplanting goat testicles into human scrotums wasn't quite as ridiculous as it might seem. As Dr. Brinkley knew, other men of medicine had experimented with the surgical transfer of animal parts into human bodies to boost virility. A French doctor named Serge Voronoff, working as a court physician to the King of Egypt, tried transplanting pieces of monkey testes into men's scrotums. The good doctor had apparently noted the high rate of illness among the court eunuchs and concluded that active genital glands were essential to male health. Dr. Voronoff claimed his surgeries boosted masculine sexual prowess, but offered no scientific evidence to back his claims up.

As Dr. Brinkley rose in prominence, mainstream medical authorities began taking note of his unusual surgical practice. Morris Fishbein, editor of the *Journal of the American Medical Association*, was particularly appalled. At the time, the AMA was working hard to establish standards and regulations for the medical profession and drive charlatans like Dr. Brinkley out of business.

To Fishbein, Dr. Brinkley was more than just a con artist taking advantage of clueless clients. He was a menace to public health, promoting a dangerous surgical procedure. According to *eSkeptic* (the e-mail newsletter of the Skeptics Society), at least 42 of Dr. Brinkley's patients died while in his hospital. Others survived the surgery but died at home. The operations were extremely risky, given the threat of infection and rejection, not to mention Dr. Brinkley's abysmal surgical skills. "His medical license was a license to kill," stated *eSkeptic*.

In 1923, Dr. Brinkley acquired a radio station in Milford, Kansas, called KFKB. He took to the airwaves, hosting a program called "Medical Question Box." The doctor would read aloud letters from people describing their symptoms and then offer advice. Dr. Brinkley would invariably recommend a quack remedy that he sold in local pharmacies.

Dr. Brinkley continued to perform goat testicle transplants. According to an estimate by Dr. Joe Schwarcz, writing for Quackwatch.org, the doctor performed over 16,000 of these surgeries throughout his career. His scamming knew no bounds. For a higher fee of $5,000 the doctor would transplant human gonads (removed from prisoners on death row) into his subjects.

Hugely wealthy, Dr. Brinkley lived large. He spent his money ostentatiously, on mansions, fancy cars, boats, and jewelry, much to the fury of Morris Fishbein.

After years of lobbying, Fishbein finally scored a major victory against the high-living doctor. In 1929, the AMA convinced the Kansas Board of Medical Registration to pull Brinkley's license, on the grounds of immorality and unprofessional conduct. One year later, the Federal Radio Commission closed KFKB for promoting fraud.

Never one to step back from a fight, Brinkley ran for governor of Kansas as a write-in candidate in the 1930 election. If he won the governorship, he could award himself a medical license again. Dr. Brinkley did reasonably well in the election (in some polls, he garnered 30 percent of voter support) but didn't win. Subsequent campaigns for governor in 1932 and 1934 were also unsuccessful.

Dr. Brinkley left Kansas and went to Del Rio, Texas. There, he set up a "border blasting" radio station just across the international border with Mexico. The station was called XERA and was licensed by the Mexican government for 300,000 watts, but could increase its power to 500,000 or even a million watts (unheard of at the time).

Once more, Dr. Brinkley used his radio station to promote fake medical concoctions (colored water in this case, passed off as powerful tonics). The doctor might have been unscrupulous, but he did have a good sense of what listeners wanted to hear. He realized that even his most devoted followers would soon tire of non-stop medical rants. As with station KFKB, he augmented his medical commentaries with country music. The soon to be world-famous Carter family got their start on XERA. The station gave national exposure to what was at the time obscure regional music and helped popularize the country genre.

If he had only concentrated on his radio career, Dr. Brinkley might have endured. But once again, he set up a clinic and began performing bogus surgeries. His focus had changed, from the scrotum to the prostate gland. He began performing prostate surgeries that were, once again, aimed at rejuvenating men's flagging sex lives. As before, the money rolled in. Dr. Brinkley lived large and again indulged in big homes, cars, and flashy living.

In the end, Dr. Brinkley's own ego brought about his downfall. After taunting the doctor for years in the pages of the AMA *Journal*, Morris Fishbein finally succeeded in goading Dr. Brinkley into suing him for libel. When Dr. Brinkley took the witness stand, his deplorable knowledge of medicine was at last made apparent. The trial revealed Brinkley as the quack he'd always been.

Thanks to this exposure, former patients of the doctor began suing him with great regularity. The XERA station was closed, and the IRS launched an investigation of Dr. Brinkley for back taxes.

Dr. Brinkley ended up going bankrupt in 1941. The doctor died on May 26, 1942, in San Antonio, Texas, and with him—hopefully forever—the notion that transplanted goat testicles can bring back a man's sexual vigor.

Further Reading

Mike Dash, "John Brinkley, The Goat-Gland Quack," *The Telegraph*, April 18, 2008.

DigitalHeritage.org, Dr. John Brinkley, http://digitalheritage.org/2010/08/dr-john-brinkly/.

Dr. Harriett Hall, *eSkeptic*, "Charlatan: Quackery Then and Now," July 9, 2008, http://www.skeptic.com/eskeptic/08-07-09/.

Kansas Historical Society, Kansapedia, John B. Brinkley, http://www.kshs.org/kansapedia/john-r-brinkley/11988.

Kansas Historical Society, KansasMemory.org, *After Twenty-One Years: The Success Story of Dr. John R. Brinkley* (archived version of booklet originally published by the Brinkley Hospitals of Little Rock, Arkansas), http://www.kansasmemory.org/item /213226.

Dr. Joe Schwarcz, Quackwatch.org, "The Goat Gland Doctor: The Story of John. R. Brinkley," http://www.quackwatch.org/11Ind/brinkley.html.

Michael Shermer, *eSkeptic*, "Faith Healing," March 27, 2008, http://www.skeptic.com /eskeptic/08-03-27/.

HEALTH CARE FRAUD

In February 2014, the Departments of Justice and Health and Human Services (HHS) issued a triumphant press release about their efforts to combat health care fraud. According to the press release, government investigators recovered a record $4.3 billion in fraudulent health spending in fiscal year 2013. This represented an increase from fiscal year 2012, when $4.2 billion was recovered.

"Over the last five years, the administration's enforcement efforts have recovered $19.2 billion, up from $9.4 billion over the prior five-year period," added the release.

Not everyone, however, was impressed with these results. An article in the May 31, 2014, edition of *The Economist* magazine, for example, described the $4.3 billion in recovered funds as "paltry" in the larger context of health care spending.

As *The Economist* pointed out, the U.S. government currently spends around $415 billion a year funding Medicaid (a government program to provide health services for the poor) and nearly $600 billion to fund Medicare (a health care program for the elderly). "Total health spending in America is a massive $2.7 trillion or 17 percent of GDP ... fraud (and the extra rules and inspections required to fight it) added as much as $98 billion or roughly 10 percent to annual Medicare and Medicaid spending—and up to $272 billion across the entire health system," wrote *The Economist*.

In light of these figures, the $4.3 billion in returned funds does seem rather paltry. Part of the problem is simply the massive size of the U.S. health care system. "The sheer volume of transactions makes it easier for miscreants to hide; every day, for instance, Medicare's contractors process 4.5 million claims," stated *The Economist* magazine.

This gargantuan system generates an equally monstrous load of paperwork: "Medicare will next year have 140,000 different codes, including nine for injuries caused by turkeys (was the victim struck or pecked? Once or more often? Did she suffer negative after affects? And so on)," stated *The Economist*.

The FBI, for its part, estimated that health care fraud—of both public and private systems—accounts for three to ten percent of total health care expenditures. The FBI has a list of common health care scams on its website. These include the following:

- Billing for services not rendered.
- Upcoding of services. "This type of scheme involves a billing practice where the health care provider submits a bill using a procedure code that yields a higher payment than the code for the service that was truly rendered," explained the FBI.
- Upcoding of items. "A medical supplier is upcoding when, for example, the supplier delivers to the patient a basic, manually propelled wheelchair but bills the patient's health insurance plan for a more expensive motorized version of the wheelchair," said the FBI.
- Duplicate claims. Simply, filing two claims for one service. The second claim is often given a different date than the first, to confuse investigators.
- Unbundling. "This is the practice of submitting bills in a fragmented fashion in order to maximize the reimbursement for various tests or procedures that are required to be billed together at a reduced cost," the FBI reports.
- Excessive services. Providing more services or products than are actually required.
- Medically unnecessary services. "A service is medically unnecessary and may give rise to a fraudulent scheme when the service is not justified by the patient's medical condition or diagnosis," stated the FBI.
- Kickbacks. The FBI states, "A health care provider or other person engages in an illegal kickback scheme when he or she offers, solicits, pays or accepts money or something of value, in exchange for the referral of a patient for health care services that may be paid for by Medicare or Medicaid. A laboratory owner and doctor each violate the Anti-Kickback Statute when the laboratory owner pays the doctor $50 for each Medicare patient a doctor sends to the laboratory for testing."

Federal officials do strive to tamp down such fraud: "In FY 2013, the Justice Department opened 1,013 new criminal health care fraud investigations involving 1,910 potential defendants, and a total of 718 defendants were convicted of health care fraud-related crimes during the year. The department also opened 1,083 new civil health care fraud investigations," stated the Justice Department/HHS press release.

Indeed, when people get caught committing health care fraud, the penalties can be harsh. In a detailed report, the Justice Department and HHS cited several cases in which individuals or companies were charged or convicted for trying to make an illegal dollar in the health care sector. "In April 2013, the owner of a mental health clinic in Miami, Florida, and three other participants in a $50 million fraud were sentenced to 30 years in prison, 25 years in prison, 262 months in prison and one year probation following their August 2012 trial convictions. The defendants caused the submission of over $50 million in false and fraudulent claims to Medicare for purported [partial hospitalization program] services at a fraudulent clinic," stated the report.

Another entry looked at crooked pharmacies: "From August 2011 through July 2013, twenty-six defendants have been convicted for their roles in a widespread scheme to defraud Medicare and Medicaid of nearly $58 million. According to the indictment, a licensed pharmacist owned or controlled 26 pharmacies in Michigan. The pharmacist concealed his ownership and control over many of his pharmacies through the use of straw owners. He offered and paid kickbacks, bribes and other inducements to providers in exchange for them writing fraudulent prescriptions for patients with Medicare, Medicaid and private insurance and directing the patients to fill their prescriptions at one of his pharmacies," stated the report.

New government initiatives such as the Affordable Care Act (ACA—better known as "Obamacare") offer fresh opportunities for scam artists. The Coalition Against Insurance Fraud, a group based in Washington DC, has warned the public about websites that purport to sign people up for ACA exchanges but instead drain their bank accounts. Another ACA-related con saw fraudsters trying to convince members of the public to register for "mandatory" ACA health cards. People who fell for this scam were duped into releasing bank account information, credit card data, and Social Security numbers.

Further Reading

Coalition Against Insurance Fraud, Fraud Statistics, http://www.insurancefraud.org/statistics.htm#Health%20Insurance.

Coalition Against Insurance Fraud, "Scams Coming with Health Reform in October, Coalition Warns," September 11, 2013.

The Economist, "That's Where the Money Is," May 31, 2014.

The Economist, "The $272 Billion Swindle," May 31, 2014.

Federal Bureau of Investigation website, "Health Care Fraud," https://www.fbi.gov/about-us/investigate/white_collar/health-care-fraud.

Nate Hendley, *The Mafia: A Guide to an American Subculture,* 2013.

James Quiggle, Coalition Against Insurance Fraud website, "Smelly Sinus Ploys Buy Nose Doc's Luxury Life," January 29, 2013, http://www.insurancefraud.org/article.htm?RecID=3239#.VZLaZtFRHIU.

Statement of John M. Taylor, Director, Office of Enforcement, Office of Regulatory Affairs, Food and Drug Administration before the Senate Special Committee on Aging, "Health Fraud," September 10, 2001.

U.S. Department of Health and Human Services, "Departments of Justice and Health and Human Services Announce Record-Breaking Recoveries Resulting from Joint Efforts to Combat Health Care Fraud," February 26, 2014.

U.S. Department of Health and Human Services and the Department of Justice, Health Care Fraud and Abuse Control Program, "Annual Report for Fiscal Year 2013," February 2014.

ENERGIZING ELIXIRS

Energy medicine is based on the idea that "the body has energy fields that can be manipulated to improve health," explained a November 21, 2007, article in the *Seattle Times*. The term "energy medicine" covers everything from Therapeutic Touch to homeopathy, acupuncture, craniosacral therapy, etc. It includes treatments that may be administered by a person or by a medical device.

Energy medicine practitioners claim all manner of miraculous physical healing from even the deadliest of ailments, such as cancer or AIDS. Skeptics, of course, remain dubious and say any "cures" are merely illusions or wishful thinking.

Here's a look at some prominent examples of energy medicine.

Therapeutic Touch

People who practice Therapeutic Touch believe that physical ailments can be detected and treated through careful manipulation of "human energy fields." Ironically, Therapeutic Touch doesn't usually involve skin contact between practitioner and subject. The former usually keeps his hands a few inches above the flesh of the latter, the better to probe his or her energy.

Therapeutic Touch (TT) is based upon the notion that "problems in the patient's energy field that cause illness and pain can be identified and rebalanced by a healer. Harmful energy is believed to cause blockages and other problems in the patient's normal energy flow and proponents of TT claim the treatment removes those blockages. TT is promoted by some to improve conditions such as pain, fever, swelling, infections, wounds, ulcers, thyroid problems, colic, burns, nausea, premenstrual syndrome, diarrhea, and headaches. They also say that TT is useful in treating diseases such as measles, Alzheimer's disease, AIDS, asthma, autism, multiple sclerosis, stroke, comas, and cancer," stated a report on alternative and complementary medicine by the American Cancer Society.

In the western world, the concept of manipulating human energy fields to affect healing can be traced to Franz Anton Mesmer. Mesmer was an eighteenth-century German doctor "who believed that illnesses were caused by imbalances in the body's magnetic forces. He believed he could restore magnetic balance through the use of soothing words and quieting gestures, a technique he called Mesmerism," continued the American Cancer Society report.

Modern historians and doctors believe that Mesmerism was basically just a form of hypnosis. Although Dr. Mesmer was quite skilled at putting people into hypnotic trances, "Mesmerism" did nothing to address their medical issues.

Mesmer's ideas were given a contemporary spin in the early 1970s, when Delores Krieger, a professor of nursing at New York University (NYU) began working with a natural healer named Dora Kunz. The pair developed what we now know as Therapeutic Touch.

It's understandable why TT is a popular choice for some people: it doesn't involve cutting a patient's body with surgical instruments or drugging them, for one thing. TT is typically performed in a soothing, supportive environment that puts a patient at ease.

But can TT actually cure people? Can TT practitioners sense a patient's "energy field" and tweak it in such a way that physical healing takes place?

"The best state of our experimental knowledge is that Therapeutic Touch does not work. It certainly has no plausible foundation and no physiological reason to suspect that the body's healing mechanisms are dependent upon some outside person waving their hands around," stated science writer Brian Dunning, in an April 27, 2010, podcast of Skeptoid: Critical Analysis of Pop Phenomenon.

Skeptoid is a science-based forum consisting of podcasts and online essays. The forum's self-described mission is to "apply critical thinking to urban legends and popular pseudoscientific subjects promoted by the mass media."

The American Cancer Society's report on complementary and alternative medicine adds, "Many researchers believe the positive results claimed to TT are due to the placebo effect. Studies suggest that the placebo effect may help many symptoms get better for a short time by using the body's own internal systems—even when fake treatments (such as pills containing only sugar or another inactive substance) or sham procedures … are given. Researchers also believe the patient's expectation of benefit or the simple presence of a person who is interested in helping can promote relaxation and increase one's sense of well-being."

Since 1996, the James Randi Educational Foundation (JREF), a group dedicated to debunking claims of medical miracles and paranormal activity, has offered a sizeable reward—currently over a million dollars—to any person who can prove the ability to detect human energy fields. Anyone trying for the award has to submit to scientific conditions specified by the *Journal*. So far, no one has collected this reward.

Homeopathy

Homeopathy is based on the theory that extremely diluted potions and pills can stimulate the body's natural healing process. The idea is that if you give a patient a minute amount of a substance that would make them sick if administered in a large dose, healing can begin.

"The word 'homeopathy' is derived from the Greek words homoios (similar) and pathos (suffering or disease)," explained Dr. Stephen Barrett in an essay on homeopathy posted on the website Quackwatch, which is dedicated to combating health fraud.

Homeopathic preparations are derived from natural substances (mineral, plant, or animal) and generally come in liquid or pill form. Liquid remedies are heavily diluted with water and/or alcohol, while pill-based remedies are pulverized together with large amounts of powdered lactose (milk sugar).

Adherents of homeopathy believe that the original substance leaves a "vibration" or "memory" in the water or milk sugar powder—a theory dismissed by mainstream medical authorities. To get the full effect, the container holding the diluted or pulverized remedies is supposed to be shaken vigorously, or "succussed," before the medicine is applied.

The "father" of homeopathy was a German physician named Samuel Hahnemann (1755–1843). Hahnemann was appalled by the crude medical care of his day, which included purging, bloodletting, and leeching. He wanted to find a less barbaric medical approach for the pre-anesthetic, pre-germ-theory era in which he lived.

"Hahnemann declared that diseases represent a disturbance in the body's ability to heal itself and that only a small stimulus is needed to begin the healing process … at first, he used small doses of accepted medications. But later he used enormous dilutions and theorized that the smaller the dose, the more powerful the effect—a notion commonly referred to as the 'law of infinitesimals,'" wrote Dr. Barrett in his homeopathy essay.

As unconventional as homeopathy may seem, it was quite popular in the Victorian era. This is understandable when we consider how toxic mainstream medicines and treatments were at the time. In many cases, patients had a better chance for survival if they stayed away from hospitals, where they were likely to contract infection from dirty surgical instruments, or the healing graces of physicians—who rarely washed their hands between operations.

According to Dr. Barrett's essay, there were roughly 14,000 homeopathy practitioners and 22 homeopathic schools in the United States at the turn of the twentieth century. The popularity of homeopathy declined sharply, however, as advances in medical science and hospital hygiene made going to the doctor a less frightening prospect. By the 1920s, the last school dedicated purely to homeopathic medical instruction in the United States closed.

Homeopathy has made something of a comeback recently, as part of the broader "alternative medicine" movement. Critics, however, remain deeply skeptical.

As Dr. Barrett notes in his essay on homeopathy, "Since many homeopathic remedies contain no detectable amount of active ingredient, it is impossible to test whether they contain what their label says. Unlike most potent drugs, they have not been proven effective against disease by double-blind clinical testing. In fact, the vast majority of homeopathic products have never even been tested."

Energy Medicine Devices

While Therapeutic Touch practitioners try to direct energy fields with their hands, some healers have relied on mechanical means to achieve this end. These efforts have typically generated much skepticism in mainstream medical and media circles.

Energy medicine tools "are not the devices in wide use by medical doctors, such as electrical stimulators used for sports injuries. Nor are they the biofeedback devices used at respected alternative-medicine centers … rather, these are boxes of wires purported to perform miracles. Their manufacturers and operators capitalize on weak government oversight and the nation's hunger for alternative therapies to reap millions of dollars in profits while exploiting desperate people," stated an investigation into energy medicine machines in the *Seattle Times*, published November 18, 2007.

Here is a look at some prominent energy machine proponents.

Dr. Albert Abrams

Dr. Albert Abrams was a pioneer in the use of energy medicine machines. Born in San Francisco in 1864 (there is some dispute about the exact year), Abrams graduated with a degree in medicine from the University of Heidelberg, Germany, in 1882.

Dr. Abrams began his career as a mainstream doctor. In the 1890s, he was hired to serve as professor of pathology at Cooper Medical College in San Francisco.

"Abrams' first clear deviation in print from medical orthodoxy came in 1909 and 1910 when he published books on a new theory of healing called Spondylotherapy. He could diagnose disease, he said, and cure it too, by a steady, rapid percussing or hammering of the spine … he began to give lectures both in San Francisco and on tour, explaining his new theories for a fee to cranks and quacks and gullible MDs," stated the book *The Medical Messiahs: A Social History of Health Quackery in Twentieth-Century America*, by Dr. James Harvey Young.

Needless to say, mainstream doctors thought Spondylotherapy was ridiculous and that Dr. Abrams was a fraud. No matter; the good doctor soon graduated to other forms of unconventional medicine and, in the process, shifted his attention from spine to stomach.

In 1916, he came up with a complex mechanical system, the first stage of which consisted of a device known as a "Dynamizer." Into this device, Dr. Abrams would place a piece of paper containing a few drops of blood from a patient. The Dynamizer was, in turn, connected to a series of mechanical devices, ending in an electrode.

"When the moment for the diagnosis came, Abrams, operating in dim light, stripped the subject to the waist, faced him westward, and affixed the electrode to his forehead. Then the doctor tapped the subject's abdomen, determining by the various areas of resonance and dullness what diseases plagued the patient, however distant, whose dried blood lay quietly four machines back up the line," stated *The Medical Messiahs*.

Dr. Abrams dubbed the system the "Electronic Reactions of Abrams" (ERA). According to its inventor, the ERA system could detect syphilis, tuberculosis, cancer, and other ailments. Dr. Abrams claimed he could even pinpoint the exact location of these diseases in a body. He could also determine the gender of the patient, just from a blood sample. If female, he could allegedly tell if they were pregnant. The doctor even claimed his system could be used to establish the religious allegiances of his patients.

The system evolved, and eventually, Dr. Abrams decided he no longer needed a blood sample to perform his magic. The doctor claimed that he could make a diagnosis from merely analyzing the signature of a patient. Dr. Abrams said he put the signatures of several famous men, including Samuel Pepys, Henry Wadsworth Longfellow, and Edgar Allan Poe, to the test. He concluded these famous figures all had syphilis.

Not only could the ERA system detect disease, it supposedly cured it too. The cure involved yet another device, dubbed the Oscilloclast. The latter produced vibrations that supposedly matched the "vibratory rates of all known diseases. Applied to a sufferer, and set by its operator to produce the proper rate, the machine stepped up the force of vibrations somehow so as to shatter and destroy the ailment," explained *The Medical Messiahs*.

"Abrams sold his diagnostic devices but would only lease the Oscilloclast. The fee was fancy and the lessee agreed by contract never to open the apparatus, which was hermetically sealed. In fact, the insides were a weird jumble of ohmmeters, rheostats, condensers and other parts, wired together without any sense at all," stated *The Medical Messiahs*.

In spite of, or perhaps because of, the bizarre medical claims he was making, Dr. Abrams attracted fans and followers from around the world. In 1922, he received high-profile support from renowned writer Upton Sinclair, author of *The Jungle*. Sinclair spent a few days at the doctor's clinic. He came away impressed by what he'd seen. Sinclair summarized his thoughts in a long letter to the *Journal of the American Medical Association* that was published April 29, 1922. In his letter, Sinclair extolled Dr. Abrams' virtues ("a devoted scientist and a great humanitarian") and defended his work ("Albert Abrams has discovered the great secret of the diagnosis and cure of all the major diseases").

Needless to say, *Journal* staff, led by quack-busting editor Morris Fishbein, were less than impressed by this touching testimonial: "Mr. Sinclair says that he has spent time in Dr. Abrams' clinic and is wonderfully impressed with Dr. Abrams' achievements. So is the small boy impressed with the marvelous facility with which the magician extracts the white rabbit from the silk hat," stated an editorial that accompanied Sinclair's letter.

The *Journal* wasn't the only mainstream publication to question Dr. Abrams' miraculous discoveries. *Scientific American* magazine ran a long series of articles critiquing the man and his methods.

Dr. Abrams died of pneumonia, on January 13, 1924, before the *Scientific American* series wrapped up. The doctor was only sixty years old. *Scientific American* continued publishing monthly articles blasting Dr. Abrams after his death. The magazine concluded that his medical devices were useless and any benefits from them an illusion.

William Nelson

In 1984, former Ohio math teacher William Nelson moved his family to Colorado. Nelson was a fan of *Star Trek* and had an autistic son. He dreamed of inventing a device as effective as the space-age tools used by *Star Trek*'s Dr. "Bones" McCoy—hand-held instruments that could cure any disease or fix any medical malady.

Nelson puttered and tinkered and eventually came up with something he called the Electro-Physio-Feedback-Xrroid System (or EPFX, for short). "The EPFX is made up of circuit boards and other computer components … during a typical EPFX treatment, a patient may watch as a computer screen displays an animation of the interior of an artery blocked by white blobs, representing cholesterol. Then, the blobs shrink and disappear," explained an article in *The Seattle Times* on November 18, 2007.

In 1989, Nelson registered his company with the Food and Drug Administration (FDA). He received approval to sell the EPFX as a biofeedback machine, not a diagnostic or treatment tool.

"Biofeedback is a relaxation technique that can help people learn to control various autonomic functions. The patient is connected to a device that continuously signals the heart rate, degree of muscle contraction or other indicator. The patient is instructed to relax so that the signals decrease to a desirable level. The patient may ultimately learn to control the body function subconsciously without the machine," explained Dr. Stephen Barrett, at the website of Quackwatch, a group devoted to exposing medical fraud.

Nelson wasn't content to sell the EPFX as a mere stress-buster, however. He insisted that the EPFX could both diagnose and cure diseases as grave as cancer by sending radio frequencies into the body. Naturally, such a miracle machine couldn't be had cheaply. Even priced at several thousand dollars apiece, the EPFX sold briskly.

In 1992, the FDA contacted Nelson to remind him that the EPFX was registered as a biofeedback device and that it was illegal to make any other medical claims for the product. Nelson continued to peddle his invention as a cure-all miracle machine. In June 1996, he was indicted on nine counts of felony fraud. Instead of sticking around to fight the charges, Nelson took off from the United States, eventually decamping to Hungary.

In Hungary, he began actively promoting and tinkering with his medical machine. As a result of this tinkering, Nelson came up with the "Quantum Xrroid Interface System" (QXCI), a supposed improvement on the original device.

"The Quantum Xrroid Interface System (QXCI)—also called EPFX or SCIO—is claimed to balance 'bio-energetic' forces that the scientific community does not recognize as real … to operate the system, a head harness, ankle straps and wrist straps are used to connect the patient to a digital box attached to a computer. After 'calibration' is done, the equipment monitors, interprets the patient's reactions to tiny electrical impulses generated by the box and advises what products to take," stated Dr. Barrett.

Like the original EPFX, the QXCI is officially marketed as a "biofeedback" device to reduce stress. The QXCI cannot be sold in the United States as a diagnostic or treatment device, but that hasn't stopped Nelson's associates from promoting it as such. A *Seattle Times* investigation into Nelson published in late 2007 made note of Nelson's propensity for exaggeration and telling tales.

"Nelson makes extraordinary claims about his life. He said he worked as a contractor for NASA, helping to save the troubled Apollo 13 mission as a teenager. He boasts that he was an alternate member of the 1968 U.S. Olympics gymnastics team. He says he has eight doctorates, including degrees in medicine and law … none of it checks out. NASA has no record of his employment, he was not an Olympic athlete. And his 'degrees' come from unaccredited schools and mail-order businesses," stated the *Times*.

Nelson is still active in Europe, selling his devices and false hope as far as his critics are concerned. The QXCI device "is promoted with elaborate pseudoscientific explanations and disclaimers intended to protect its practitioners from prosecution. Use of the device can cause unnecessary expense as well as delay in getting appropriate treatment," stated Dr. Barrett.

Further Reading

"Albert Abrams—A Defense by Upton Sinclair," *Journal of the American Medical Association*, April 29, 1922.

"Albert Abrams," *Journal of the American Medical Association*, June 10, 1922.

Albert Abrams, MuseumofQuackery.com, http://www.museumofquackery.com/amquacks/abrams.htm.

American Cancer Society website, http://www.cancer.org/.

American Cancer Society website, Therapeutic Touch, http://www.cancer.org/treatment/treatmentsandsideeffects/complementaryandalternativemedicine/manualhealingandpsychicaltouch/therapeutic-touch. (Webpage no longer online.)

Dr. Stephen Barrett, Quackwatch.org, "Homeopathy: The Ultimate Fake," http://www.quackwatch.org/01QuackeryRelatedTopics/homeo.html.

Dr. Stephen Barrett, Quackwatch.org, "Some Notes on the Quantum Xrroid (QXCI) and William Nelson," http://www.quackwatch.org/01QuackeryRelatedTopics/Tests/xrroid.html.

Michael J. Berens and Christine Willmsen, "How One Man's Invention Is Part of a Growing Worldwide Scam That Snares the Desperately Ill," *The Seattle Times*, November 18, 2007.

Michael J. Berens and Christine Willmsen, "Spread of Illegal Devices Causes Alarm," *The Seattle Times*, November 21, 2007.

Brian Dunning, "Therapeutic Touch," Skeptoid #204 podcast, April 27, 2010.

Dr. G. E. Hartshorne, "The Abrams Cult Again," *Journal of the American Medical Association*, December 8, 1923.

Dr. Harriett Hall, "Energy Medicine," *Skeptic Magazine*, Volume 11, Number 3, 2005.

Dr. Harriett Hall, "Gary Schwartz's Energy Healing Experiments: The Emperor's New Clothes?" *Skeptical Inquirer*, March/April 2008.

House of Commons, Science and Technology Committee, "MPs Urge Government to Withdraw NHS Funding and MHRA Licensing of Homeopathy," press release, February 22, 2010.

House of Commons, Science and Technology Committee, "Science and Technology Committee—Fourth Report, Evidence Check 2: Homeopathy," fourth report of Session 2009–10, February 22, 2010.

Joe Nickell, Center for Inquiry blog, "The New Snake Oil," March 4, 2009, http://www.centerforinquiry.net/blogs/entry/the_new_snake_oil/.

Steven Novella, "Magnetic Healing: An Old Scam That Never Dies," *Skeptical Inquirer*, January/February 2011.

Benjamin Radford, "Is There a 100C Grain of Truth to Homeopathy?" *Skeptical Inquirer*, July/August 2011.

Emily Rosa, Linda Rosa, Larry Sarner, Dr. Stephen Barrett, "A Close Look at Therapeutic Touch," *Journal of the American Medical Association*, 1998.

Phillips Stevens, Jr., "Magical Thinking in Complementary and Alternative Medicine," *Skeptical Inquirer*, November/December 2001.

U.S. Department of Health and Human Services, Food and Drug Administration, "Guidance for Industry on Complementary and Alternative Medicine Products and Their Regulation by the Food and Drug Administration," draft guidance, December 2006.

U.S. Department of Health and Human Services, National Institutes of Health, National Center for Complementary and Alternative Medicine website, Complementary, Alternative, or Integrative Health: What's in a Name? https://nccih.nih.gov/health/integrative-health.

Richard Van Vleck, "The Electronic Reactions of Albert Abrams," *American Artifacts*, No. 39, http://www.americanartifacts.com/smma/abrams/abrams.htm.

Dr. James Harvey Young, *The Medical Messiahs: A Social History of Health Quackery in Twentieth-Century America*, 1967.

PSYCHIC SURGERY

"Psychic surgeons" are individuals with minimal or no medical training who perform operations with their fingers or rudimentary tools such as kitchen knives. These "operations" typically involve plenty of blood and gore but little pain and no scarring. Often the "surgeons" say they're guided by God or some kind of spirit power.

Psychic surgeons claim they have the ability to remove tumors, cancers, and other malignancies. But according to skeptic James Randi, psychic surgeons are phonies using sleight-of-hand and animal parts to fake their way through medical procedures.

"Apparently by means of psychic—or divine—powers, these healers can reach their hands into the bodies of their patients, extracting deadly tumors and other substances along with quantities of blood. In most cases, there is no trace of an incision on the body of the patient afterwards ... to any trained conjuror, the methods by which these seeming miracles are produced are obvious. But inexperienced observers quite naturally do not see the trickery and, if they are predisposed to believe in magic, they are prepared to accept that something supernatural has taken place," wrote Randi, in his book *James Randi: Psychic Investigator.*

While the epicenters of psychic surgery are in Brazil and the Philippines, this sham attracts devotees from all over the world. It has also attracted the attention of legal authorities. The Federal Trade Commission (FTC) has charged U.S. travel agencies that arrange visits to foreign psychic surgeons, with falsely promoting such surgery as genuinely helpful medical treatment. Psychic surgeons making tours of the United States have been arrested for fraud and practising medicine without a licence.

Although similar to faith healing—in which individuals are supposed to be cured of various ailments by God's grace or by the healing touch of a religious figure—psychic surgery is a newer phenomenon. As far as anyone can tell, psychic surgery originated in rural areas of the Philippines in the 1940s.

"Certain local 'healers' are believed to act as mediums for healing forces that enable them to perform painless surgery using their fingers and/or unsterile tools," stated an article on psychic surgery in the May/June 1990 issue of *CA—A Cancer Journal for Clinicians.*

Eleuterio Terte "was reportedly the first Filipino healer to perform fake operations in his healing rituals. In the 1940s, Terte incorporated a few sleight-of-hand techniques using chicken guts, red dye and cotton," continued the article.

These performances caught the attention of ailing peasants, who began flocking to Terte. Terte acquired students, eager to learn his chicanery. One of his most talented pupils was a man named Tony Agpaoa. Films and media articles about Terte and Agpaoa brought their unusual skills to world prominence in the 1960s. People from around the world started to travel to the Philippines to seek out this unconventional surgery: "In 1967, 109 ailing Detroit residents travelled to Manila for treatment by Agpaoa. When they returned, several dissatisfied group members claimed they had been bilked," wrote the *CA* journal.

While on a healing tour of Michigan, Agpaoa was arrested and "indicted on three counts of using the telephone wires to defraud by representing himself as able to perform psychic surgery and one count of foreign transportation of $72,000 obtained by fraud. He fled to the Philippines before coming to trial, forfeiting the $25,000 bail raised by his supporters," continued the article.

In August 1986, Gary G. Magno (aka "The Reverend Monsignor") was arrested in Phoenix, Arizona, while performing an "operation" in the home of a follower. He was apparently seeing a hundred patients a day, charging $75 for an initial visit and $50 for follow-up "surgeries." "At the time of his arrest, Magno was found to have vials of red fluid and packets of meat tucked under his waistband," stated *CA*.

That same year, a psychic surgeon named Jose "Brother Joe" Bugarin performed hundreds of "operations" in three days, under the sponsorship of a Denver church. Brother Joe charged $45 for each surgery. Upon examination, it was revealed that the blood in his operations came from chickens. Charged with practising medicine without a licence, Bugarin was slapped with a nine-month jail sentence in Sacramento County, California, in October 1988.

In February 1989, psychic surgeon Placido Palatayan was arrested at a house in Colville, Washington. He was scheduled to perform over 100 surgeries in two days, at a price of $75 per operation. Palatayan was charged with theft and practising medicine without a licence.

"A bucket containing blood and tissue that purportedly had been removed from patients was found to contain tissue from a bovine animal. Palatayan is known to have treated at least 1,200 people in Colville during the six or seven visits he made since 1984," stated *CA*.

Groups trying to make money from psychic surgery have also found themselves under investigation. In January 1974, the FTC charged 11 respondents (four West Coast travel agencies and seven of their officers/shareholders) with falsely representing psychic surgery in the Philippines as a legitimate form of medical treatment.

Brazil is also a hotspot for psychic surgery, as exemplified by the bizarre story of "Doctor Fritz." According to an article in the January 12, 1996, *New York Times*, Dr. Adolf Frederick Yeperssoven was supposedly a German doctor who died in the First World War. For unclear reasons, his spirit apparently started possessing people in Brazil several decades ago, imbuing them with amazing healing abilities.

The first possessed healer was Jose Pedro de Freitas, who began performing psychic surgery in the 1950s, after the spirit of Dr. Fritz (as the German doctor was nicknamed by his Brazilian believers) took hold. Jose became widely known under the name "Ze Arigo." Ze Arigo was fond of using kitchen knives in his "operations" and asking Jesus to stop the bleeding. Needless to say, Ze Arigo became hugely popular and wealthy.

While Ze Arigo died in a car crash in 1971, the spirit of Dr. Fritz lived on. He inhabited a series of new healers, who also used dirty utensils to perform their "operations" and sometimes spoke in a German accent.

One of the most popular contemporary psychic surgeons in Brazil is João Teixeira de Faria, aka "John of God," who operates a "spiritual healing centre" in a small town called Abadiania. A farmer by background, John of God receives thousands of sick visitors a year. He was the subject of an ABC News Primetime special broadcast February 12, 2005, that demonstrated some of his more popular "surgical" routines. These included shoving forceps up people's noses and scraping eyeballs with a knife.

James Randi, who was interviewed for the Primetime special, is openly critical of John of God's procedures. In a report posted February 18, 2005, for the online newsletter of the James Randi Educational Foundation, he pointed out that the forceps-up-the-nose act was simply a new version of an old stunt that people had been performing at carnivals and sideshows for decades.

The eyeball-scraping procedure also came under withering fire: "I believe that this is a variation of the usual trick—in which a knife-blade is inserted under the eyelid of a subject with little or no resulting discomfort. With the Brazilian faker, the 'scraping' motion gives it a much more fearsome aspect but for several good reasons I doubt that any contact takes place with the cornea," wrote Randi.

Randi also pointed out that the sclera, or the white part of the eye, "is relatively insensitive to touch" and that many onlookers reflexively flinch or look away when John of God does this trick (making it likely they don't get a clear view of what was really going on). He suggested that if contact was made between knife and eye, it was possible John of God introduced a local anaesthetic to the eye surface to make it numb to the touch.

In the newsletter report, Randi also noted that "the John of God organization has set up a situation in which they simply cannot fail; if recovery is not experienced by their patients, it's not a failure of the magical forces, but the fault of the patient … they say one has to wait at least 40 days to see any healing … and sometimes up to two years have to pass before any effect will be seen. All this is a fail-safe scenario, one I've come upon many times in the faith-healing racket."

Such criticisms haven't stopped other U.S. media outlets from featuring John of God. He has received ample publicity over the years from Oprah Winfrey, for example, in her magazine and on her TV show.

Anyone actually afflicted with a life-threatening illness would be well advised to steer clear of psychic surgery charlatans. "After study of the literature and other available information, the American Cancer Society has found no evidence that 'psychic surgery' results in objective benefit in the treatment of any medical condition. Lacking such evidence, the American Cancer Society strongly urges individuals who are ill not to seek treatment by psychic surgery," stated *CA* magazine.

"The alleged removal of diseased tissue from the body without leaving an incision as has been practiced in the Philippines for some years is denounced as a complete fraud; not only does it waste money and cause psychological harm through promoting false hope, it can keep people from seeking valuable health care before it becomes too late for effective therapy," added the National Council Against Health Fraud.

Further Reading

American Cancer Society, http://www.cancer.org/.

Dr. Stephen Barrett, "Questionable Cancer Therapies," Quackwatch.org, http://www.quackwatch.org/01QuackeryRelatedTopics/cancer.html.

Federal Trade Commission, "In the Matter of Travel King, Inc., et al.," Docket 8949, Amended Complaint, May 17, 1974—Order, September 30, 1975.

From the Heart Foundation, Father Joshua, http://www.psychicsurgeon.org/.

National Council Against Health Fraud, NCAHF Consumer Information Statements on Faith Healing and Psychic Surgery, 1987, http://www.ncahf.org/pp/faith.html.

James Randi, "From the Archives: Randi's Inside Scoop into ABC News' 'John of God' Investigation," *Swift,* the online newsletter of the James Randi Educational Foundation, February 18, 2005, http://web.randi.org/home/from-the-archives-randis-inside-scoop-into-abc-news-john-of-god-investigation-2005.

James Randi, *James Randi: Psychic Investigator,* 1991.

Diana Jean Schemo, "Rio Journal; Live, in Brazil (Again): The Reincarnated Dr. Fritz," *New York Times,* January 12, 1996.

"Unproven Methods of Cancer Management: 'Psychic Surgery,'" *CA—A Cancer Journal for Clinicians,* May/June 1990.

RADIUM MEDICINE

In 1927, a Pittsburgh steel industrialist named Eben Byers fell out of an upper berth on a train while coming home from a Yale–Harvard football game. Byers injured his arm and found himself in persistent pain after the accident. His doctor recommended something called Radithor, which was a patent medicine consisting of water with trace amounts of the radioactive element radium. Byers started using Radithor with great enthusiasm, drinking upwards of three bottles a day. He said the stuff cured his pain and generally invigorated him.

Byers was not the only person at the time with a predilection for radium. Radium-infused medicines were hugely popular during this era, while radium paint was used to highlight watch and clock faces so the numerals glowed in the dark. This wasn't modern radiation therapy, a common cancer treatment conducted under strict medical conditions. This was unregulated use by citizens lacking the medical skill and scientific knowledge to use radium safely.

As Byers was to discover, radium medicine came with some nasty side-effects. His bones began deteriorating, mostly notably in his jaw, which fell apart, while holes appeared in his skull. Byers died in 1932 of radiation poisoning, having consumed nearly 1,500 bottles of Radithor. He was buried in a lead-lined coffin.

The discovery of the radioactive element radium can be attributed to pioneering female scientist Marie Curie, in the late Victorian era. Radium came to America in the late 1890s via the scientific lecture circuit, in which the public paid to hear presenters discuss the latest breakthroughs in science and medicine. Presenters extolling the virtues of radium would dim the lights during their talks, to demonstrate how radium samples glowed in the dark with a greenish hue that never diminished.

Radium-based medicine soon became a huge craze. The press at the time was filled with stories about the supposed cure-all properties of the element. It was said to be great at killing bacteria and treating everything from acne to melanomas (basically, by burning off the afflicted tissue).

Radium nasal sprays and radium-infused rooms called "inhalatorias" or "emanatorias" became widely popular. These were places where people could sit and soak in radioactive emanations. Other frightening uses of the element included radium condoms, suppositories, and facial cream.

The patent medicine industry was quick to respond to the popularity of radium. Radithor was only one of the more common radium-based medicines on the market. A 2013 article in *Skeptic Magazine* titled "The Great Radium Craze" estimates that up to half a million bottles of Radithor were sold from the years 1925 to 1929.

People could also purchase ceramic or glass jars lined with radium-infused clay. Consumers were instructed to fill these jars with regular drinking water. The radium-infused clay would turn the water radioactive, at which point it was swallowed. Radium-water in general was widely used.

Doctors inserted radium concoctions in patients, surgically or through body cavities. Radium salts, meanwhile, could be swallowed by mouth or injected.

The public was also quick to embrace radium's glow-in-the-dark properties. A radium-based paint called "Undark" was applied on everything from doorbells and house numbers to signs in mines, fishing lures, and eyes on toy dolls.

The radium craze was even noted by Broadway. The musical *Piff Paff Pouf* (which opened in April 1904) offered a number called the "Radium Dance." This bit featured dancers prancing about in the dark in outfits decorated with radium paint. Radium-painted props such as ropes were also used for dramatic effect in the number.

"Radium was everywhere. And people were being sold on the idea that it was good for you," stated *Skeptic Magazine*.

People did, however, gradually become aware of radium's lethal effects. In the 1920s and 1930s, there were lurid newspaper accounts of dying or deformed "Radium Girls"—workers, mostly young women, who toiled in factories, applying radium paint on watch and clock faces. The girls often used camel-hair brushes, which they would insert in their mouths to keep the point sharp. In this manner, they regularly ingested radium. Once in the bones, radium can lead to cancer. One particularly horrifying ailment, known as "Radium Jaw," saw the sufferer's jaw decay to pieces.

Hugo Gernsback, publisher of *Everyday Science and Mechanics*, decided to do some investigating. Gernsback sent out questionnaires to six medical authorities who were experts on radium. The doctors' replies were featured in an article called "Radium—Boon or Menace?" in the June 1932 issue of *Everyday Science and Mechanics*. The article represented one of the first major media investigations into the dangers of radium.

"Every respondent said the same thing: radium is safe in the hands of someone trained for the work … and that it was dangerous in the hands of anyone else. Further, they were unanimously against home-use products," states *Skeptic Magazine*.

Awareness of the dangers of radium led to restrictions on the sale of radium-based patent medicines. In professional medical circles, however, radium treatment continued to be a popular option. From 1940 through to 1970, doctors used radium therapy to reduce swollen tissue in nasal cavities. Two sealed cylinders containing radium sulfate would be inserted through the nostrils and into the nasal region for a short period of time. The idea was that the radiation emitted would reduce swollen tissue and shrink tonsils and adenoids. It was a very common procedure in North America and Europe. The *Skeptic Magazine* piece on radium estimated that between 500,000 and 2.5 million children had this treatment in the United States alone, along with 8,000 military personnel. There have been reports of increased rates of cancer among people who received this therapy but nothing definite has been confirmed.

Further Reading

Oak Ridge Associated Universities, Radioactive Quack Cures, http://www.orau.org/ptp/collection/quackcures/quackcures.htm.

"Radium Ore Revigator," *Journal of the American Medical Association*, November 21, 1925.

David Stipp, "A Little Poison Can Be Good For You—The Received Wisdom About Toxins and Radiation May Be All Wet," *Fortune*, June 9, 2003.

Ray Sutera, "The Great Radium Craze," *Skeptic Magazine*, Volume 18, Number 3, 2013.

REPRESSED MEMORIES AND MULTIPLE PERSONALITY DISORDER

"Sybil Dorsett" was the alias of the real-life psychiatric patient at the center of the hugely popular book *Sybil*. Written by Flora Rheta Schreiber, the 1973 best seller centered on a young woman who allegedly had 16 distinct identities. These identities emerged during a decade of therapy with a psychiatrist named Cornelia Wilbur. Sybil allegedly took on these different personalities as a response to horrific childhood abuse, the memories of which she had deeply repressed.

A smash hit with the public, the book was turned into a hugely popular television mini-series in 1976, featuring Sally Field as Sybil and Joanne Woodward as Dr. Wilbur.

Sybil, the book and mini-series, helped popularize the concept of Multiple Personality Disorder (MPD—now called Dissociative Identity Disorder, or DID for short). Patients with DID supposedly house more than one personality. Often these personalities are in conflict with each other; one personality might be gregarious and flirtatious, while another is demure and puritanical.

Before the book was released, "only a handful of DID cases had previously been reported in the scientific literature. After *Sybil*, the number skyrocketed into the thousands," according to an article in the March/April 2012 edition of *Skeptical Inquirer*.

Sybil did more than just popularize the concept of multiple personalities. The book and mini-series both explicitly tied DID with childhood trauma. This gave rise to the notion that people who suffered abuse as children often "repressed" these memories in an effort to stay sane. This repression, however, could cause anxiety, neurosis, and other mental woes. Therapeutic intervention was necessary to bring these bad memories to the fore, the first step to a cure.

Today, researchers doubt the veracity of the Sybil story, while many psychiatrists and mental health experts are no longer certain that DID even exists.

The woman given the alias "Sybil" in the book was really named Shirley Ardell Mason. She grew up as an only child in small-town, conservative Dodge Center, Minnesota. Her parents, Mattie and Walter Mason, were devout Seventh-Day Adventists. Walter Mason worked as a hardware store clerk and carpenter while Mattie focused on housewife duties.

When interviewed decades after the book was released, Dodge Center residents recalled Mattie Mason as an overprotective mother and Shirley as a quiet, timid child who excelled at painting. Mattie was known to be a bit eccentric, but no one in Dodge Center reported knowing anything about the horrific abuse alleged in the book.

"Shirley was a creative, imaginative, artistic, suggestible, easily hypnotized, vulnerable patient. She had always been a daydreamer who had difficulty separating fact from imagination," according to a 2012 story called "Multiple Personality Delusions" in *Skeptic Magazine*.

In 1941, Shirley went to what is today called the Minnesota State University in Mankato, Minnesota. She apparently suffered some kind of breakdown and did not graduate until 1949. At some point during her breakdown, Shirley encountered psychiatrist Cornelia Wilbur and received therapy. Shirley's main problems at the time were anxiety and blackouts.

In the early 1950s, Shirley moved to New York City to study art at Columbia University. She re-united with Dr. Wilbur, who now worked out of a Park Avenue office in Manhattan. Suffering from anorexia, anxiety, and feelings of inferiority, Shirley started a fresh round of therapy with Wilbur. These sessions would last for more than a decade.

Unusually for a psychiatrist, Wilbur talked about her own life during therapy sessions. Wilbur had an interest in multiple personalities and some experience dealing with hysteric patients. Shirley became infatuated with Wilbur, who served as something of a mentor as well as a therapist. Wilbur told Shirley she could get her a job as an art therapist at a mental health facility for children. Shirley revealed that she dreamed of becoming a doctor herself (a psychiatrist, to be precise) but that her parents discouraged this ambition, telling their daughter she was too timid to handle such a job. Wilbur told Shirley to embrace her dream. She also encouraged her patient to keep a "therapy diary."

Therapy sessions began to involve the use of powerful drugs, including Seconal, a tranquilizer prescribed by Wilbur to allow Shirley to sleep. Seconal is now understood to be highly addictive.

In late winter 1955, Shirley mentioned to Wilbur how she sometimes found herself in strange locales, with no idea how she got there. This revelation excited the doctor, who suspected Shirley was suffering from "fugue states"—a rare form of hysteria in which patients drift into unplanned wandering, often taking on a new identity, then experience amnesia about the whole episode.

At a subsequent session, Shirley surprised Wilbur again, by speaking in a different voice and using new mannerisms. Shirley informed the psychiatrist that she was actually Peggy Lou, a dark-haired little girl. Unlike real-life Shirley, Peggy Lou was fun-loving and had a strong personality.

Other identities emerged, including warm and cultured Vicky, and Peggy Ann—less blunt than the other Peggy but also more timid.

Wilbur concluded that her patient had the very rare syndrome then called Multiple Personality Disorder. Wilbur informed her patient of this conclusion (apparently Shirley was relieved, not horrified, when told she had MPD) and started treating her for free.

When in "Vicky" mode, Shirley alluded to childhood abuse. Wilbur began dosing Shirley with sodium pentothal—a barbiturate commonly called "truth serum" that induces a relaxed state which allegedly makes patients more honest—and tape-recording their sessions.

Wilbur pressed "Vicky" on her tales of abuse. Vicky/Shirley spoke about being drugged as a child, and having flashlights shined in her eyes and smothering blankets placed over her face. Contemporary researchers have traced this memory to a traumatic tonsillectomy Shirley had at age seven, when she was administered chloroform and operating on without advance warning from her parents or doctor. Wilbur, however, concluded that Shirley had been raped as a child. The doctor also surmised, on minimal evidence, that Mattie Mason was a paranoid schizophrenic who tortured her offspring.

More personalities emerged during further sessions. In addition to Vicky and the two Peggys, there was religious homebody Mary; Marcia, a passionate artist who spoke with an English accent; Nancy, a paranoid case big on conspiracy theories; Ruthie, a little child; and others. In total, Shirley proffered 16 different personalities.

Interestingly enough, these different identities "only displayed themselves in the therapy sessions; no one else in Shirley's life ever observed them," reported the "Multiple Personality Delusions" article in *Skeptic Magazine*.

In the late 1950s, the relationship between Shirley and Wilbur almost ground to a halt. Shirley presented her doctor with a four-page, neatly typed note in which she denied having multiple personalities and denied that her mother had abused her. Shirley stated that she had assumed various identities merely to please Wilbur. Instead of terminating therapy, Wilbur took this note as a sign of denial on Shirley's part. The intense therapeutic sessions continued, and Shirley resumed her personality free-for-all.

In 1965, Wilbur decided that Shirley had been "cured." The psychiatrist claimed to have "integrated" her patient's various personalities into one solid identity. The doctor and patient remained close, however, collaborating on a book detailing Shirley's experience. The actual book writing was handled by journalist Flora Schreiber. She based her research on transcripts of tape-recorded therapy sessions and various patient diaries. In this manner, Schreiber produced the manuscript that became the best-selling *Sybil*. In an unusual arrangement, the author, doctor, and patient all shared in the royalties from the book.

Shirley kept a low profile after the book and mini-series about her life were released. She eventually followed Wilbur to Lexington, Kentucky, where the doctor taught at the University of Kentucky.

Author Schreiber died in 1988. Prior to her death, Schreiber asked librarians at the John Jay College of Criminal Justice in New York City to guard her Sybil-related research material. The librarians agreed and sealed the documents.

In 1990, Wilbur diagnosed Shirley with breast cancer. Shirley did not enter treatment, however, and the cancer went into remission. Wilbur herself came down with Parkinson's disease and died in 1992. She left Shirley some $25,000 in her will.

With Wilbur's death, Shirley became something of a recluse. She maintained little contact with old friends and family, spending most of her time with her cats and painting.

In 1997, Shirley's cancer returned. Again, she refused medical treatment. Shirley began giving away possessions and seemed reconciled with dying. On February 26, 1998, Shirley died of untreated breast cancer.

Upon discovering that Shirley was deceased, librarians at the John Jay College released Schreiber's *Sybil* research material for all to see. What the transcribed tapes revealed was a pushy psychiatrist imposing her views on a gullible patient.

The whole *Sybil* story had started to unravel, however, even before these documents were released. In the mid-1990s, it was revealed that a well-regarded New York psychiatrist named Dr. Herbert Spiegel had also interacted with Shirley Mason. Apparently, Wilbur had approached Dr. Spiegel for a second opinion on Shirley. Wilbur told Dr. Spiegel that she had initially viewed Shirley as a schizophrenic but now wasn't sure. Wilbur asked the doctor if he would examine Shirley to help determine the true nature of her mental malady. Dr. Spiegel worked with Shirley on other occasions as well, when Wilbur was busy.

Early on in their interactions, Shirley apparently asked Dr. Spiegel if he wanted her to assume a different identity. The startled doctor discovered that Wilbur had been encouraging Shirley to try on various identities in their therapy together.

Dr. Spiegel found Shirley highly hypnotizable, which hinted that she was very suggestible. Shirley also revealed that to please Wilbur, she had read *The Three Faces of Eve*, a popular book offering an account of DID, as well as literature on multiple personalities.

"I think she was a wonderful hysterical patient with role confusion, which is typical of high hysterics … I saw her 'personalities' rather as game-playing," stated Dr. Spiegel of Shirley, in an interview published in the 1997 *New York Review of Books*. Dr. Spiegel refused to work with Schreiber and Wilbur on the *Sybil* book.

In 2011, investigative journalist Debbie Nathan came out with an exposé called *Sybil Exposed*. "Nathan demonstrates that *Sybil*, both the book and the mini-series, were packed with lies and distortion," stated a story in the March/April 2012 issue of *Skeptical Inquirer*.

The book *Sybil Exposed* makes it clear that Shirley never displayed multiple personalities until she started therapy with Wilbur. "The young patient's florid symptoms emerged and morphed over a period of years as she and Wilbur engaged in a complicated dance of mutually reinforced self-deception.

According to her own admission, Shirley pretended to have alter personalities because she wanted Wilbur's attention. The doctor quickly became fascinated by the personalities and began planning how she might attain professional fame and money by publishing about them," stated the March/April 2012 *Skeptical Inquirer.*

Nathan's book also took aim at the assertion that Shirley's mother was mentally ill. In the book *Sybil*, Shirley's father admits to Wilbur that Mattie Mason had been diagnosed as schizophrenic. There is little evidence, however, that this confession ever occurred. Although Mattie Mason was an odd character, she was never diagnosed with a serious mental illness.

The very diagnosis of MPD/DID has come under fire as well, particularly the attributing notion of "repressed memories" of childhood abuse. It has been pointed out that children incarcerated in concentration camps or forced to serve as prostitutes, far from repressing such awful memories, often have crystal-clear recall of their experiences.

"Few topics in modern psychiatry arouse more controversy than MPD/DID. Many mental health professionals question whether the disorder even exists. According to these skeptics, MPD/DID is usually or always a socially created condition, fostered and reinforced in patients by suggestive therapists such as Wilbur. These skeptics contend that much of the supposed evidence for MPD/DID is based on shaky stories, weak methodology and questionable data sources," stated the March/April 2012 *Skeptical Inquirer.*

The doctor who treated Shirley Mason has also been called out for criticism: "Dr. Wilbur was guilty of multiple ethical violations and gross malpractice. She should have lost her license; instead, she became world-famous, made big bucks and spread false ideas that led to untold harm," stated *Skeptic* magazine.

Further Reading

Mikkel Borch-Jacobsen and Dr. Herbert Spiegel, "Sybil: The Making of a Disease: An Interview with Dr. Herbert Spiegel," *New York Review of Books*, April 24, 1997.

Harriet Hall, "Multiple Personality Delusions," *Skeptic Magazine*, Volume 17, Number 3, 2012.

Elizabeth F. Loftus and Melvin J. Guyer, "Who Abused Jane Doe? The Hazards of the Single Case History," *Skeptical Inquirer*, May/June 2002.

Mark Miller, "Unmasking Sybil," *Newsweek*, January 24, 1999.

Debbie Nathan, "A Girl Not Named Sybil," *New York Times*, October 14, 2011.

Mike Pendergrast, *Victims of Memory: Sex Abuse Accusations and Shattered Lives*, 1996.

Elaine Showalter, *Hystories: Hysterical Epidemics and Modern Media*, 1997.

James Wood, "End to a Twisted and False Episode in Psychiatry," *Skeptical Inquirer*, March/April 2012.

SECTION SEVEN
ONLINE SCAMS

INTRODUCTION

The advent of the Internet has created a new world of opportunity for con artists and criminals. Some online swindles, such as the "Nigerian Letter" are variations of old, existing cons—in this case, the "Spanish Prisoner" scam. Other online scams, involving phishing, vishing, and malware, are of more recent vintage. As with any other rip-off, online scams take advantage of human gullibility in the face of sometimes ridiculous schemes.

The difference between scams of old and online hustles is scope: thanks to the Internet, confidence artists have been able to massively expand their feeding grounds, utilizing a worldwide computer network to hunt fresh prey.

INTERNET DATING FRAUD

Paul Frampton was lonely. An Oxford-educated physics professor at the University of North Carolina, Frampton had been separated from his wife, Anne-Marie, for years. Like a lot of lonely people, he decided to try his luck at online dating.

Frampton, who was in his late 60s at the time, began his online adventures in late 2011. Much to his surprise, Frampton soon hit it off with a young woman who seemed genuinely taken by him. The woman's profile identified her as a 32-year-old Bolivian bikini model named Denise Milani. Her pictures depicted a striking woman with dark hair and a well-proportioned physique. An online search revealed that Ms. Milani was the winner of the coveted Miss Bikini World 2007 title.

Frampton traded hundreds of e-mails with Milani. He indicated surprise that such a voluptuous young woman would have romantic stirrings for an aging academic. Milani told him that men her age only chased her for her appearance and that she was looking for a mature man. While Frampton was clearly impressed by Milani's physical attributes, he appreciated the interest she showed in his work and university-based life.

It was decided that Frampton would fly to Bolivia and meet his sweetie face-to-face. In reality, he was being set up. While there really was a bikini model named Denise Milani, she wasn't communicating with Frampton. Milani's real-life image, background, and name had been borrowed by drug traffickers to create a fake Internet dating site profile. The real Milani was completely oblivious to all these machinations.

Frampton left for Bolivia without taking the precaution of speaking to Milani on the phone first, to confirm that her voice matched her appearance. In an article published February 25, 2015, in Great Britain's *Daily Mail* newspaper, Frampton admitted that he had been "incredibly naïve."

Once he reached La Paz, Bolivia, Frampton received distressing news. Milani said she wasn't in Bolivia, but had in fact flown to Brussels for a photo shoot. She would be delighted to meet her online lover in Belgium. And would he be so kind as to pick up a suitcase she had foolishly left behind and take it with him to Brussels? When Frampton agreed to this arrangement, a man met him at his hotel and handed off a suitcase.

Irked at not being able to connect with Milani in Bolivia, Frampton decided to fly home rather than jet off to Belgium. With the extra suitcase in tow, Frampton arranged to fly to the United States via Argentina.

While at Ezeiza International Airport in Buenos Aires, in January 2012, Frampton was stopped by customs officers. They wanted a closer look at the extra suitcase he was traveling with. Authorities examined the suitcase and discovered two kilos of cocaine. Frampton's protests of innocence achieved nothing, and he was hauled off to jail. Frampton later told reporters it hadn't occurred to him that the lost piece of luggage might contain contraband.

As an unwitting drug mule, Frampton was sentenced to four years and eight months in jail. This was reduced to four years after he appealed. Frampton served his time at the Villa Devoto jail in Buenos Aires, which was overcrowded and notorious for its harsh conditions. Needless to say, Frampton lost his job at the University of North Carolina.

Frampton was housed in a section of jail with 80 foreign drug smugglers in one large room. There were 40 bunks attached to the floor. Food was mostly stale bread. Frampton lost 25 pounds during his stay. He also witnessed a brutal murder when an inmate was stabbed to death right in front of him, allegedly by a hit man from the Medellin cocaine cartel.

In total, Frampton spent nine months in jail. He was released for health reasons and allowed to serve the rest of his sentence under house arrest at a friend's residence in Buenos Aires. He stayed under house arrest until June 2014. In early 2015, Frampton moved back to his homeland of Great Britain.

While Frampton's experience was extreme, online dating fraud is not. The Internet Crime Complaint Center (IC3, a partnership between the FBI and the National White Collar Crime Center), received 5,883 complaints of online romance fraud in 2014. Total losses among people who reported being scammed ran to nearly $87,000,000. Women were more likely to be scammed; there were 4,088 complaints from women versus 1,795 for men. The most likely age group to be scammed were people 50 to 59 years old.

These statistics closely match FBI research. According to a February 14, 2013, press release from the FBI's San Diego Division, the typical target of online dating scams "are women over 40 who are divorced, widowed and/or disabled … but every age group and demographic is at risk."

The FBI press release explained how a typical Internet dating scam goes down: "You're contacted online by someone who appears interested in you. He or she may have a profile you can read or a picture that is e-mailed to you. For weeks, even months, you may chat back and forth with one another, forming a connection. You may even be sent flowers or other gifts. But ultimately, it's going to happen—your newfound 'friend' is going to ask you for money."

The first request is not going to be the last request either. The requests will likely keep on coming for as long as the online dating scammer can gull his victim. In some cases, such as that of Paul Frampton, scammers have bigger plans for their prey than just ripping them off for quick cash.

The website RomanceScams.org offers more insights into online dating fraud dynamics. The site was founded June 6, 2005, as a Yahoo group for people who had been scammed by online dating predators. "The mission of RomanceScams.org, an information and advocacy organization, is to create public awareness, provide accurate information and expertise to assist in the successful demise of online romance scams, and help people learn, heal, and experience a safe online environment," stated the site.

RomanceScams.org offers helpful warning signs of a date site scammer. For example:

- Do they profess to be in love with you within hours of your first contact?
- Do they immediately pester you to leave the dating site and communicate by Instant Messenger or e-mail?
- Do they claim to be from the United States but are working overseas (usually in Nigeria or the UK)?
- Do they ask you for money or to cash a check?
- Do they make arrangements to visit you that always fall through for some reason?
- Do they claim not to have any close family, friends, or business associates who could help them through a financial crisis?
- Do they immediately start using "pet" names with you, such as hon/hun, baby/babe, or sweetie?
- Do the details they give you during chats regarding their height, weight, age, and birth date not match with the details in their profile?
- Do their profile pictures look like they came from a glamor magazine?
- Do they claim God brought you together?
- Do they sometimes call you by a different name? This is a clue that your paramour is in contact with more than one person and is getting names mixed up.
- Do they send you generic love poems?

These schemes are designed for one purpose: "in all cases, the plea for financial assistance is the key to the scam," noted RomanceScams.org.

Requests for money can be quite creative. The mysterious online paramour who's been wooing you might claim to be in a hotel where she can't pay the bill, or he's been mugged, or she may be in the hospital and won't be discharged until the fee is settled.

Online dating site scam artists often hail from abroad. Tipoffs that you're dealing with someone who is lying about his or her citizenship include time zone confusion (your online paramour isn't sure what the time is supposed to be in the place they're supposed to be in); unfamiliarity with common U.S. landmarks, attractions, and history; unfamiliarity with American slang; terrible spelling; and weird, stilted syntax, according to RomanceScams.org. It's also a giveaway if you have a phone conversation with your online suitor and realize she can barely speak English, or if you have difficulty hearing him above background noise—a possible sign he's at an Internet café.

While websites such as RomanceScams.org do their best to spread the word about online dating fraud, there is no shortage of new victims willing to do anything for their Internet sweethearts. The *National Post* newspaper of Canada, for example, ran a story on April 29, 2015, about a Vancouver man named Jake Malone who wandered around China in search of his Internet love.

Sixty-year-old Malone had apparently fallen in love with a young Chinese woman with the username RiLi through an online dating site. After exchanging close to 400 e-mails, Malone decided it was time to fly to Shenzhen, China, where the object of his affections claimed to live. RiLi demurred, fretting that an in-person meeting might ruin their unique online chemistry, but Malone wasn't deterred and hopped on a flight.

Once he landed in Shenzhen, Malone sought out the clothing company that RiLi claimed she owned. No doubt he had in mind romantic notions of meeting his love at work and sweeping her off her feet. When he went to the address of the clothing company, however, he found that the place had been shuttered for years. Undaunted, Malone took to walking around Shenzhen with a billboard hanging from his neck, containing a photo of RiLi and a message in Chinese informing her he was in town looking for her.

To the media, Malone admitted that his searching hadn't produced any results. He seemed unworried by suggestions that "RiLi" might have just been looking to chat with someone online or was even trying to scam him. Once they finally connected, Malone said he was willing to relocate and live in China with his lady-love. "I believe in her. I can feel from her letters that she loves me," Malone was quoted in the *National Post* as saying.

Further Reading

Ian Austin, "Vancouver Man Wanders Streets of Shenzhen, China, Looking for an Online Love He's Never Met," *The National Post*, April 29, 2015.

Federal Bureau of Investigation and National White Collar Crime Center, The Internet Crime Complaint Center, "2014 Internet Crime Report," http://www.ic3.gov/media/annualreport/2014_IC3Report.pdf.

Federal Bureau of Investigation, San Diego Division, "Looking for Love? Beware of Online Dating Scams," February 14, 2013, https://www.fbi.gov/sandiego/press-releases/2013/looking-for-love-beware-of-online-dating-scams.

Jennifer Quinn and Robert Cribb, "Online Dating Relationship Ends Badly, $1.3M Later," *Toronto Star*, November 30, 2013.

Romance Scams website, http://www.romancescams.org/.

Tom Worden, "'I Was Conned into Smuggling Cocaine by a Voluptuous Bikini Model—Then Locked Up in an Argentinian Hellhole Where an Inmate Was Butchered in Front of Me': Incredible Tale of 'Naïve' Professor, 71," *Daily Mail* online, February 25, 2015, http://www.dailymail.co.uk/news/article-2968276/He-went-straight-neck-decapitated-Professor-fell-honeytrap-cocaine-sting-relives-horrifying-moment-prisoner-butchered-eyes-notorious-Argentinian-jail.html.

MALWARE

On June 22, 2011, the U.S. Department of Justice announced the results of "Operation Trident Tribunal"—two separate investigations into cybercrime. Over one million computer users worldwide were victimized in the two schemes with total losses of more than $74 million, said the Department of Justice.

Both scams involved "scareware"—a type of malware (malicious software that serves only to sabotage people's computers as a means to extract cash). A U.S. Department of Justice press release explained that scareware "poses as legitimate computer security software and claims to detect a variety of threats on the affected computer that do not actually exist. Users are then informed they must purchase what they are told is anti-virus software in order to repair their computers. The users are then barraged with aggressive and disruptive notifications until they supply their credit card number and pay for the worthless 'antivirus' product. The product is, in fact, fake."

Operation Trident Tribunal's first investigation was spearheaded by the FBI's Seattle office. Authorities focused on a band of criminals in Kiev, Ukraine, who "infected hundreds of thousands of computers with scareware and sold more than $72 million of fake antivirus product over a period of three years," stated the U.S. Department of Justice.

The scareware purveyors used several tactics to infect computers. They created web pages advertising computer scans that could search for undetected viruses. Any computer user who clicked on the page downloaded scareware. Next thing users knew, they received urgent messages warning that their computers were teeming with viruses. The only way to get rid of these viruses was by purchasing a $129 "antivirus software" program from the criminal gang. The antivirus program in reality did nothing, because users' computers weren't infected with anything beyond the scareware itself.

The U.S. Department of Justice estimated that some 960,000 computer users were victimized in total. A dozen countries participated in the investigation, including the U.S., Ukraine, Latvia, Germany, the Netherlands, Cyprus, France, Sweden, Lithuania, Romania, Canada, and the United Kingdom. Authorities seized 22 computers and servers in the United States and 25 computers and servers in various European locales. Police in Latvia also closely examined five bank accounts that were allegedly used to channel profits to the leaders of the gang.

The second Operation Trident Tribunal investigation was led by the Minneapolis FBI office and concerned a case of online "malvertising." Two defendants in Latvia were arrested on behalf of U.S. authorities. The pair was charged with two counts of wire fraud, one count of conspiracy to commit wire fraud, and computer fraud.

The Latvians were accused of creating a phony advertising agency, then contacting startribune.com, the website of the *Minneapolis Star Tribune* newspaper.

The pair said their ad agency represented a hotel chain that wished to purchase online advertising space on startribune.com. The pair provided the newspaper with an electronic version of their ad. Startribune.com staff checked the ad out and found nothing amiss. Once the ad was running on startribune.com, however, the couple who created it allegedly changed the computer code in the advertisement. Visitors to the *Star Tribune* website suddenly were at risk of picking up a scareware program. Once downloaded, the scareware froze users' computers, then generated a series of annoying pop-up ads for an antivirus software that would unfreeze the screen.

If a user purchased the "antivirus" software, their screens unfroze, but the scareware remained in the system. Anyone who failed to purchase the fake antivirus software found that all their information, data, and files stored became inaccessible, said the U.S. Department of Justice. Total losses from this second scheme ran to about $2 million.

While the U.S. Department of Justice didn't say so, the malware used to infect startribune.com could actually be considered a variant of scareware called "ransomware." If downloaded, ransomware will restrict users' access to their own computer systems. In order to recover access, users must pay a "ransom" to whoever sent or created the malware.

The Internet Crime Complaint Center (IC3), a partnership between the FBI and the National White Collar Crime Center (NW3C) recorded 991 complaints about ransomware in 2013 (the most recent year for which figures are

How to Protect Yourself from Malware

- Make sure you have anti-virus protection on your computer and that it's periodically updated
- Don't click on e-mail attachments from unsolicited senders. Be wary of messages supposedly from your bank branch or the Federal Reserve, saying your bank account has been compromised and you have to click a link to fix the problem. Instead, go directly to your financial institution's website to see if there is indeed a problem with an account.
- Don't accept unsolicited jobs online that require you to receive funds from various bank accounts then wire-transfer the money to overseas bank accounts. This reeks of scam. If you ignore the warnings and wire-transfer cash as requested, you might find yourself part of a criminal investigation.

Source: FBI website, https://www.fbi.gov/news/stories/2015/january/ransomware -on-the-rise

available). Combined losses from these complaints came to $539,562. The majority of people registering complaints were male (596 men versus 395 women). Men over 60 and women aged 40 to 49 were the demographics most likely to report a complaint.

"The IC3 has received multiple complaints surrounding ransomware/scareware schemes. These schemes are used to target and extort funds from victims by intimidating them. These scams began years ago with false claims in which the perpetrators pretended to be federal government officials who were watching and monitoring the victims' Internet usage," stated IC3's 2013 Internet Crime Report.

The Crime Report cited common ransomware programs such as "CryptoLocker": "The IC3 became aware of the CryptoLocker scheme in October 2013. It spreads via e-mail and propagates rapidly. The virus encrypts various file types and then a pop-up window appears on the victims' computer that states their data has been encrypted. The only way to get it back is to send a specified monetary payment to the perpetrator. This ransomware provides the victim with a timeline to pay via a displayed countdown clock. If victims do not pay on time, they lose the ability to pay and risk having their data permanently encrypted and rendered unusable. Perpetrators are demanding a $300 to $700 payment sent to the perpetrator using various methods," stated the 2013 Internet Crime Report.

Another reoccurring scareware/ransomware scam raises the ugly specter of child pornography. In this scam, malware is transmitted when a computer user visits an infected website. Once the scareware/ransomware takes root, the user's computer freezes up and a pop-up warning tells the user they've violated U.S. federal law.

"Child pornography is either embedded in a banner image that appears on the victims' screen or revealed via an automatic browser redirecting them to a child pornography website. The scareware is used as an extortion technique by threatening prosecution for visiting or viewing these images. The victim is also informed that they have been recorded using audio, video and other services. The only way to unlock the computer is to pay the fine, usually between $300 and $5,000," stated the IC3 report.

Needless to say, the fear of being reported for possessing child pornography, just like the fear of losing control of your own computer, prompts many victims to simply pay up instead of fighting back.

Further Reading

Federal Bureau of Investigation and National White Collar Crime Center, The Internet Crime Complaint Center, "2013 Internet Crime Report," http://www.ic3.gov/media /annualreport/2013_IC3Report.pdf.

Federal Bureau of Investigation website, "Malware Targets Bank Accounts—'Gameover' Delivered via Phishing E-Mails," January 6, 2012, https://www.fbi.gov/news/stories /2012/january/malware_010612/malware_010612.

Federal Bureau of Investigation website, "New Internet Scam—'Ransomware' Locks Computers, Demands Payment," August 9, 2012, https://www.fbi.gov/news/stories /2012/august/new-internet-scam.

Federal Bureau of Investigation website, "'Scareware' Distributors Targeted—12 Nations Coordinate Anti-Cyber Crime Effort," June 22, 2011, https://www.fbi.gov /news/stories/2011/june/cyber_062211/cyber_062211.

U.S. Department of Justice, "Department of Justice Disrupts International Cyber Crime Rings Distributing Scareware," June 22, 2011.

THE NIGERIAN LETTER

Anyone who has ever used e-mail has probably received a spam message supposedly from a Nigerian prince or other dignitary, promising millions for participation in a scheme to access an even bigger fortune. These messages typically contain a great deal of spelling mistakes, odd syntax, and stiffly formal salutations (e.g., "Dear Good Sir, We humbly request your attention to a financial matter of which your personal involvement may enrich you to a considerable sum"). Readers are instructed to provide their banking information and/or pay a small fee as part of the plan to recover the letter writer's fortune. This is the so-called "Nigerian Letter" scam at play.

Also known as the "419 scam," after the section of the Nigerian criminal code dealing with such offenses, the Nigerian Letter scam is a modern-day version of the centuries-old "Spanish Prisoner" con (which was covered in the section "Classic Confidence Scams"). In the Spanish Prisoner con, people would receive personal letters, supposedly smuggled out of jail, from a royal figure being held against his will behind bars in Spain. The prisoner required an outsider to help them access their wealth. All the letter recipient had to do was provide his bank account numbers and send a small fee to an enclosed address.

The Nigerian Letter scam, like its Spanish Prisoner predecessor, can be categorized as a form of advance fee fraud (AFF). In such frauds, a targeted individual is convinced they can obtain wealth or a romantic relationship as long as they pay a fee in advance.

"Names and addresses of potential victims are obtained through various trade journals, business directories, magazine and newspaper advertisements, Chambers of Commerce, and the Internet," stated an April 1997 warning on Nigerian advance fee fraud issued by the U.S. Department of State, Bureau of International Affairs and Law Enforcement Affairs.

There are several reasons why Nigeria has become the epicenter of advance fee fraud. For one, Nigeria is the most populous country in Africa, with a large English-speaking population. It is believed that the Nigerian Letter scam emerged in the 1980s, following the collapse of world oil prices (the Nigerian economy is heavily resource-based). University-educated Nigerians, finding themselves out of work, turned to criminality and revived the Spanish Prisoner con with the help of then-cutting-edge fax machines.

In the mid-1990s, following the commercialization of the Internet, Nigerian scammers turned to e-mail as their prime vehicle of communication. It was an extremely inexpensive and easy way to find new prey. Some Nigerian scammers began sending millions of messages to random e-mail addresses.

However the victims are found, the structure of the con is generally the same: anyone who responds positively to a Nigerian Letter will enter into a period of back-and-forth communication with their supposed benefactor. A long, sad tale will unfold, as the letter writer explains how he came to his position. Sometimes the scammer pretends to be a royal figure or dignitary who requires outside assistance to access his wealth. Other times, the scammer introduces an element of thievery into the proceedings, claiming to be a Nigerian civil servant who stumbled upon millions in "forgotten" government money he needs your help in embezzling.

However the victim is hooked, the scammer soon starts making demands. "Those willing to assist are asked to provide their banking account number (for 'safekeeping' the funds) and Social Security number, birth date or other personal information. Or they are asked to send money to the letter-sender for taxes and various fees," reported the Better Business Bureau of Metropolitan New York, Long Island and the Mid-Hudson Region.

In the short-term version, the scam is over the moment the dupe gives up their bank account number or wires in a "fee." Other times, the scammer strings his victim along and attempts to rip him off repeatedly. In such cases, the scam artist frequently requests company letterhead or various other corporate documents from wherever the victim works. Such items are subsequently used in future cons. In the meantime, the scammers send their dupe reams of documents supposedly from Nigerian banks, government agencies, or corporations, in an attempt to establish legitimacy. All of these documents are either forged or stolen. None will actually help the mark recover his money once the scam is up.

After a few days of back-and-forth banter, the long-term version of the scam enters a crucial phase: "A victim will be advised that the deal is near completion, however, an emergency has arisen and money is needed to pay an unforeseen government fee or tax before the money can be released. If the fee is paid, the criminals will come up with another 'problem' that requires immediate payment by the victim. Each 'problem' is supported by 'official' documentation … the criminal can run this ruse for months or even years depending on the gullibility of the victim or his or her desperation to recoup losses," explained the 1997 U.S. Department of State warning on Nigerian advance fee fraud.

Sometimes, the scammers will request that their dupe travel to Nigeria or a bordering nation to seal the deal in person. The scam artists might request that the victim bring along pricey watches or men's suits, which will allegedly be used to bribe officials but in fact will only enrich the fraudsters.

The U.S. Department of State warning continues: "Once in Lagos, the victim will be housed in one of the many small hotels (euphemistically known as "419" hotels) located primarily around [the airport]. At this point, the victim is totally immersed in the scam and the criminals have total control over the victim's every move. The victim is taken to meetings with criminals posing as Nigerian government officials or possibly corrupt government officials to final-ize the deal. These meetings can take place in government offices or annexes that are 'rented' by the criminals or an office that is set up to resemble a gov-ernment office."

If the victim continues to go along with the scam, he will likely be fleeced of his money but sent home alive. Should he cotton on and refuse to play along or pay any more "fees," the scammers might turn to threats or physical violence. "In the 1990s, at least 15 foreign businessmen, including one American, were killed after being lured to Nigeria by 419 scammers," stated the May 15, 2006, *New Yorker* magazine.

Even for those people who don't travel to Nigeria, the experience of dealing with Nigerian Letter scammers can be searing. "Any money wired to [Nigerian Letter scammers] will be forever lost and irretrievable. If they hook a victim, they will always insist money be wired through Western Union or Money-Gram. They prefer Western Union and MoneyGram because these funds can be easily retrieved at any branch (thousands of them) throughout the country using their false IDs," stated a warning from the U.S. Embassy in Cote d'Ivoire.

There are many variations of the Nigerian Letter scam. In some versions, a dupe is told they are the beneficiary of a will. An obscure relative who made a fortune in Africa died, leaving his million-dollar fortune to his next-of-kin. The victim is told he is the next-of-kin. In order to retrieve his inheritance, he will first have to pay a few "processing" and "administrative" fees.

In another version, spam e-mails request contributions to fight poverty, dis-ease, or dictatorship in Africa. Anyone who responds to these missives is asked to provide bank account information to speed up the donation process.

The Nigerian Letter scam often involves counterfeit checks. A dupe is sent a large check from the scammers, who ask that he deposit it in his bank account and then wire the majority of the funds to another account. The dupe will be allowed to retain ten percent of the cash in the form of a fee. The victim cashes the check and wire-transfers the money, only to discover a few days later that the check has bounced. The bank is demanding that the dupe make good on the entire amount of the phony check.

In some cases, the scamming takes a romantic twist. The scammer seeks out victims on dating websites, looking for profiles from lonely or desperate people. After contacting the dupe, the scammer quickly expresses deep love, sending romantic musings. At some point, the scam artist asks his prey to cash a check for him and wire the proceeds. Or he pleads poverty and asks the dupe to send money for a round-trip airline flight from Africa, so the two online lovers can meet. Needless to say, none of these romantic overtures ever amount to anything.

The Nigerian Letter is based on the same marketing strategy that guides door-to-door sales and other "hard-sell" business dealings. The vast majority of people who receive Nigerian Letter e-mails will delete them without a second thought. The scammers know this and don't care. Like the door-to-door salesman, they know that persistence will pay off. If one in a thousand people responds to an e-mail plea for assistance in recovering a fortune, the scam artists' efforts have been amply rewarded.

Sometimes the victims of the Nigerian Letter scam are not who you might expect. The May 15, 2006, edition of the *New Yorker* contained a long profile

How to Protect Yourself from the Nigerian Letter Scam

- Don't reply to any e-mails or letters from anyone from Nigeria asking you to send personal or banking information. Delete such e-mails and throw out paper letters and faxes of this nature.
- If you have responded to such an inquiry, or know someone who is communicating with supposed millionaires in Nigeria, contact the U.S. Secret Service.
- Be immediately suspicious of a stranger who seems eager to place a large amount of money at your disposal in exchange for your bank account number or other personal financial information.
- Cashier checks and money orders can be faked, just like actual currency. If a stranger sends you a check or money order to buy a product or service from you, confer with your bank about how long it will take to verify the check, then wait for the funds to clear before doing anything else (despite the stranger's loud protests to send the cash right away).

Note: Anyone who is scammed can also report the Internet Crime Complaint Center (IC3), a partnership between the FBI and National White Collar Crime Center (NW3C).

Source: Better Business Bureau of Metropolitan New York, Long Island and the Mid-Hudson Region, https://www.bbb.org/new-york-city/get-consumer-help /articles/the-nigerian-prince-old-scam-new-twist/

of one John W. Worley, a 57-year-old ordained minister who lived in Massachusetts and worked as a Christian psychotherapist. Worley was well-educated and worldly, yet he fell for the Nigerian scam, stated the article, titled "The Perfect Mark." His initial contact came via e-mail. A stranger, who said he was Captain Joshua Mbote, former head of security for a Congo leader, requested help getting funds out of South Africa that had been earmarked to buy weapons. Anyone who provided assistance could expect a sizeable share of the proceeds, according to Captain Mbote.

Over a period of months, Worley wire-transferred thousands of dollars of his own money to scammers in Nigeria. He also cashed checks they sent him and wired most of the funds to other banks, only to discover the checks were fake and he was on the hook for them.

Worley was brilliantly conned by several different scammers. When he became suspicious of one ruse, the scam artists would abandon it and announce a new scheme and a new contact. At one point, Worley thought he was helping a "Mrs. Abacha," widow of a Nigerian dictator, who required assistance retrieving a fortune embezzled from the Nigerian bank.

After numerous e-mails, phone calls, faxes, and bank transfers, Worley finally realized he'd been had. He also found himself on trial in May 2005 in U.S. District Court in Boston, charged with bank fraud, money laundering, and possession of counterfeit checks. The scammers were not charged, because authorities in North America weren't sure who they were. Worley had sent the scam artists more than $40,000 of his own money and nearly $600,000 from bad checks. Add in fees such as credit card interest, cost of wiring money, long-distance phone bills, and a tax lawyer, and Worley's direct personal losses (not counting bad checks) were more like $80,000.

Worley's lawyer tried to portray his client as a naïve man who genuinely thought he was helping Nigerians in financial straits. The jury didn't buy it. In February 2006, Worley was found guilty on all charges. He was sentenced to two years in jail, plus restitution of nearly $600,000.

During the trial, the contents of hundreds of e-mails between Worley and various scammers were revealed. "It is clear that the Nigerians were able to take advantage of his religious convictions, his stubbornness, and his desire to be a hero to Mrs. Abacha and to his family. Patiently and persistently, the Nigerians turned Worley's skepticism into suspension of disbelief, to the point where he seemed to worry that they might not trust *him*. They made Worley the perfect mark," reported the May 15, 2006, *New Yorker*.

Further Reading

Better Business Bureau, Metropolitan New York, Long Island and the Mid-Hudson Region, "The Nigerian Prince: Old Scam, New Twist," http://www.bbb.org/new-york -city/get-consumer-help/articles/the-nigerian-prince-old-scam-new-twist/.

Embassy of the United States Abidjan, Cote d'Ivoire, "419 Scams," http://abidjan
.usembassy.gov/art_of_scam.html.

Federal Bureau of Investigation website, "Nigerian Letter or '419' Fraud," https://www
.fbi.gov/scams-safety/fraud.

Steve Lohr, "'Nigerian Scam' Lures Companies," *New York Times*, May 21, 1992.

Dave Stancliff, "As It Stands: Why Nigeria Became the Scam Capital of the World,"
Times Standard, February 12, 2012.

United States Department of State, Bureau of Consular Affairs, "Inheritance and Money
Laundering Scams," http://travel.state.gov/content/passports/english/emergencies
/scams/inheritances.html.

United States Department of State, Bureau of International Narcotics and Law Enforcement Affairs, "Nigerian Advance Fee Fraud," April 1997, http://www.state.gov
/documents/organization/2189.pdf.

Mitchell Zuckoff, "The Perfect Mark," *The New Yorker*, May 15, 2006.

PHISHING/VISHING

"Phising" e-mails contain warnings that that hackers have accessed the bank account or credit card of the e-mail recipient. At first glance, such missives appear to be from legitimate sources.

Phishing e-mails are "designed to look like they come from well-known and trusted businesses, financial institutions and government agencies in an attempt to collect personal, financial and sensitive information," explained the website to the Royal Canadian Mounted Police (RCMP).

"The content of a phishing e-mail or text message is intended to trigger a quick reaction from you," continued the RCMP. "It can use upsetting or exciting information, demand an urgent response or employ a false pretense or statement. Phishing messages are normally not personalized ... typically [these messages] will ask you to 'update', 'validate', or 'confirm' your account information or face dire consequences."

Usually, a link is provided to a website, where all can be supposedly sorted out. Anyone who clicks on the link and fills in information on the site provided risks being scammed for real.

Some criminals go so far as to include official-looking logos and other online identifiers from actual financial institutions or credit card companies in their messages, to make them look more like the real thing. The information the criminals are after can include the victim's Social Security number, date of birth, full name, full address, mother's maiden name, username and passwords to websites victims frequent, driver's license number, personal identification numbers (PINs), and credit card and bank account numbers. With this kind of data, cybercriminals can access victims' financial accounts, open new bank accounts in their name, transfer money from their accounts, apply for loans or credit, purchase goods and services, etc.

Fortunately, there are numerous red flags to indicate you have received a phishing message. Poor command of the English language is an immediate giveaway: "Cybercriminals are not known for their grammar and spelling. Professional companies or organizations usually have a staff of copy editors that will not allow a mass e-mail [full of mistakes] to go to its users. If you notice mistakes in an e-mail, it might be a scam," warns the Microsoft Safety & Security Center webpage.

Any e-mail or text message containing urgent requests for personal or financial information is suspicious. Financial institutions and credit/debit card companies generally don't confirm an existing client's information via e-mail. If you receive an e-mail along these lines, check with your financial institution or credit card company to see if all is well with your account.

Phishing isn't just a small-time con. On May 20, 2008, the FBI announced the results of two investigations into phishing. A total of 38 people "with links to global organized crime—mostly working out of Romania and the U.S. but also operating in Pakistan, Portugal and Canada—were indicted for engineering a decidedly 21st-century cyber-based scheme," stated a post on the FBI website.

According to the FBI, the worldwide scam ran as follows: fraudsters, primarily in Romania, known as "suppliers" went phishing by sending out vast amounts of spam. Anyone who responded to this spam got potentially caught in their net. The suppliers passed on information regarding bank and credit accounts and other details from thousands of victims to partners in the U.S. The American partners (known as "cashiers") took this data and manufactured

How to Prevent Phishing

- Never send personal or financial information via e-mail.
- Avoid embedded links in an e-mail claiming to take you to a secure site.
- If an e-mail contains a link to a site you've frequently visited, and the URL is different from what you're familiar with, don't click on it.
- Regularly update your computer's anti-virus software, spyware filters, e-mail filters, and firewall programs.
- Make a regular habit of checking your bank and credit or debit card statements, to make sure all transactions are legitimate. Contact your bank or credit/debit card company immediately if you find any suspicious-looking transactions.

Source: Royal Canadian Mounted Police website, http://www.rcmp-grc.gc.ca/scams-fraudes/phishing-eng.htm

counterfeit credit, debit, and gift cards encoded with stolen financial information. These cards were then used in ATMs and point-of-sale terminals to withdraw cash and make purchases. The cashiers would wire transfer a portion of their proceeds to the suppliers in Romania, their reward for providing banking/personal information from unwitting victims.

As with many high-tech scams, there are some common variations on the phishing theme. "Smishing," for example, refers to phishing via Short Message Service (SMS) text. "Vishing" refers to phishing via voice.

The FBI website explained how smishing and vishing work: criminals establish an automated dialing system that will text message or call people on the phone in a given region or area code. The message is usually a warning, along the lines that there is a problem with a person's bank account or ATM/credit card that requires immediate attention. Fortunately, said problem can be easily resolved, by simply calling a given phone number or visiting a particular website. Anyone who calls the phone number or visits the website will be asked to provide personal/financial information to "verify" their identity.

A November 24, 2010, FBI website posting on "Smishing and Vishing" warned, "Sometimes, if a victim logs onto one of the phony websites with a smartphone, they could also end up downloading malicious software that could give criminals access to anything on the phone. With the growth of mobile banking and the ability to conduct financial transactions online, smishing and vishing attacks may become even more attractive and lucrative for cyber criminals."

Further Reading

Federal Bureau of Investigation website, "Gone Phishing—Global Ring Gets Rather Slick," May 20, 2008, https://www.fbi.gov/news/stories/2008/may/phishing052008.

Federal Bureau of Investigation website, "Something Vishy—Be Aware of a New Online Scam," February 23, 2007, https://www.fbi.gov/news/stories/2007/february/vishing _022307/.

Microsoft.com, "How to Recognize Phishing E-mail Messages, Links or Phone Calls," http://www.microsoft.com/security/online-privacy/phishing-symptoms.aspx.

Royal Canadian Mounted Police, "E-mail Fraud/Phishing," http://www.rcmp-grc.gc.ca /scams-fraudes/phishing-eng.htm.

PHONY RENTALS AND AUCTIONS

Phony online property rentals can result in depleted bank accounts, ruined holidays, and embarrassed travelers and homeowners alike. Phony online car ads typically produce similar results: no car, no actual seller, and little chance of getting your money back.

A consumer alert posted July 29, 2009, on the FBI's website outlined how phony online rental scams work: "Criminals search websites that list homes for sale. They take the information in those ads—lock, stock, and barrel—and post it with their own e-mail addresses in an ad on Craigslist (without Craigslist's consent or knowledge) under the housing rental category. To sweeten the pot, the houses are almost always listed with below-market rental rates."

The FBI consumer alert continued, "An interested party will contact the 'homeowner' via e-mail, who usually explains that he or she had to leave the U.S. quickly because of some missionary or contract work in Africa. Victims are usually instructed to send money overseas—enough to cover the first and last month's rent—via a wire transfer service (because the crooks know it can't be traced once it gets picked up on the other end)."

Some particularly malicious scammers victimize their prey twice. During "negotiations" for the property, the con artist might request that the dupe fill out a credit application, including their credit history and Social Security number. This information is used to rip the dupe off even further.

In a variation of this scam, a cash-strapped homeowner facing imminent foreclosure for failing to make their payments abandons their property and puts it up for rent. An unsuspecting tenant pays first and last month's rent, then moves in. Mere days after their arrival, a sheriff or other authority figure comes knocking at the door with an eviction order. Although the eviction order is directed at the actual owner, the renter might also be forced to leave.

People who have been defrauded by such scams can report their experience to the Internet Crime Complaint Center (IC3). A partnership between the FBI and the National White Collar Crime Center, IC3 keeps tabs on various online scams. In the Center's report for 2014, some 9,955 people registered complaints regarding online real estate fraud, with total reported losses of $19,800,172. Females were more likely to be scammed (the IC3 registered 5,921 complaints from women and 4,034 complaints from men). The most frequently scammed age bracket was people 20 to 29 years old.

The Internet has also proven a boon to con artists peddling fake car ads. Once again, the criminal advertises an attractive vehicle on Craigslist or another site at a discount price. The victim contacts the fraudster via e-mail—and the scammer jumps at the opportunity to skin another dupe.

"Often criminals claim they must sell the vehicle because they are moving or being relocated for work. Due to the pending move, the criminals often refuse to meet with the potential buyers or allow vehicle inspections and ultimately try to rush the sale," stated the IC3 report for 2013. Needless to say, once money has been sent via wire transfer, the victim never actually receives the car in question. Most times, the scam artist doesn't even own the vehicle they've advertised for sale.

The IC3 recorded a total of 16,861 complaints about phony online vehicle auctions in 2014, for total losses of $56,222,655. The majority of victims were male (10,635 complaints from men versus 6,226 from women), while the age group most likely to be victimized were those 40 to 49 years old.

Fortunately, with either the fake rental or fake car auction, it is fairly simple to avoid being ripped off. In the case of fake property rentals, the FBI urges people to only deal with local landlords, to not send any money via wire transfer (asking for cash this way is a major red flag), and to be suspicious of e-mail correspondence from a supposed landlord that's full of spelling mistakes and broken English. It's also worthwhile to investigate average rental prices in the area; if a property is being advertised at considerably below the average price, there is a good chance it's a scam. Likewise, don't give out personal information such as Social Security numbers or bank/credit information on rental applications.

Another simple method of smoking out con artists is to ask them for identification, such as a driver's license. Search the county website to see if the person you're dealing with actually owns the property that's been advertised for rent. This information might be stored in the webpages for the recorder of deeds or assessor's office.

Much of the same advice applies to online automotive sales, with the proviso that to be really safe, only purchase a vehicle from a licensed, recognized dealer.

Further Reading

Federal Bureau of Investigation and National White Collar Crime Center, The Internet Crime Complaint Center, "2014 Internet Crime Report," http://www.ic3.gov/media/annualreport/2014_IC3Report.pdf.

Federal Bureau of Investigation and National White Collar Crime Center, The Internet Crime Complaint Center, "2013 Internet Crime Report," http://www.ic3.gov/media/annualreport/2013_IC3Report.pdf.

Federal Bureau of Investigation website, "Consumer Alert, Online Rental Ads Could Be Phony," July 29, 2009, https://www.fbi.gov/news/stories/2009/july/housingscam_072909.

Lew Sichelman, "Rental Scams Can Target Either Landlords or Tenants," *Los Angeles Times*, March 25, 2012.

PHONE FRAUD
Cramming

The modern-day Mafia has proven very capable of finding new ways to extract money from old technology. In February 2004, for example, federal authorities in New York state arrested two Gambino Mafia family members and various associates for racketeering and money laundering in connection with phone fraud.

According to the U.S. government, the Gambino Mafiosi worked with corrupt telephone executives on a scam that generated phony charges on phone bills. "Forget gambling, loan-sharking and labor racketeering, New York organized crime figures bilked millions of unsuspecting consumers out of more than $200 million over five years by piggybacking bogus charges on their telephone bills, federal authorities said yesterday ... the scheme ... marked what federal authorities believe was the first time organized crime figures have been charged with using the billing fraud known as "cramming" to fill mob coffers ... [Cramming] is the common term for larding a telephone bill with unauthorized charges," stated the *New York Times* on February 11, 2004.

The *Times* continued, "The nationwide scheme was sophisticated, officials said, but the idea was simple: callers responding to advertisements for free samples of services like psychic phone lines, telephone dating services and adult chat lines were unknowingly charged up to $40 a month on their phone bills for services they never requested and never used."

To find out if you've been a victim of "cramming," closely examine your phone bill. Calls with strange area codes, charges for collect calls the consumer never accepted, and calls to sex or entertainment lines that the consumer never made are tipoffs that someone has been making phony charges against your number.

Further Reading

Nate Hendley, *The Mafia: A Guide to an American Subculture*, 2013.

Corey Kilgannon, "Phone Executive Admits Conspiracy in Mob Fraud," *New York Times*, January 9, 2005.

William K. Rashbaum, "Officials Say Mob Stole $200 Million Using Phone Bills," *New York Times*, February 11, 2004.

Jury Duty Scam

The Jury Duty scam is simple and very effective. A con artist calls a victim, claiming to be an officer of the court. The alleged officer asks the victim why they didn't show up for jury duty. The victim pleads ignorance. The court officer says a notice was sent to the victim's home, which they obviously ignored. Failing to appear for jury duty is a criminal offense, warns the officer. The victim is told a warrant has been issued in their name.

By now, if the con artist has a good phone manner and sounds believable, the victim is terrified. They've never been arrested before in their lives. This obviously is some mistake, they claim. Isn't there some way they can rectify the situation? In fact, there is, says the scammer. Please provide some personal details—say, your Social Security number and a credit card number—so the court can confirm your identity and clear this matter up. If the victim balks, the "court officer" warns that refusing to cooperate might result in a hefty fine, in addition to arrest.

"The scam's bold simplicity may be what makes it so effective. Facing the unexpected threat of arrest, victims are caught off guard and may be quick to part with some information to defuse the situation," stated a warning about the Jury Scam on the FBI's website.

A basic understanding of courthouse procedure is good inoculation against this scam: "Federal courts do not require anyone to provide any sensitive information in a telephone call. Most contact between a federal court and a prospective juror will be through the U.S. Mail, and any phone contact by real court officials will not include requests for Social Security numbers, credit card numbers or any other sensitive information," stated a bulletin from the Administrative Office of the U.S. Courts, on behalf of the federal judiciary.

Further Reading

Administrative Office of the U.S. Courts, "Warning: Bogus Phone Calls on Jury Service May Lead to Fraud."

Federal Bureau of Investigation website, "Telephone Fraud Involving Jury Duty," September 28, 2005, https://www.fbi.gov/news/pressrel/press-releases/telephone-fraud-involving-jury-duty.

Federal Bureau of Investigation website, "The Verdict: Hang Up—Don't Fall for Jury Duty Scam," February 6, 2006, http://www.fbi.gov/news/stories/2006/june/jury_scam060206.

Telemarketing Fraud

Telemarketing fraud has been around almost as long as telephones. While e-mail spam and online scams get more attention these days, the old-fashioned telephone is still a handy tool for con artists looking for victims to fleece. Common telemarketing schemes include fake charities ("Donate now to save the starving children of Abyssinia"), offers of products or services ("We'll be happy to paint your house once you provide us with a down payment from your credit card"), and fake lotteries.

Some telemarketing frauds are aimed specifically at businesses or government offices, not individuals. One such fraud can be dubbed the Business Directory scam. A random caller contacts the human resources or marketing department of a company and asks for their mailing address. The caller wants to send your firm a corporate or government directory, containing your company's contact information. The caller implies that your office has been listed in this directory for years.

The fraudster is counting on bureaucratic inertia and unwieldy size to pull their scam. In a really big company or government office, it can be hard to keep track of who ordered what product from where. If the caller sounds sincere, a hapless bureaucrat or administrator might think the offer is legitimate. Obviously, someone somewhere in the chain of command must have given approval for the listing at some point in time. Why else would the directory representative be calling?

Of course, once the order has been made, the company will never receive the promised business directory. Or if they do receive a directory, it will be filled with information easily available elsewhere. Nonetheless, the office responsible for ordering the directory can expect a large bill.

Individuals or businesses alike can avoid being victims of telemarketing fraud by following some simple steps:

- Never purchase anything from a company you've never heard of, whose representatives are loath to offer too many details about their firm over the phone.
- Never feel compelled to "act immediately" in response to an offer received over the phone.
- Always ask for written material before giving any money.
- Check to see whether the company or charity that claims to be calling is listed in the Better Business Bureau or other fraudster watchdog groups.
- If you're dealing with a charity, ask what percentage of your donation will actually go to help the needy. A legitimate charity will be forthcoming with such information. If only a tiny fraction of your donation actually helps the purported recipients of the charity, don't make a payment.
- Ask the phone representative for their name, the name of the company they claim to be from, the mailing address of said company, and a phone number where you can call them back. Failure to offer such details should be an immediate red flag.
- If offered services, such as house-painting or yard work, don't pay in advance. Only pay after the services have been rendered to your satisfaction.
- If you've won a lottery or some kind of prize, be wary if you're told you have to pay taxes or fees to collect it.
- If you don't understand the offer, don't accept it.
- Trust your instincts. If you sense the caller is lying or deceiving you, hang up.

Fake Tech Support

In late 2012, the Federal Trade Commission (FTC) announced a crackdown on companies that arranged fraudulent "tech support" calls. The FTC set their sights at six firms. Most of these were based in India, while their victims were generally based in English-speaking nations, including Canada, the United States, Australia, New Zealand, Ireland, and the United Kingdom.

Indian-based staff working for the fraudsters made random calls to individuals whose numbers were gleaned from phone directories. Anyone who answered such a call was told they were speaking to a computer support person from a legitimate company, such as Microsoft or Dell. The tech support person claimed to have noticed that the computer belonging to the person they were calling was infected with viruses and badly in need of care. To further prove their point, scammers pointed to online "warning messages" about viruses (actually generic error notices from Windows Event Viewer).

If given the opportunity to control the victim's computer remotely, the con artists would download free anti-virus software, then charge a fee for their services—generally, between $50 and $500. In addition to getting rid of non-existent viruses, the fraudsters sometimes took the opportunity to snoop for passwords and financial information while controlling a victim's computer remotely.

Just as with old-fashioned phone fraud, the best way to ward off con artists plying the fake tech support staff scam is to refuse their services or start asking questions, such as, What company do you work for again? What is your full name? What is a contact number I can call to reach you? What is specifically wrong with my computer? How did you get my number?

Further Reading

Federal Bureau of Investigation website, "Common Fraud Schemes," https://www.fbi.gov/scams-safety/fraud.

Federal Bureau of Investigation website, "The Latest Phone Scam Targets Your Bank Account," June 21, 2010, https://www.fbi.gov/news/stories/2010/june/phone-scam.

Federal Trade Commission, "FTC Halts Massive Tech Support Scams," October 3, 2012.

SECTION EIGHT

PARA-ABNORMAL FRAUD

INTRODUCTION

From best sellers about haunted houses to celebrity psychics, our society is fascinated with the paranormal, the uncanny realm of the weird and unexplained. This interest in all things supernatural has deep roots; the Fox sisters, for example, enthralled nineteenth-century audiences with their apparent ability to communicate with the dead.

Even the U.S. government has shown interest in this field. From the 1970s through the mid-1990s, various intelligence agencies funded research into "remote viewing"—the supposed ability to mentally travel to distant locales and investigate people's thoughts.

Although skeptics scoff at such claims, the notion of ghostly spirits and inexplicable psychic power is very real to a large segment of the public. Some individuals, their motivations cynical or sincere, are willing to play upon such beliefs to profit from the paranormal. When such individuals knowingly peddle falsehoods and delusions, however, their actions are best described as fraudulent, not psychic.

THE AMITYVILLE HORROR

In the summer of 1975, George and Kathy Lutz were looking for a new house for their family. On one of their house-hunting expeditions, they spotted a three-story, six-bedroom Dutch Colonial–style home in the quaint town of Amityville, New York. The handsome house was located at 112 Ocean Avenue, in a pleasant suburban setting.

Built in the 1920s, the home had some history to it. On November 13, 1974, six members of the DeFeo family were shot dead in the house as they slept. The dead included Ronald DeFeo Sr., his wife, Louise DeFeo, and two sons and two daughters. All were killed with a .35-caliber Marlin rifle. The only family member who wasn't killed—one Ronald Jr. (aka "Butch")—quickly confessed to the slaughter.

In early December 1975, "Butch" DeFeo received a sentence of 25 years to life for murder. Two weeks later, on December 18, 1975, the Lutzes moved into 112 Ocean Avenue. They were fully aware of the horrendous events that had taken place in the home but seemed unfazed by the prospect of living in a former crime scene.

George Lutz's wife, Kathy, had three children from a previous marriage. The family seemed delighted to have found such a large, expansive home in such a pleasant community. Little did any of them suspect they were going to spend less than 30 days in the place, allegedly driven out by an intense bout of supernatural horror.

According to the Lutzes' later account, strange things began happening in the home almost immediately. The family sensed cold spots in random locations around the house. Lingering odors could sometimes be scented—sometimes perfume, other times excrement. Jolting sounds could be heard at night, and a sinister mood prevailed. George Lutz began to mysteriously cut himself off from his family, brooding next to a fireplace.

Kathy Lutz had her own woes, or so the family said. It felt like an invisible person was touching her as she slept. Once, upon waking from a refreshingly deep slumber, Kathy looked in the mirror and discovered her face had turned into the visage of a horrible old lady. Reportedly it took hours for the transformation to wear off.

The Lutzes' list of mysterious happenings included odd behavior on the part of the children. Youngest child, Missy, talked about the angel that happened to be living in her room. This angel had a name ("Jodie") and could apparently change shape when it wanted to. Sometimes, for unclear reasons, the angel appeared as a large pig. George and Kathy Lutz reported seeing two evil red eyes staring at them through the upstairs bedroom windows. Missy believed this was Jodie, eager to come inside.

The horrors kept coming, claimed the family: a mysterious force ripped a heavy door open, almost tearing it completely off the hinges. Windows opened and shut on their own. Some sort of slimy green substance oozed from ceilings. The family found tracks in fresh snow outside their home, from a cloven-hooved creature. In the middle of winter, one room in the house became infested with an Egyptian plague's worth of flies. A priest who came around to bless the home left with blisters on his hands.

The alleged eeriness began to evoke the fate of the previous tenants. George Lutz found himself constantly waking up at 3:15 a.m.—supposedly the same time the DeFeo murders took place. He discovered a small room behind some shelving in the basement that wasn't on the blueprints of the house. The room was about four feet by five feet and painted a creepy shade of red. The family dog didn't want anything to do with the newly discovered space and seemed quite put off by the red room.

Soon the ghost story took on a hallucinatory aspect. When the Lutz parents poked the logs in the fireplace, they saw a demonic image, missing half of its head. George Lutz heard the front door slam one night. Racing downstairs to investigate, he noticed the family dog sleeping peacefully. Other times, Lutz swore he heard what sounded like a marching band tuning their instruments or a clock radio that hadn't synched on a frequency. Kathy Lutz, meanwhile, discovered weird red welts on her chest. She supposedly levitated off her bed one night as her husband lay paralyzed and helpless. George Lutz swore he could sense a new, unseen presence enter the bed, taking his wife's spot.

At some point in the Lutzes' narrative, they claimed strange green slime began pouring from walls, and from the keyhole to an attic door to a playroom. Missy started singing all the time when she was in her room. Whenever she left the room, she would stop singing, only to resume her song exactly where she left it upon her return.

On January 8, 1976, George and Kathy Lutz decided to tap into some spiritual power. George Lutz toted a crucifix around the house as the couple recited the Lord's Prayer. While in the living room, George Lutz supposedly heard what sounded like a chorus of voices demanding that he stop.

At this point, the Lutzes decided that discretion was the better part of valor. They took some of their possessions and made plans to live briefly with Kathy's mother in the nearby community of Deer Park. The couple hoped to stay temporarily as they tried to determine what exactly was going on in their new dream home. Only, according to later written accounts, the horrors followed them to their new locale, in the form of green-black slime oozing up the stairs toward the Lutz clan.

This slime proved the proverbial last straw. On the afternoon of January 14, 1976, the Lutz family fled 112 Ocean Avenue for good, leaving everything behind. Oddly enough, a mover who arrived shortly thereafter to clear the furniture out didn't seem to notice anything amiss with the supposedly haunted house. Nor has anyone else who visited or lived in the place experienced anything ghostly or unworldly. No demonic pigs, no clouds of flies, no invisible presences, and no evil slime oozing from the walls.

Channel 5, a local New York TV station, got wind of the Lutzes' situation and figured their house of horrors was worth investigating. The station arranged for a self-described "demonologist" named Ed Warren and his wife, Lorraine, who was said to be clairvoyant, to check on the property. The couple dutifully held a séance in the supposedly evil house. Lorraine declared that the home was inhabited by a negative entity of some kind. The couple couldn't get to the root of the problem, but it was strongly suggested that demonic spirits infested the home.

The Lutzes' tale of horror would soon receive a broad audience. An editor at publishing house Prentice Hall introduced the Lutzes to a professional writer named Jay Anson, with a view to putting together a book about the family's haunting. Anson didn't interview the Lutzes directly, to write his tome, but relied on some 45 hours of recollections recorded on cassette tape by the Lutz parents.

In September 1977, Anson's book, *The Amityville Horror*, was released and became a smash hit best seller. Two years later, a hugely popular movie based on the book was released, starring James Brolin and Margot Kidder as the unlucky Lutz parents. This top-grossing film was followed by a series of lesser sequels and later, a remake.

The big selling point behind the books and movies was that the horrors endured by the Lutzes were real. By contrast, no one who took possession of the house after the Lutz family had any trouble with demons and evil spirits. "Indeed, a man who later lived there for eight months said he experienced nothing more horrible than a stream of gawkers who tramped onto the property," read an article from the January/February 2003 issue of the *Skeptical Inquirer*.

In a similar fashion, James and Barbara Cromarty, a couple who moved into 112 Ocean Avenue immediately after the Lutzes departed, said nothing evil ever happened. People began poking around the Lutzes' story. It was noted that the day the Lutz family claimed to have seen cloven-hoofed footprints in the snow, it hadn't actually snowed.

When asked, the Cromarts also had interesting things to say about the supposed horrors at their Dutch Colonial manse: "recalling the extensive damage to doors and windows detailed by the Lutzes, [Barbara Cromarty] noted that the old hardware—hinges, locks, doorknobs, etc.—were still in place. Upon close inspection, one could see that there were no disturbances in the paint and varnish," stated the January/February 2003 *Skeptical Inquirer*.

Eventually, William Weber, the attorney representing Ronald DeFeo Jr., revealed that he had met the Lutzes after they abandoned their house. The Lutz parents apparently regaled Weber with tales of what happened during their stay. Over the course of a wine-fueled meeting, Weber and the Lutzes embellished upon these anecdotes.

"'We created this horror story over many bottles of wine that George Lutz was drinking,' Weber later told the Associated Press. 'We were creating something the public wanted to hear about.' Weber later filed a two-million-dollar lawsuit against the couple, charging them with reneging on their book deal," stated the *Skeptical Inquirer*.

Weber wasn't the only one to sue either. The Cromartys also launched a suit against the Lutz parents, author Anson, and his publisher. The basis of their suit was that all the attention stirred up by tales of terror in the Amityville home "had resulted in sightseers destroying any privacy they might have had. During the trials, the Lutzes admitted that virtually everything in The *Amityville Horror* was pure fiction," continued the *Inquirer*.

In 2013, a whole new theory was presented by Daniel Lutz, one of the children of the family. He claimed that the Amityville events were real. A counter-claim suggested that Daniel, in fact was responsible for most of the events that happened in the home. Daniel faked a haunting as a way to get back at his step-father, George Lutz, with whom he apparently had a difficult relationship.

The Center for Inquiry, a Washington DC–based nonprofit group supporting science, reason, and humanism, offered another take. Among other activities, the Center publishes *Skeptical Inquirer* magazine, which has been withering in its criticism of the Amityville case. "Unfortunately for the poltergeist-mimicking hypothesis, however, there is much better evidence as to what really happened at Amityville. The tale was deliberate fiction. Some of the reported events were simply made up, while others were exaggerations of mundane occurrences," stated a March 20, 2013, blog posting from the Center for Inquiry.

Further Reading

Jay Anson, *The Amityville Horror*, 1977.

Joe Nickell, "Amityville: The Horror of It All," *Skeptical Inquirer*, January/February 2003.

Joe Nickell, "Horrors! Amityville Returns!" Center for Inquiry blog, March 20, 2013, http://www.centerforinquiry.net/blogs/entry/horrors_amityville_returns/.

Benjamin Radford and John Gaeddert, "Reel or Real? The Truth Behind Two Hollywood Ghost Stories," *Skeptical Inquirer*, March 2005.

Village of Amityville, Long Island, New York, website, http://amityville.com/.

SYLVIA BROWNE

The March/April 2010 issue of the *Skeptical Inquirer* magazine contained a damning investigation into the accuracy of predictions made by psychic superstar Sylvia Browne. Hugely famous through a series of books and television appearances, Browne claimed a psychic success rate of around 90 percent. She modestly declared that only God was 100 percent correct all the time.

Against this background, a clutch of investigators at *Skeptical Inquirer*, the James Randi Educational Foundation forum, and the website StopSylvia.com took Browne at her word. These investigators examined 115 criminal cases in which Browne had offered a confirmed opinion. Most of these cases revolved around missing persons or unsolved homicides.

"The criteria for a correct prediction is that it mostly matches a case referenced in a newspaper and the criteria for a wrong prediction is that Browne's claim is the opposite of what actually occurred," explained the March/April 2010 *Skeptical Inquirer* article, which was titled "Psychic Detective: Sylvia Browne's History of Failure."

Investigators revealed that Browne was a bit off in gauging her success rate: "As this article shows, in the 115 available cases, Browne was correct zero times and wrong 25 times. Ninety out of the 115 cases have unknown outcomes … when we began to research this, we expected Browne to have been correct at least a few times but as the list demonstrates, she was not. The references show that the only cases in which Browne was not proven wrong are those that remain unsolved," read the March/April 2010 *Skeptical Inquirer*.

Browne was born Sylvia Shoemaker October 19, 1936. She was raised in Kansas City, Missouri, and allegedly developed her paranormal powers at a very young age: "Sylvia manifested her psychic ability at the age of three … for many years, she shared her gift with friends and family and became very well known for helping people to see their future. Moving to California in 1964, she continued assisting people privately," stated SylviaBrowne.com, her official website.

When she wasn't making predictions and seeing into peoples' souls, Browne worked as a Catholic high school teacher in San Jose. She apparently taught English and World Religions. According to Novus.org, a website for Browne's mystical musings, Browne's career as a professional psychic was launched May 8, 1973, when she hosted a small gathering in her home for paranormal purposes. Her psychic practice apparently caught on quickly, and in 1974 she incorporated her company as the nonprofit Nirvana Foundation for Psychic Research.

Like other psychics before her, Browne claimed she fell into trances in which bits of paranormal wisdom were revealed to her. In this manner, she said she could read peoples' past lives (reincarnation was one of Browne's key beliefs) and determine the fate of people missing or murdered.

Browne continued making predictions, taking the time to found another organization, called the Society of Novus Spiritus in 1986. "Novus is Sylvia's monument to God, a forum to express the joy and love that is God—with no fear, no guilt, no sin, no hell and no Satan. Through Novus, Sylvia gives the world a means to understand God, Life and the reason for being," explained Novus.org.

Browne's spiritual development occasionally hit a few real-world roadblocks, including a conviction for investment fraud: "In 1992, Sylvia and [her husband at the time] Kensil Brown were accused of illegally selling securities that had not been registered with the State of California. Both were also charged with misrepresentations and grand theft and Kensil was additionally charged with fraud," wrote Dr. Stephen Barrett in a December 14, 2013, article posted to Quackwatch, a website devoted to fighting medical fraud.

The charges stemmed from selling securities without a permit and misleading investors about a gold-mining venture. On March 8, 1993, Browne (who spelled her name without an "e" at the time, like her husband) and her partner pled no contest to the charges. They were given a year of probation and ordered to pay restitution.

A detailed synopsis of the case, put together by Dr. Barrett, can be found on Casewatch, a sister site to Quackwatch, devoted to health-related legal matters. The Casewatch posting included the contents of a May 26, 1992, arrest warrant for the Browns issued by the Municipal Court of California, Santa Clara County Judicial District, San Jose Facility. Also available on the site is a scanned copy of the court report documenting Sylvia Browne's no contest plea.

Such a setback didn't impede Browne's rise as a media-savvy psychic diva, however. From the early 1990s through to 2008, she appeared numerous times on *The Montel Williams Show*, a popular talk show, dispensing advice and psychic visions. She also appeared on *Larry King Live* and in major print publications such as *People* and *Cosmopolitan* magazines. Along the way, she also found time to write some 40 books, with titles such as *Life on the Other Side: A Psychic's Tour of the Afterlife*, *All Pets Go to Heaven: The Spiritual Lives of the Animals We Love*, *Contacting Your Spirit Guide*, and *Past Lives, Future Healing*. Many of these books were best sellers.

Browne said she shared some of her psychic visions with police and law authorities investigating homicides and missing persons cases at no cost. For others, she charged up to $700 for 30-minute phone sessions, tapping her paranormal abilities to solve ordinary people's problems.

For all her fame and wealth, Browne was notoriously inaccurate, as the *Skeptical Inquirer* investigation proved: "These 115 cases prove devastating to Browne's claims of helping police and families. It is hard to understand how someone with such a dismal record continually tops best-seller lists and maintains a following," stated the report on the investigation.

Examples of Browne's botched predictions abound: on September 30, 1999, for example, during a *Montel Williams* appearance, she told the family of a missing girl named Eve Brown that their daughter was alive and well in Florida. A year after this prediction was made, Eve Brown's body was located in a construction site in Brooklyn, New York, only 13 miles from where she was last seen alive. The case has still not been solved.

On February 26, 2003, also on *Montel*, she told the parents of Shawn Hornbeck that their missing son, Shawn, was dead. The young boy had disappeared four months before the taping. For good measure, Browne also said Shawn had been kidnapped by a man with dark skin and dreadlocked hair. A few years after the show aired, Shawn Hornbeck was found very much alive, having been kidnapped and held prisoner with another boy by a miscreant in St. Louis.

In 2004, once again on *Montel Williams*, she informed the mother of Amanda Berry, a teenager in Cleveland, Ohio who vanished right before her seventeenth birthday, that their daughter was dead. In reality, Amanda was one of three women being held captive by a Cleveland sociopath named Ariel Castro.

Browne predicted she would die at age 88. She expired 11 years earlier than that, on November 20, 2013, in a San Jose hospital. Upon her death, professional magician/escape artist turned paranormal skeptic/debunker James Randi issued a blistering broadside on his website: "I agree with [James Randi Educational Foundation] president D. J. Grothe that we do not celebrate her death, even as we criticize the way she lived. But I'll be frank with you, I cannot mourn at Browne's passing—she really hurt far too many people and always so unapologetically … it's unfortunate that she only stopped hurting so many people by dying," wrote Randi.

Further Reading

Dr. Stephen Barrett, "Sylvia Browne's Criminal Conviction," Casewatch.org, December 12, 2013, http://www.casewatch.org/crim/browne/complaint.shtml.

Dr. Stephen Barrett, "Sylvia Browne: Psychic or Con Artist?" Quackwatch.org, December 14, 2013, http://www.quackwatch.com/11Ind/browne.html.

David Moye, "Sylvia Browne: Dead Psychic's Legacy Riddled with Failed Predictions, Fraud," The Huffington Post, November 21, 2013, http://www.huffingtonpost.com/2013/11/21/sylvia-browne_n_4317470.html.

Joe Nickell, "Another Sylvia Browne Failure," Center for Inquiry blog, May 9, 2013, http://www.centerforinquiry.net/blogs/entry/another_sylvia_browne_failure/.

James Randi, "Message from James Randi on Sylvia Browne's Death," Randi.org, November 21, 2013, http://archive.randi.org/site/index.php/swift-blog/2273-message-from-james-randi-on-sylvia-brownes-death.html.

Ryan Shaffer and Agatha Jadwiszczok, "Psychic Detective: Sylvia Browne's History of Failure," *Skeptical Inquirer*, March/April 2010.

Ingrid Hansen Smythe, "Sylvia Browne Takes the Case!" *Skeptic Magazine*, Volume 18, Number 3, 2013.

Society of Novus Spiritus website, http://novus.org/home/index.cfm.

Sylvia Browne website, http://sylviabrowne.com/.

DOWSING FOR WATER—OR BOMBS

Dowsing, typically for water but sometimes for oil or minerals, is a centuries-old tradition that's been given a new spin in war-torn and crime-ridden regions. Dowsing involves walking outdoors and using a stick or pole (called a "divining rod" by believers) to "sense" the presence of underground water. Dowsing was mentioned in print as far back as the 1500s and is common to many cultures.

Magician and escape artist turned paranormal debunker James Randi posted a commentary to his website explaining how divining rods are supposed to work: "The traditional method is to use a flexible green forked stick … hazel and willow are the preferred woods. The Y is inverted and the forked parts are grasped, one in each hand, palms up, usually with the thumbs pointing away from the body in opposite directions and the elbows tightly against the body … the dowser attempts to keep the stick parallel with the ground and as he walks about, it is believed that subtle influences from water, metal, oil or any other substance will cause the stem of the stick to either rise or depress from the horizontal position."

Some versions of dowsing involve two sticks or rods. "Map dowsing" involves the use of a pendulum held over a map to locate things. Whatever approach is taken, dowsers generally claim they can detect energy, rays, or vibrations that might be unnoticed by anyone else.

The most likely explanation, however, is that small, involuntary twitches or movements of the dowser's hand causes the divining rod to bounce around. In his online article, Randi noted that the dowsing stick or pole is balanced "in very unstable equilibrium. Since force is being applied to the stick, the tendency is for the stem to whip up or down unless care is taken to balance it. There is thus potential energy stored in the system and the slightest inclination, tensing or relaxation of either hand, or both hands, must result in the stick moving violently. This motion is taken by dowsers as evidence that there is a supernatural external force acting upon the device."

One of the few comprehensive, scientific tests of dowsing took place in Kassel, Germany, north of Frankfurt, in 1992. German scientists and skeptics belonging to the Gesellschaft zur wissenschaftlichen Untersuchung von Parawissenschaften (GWUP) or the Society for the Scientific Investigation of Parasciences, held a three-day controlled test. Some 30 dowsers, most of them German, were put through their paces as television cameras caught the drama. GWUP personnel arranged for a plastic pipe to be buried about 20 inches deep in a flat field. Testers could control the flow of water into this pipe. The pipe's position on the surface was noted by a colored stripe. Using only their divining rods, dowsers had to determine whether water was running through the pipe at a given moment. Over the course of three days, the dowsers were tested repeatedly.

The results were not promising for the credibility of dowsing. "A summary of their results produced just what would be expected according to chance," noted Randi on his website. In other words, the dowsers scored no better on the test than if they had simply guessed whether water was running through the pipe at a given moment.

While the Kassel tests didn't include an actual search for water, this part of dowsing is also dismissed as guesswork by skeptics. As Randi pointed out, if you drill a well in ground that's geologically capable of housing water, chances are good you will eventually find what you're looking for. This has less to do with the power of divination than the simple fact that there is lots of ground-water in the earth.

While traditional water dowsing might be out of fashion today, the concept behind it—that is, using a divining rod to find things quickly—is alive and well in huckster circles. Modern-day dowsing rods, boasting electronic circuitry and plastic handles, are being used to detect drugs and bombs.

A British company called Global Technical Ltd. produced a black plastic wand called the GT 200, which they sold to the Mexican military and the police and army in Thailand. The Mexicans used the GT 200 to find drugs, while Thai authorities used it to find bombs. There have been reports of deaths of Thai police and civilians after the GT 200 failed to uncover the presence of explosives.

On March 15, 2010, the *New York Times* ran a story detailing British efforts to warn Mexican officials about the GT 200's dubious benefits. The warnings came after Mexico's National Defense Secretariat spent over $10 million purchasing hundreds of these supposed bomb and drug detectors.

"Although critics have called them nothing more than divining rods, Mexican defense officials praise the devices as a critical part of their efforts to combat drug traffickers … [GT 200 devices] are widely used nationwide at checkpoints to search for contraband inside vehicles as well as to canvass neighborhoods in drug hotspots for drugs and weapons stash houses," reported the *Times*.

The newspaper noted that the U.S. Drug Enforcement Administration didn't use the detectors. In fact, tests done for the Defense Department by the National Explosive Engineering Sciences Security Center at Sandia National Laboratories in New Mexico, found the devices highly ineffective.

Additionally, a lobby group called Human Rights Watch released a statement in February 2010, asking the government of Thailand to stop making arrests based on results derived from GT 200 detectors. Human Rights Watch referred to the GT 200 as a "magic wand" that "performs worse than a roll of the dice," reported the March 15, 2010, *New York Times*. The group was appalled that people were being arrested and charged in Thailand based entirely on readings from the GT 200.

In a similar vein, the Iraqi government spent over $80 million on a device called the ADE 651, which U.S. authorities said was money completely wasted.

The ADE 651, as made by a company called ATSC (UK) Ltd., could allegedly detect the presence of explosives. "Nearly every police checkpoint and many Iraqi military checkpoints have one of the devices, which are now normally used in place of physical inspections of vehicles," stated a November 3, 2009, piece in the *New York Times*.

The *Times* continued, "ATSC promotional material claims that its devices can find guns, ammunition, drugs, truffles, human bodies and even contraband ivory at distances up to a kilometer, underground, through walls, underwater or even from airplanes three miles high. The device works on 'electrostatic magnetic ion attraction' ATSC says ... to detect materials, the operator puts an array of plastic-coated cardboard cards with bar codes into a holder connected to the wand by a cable."

Tests of the ADE 651 by the National Explosive Engineering Sciences Security Center found it to be as worthless as the GT 200: "The device works 'on the same principle as a Ouija board'—the power of suggestion—said a retired United States Air Forces officer, Lt. Colonel Hal Bidlack, who described the wand as nothing more than an explosives divining rod," stated the *Times*.

The paper made it clear why Iraq chose to go with the ADE 651, in spite of such criticism. Even at thousands of dollars apiece, the ADE 651 detectors were far cheaper than traditional remote explosives detection machines, which are typically found at airports. While Iraqi authorities conceded that sniffer dogs would have been even cheaper, they said canines took too long to conduct bomb searches. Using the ADE 651 wands sped up inspections to the point that it took only a few seconds to "clear" vehicles at checkpoints, reported the *Times*.

Iraqi officials insisted that any failings of the ADE 651 were the result of human error. To work properly, said Iraqis, the ADE 651 needed to be handled by an operator with a steady pulse, walking a certain way while holding the device in a certain manner.

"'It would be laughable,' Colonel Bidlack said, 'except that someone down the street from you is counting on this to keep bombs off the street,'" noted the *Times*.

Further Reading

J.T. Enright, "Testing Dowsing: The Failure of the Munich Experiments," *Skeptical Inquirer*, January/February 1999.

Marc Lacey, "Mexico Is Warned on Drug Detector," *New York Times*, March 15, 2010.

Rod Nordland, "Iraq Swears by Bomb Detector U.S. Sees as Useless," *New York Times*, November 3, 2009.

James Randi Educational Foundation, An Encyclopedia of Claims, Frauds, and Hoaxes of the Occult and Supernatural: Dowsing, https://web.archive.org/web/20140707120029/http://www.randi.org/encyclopedia/dowsing.html.

James Randi. *James Randi: Psychic Investigator*, 1991.

THE FOX SISTERS

In the early spring of 1848, the Fox household in bucolic Hydesville, New York, began to play host to strange aural phenomena. A series of raps and taps could be heard in the house, on floors, furniture, and walls. For some reason, the rapping and tapping noises only seemed to occur when the household's two youngest occupants, sisters Margaret and Kate, were present.

Margaret was eight, and Kate was six-and-a-half. Their father, who worked as a blacksmith, and mother, who was a housewife, were flabbergasted at the strange noises in their abode. The parents sternly asked their daughters if they had anything to do with the weird noises. Kate and Margaret both denied having anything to do with the uncanny sounds.

The Fox parents brought neighbors over so they too could hear the strange taps and raps. A theory began to emerge in the small village, that the Fox house was haunted by some kind of disembodied spirit. There were rumors that the spirit belonged to an unfortunate soul, thought to be a peddler, who had been murdered at the house before the Fox family took possession.

At this point, the odd noises might have remained a local curiosity, except for a highly fortuitous visit by the Fox family's eldest daughter, Leah Fish. Leah, who was 23 years older than Margaret, took in the strange sounds and came up with what would be described today as a marketing plan: "She seems to have grasped instantly the possibilities in the 'occult' powers of her little sisters and to have taken complete command of the Fox family's affairs at once. Her first move was to organize a 'Society of Spiritualists' and encourage crowds to come see the children," stated escape artist turned paranormal debunker Harry Houdini, in his 1924 book, *A Magician Among the Spirits*.

Houdini himself played no role in debunking the Fox sisters; he hadn't been born yet when Margaret and Kate emerged as psychic celebrities. His book, however, offers a detailed account of the Fox Sisters and similar characters who claimed supernatural powers.

As the crowds at the Fox home grew larger, questions were raised. Some observers found it odd that the weird raps and taps only ever happened when the two youngest Fox sisters were around. Was it possible the little girls were having the grown-ups on? Nonsense, insisted Leah. Leah "replied, with a great deal of haughtiness" that the spirits "wished to communicate with the world but only through her sisters," according to *The Crooked Lake Review*, a local history journal for the part of New York state where the Fox sisters resided.

At Leah's urging, Margaret and Kate were whisked out of Hydesville and exhibited in Rochester, New York. After that, they hit New York City. Large paying crowds marveled at how the two Fox sisters could seem to conjure spirits from beyond at will. By this point, the spirits had settled on a kind of code that they used to answer simple questions. One rap meant "no," while three raps meant "yes."

Leah arranged for her younger siblings to become the main attraction at séances—gatherings, usually around a table, in which "mediums" (people with "psychic" ability) try to contact the dead. For unclear reasons, the spirits tended to make themselves present only in conditions of near-total darkness. Darkened séances became a cornerstone of the "Spiritualist" movement (a movement dedicated to the idea that live humans could communicate with dead spirits) and a common part of nineteenth-century American life.

Margaret eventually became involved with the Catholic Church. With penitence on her mind, Margaret came clean. In a signed confession, published by the *New York World* newspaper on October 21, 1888, she admitted all: "My sister Katie and I were very young children when this horrible deception began. I was only eight, just a year and a half older than she. We were very mischievous children and sought merely to terrify our dear mother, who was a very good woman and very easily frightened," read the confession.

At first, Margaret and Kate were content to fling an apple on a string around their shared bedroom. They made the apple bump on the floor and wall and make strange sounds. The girls' mother almost brought the prank to an end by bringing in the neighbors to hear the apple-bonking sounds. "All the neighbors around, as I have said, were called in to witness these manifestations. There were so many people coming to the house that we were not able to make use of the apple trick except when we were in bed and the room was dark," Margaret stated in her confession.

After being taken to Rochester on exhibit, the girls came up with a simple, ingenious way to make their raps and taps. They discovered that by cracking their knuckles in their hands or the joints in their feet, they could make all kinds of odd noises. They also practiced knocking their feet against the floor in a manner that created a ghostly sound but wasn't visible to the eye.

In her confession, Margaret noted she and her sister were aided by the power of suggestion. During a séance for some wealthy people, one of the girls made a rapping sound, at which an attendee announced that a spirit was tapping her shoulder.

Leah's role in the machinations was also laid bare in Margaret's confession. In addition to making money off the girls, Margaret accused her older sister of trying to "establish a new religion" built around the "messages from spirits." Apparently, Leah knew the girls were faking it, but was willing to overlook this fact if it helped grow her spiritualist movement.

The same day that Margaret's confession ran in the *New York World*, she did a show at New York City's Academy of Music. In front of some 2,000 people, she repeated her confession and demonstrated some of her joint cracking and foot tapping tricks. Spiritualist supporters in the audience were not impressed and hissed and booed. Kate, however, was in the audience too and was seen nodding enthusiastically to her sister's confession.

A year after her appearance, Margaret "recanted" her confession and went back to doing séances. Her change-of-heart was largely due to strained finances. As Houdini wrote in *A Magician Among the Spirits*, "once more she resorted to Spiritualism as a means of livelihood, giving séances and mediumistic meetings in a number of cities throughout the United States."

According to Houdini, the general public was indifferent to her attempted comeback. "Having confessed to deceit once, no amount of persuasion on her part could convince the public that she was genuine," wrote Houdini. However, while most people viewed her as a self-confessed fraud, Margaret still had supporters within the Spiritualist movement. Margaret died on March 8, 1895. Moved by her recantation, thousands of Spiritualists attended her funeral.

Further Reading

Harry Houdini, *A Magician Among the Spirits*, 1924.
John H. Martin, "Saints, Sinners and Reformers," *The Crooked Lake Review*, Fall 2005.
Joe Nickell, "A Skeleton's Tale: The Origins of Modern Spiritualism," *Skeptical Inquirer*, July/August 2008.

REMOTE VIEWING

For a brief period, the U.S. government funded and studied psychic research to try to gain an edge in the Cold War. Federal authorities wanted to determine whether there was anything tangible about "remote viewing," an alleged psychic power involving telepathy and clairvoyance.

Telepathy is basically mind-reading—being able to "read" people's thoughts. Clairvoyance is mind-projection—being able to "travel" to any location with your mind's eye. The umbrella term "remote viewing" was invented by a researcher at Stanford Research Institute (SRI), a California think-tank, to give such concepts more scientific legitimacy.

The 1960s and 1970s saw an explosion of interest in paranormal and psychic phenomenon, from telepathy to telekinesis (moving objects with your mind). At the time, the United States was locked in a "Cold War" with the Soviet Union. U.S. authorities feared that the USSR was pulling ahead on the psychic front.

"In 1972, U.S. analysts from the Defense Intelligence Agency (DIA—a branch of the Department of Defense) issued a report warning that Soviet 'psi research' might eventually permit the adversaries to learn the contents of secret documents, divine the movements of troops and ships, discern the location and purpose of installations, even 'mold the thoughts' of American leaders," stated an article in the March 2001 edition of the *Skeptical Inquirer*.

Even worse, some analysts fretted that Soviet psychic warriors could use their paranormal powers to kill American officials or disable military equipment. While this may sound like something from a bad science fiction film, U.S. authorities wanted to determine how real the threat was.

In late 1972, the Central Intelligence Agency (CIA) funded a $50,000 study by the Stanford Research Institute to look into remote viewing. The program was expanded and funding greatly increased, to about $1.5 million a year, but the results were scanty. The CIA grew disinterested and withdrew its funding in the late 1970s. The DIA, however, had other ideas. The DIA took over the abandoned psychic research program and ran it as a secret project dubbed "Star Gate."

As the March 2001 *Skeptical Inquirer* states, "Star Gate had three components: one attempted to track other countries' psychic warfare projects; another provided six (later only three) 'remote viewers' to any government agency desiring to use them; and the third continued the laboratory work initiated at SRI (and subsequently transferred to another think-tank at Palo Alto, California, called Science Applications International Corporation)."

The *Inquirer* article outlines the structure of a typical remote viewing experiment: a person with alleged remote viewing abilities would be isolated in a secure locale with an experimenter. In another locale, a person designated the "sender" would examine a "target" selected at random from a series of other targets. Most of the "targets" consisted of pictures culled from *National Geographic* magazine. It was up to the viewer to figure out what the sender was looking at. To this end, the remote viewer would draw pictures or write down words that popped into his or her mind while the sender concentrated on the target.

After a given time, the viewer's words and images ("the description") would be given to a judge, along with five pictures. One of the five pictures was the original "target" that the sender was supposed to focus on. The other pictures were decoys. It was up to the judge to determine which picture most closely matched the notes and scribbled drawings made by the remote viewer. If the judge selected the target picture, that was considered a "hit." Since there was a one-in-five chance the judge would randomly select the target picture, experimenters set their baseline at 20 percent. If a viewer scored higher than 20 percent on a series of tests, it was seen as possible evidence of psychic ability.

These psychic experiments were suspended in 1995. That same year, the CIA hired the American Institutes for Research (AIR) to review the years of laboratory tests to see whether they could uncover any important insights on remote viewing. AIR established a panel to look into the accumulated research. The panel included Dr. Jessica Utts (a professor of statistics at the University of California at Davis) and Dr. Ray Hyman (a professor of psychology at the University of Oregon). Dr. Utts was known to be open-minded about the paranormal, while Dr. Hyman was a skeptic. (Hyman was also a fellow with the Committee for the Scientific Investigation of Claims of the Paranormal, CSICOP—now known as the Committee for Skeptical Inquiry.) Dr. Utts and Dr. Hyman worked independently of each other to create separate reports.

Dr. Utts and Dr. Hyman's findings were included in a paper called "An Evaluation of Remote Viewing: Research and Applications," released by AIR on September 29, 1995. The report was damning: "Both Utts and Hyman agreed that a group of the 10 best experiments did produce 'hit' rates that were consistently above chance. However, they also agreed that the studies were flawed in that they involved a single judge, who was also the main instigator, and that it needed to be demonstrated that significant scores would still be obtained when independent judges were employed," reported the March 2001 *Skeptical Inquirer*.

The Charlie Jordan Case

Supporters of remote viewing frequently cite the case of rogue drug agent Charlie Jordan as a successful example of psychic sleuthing.

Jordan was an agent for the U.S. Customs section of the Drug Enforcement Administration (DEA) based in south Florida. He was supposed to be combatting drug smuggling around the Florida coast and the Florida Keys, but began to accept bribes from dealers to look the other way. When Jordan realized his superiors were on to him, he fled. For two years, Jordan was at large.

In the spring of 1989, the Customs Service tapped the Defense Intelligence Agency's (DIA) remote viewing team. Psychics "spotted" Jordan all over the place, from Central America to the Caribbean. One psychic, later identified as Angela Dellafiora, claimed to have detected Jordan in northern Wyoming. Sure enough, a few weeks after Dellafiora made her pronouncement, Jordan was captured by police—in northern Wyoming.

As impressive as this case sounds, it should be pointed out that authorities were already on Jordan's trail in Wyoming. It was also unclear how many incorrect sightings were made by Dellafiora in the course of her remote viewing experience.

"In the Jordan case, several remote viewers were utilized in 18 sessions logged in 1989 in the attempt to locate Jordan … all of these were apparently worse than useless, except for the alleged offerings of Dellafiora," reported the March 2001 edition of the *Skeptical Inquirer*.

The *Inquirer* also questioned whether Dellafiora's vision was a true example of remote viewing or the result of random guesswork—of throwing out a series of locales where Jordan might be hiding.

Certainly skeptics weren't impressed: "In summary, the Charlie Jordan case, touted as one of the most successful examples of remote viewing in the U.S. government's psychic-spying project is not convincing evidence of anything save perhaps folly," reported the *Inquirer*.

The *Inquirer* continued: "Other evaluators—two psychologists from AIR—assessed the potential intelligence gathering usefulness of remote viewing. They concluded that the alleged psychic technique was of dubious value and lacked the concreteness and reliability necessary for it to be used as a basis for making decisions or taking action. The final report found 'reason to suspect' that in 'some well publicized cases of dramatic hits,' the remote viewers might have had 'substantially more background information' than might otherwise be apparent." In other words, in situations where remote viewers enjoyed high "hit" rates, they might have been coached with hints and clues from experimenters.

Then there was the fact that the remote viewers were maddeningly vague about what they viewed. "The remote viewing reports failed to produce the concrete, specific information valued in intelligence gathering ... the information provided was inconsistent, inaccurate with regard to specifics and required substantial subjective interpretation—in no case had the information provided ever been used to guide intelligence operations. Thus remote viewing failed to produce actionable intelligence," stated the Evaluation of Remote Viewing report.

The report concluded that the results didn't justify the use of remote viewing for military intelligence purposes. While "a statistically significant effect has been observed in the laboratory," it wasn't clear whether this was proof of anything, stated the report.

"Thus we conclude that continued use of remote viewing in intelligence gathering operations is not warranted," the report determined. In the wake of the scathing report, the U.S. government did not resume remote viewing research—as far as anyone knows.

Further Reading

Michael Mumford, Andrew M. Rose and David A. Goslin, "An Evaluation of Remote Viewing: Research and Applications," prepared by the American Institutes for Research, September 29, 1995.

Joe Nickell, "Remotely Viewed? The Charlie Jordan Case," *Skeptical Inquirer*, March 2001.

Douglas Waller, "The Vision Thing," *TIME*, December 11, 1995.

SECTION NINE

POP CULTURE CONS

INTRODUCTION

Pop culture has been kind to con artists. When portrayed on screen, confidence men tend to be depicted as loveable rogues rather than cold-hearted criminals. This depiction isn't exactly accurate, but isn't completely wrong either. As film critic Roger Ebert astutely noted, con artists are often quite charming individuals who specialize at gaining people's trust, before swindling them.

Besides movies, this section examines other pop culture controversies such as the 1919 World Series (was it really "fixed" by gangsters?), "subliminal messaging" (do musicians really put secret messages in their songs that are perceived subconsciously?), and Buffalo Bill and the "Wild West." Buffalo Bill was not a con artist, but he was responsible for helping shape a deliberately skewed version of U.S. history.

This chapter also looks at authors Forrest Carter, a white racist who reinvented himself as a sensitive chronicler of Indian culture, James Frey whose grossly exaggerated account of time in drug and alcohol rehab fooled Oprah Winfrey, and Damon Runyon, who wrote about con artists in a multitude of short stories.

The politics sub-section examines two dubious elections—the presidential election of 1876 and Lyndon Johnson's campaign in a 1948 Texas primary—the infamous Teapot Dome scandal, which occurred under the watch of amiable President Warren Harding, and William "Big Bill" Thompson, selected by academics as the worst big-city mayor in American history.

Also profiled is the little-known world of counterfeit sports/celebrity memorabilia. The following section cites these and other examples of cons, swindles, and hoaxes in the pop culture realm of sports, politics, and entertainment.

BUFFALO BILL AND THE MYTH OF THE "WILD WEST"

Born in Le Claire, Iowa, on February 26, 1846, William Frederick Cody—aka "Buffalo Bill"—is responsible for helping popularize a mythical view of the American West that exists to this day. Along the way, Cody became a much-lauded and internationally renowned showman. Indeed, "at the turn of the twentieth century, 'Buffalo Bill' Cody was the most famous American in the world," states The William F. Cody Archive, a scholarly digital collection of all things Buffalo Bill–related.

Cody's family moved to Kansas Territory when he was a child. In the 1850s, Kansas Territory (which had yet to become a state) was deeply riven by pro- and anti-slavery factions. This violence became personal for Cody in June 1856, when his father—a farmer who opposed the spread of slavery into new states—was stabbed by pro-slavery supporters. Cody's father succumbed to his injuries one year later. "Father died in the little log-house, the first man to shed his blood in the fight against the extension of slavery into the Northern Territories," wrote Cody, in his autobiography, published in 1920.

According to his memoir, Cody became chief breadwinner for his family at age 11, trapping game and harvesting crops. Following the outbreak of the Civil War in 1861, Cody joined a group of scouts who protected Kansas from incursions by pro-Confederate bandits, such as William Quantrill and the James brothers, Jesse and Frank.

In 1864, Cody enlisted in a Kansas volunteer cavalry unit that fought on the Union side. He served as a private in this outfit for a year and a half, until the end of the Civil War. After the war, Cody married Louisa Frederici, of St. Louis, with whom he would have four children.

Cody acquired the nickname "Buffalo Bill" for his skill in hunting bison. Starting in 1866, he spent 18 months killing buffalo for hungry railroad workers to eat. When not shooting buffalo, Cody earned extra cash guiding wealthy Easterners and Europeans on hunting expeditions. During this period, Cody claimed to have killed a staggering 4,280 buffalo.

In 1868, Cody began working with the military as a hunter and guide. He eventually rose to the position of scout, earning around $75 a month. He guided troops, carried messages, and sometimes hunted game animals.

As a scout, Cody took part in a few odd skirmishes with Indians. He also began to develop his public persona. Cody modeled himself, to an extent, after one of his acquaintances, "Wild Bill" Hickok. Like Hickok, Cody sported shoulder-length hair, a bushy moustache (complemented by a goatee) and buckskin outfits. Cody drew the attention of a writer named E. Z. C. Judson—better known by his penname, Ned Buntline. In 1869, a novel by Buntline called *Buffalo Bill, King of the Border Men* was published as a serial by a New York magazine.

Buntline specialized in "dime novels"—cheaply made, quickly written tales of bravado and manly daring-do. Such books served as pulp fiction for post-Civil War nineteenth-century American society. Buntline's greatly embellished accounts of Wild West figures such as Cody and Hickok thrilled readers. Over the next few decades, hundreds of dime novels would be published, featuring Cody and other Westerners.

With the encouragement of Buntline, Cody launched a stage career in 1872. Cody played himself in a melodrama written by Buntline called *Scouts of the Prairie*. Cody wasn't much of an actor, but he did have the gift of gab. Cody's experience as a hunting guide had made him a great storyteller, and he made his theatrical debut in Chicago. Gauging audience reaction, Buntline reshaped the play to incorporate Cody's improvisational talents.

Critics hated *Scouts of the Prairie*, which they slammed as being no better than a dime novel put to stage. No matter: the public loved it, and Cody sensed the possibilities offered by performing. Cody broke with Buntline and formed a theatrical troupe with Hickok and other equally colorful characters. The troupe toured for the next ten years, adding new performers when necessary. (Hickok, for example, was killed in 1876, in a notorious saloon shooting.) Usually, the troupe confined their performances to winter, fall, and spring so Cody could resume his scouting duties for the army each summer, as well as leading hunting parties.

In 1875, Cody moved his family to Rochester, New York. One year later, following the death of George Armstrong Custer at the hands of native Indians at Little Bighorn, Cody went back to scouting for the military. Again, he was involved in skirmishing with Indians. During this period, Cody wore a rather theatrical outfit consisting of a scarlet shirt and black velvet pants—neither of which exactly blended in with the Western scenery. The outfit was actually entirely appropriate, however, given the degree to which Cody was blurring the distinction between his real-life achievements and on-stage persona.

After finishing his scouting adventures, Cody returned to the stage, wearing the same outfit and "brandishing his war trophies, including Yellow Hair's war bonnet, shield and scalp," according to The William F. Cody Archive. Yellow Hair was the name of an Indian warrior Cody killed.

In 1879, Cody published his autobiography, *The Life of Hon. William F. Cody*. "The memoir is a mixture of Cody's experiences from his first 33 years and tall tales that draw on dime novel language and plots to shape the persona of Buffalo Bill. Historians have cast doubt on a number of claims made in the autobiography, including his account of riding for the Pony Express. However, Cody would continue to promote these biographical details on stage and showground throughout his career," states The William F. Cody Archive.

Cody moved his family to Nebraska. Then he established the revue that would make him world famous. Buffalo Bill's Wild West was an outdoor extravaganza featuring cowboys, Indians, and Mexican *vaqueros*, among others. The first show took place in Omaha in May 1883. A long series of engagements followed. A typical performance included demonstrations of marksmanship and horsemanship, along with staged Indian "attacks" on a settler's cabin or stagecoach. Some shows featured a "buffalo hunt," while others featured reenactments of famous battles, including Little Bighorn. Cody served as ringmaster and took part in many of the performances.

Cody recorded in his autobiography, "I worked hard on the program of the entertainment, taking care to make it realistic in every detail. The wigwam village, the Indian war-dance, the chant of the Great Spirit as it was sung on the Plains, the rise and fall of the famous tribes, were all pictured accurately … for my grand entrance, I made a spectacle, which comprised the most picturesque features of Western life. [American Indians] in war paint led the van, shrieking their war-whoops and waving the weapons with which they were armed in a manner to inspire both terror and admiration in the tenderfoot audience."

The Wild West show made a star out of Annie Oakley, a female sharpshooter who joined in 1884. The following year, prominent Indian chief Sitting Bull took part in the revue for four months. He was one of hundreds of Indians who participated in the show over the decades.

Cody paid his performers decently and treated his native Indian performers in particular with respect. The latter received $25 a month, for not particularly hard work. Cody's outsized public image blossomed in this period, thanks to the Wild West exhibition and his recurring appearances in dime novels.

In May 1887, Cody took Buffalo Bill's Wild West Show on a year-long tour of England, where it proved to be a sensation. He did command performances in front of Queen Victoria, then traveled to continental Europe. One European performance boasted an audience including Pope Leo XIII.

The content of the Wild West Show wasn't a lie. There really were gunfights, stampedes, Indian attacks, and battles in the Wild West—but they only happened sporadically. Buffalo Bill's shows offered an exaggerated version of reality, while overlooking some of the grimmer aspects of the real Wild West, such as army massacres of Indian civilians. Needless to say, the show glorified white settlers and soldiers. Custer, for example, was portrayed as a hero who went down fighting hordes of Indian warriors.

Cody died on January 10, 1917, at his sister's residence in Denver, Colorado. The William F. Cody Archive sums up his life thus: "William F. Cody painted his public life in broad strokes—frontiersman, showman, bon vivant, raconteur, gentleman, entrepreneur … he perpetuated the myth of the West with grace and style … whether we see Cody as an imposter or as a hero, we cannot debate his significant contributions to the world."

Further Reading

Buffalo Bill Center of the West, http://centerofthewest.org/.
Colonel William F. Cody ("Buffalo Bill"), *The Adventures of Buffalo Bill*, 1904.

William F. Cody ("Buffalo Bill"), *An Autobiography of Buffalo Bill (Colonel W. F. Cody)*, 1920. University of Nebraska Lincoln, Buffalo Bill Center of the West, The William F. Cody Archive (scholarly digital archive), http://codyarchive.org/life/wfc.bio.00002.html.

FAKE SPORTS/CELEBRITY MEMORABILIA

On July 21, 2005, the FBI held a press conference in San Diego to announce a major victory in the war on counterfeit sports/celebrity memorabilia. In a press release issued the next day, the FBI announced that 63 people had been "charged and convicted; 18 forgery rings dismantled; tens of thousands of forged baseballs, basketballs seized." The convictions stemmed from a pair of FBI initiatives called Operation Foul Ball and Operation Bullpen.

A report on Operation Bullpen, released in April 2000 by the FBI's San Diego division, cited the massive scale of the fraudulent sports/celebrity memorabilia market: "While it is impossible to definitely estimate the percentage of forged memorabilia, most industry experts concede that over half of the autographed memorabilia is forged. In fact, some cooperating subjects and memorabilia experts believe that up to 90 percent of the memorabilia on the market is forged. Industry experts estimate that the autographed memorabilia market in the United States is approximately $1 billion per year. Using these estimates, forged memorabilia comprises between $500,000,000 and $900,000,000 of the market," stated the San Diego FBI report.

Operation Foul Ball began in the mid-1990s. Initially, it was just a local investigation by the Chicago FBI office into forged autographs from various Chicago sports figures, such as Michael Jordan. The Bureau quickly realized that the fraud was more wide-reaching than originally thought: "arrests were made in five states before 'Operation Foul Ball' was over," stated an October 15, 2003, press release from FBI headquarters. Operation Foul Ball led directly to Operation Bullpen, a larger investigation with global implications.

For Operation Bullpen, the FBI invited the Internal Revenue Service, Criminal Investigation Division, to join forces. The IRS could offer insights on money laundering, tax violations, and cash-only transactions in the counterfeit memorabilia milieu. The FBI also enlisted the support of legitimate memorabilia dealers and professional athletes, such as baseball players Tony Gwynn of the San Diego Padres and Mark McGwire of the St. Louis Cardinals. These athletes helped the Bureau by confirming the authenticity of autographs of their names.

Operation Bullpen also involved clandestine intrigue: "In 1997, the government devised an undercover scenario in which an undercover agent would pose as a distributor of American memorabilia in Asia. The scenario enabled the FBI to purchase evidence without being forced to sell forged items to the public. It also made the criminals more likely to openly discuss the counterfeit nature of the memorabilia because it was 'going overseas,' beyond the reach of the U.S. law enforcement agencies," stated the April 2000 report by the FBI's San Diego division on Operation Bullpen.

To enhance undercover credibility, the Bureau established a phony memorabilia distributor called the Nihon Trading Company, based in Oceanside, California. The presence of this faux firm made it easier for the FBI to infiltrate the counterfeit memorabilia market "and obtain recorded statements from individuals who were identified as forgers, authenticators and distributors of fraudulent memorabilia," stated the San Diego report.

Fake sports/celebrity memorabilia was sold via trade publications, trade shows, in retail businesses, online, and through television shopping channels.

On October 13, 1999, after two years of gathering evidence, the FBI and the IRS carried out 60 search warrants on residences and businesses of people in the counterfeit memorabilia sector. These raids were conducted by over 400 special agents in five states: California, New Jersey, Nevada, Pennsylvania, and

How to Avoid Buying Fake Sports/Celebrity Memorabilia

- Bargain prices. If a piece of sports/celebrity memorabilia seems priced far below what you might expect, there's a good chance it's fake.
- Phony certificates of authenticity. A certificate of authenticity doesn't necessarily guarantee that a piece of memorabilia is actually authentic. The authenticator might be working for memorabilia counterfeiters or might not be competent enough to properly certify the item.
- A far-fetched backstory. Be wary of an item that is accompanied by a hard-to-believe (and harder-to-confirm) backstory. An example might be a baseball autographed by Babe Ruth that is supposedly the last (or first) home run ball he ever hit. Likewise, a guitar pick supposedly used by John Lennon on the Beatles' first hit single might just be a generic pick selected at random by a merchant of phony memorabilia.
- Try to obtain the autograph in person. The only way to make 100 percent sure a piece of sports or celebrity memorabilia is genuine is to get it signed by the athlete or celebrity in your presence.
- Do some research. If you are looking at a piece of memorabilia from a deceased person, take time to investigate the company selling the item. Check online to see if there are consumer complaints about the firm or any media articles that cast light on how reputable the company is.

Source: San Diego FBI Report on Operation Bullpen, April 2000, https://www .fbi.gov/sandiego/about-us/history/operation-bullpen

Florida. In total, the FBI and IRS seized over $500,000 in cash and $10 million worth of phony athlete/celebrity memorabilia.

"The seized memorabilia included over 10,000 forged baseballs, signed by a variety of athletes and celebrities. Some of the autographs included: Mother Teresa, President Ronald Reagan, Babe Ruth, Ty Cobb, Mickey Mantle, Roberto Clemente, Mark McGwire, Sammy Sosa [and] Tony Gwynn," noted the April 2000 San Diego FBI report.

The raids also turned up hundreds of so-called "cut" autographs. A "cut" autograph consists of a scrap of paper with the signature of a deceased individual. The FBI and IRS seized cut autographs containing phony signatures of President George Washington, President Abraham Lincoln, President Theodore Roosevelt, President John F. Kennedy, James Dean, Marilyn Monroe, Elvis Presley, James Cagney, Walt Disney, Charlie Chaplin, Ty Cobb, Babe Ruth, Christy Mathewson, Cy Young, Roberto Clemente, and more. To produce these cut autographs, counterfeiters wrote in ink on blank pages from aged books they acquired from second-hand bookstores and thrift shops.

A second phase of Operation Bullpen broadened the investigation to include fake memorabilia marketers operating on the Internet. Phase two also relied on undercover operations and recordings made of counterfeiters discussing their trade. "Conspirators bragged how their forgeries were better than those of other forgers ... a total of 18 searches were conducted in 12 states, resulting in 36 additional convictions [in phase two]," stated a July 2005 Operation Bullpen overview posted on the FBI website.

Persons charged in both phases of Operation Bullpen were accused of fraud and various tax offenses. In addition to making individual arrests, Operation Bullpen resulted in the dismantling of "a major nationwide network of forgers, authenticators, wholesalers and retailers. This organization is responsible for the creation and sale of up to $100 million of forged memorabilia," stated the April 2000 San Diego FBI report.

The widespread sale of fake sports/celebrity memorabilia can be blamed in part on "the role played by authenticators who fraudulently (or mistakenly) certify forgeries as genuine signatures," continued the same report.

In announcing the outcome of Operation Bullpen, the Bureau urged collectors to use a degree of caution and common sense when purchasing sports/celebrity memorabilia. "When you see that irresistible autograph of Manny Ramirez ... Jason Giambi ... Ivan Rodriguez ... or Sammy Sosa ... Well, you just might want to step back from the plate for a moment ... to keep from striking out," stated an October 15, 2003, press release from FBI headquarters.

Further Reading

Federal Bureau of Investigation, "America's National Pastime," October 15, 2003.
Federal Bureau of Investigation, "Hey, Wanna Buy a Baseball Autographed by ... Mother Teresa?" press release, July 22, 2005.

Federal Bureau of Investigation, San Diego Division, Operation Bullpen, April 2000.
Federal Bureau of Investigation, Operation Bullpen: Overview, July 2005.

JAMES FREY: A MILLION LITTLE FALSEHOODS

A Million Little Pieces was a powerful book that detailed author James Frey's intense struggle with substance abuse. Published in 2003 by the Doubleday division at Random House, Frey's gripping book was billed as a true-life story of recovery from a life of violence, crime, and intoxication. The events in the book were said to have taken place in the 1980s and 1990s in Michigan, Ohio, and other states, when Frey was a teenager and young adult.

The memoir was a massive success, selling upwards of 3.5 million copies and topping the *New York Times* nonfiction paperback best-seller list. Frey gave countless interviews, in which he stressed that all the horrifying stories in *A Million Little Pieces* were true. In his book, Frey said he had been arrested nearly a dozen times before turning 19, that he used methamphetamine, PCP, and cocaine in college, and that he was wanted for drug offenses in three states when he went into rehab at age 23. According to Frey, the FBI investigated him for drug trafficking, police beat him after he drunkenly struck a patrolman with his car, and his only friend in grade school was killed in an automobile accident with a train.

A Million Little Pieces caught the attention of media mogul Oprah Winfrey. During an October 26, 2005, broadcast of *The Oprah Winfrey Show*, the TV hostess personally endorsed Frey's book and added it to her list of recommended reads. Other authors in Oprah's highly coveted TV book club included William Faulkner, Pearl Buck, Leo Tolstoy, and Carson McCullers. Frey appeared as a guest during the broadcast, affirming once again that the incredible events in his book actually happened.

Shortly after the show aired, a website called The Smoking Gun (TSG) decided to do some basic research into Frey's claims. Founded in April 1997, The Smoking Gun bills itself as an online investigative site whose self-declared mission is to post "exclusive documents … that can't be found elsewhere on the Web." These documents are secured from government and law enforcement sources "via Freedom of Information requests and from court files nationwide," stated The Smoking Gun.

A TSG article titled "A Million Little Lies," posted January 8, 2006, stated, "It was after the Oprah show that TSG first took a look at Frey. We had simply planned to track down one of his many mug shots and add it to our site's large collection. While Frey offers no specific details about when and where he was collared, the book does mention three states where he ran into trouble: Ohio, Michigan and North Carolina. While 9 of Frey's 14 reported arrests would have occurred when he was a minor, there still remained five cases for which a booking photo (not to mention police and court records) should have existed."

However, the article continued, "Repeated dead-ends on a county-by-county records search turned our one-off hunt for a mug shot into a more prolonged review of various portions of Frey's book. In an attempt to confirm or disprove his accounts, we examined matters for which there would likely be a paper trail at courthouses, police departments or motor vehicle agencies."

Such evidence was vital for corroboration, because the colorful supporting characters cited in *A Million Little Pieces* who might have been able to backup Frey's claims were largely unavailable. These characters included fellow drug addicts, criminals, and reprobates. By the end of the book, most of these acquaintances were either dead (through suicide, murder, or AIDS), serving life in prison, or residing in mental hospitals.

TSG made a six-week investigation. Frey was interviewed and given a chance to explain himself as part of this inquiry. The Smoking Gun concluded that Frey had made up most of his book. A follow-up book called *My Friend Leonard* also contained bogus material presented as true stories.

"Police reports, court records, interviews with law enforcement personnel and other sources have put the lie to many key sections of Frey's book," reported the "A Million Little Lies" article. "The 36-year-old author, these documents and interviews show, wholly fabricated or wildly embellished details of his purported criminal career, jail terms and status as an outlaw … in addition to these rap sheet creations, Frey also invented a role for himself in a deadly train accident that cost the lives of two female high school students … Frey appears to have fictionalized his past to propel and sweeten the book's already melodramatic narrative and help convince readers of his malevolence."

In *A Million Little Pieces,* Frey said his family moved from Cleveland to a rich Michigan suburb called St. Joseph when he was 12 years old. Frey wrote that he had few friends and hated living in St. Joseph. In his book, Frey claimed he developed a reputation as a wild kid who readily got in fistfights with his bullying peers. TSG spoke to Frey's classmates, who described him as a rather ordinary child who was far from being a wild, angry rebel.

TSG also cast doubt on Frey's account of being arrested and held in jail for drunk driving while in high school. "A thorough review of court and police records in the city and township of St. Joseph, the larger Berrien County and surrounding counties turned up only one case which landed Frey in a Michigan District Court around the time of his high school graduation. Here's how he succinctly described that drunk driving bust in *A Million Little Pieces:* 'Got first DUI. Blew a .36 and set a County Record. Went to Jail for a week.'"

In reality, this arrest was far less dramatic. TSG cited a police report from St. Joseph Township that described the June 8, 1988, traffic stop involving Frey. An officer noticed Frey's erratic driving and pulled him over. The officer observed that Frey's eyes were glassy, and that he smelled of alcohol and seemed out of it. Frey failed a series of field sobriety tests and was arrested for drunk driving and driving without his license. He was taken to the Berrien County Sheriff's Office, where he agreed to take a Breathalyzer test.

"Though he would later write of setting a .36 county record, Frey's blood alcohol level was actually recorded in successive tests at .21 and .20 (about twice the legal limit). As for his claim to have spent a week in jail after the arrest, the report debunks that assertion. After Frey's parents were called, he was allowed to quickly bond out," reported TSG, adding that police were eager to get the young man to leave because he had chicken pox (clearly visible in the mug shot of Frey posted by TSG) and they didn't want him to spread it during his stay.

Two weeks after the arrest, "court records show he pleaded guilty to a reduced charge of reckless driving and was fined $305. No jail, no framed certificate for setting the Berrien County Blood Alcohol Content record," continued the "Million Little Lies" article.

Three months after the arrest, Frey entered Denison University, a small liberal arts school in small-town Granville, Ohio. During his academic career, Frey supposedly blacked out from drinking on a daily basis, abused hard drugs, and was arrested multiple times. He somehow managed to graduate on time, however, in 1992.

The Smoking Gun was able to confirm only one arrest in this troubled period of Frey's life, in the fall of 1992. This run-in with the law—which happened about five months after Frey graduated—is described in vivid detail in *A Million Little Pieces*.

According to Frey, the trouble started when he tried to reunite with an ex-girlfriend in Ohio. She didn't care to get reacquainted, so Frey said he drank heavily, smoked crack, then drove to a local bar to search for the young woman in order to further their discussion. Frey drove up on the sidewalk and hit a policeman on foot patrol. Although Frey claimed to only be going five miles an hour, the constable was outraged and called for backup. A posse of police forcibly removed a swearing and fist-swinging Frey from his car then beat him with their truncheons. Police retrieved a bag of crack cocaine from his car and later recorded his blood alcohol level at .29.

As a result of this incident, Frey received a series of charges. TSG summarized these charges as follows, reflecting Frey's stylized use of capital letters: "Assault with a Deadly Weapon, Assaulting an Officer of the Law, Felony DUI, Disturbing the Peace, Resisting Arrest, Driving Without a License, Driving Without Insurance, Attempted Incitement of a Riot, Possession of a Narcotic with Intent to Distribute, and Felony Mayhem."

A Million Little Pieces doesn't identify where and when this dramatic arrest took place. The Smoking Gun later determined that it occurred October 25,

1992, in Licking County, Ohio, which includes the town of Granville and the Denison University campus.

At this point in the book, Frey enters treatment at the famous Hazelden rehab facility in Minnesota. In a scene with his parents and a lawyer named Randall, Frey is told he is in serious trouble. Ohio authorities wanted to make an example of Frey, stated Randall. Randall informed Frey that if he pled guilty to the charges stemming from his Ohio arrest, prosecutors would ask for a three-year sentence in state prison, followed by probation, a $15,000 fine, and 1,000 hours of community service upon release. Should Frey refuse the deal and go to trial, he faced a sentence of eight-and-a-half years. Naturally, the prospect of serious jail time terrified him, wrote Frey.

In a follow-up meeting, Randall had good news. Evidence had gone missing and some people vouched for Frey's good name. The prosecution now offered Frey the option of serving three to six months in county jail, and having his felony charges reduced to misdemeanors and his record cleared if he successfully completed probation. In Frey's telling, two friends from Hazelden—a gangster named Leonard (the same character referenced in the title of Frey's follow-up book) and Miles, a New Orleans federal appeal judge—"fixed" the case for him.

The Smoking Gun tracked down the actual story behind Frey's October 25, 1992, arrest. The website was unable to locate any jail records relating to this arrest, a sign that Frey didn't actually spend any time behind bars. A Licking County prosecuting attorney who was serving at the time of the arrest told TSG his office was never involved in any felony prosecutions against Frey. The same attorney also noted that there was no such offense as "felony mayhem" in Ohio's criminal code and that "felony DUI" didn't exist as an offense until the mid-1990s.

TSG did track down a mug shot of Frey and a Granville Police Department arrest report about the events of October 25, 1992. According to the report, the incident began around 11 p.m. on October 24, 1992, when a police officer observed Frey trying to park his car in a no-parking zone. In the process, Fry drove up onto the curb and almost hit a power pole. The investigating officer noticed that Frey's eyes were bloodshot and that he smelled of alcohol. There was a half-full bottle of beer in the car—but no crack. Frey failed field sobriety tests and was driven by a backup officer (the original investigating patrolman was on foot) in a vehicle to police headquarters. Although Frey refused to take a blood alcohol test, he was otherwise polite and cooperative, stated the arrest report, which was written at 4 a.m. on October 25, 1992.

The police station lacked a jail cell, so Frey wasn't put behind bars but was simply kept in a room for a few hours. He received two traffic tickets, "one for driving under the influence and another for driving without a license and a separate misdemeanor criminal summons for having that open container [of beer]. He was directed to appear in Mayor's Court in 10 days. Frey was then released on $733 cash bond, according to the report," stated The Smoking Gun.

TSG estimated that Frey's total "time in custody did not exceed five hours." *My Friend Leonard*, however, offered a detailed account of Frey's supposed three-month stay in Licking County Jail. Frey said he befriended a 300-pound inmate called Porterhouse, to whom he read aloud books of classic literature in his cell. Male inmates in the Licking County facility wore blue and yellow jumpsuits, and the place had a 15-foot fence topped with razor wire, wrote Frey.

A Licking County sheriff told TSG, however, that inmates of the county jail actually wore orange jumpsuits and that the place lacked a 15-foot-high razor wire fence. The sheriff also suggested it was unlikely that guards would allow two prisoners to spend so much time together in a single cell, out of sight of supervisors.

TSG debunked other claims as well. In *A Million Little Pieces*, Frey said he had sold large quantities of drugs at university and was investigated by the FBI. Granville police said the actual investigation involved tiny quantities of illegal substances and no FBI. Frey wasn't even questioned in the affair, added police. Frey said he was wanted on drug charges in Michigan and North Carolina, but TSG found no record of this.

In *A Million Little Pieces*, Frey claimed a close connection with a girl who died in a car accident. This anecdote was based on a real-life tragedy. On November 15, 1986, in St. Joseph Township, a teenage boy driving a pair of high school girls, Jane Hall and Melissa Sanders, tried to race past a train at a railway crossing. The driver was unsuccessful, and his car hit the train. The two girls were killed and the driver, badly injured.

In *A Million Little Pieces*, Frey refers to Melissa as "Michelle" and said she was a cheerleader, a classmate, and his only friend in eighth grade after he moved to St. Joseph. Frey said he had agreed to pretend to be on a movie date with Michelle, who used him as cover for a real date with a high school boy. Frey said he went along with this lie because Michelle might get in trouble if her parents knew the age of her real paramour. Frey went to the movies with Michelle, and she was then picked up by the high school boy, who proceeded to plow into a train, killing her. For unclear reasons, everyone blamed Frey for this tragedy, he stated.

As The Smoking Gun discovered, however, Frey's name wasn't even mentioned in the final, 16-page police report on the accident. When asked by TSG, Melissa's parents had only dim recollections of Frey. They also stated that their daughter wasn't a cheerleader and was in high school, not grade eight, when she died.

As part of their investigation, The Smoking Gun conducted a series of interviews with Frey. In these interviews, Frey admitted to exaggerating the nature of his arrests, though he claimed that the broad outlines of his story were true.

When posted in early 2006, The Smoking Gun's report drew an immediate reaction. On January 26, 2006, Frey appeared again on Oprah's show, only now she berated him instead of praising him. He admitted that TSG's report was largely true, and that he never served three months in jail and hadn't experienced the degree of debauchery and criminality cited in his book. Winfrey angrily withdrew her Book Club endorsement of *A Million Little Pieces*.

A representative of Doubleday admitted that the publisher hadn't fact-checked the book. According to the Doubleday representative, "the company first learned that parts of the book had been made up when The Smoking Gun published its report, nearly two years after the memoir was first published," noted a January 27, 2006, story in the *New York Times*.

Other accounts indicated Frey had in fact been fairly upfront prior to publication about the fictionalized nature of his book: "Mr. Frey had previously said he offered *A Million Little Pieces* to publishers first as a work of fiction, then as a memoir. But he has also said that in changing the book's designation from fiction to nonfiction, he did not change anything in it," stated the January 27, 2006, *Times*.

Random House offered small refunds to readers who felt duped by Frey's book. While Random House and Frey were ready to pay up to $2.35 million in settlement fees, only 1,345 people applied for a refund in the months after it was offered, reported The Smoking Gun on October 1, 2007.

In 2010, Frey founded a publishing company called Full Fathom Five, which is devoted to producing fiction. He continues to write.

Further Reading

David Carr, "How Oprahness Trumped Truthiness," *New York Times*, January 30, 2006.
James Frey, *A Million Little Pieces*, 2003.
Hilary Hylton, "Oprah vs. James Frey: The Sequel," *TIME*, July 30, 2007.
Janet Maslin, "Cry and You Cry Alone? Not If You Write About It," *New York Times*, April 21, 2003.
New York Times, "Author Is Kicked Out of Oprah Winfrey's Book Club," January 27, 2006.
The Smoking Gun.com, "A Million Little Lies," January 8, 2006.
The Smoking Gun.com, "A Thousand Little Refunds," October 1, 2007.

THE MIS-EDUCATION OF LITTLE TREE

In 1976, a book aimed at young people called *The Education of Little Tree* was published. The book concerned an orphan boy who comes to appreciate his Native American heritage and the beauty of the natural world. Forrest Carter, author of *Little Tree*, said the book was autobiographical and based on his own Cherokee childhood. Carter claimed "he had Cherokee family in north Alabama and that he was an official 'story teller' and 'oral historian' for the

Cherokee nation … he performed what he called Cherokee songs and dances for his friends," stated a December 20, 2001, article posted in online magazine Salon.

Little Tree became a huge hit, earning "rave reviews in the *New York Times*, the *Atlantic Monthly* and elsewhere," reported Salon. Critics, however, said Carter was hiding a hateful past behind a new name and Native American persona.

"[Forrest] Carter was identified as Asa Earl Carter, a member of the Ku Klux Klan and speechwriter for Alabama Governor George Wallace," wrote the *Washington Post*, on November 6, 2007. Asa Carter also co-founded a racist, pro-Confederate magazine and ran for Governor of Alabama in 1970 on an unabashed platform of white supremacy.

All of which strands in ironic contrast to the content of *The Education of Little Tree*. Originally marketed as a work of nonfiction, *Little Tree* is set during the Great Depression. An orphan boy is taken in by his Cherokee Indian grandparents, who live in the Appalachian mountain region of Tennessee. The orphan is given the nickname "Little Tree" by his grandparents, who instruct him in traditional Native American hunting and survival techniques. Little Tree is taught to respect nature and be wary of bigoted white people who might not appreciate his Indian background. The book was widely praised for its message of respecting Native American culture and living in harmony with the environment.

"Unfortunately, *The Education of Little Tree* is a hoax. The carefully constructed mask of Forrest Carter—Cherokee cowboy, self-taught writer and spokesman for Native Americans—was simply the last fantasy of a man who reinvented himself again and again in the 30 years that preceded his death in 1979," stated an October 4, 1991, *New York Times* article.

In a biography provided for his gubernatorial run, Asa Carter said he was born September 4, 1925, in Oxford, Alabama. He said his parents were dairy farmers and that his family had Cherokee roots. (Apparently, having Native Indian ancestors was a point of pride among some white racists, said Salon. Nonetheless, Carter's alleged Native heritage was hotly contested by some of his relatives.) Carter graduated from high school in 1942. With World War II raging at the time, he joined the Navy. When the war ended, Carter married Thelma India Walker, whom he had dated in high school. He moved to Colorado, where he studied at the state university, then returned to Alabama.

Back in Alabama, Carter earned a reputation as a very public racist and anti-Semitic rabble-rouser. He helped found a publication called *The Southerner*, "a monthly magazine devoted to white supremacy," according to the December 20, 2001, article in Salon.

Carter formed a group called the White Citizens Council, "an organization that espoused the same fundamental views as the KKK," reported Salon. He went on to form another racist group called the Original Ku Klux Klan of the

Confederacy. The Original KKK achieved notoriety when members attacked African American singer Nat King Cole during a concert in Birmingham, Alabama, in 1956. The same organization, without Carter present, was accused in 1957 of kidnapping African American handyman Edward Aaron, "who had offended members of Carter's group with inflammatory talk of forced integration." Aaron was castrated and had turpentine poured on his wounds, reported the December 20, 2001, Salon article.

In 1958, Carter quit his KKK group over disputes about leadership. He ran for lieutenant-governor of Alabama, finishing poorly. The same year, a circuit judge named George Wallace lost the Democratic primary to run as governor of Alabama. Wallace blamed his loss on the perception that he was a racial moderate by the standards of the day. According to the December 20, 2001, Salon report, Wallace aides hired Carter as a speechwriter to beef up their candidate's racist credentials.

Wallace won the 1962 election for governor and, the following year, made an infamous Inauguration Day speech on the Alabama capitol steps, pledging, "Segregation now! Segregation tomorrow! Segregation forever!" The words—spoken in favor of "segregating" blacks and whites by maintaining separate public facilities—were penned by Carter, reported the October 4, 1991, *New York Times*.

Carter continued to toil as a Wallace speechwriter, though he worked through intermediaries and was kept at a distance from the man himself. Carter was fired when Wallace entered the 1968 presidential race and toned down his racist rhetoric to earn greater public support. Wallace's bid for president was not successful, and he soon eyed a return to the governor's mansion. Carter had similar plans. "Deserted and, he felt, betrayed, Carter ran against Wallace for the Governor's seat in 1970," stated the December 20, 2001, Salon report.

Pamphlets and radio messages issued by Carter for the campaign blasted Jews for supposedly financing the Russian Revolution and warned of the dangers posed by black policemen to white wives and daughters. Carter lost the race. Three years later, he sold his Alabama home and moved his family to Florida.

In the Sunshine State, Carter changed his first name to Forrest (in honor of Nathaniel Bedford Forrest, a Confederate cavalry general and founder of the Ku Klux Klan, according to Salon). He adapted a new persona, as a folksy writer with a Native American background and pro-wilderness attitude, and began to spend much time in Texas. Carter penned a book, published in 1973, called *The Rebel Outlaw: Josey Wales*. The book sold reasonably well and was turned into a hit movie in 1976, starring Clint Eastwood as the embittered, ex-Confederate soldier of the title. The same year the Eastwood movie came out, *The Education of Little Tree* was released as a book.

Carter's new persona began to unravel, however, due to the publicity stirred up by his books and the Eastwood movie. In 1975, Carter was interviewed on television by Barbara Walters. He wore a black cowboy hat and played up his Texas/Cherokee image for the occasion. Not all viewers were taken in, however. NBC, the station that broadcast the interview, received several calls from Carter's acquaintances and friends back in Alabama. These associates made it clear that Forrest Carter was none other than Asa Earl Carter, wrote Salon.

Carter denied he had changed identities. Evidence was mounting, however, about his earlier life as an embittered racist. A childhood friend of Carter's named Buddy Barnett owned an autographed first edition of *The Rebel Outlaw: Josey Wales*. The inscription read, "Forrest (Asa) Carter." The handwriting in the inscription was compared with a handwriting sample from the biography Carter provided for the 1970 Alabama governor's race. The handwriting matched, reported Salon.

The man claiming to be Forrest Carter died of heart failure on September 4, 1979, and was buried near Anniston, Alabama. The tombstone his family eventually settled on, after having the initial grave marker removed, read "Asa Earl Carter," not Forrest.

In spite of such revelations, which were published in the media, *The Education of Little Tree* continued to sell well. "The book became a million seller and sentimental favorite. In 1991, the American Booksellers Association gave Little Tree its first ever ABBY award, established 'to honor the 'hidden treasures' that ABA bookstore members most enjoyed recommending,'" stated the November 6, 2007, *Washington Post*.

A news article published in 1991 in the *New York Times*, headlined, "The Transformation of a Klansman," reminded readers of the true origins of the *Little Tree* author. Such exposés didn't diminish the book's popularity—although it was rebranded as a work of fiction. The *Washington Post* article noted that *Little Tree* had received TV diva Oprah Winfrey's approval in 2007. Once Winfrey was brought up to speed on the nature of the book's author, this approval was rescinded. Winfrey pulled the "discredited children's book … from a list of recommended titles on her website, blaming an archival 'error' for including a work considered the literary hoax of a white supremacist," noted the November 6, 2007, *Post* article.

In 1997, a movie based on *The Education of Little Tree* was released, featuring well-known actor James Cromwell and Native Indian character actor Graham Greene. The film, however, was not a big hit. According to the website Box Office Mojo (which tabulates how much money a given film earned in its theatrical run), the movie's gross came to only $323,411. It is unclear how many moviegoers were aware of the controversial origins of the book from which the movie took its plot and characters. *The Education of Little Tree* novel is still widely available, online and in bookstores.

Further Reading

Allen Barra, "The Education of Little Fraud," Salon, December 20, 2001, http://www
.salon.com/2001/12/20/carter_6/

Box Office Mojo.com, "The Education of Little Tree," http://www.boxofficemojo.com
/search/?q=the%20education%20of%20little%20tree.

Dan Carter, "The Transformation of a Klansman," New York Times, October 4, 1991.

Forrest Carter, The Education of Little Tree, 1976.

Hillel Italie, "Disputed Book Pulled from Oprah Web Site," Washington Post, November
6, 2007.

MOVIE CONS

Con artists have long fascinated moviemakers and moviegoers alike. "Con men are more appealing than run-of-the-mill villains, who want to take your money because they are stronger or more dangerous than you are. Con men want to take it because they're smarter than you are. And there is hardly ever a con man who isn't likable, because, after all, if he can't win your confidence, how can he take your money?" wrote film critic Roger Ebert, in a review of *The Grifters*.

The Grifters is one of several movies to focus on scam artists and the cons they pull. As Ebert noted, confidence artists are usually portrayed much more sympathetically onscreen than, say, serial killers or sex offenders. The two con men at the center of *The Sting*, a blockbuster hit from the 1970s, are seen as adorable, even as they cheat and steal. Other films don't go quite as far but still tend to romanticize confidence artists as likeable characters rather than sociopathic felons.

The following are some notable big-screen depictions of con men and women.

The Grifters (1990)

In his classic study of confidence artists, academic David Maurer discussed the difference between the "short con" and the "big con." Put simply, a short con is something done on the spot for a relatively modest amount of money, while a big con is an elaborate ploy involving many different characters, played out over a period of time. This movie aptly underscores the difference.

The film centers on a young man named Roy. As played by John Cusack, Roy is a small-time "grifter," someone who "grifts"—i.e., rips people off—then drifts away. At the beginning of the movie he tries to fool a bartender into giving him more change by switching a $20 bill for a lower denomination. This petty scam fails miserably, and Roy gets beaten up so badly by the barkeep that he has to recuperate in hospital.

We learn that Roy's mother, Lily Dillon (played by Anjelica Huston), and his girlfriend Myra (played by Annette Bening) are also con artists, though much more accomplished. Lily, a heartless woman who never paid much attention to her son, works for organized crime, going around the United States to horse tracks to place bets designed to change the odds. Myra, meanwhile, is chummy with major-league criminals in Texas and Oklahoma.

Roy gets out of the hospital, and much complex intra-family scamming ensues. Roy ends up tricked and manipulated, then abandoned, by his own mother, who is much more criminally astute than he.

Film critic Roger Ebert considered *The Grifters* one of the best films of the year. He described it as "the story of a young man who thinks he is an expert at playing the confidence game—until he runs into two women who really are experts, who destroy every illusion he ever had that he could count on someone or love someone."

American Hustle (2013)

American Hustle is a crime comedy loosely based on the FBI's Abscam sting operation of the late 1970s and early 1980s. Abscam caught various politicians on videotape accepting bribes on behalf of wealthy Arabs.

"The real story of Abscam, the sweeping and still controversial federal corruption investigation that played out from Jersey to Florida in the late 1970s and early 1980s, turned out to be far more bizarre and outrageous than anything Hollywood could ever imagine ... the elaborate sting ensnared seven members of Congress, including six in the House of Representatives and a veteran U.S. Senator, along with a powerful New Jersey state legislator, three Philadelphia councilmen and a number of high-level political operatives," stated a November 25, 2013, article on the NJ.com website.

In the movie, Christian Bale plays "Irving Rosenfeld," a rumpled, crude, and canny hustler. Rosenfeld is an alias for Mel Weinberg, a very real character who assisted the FBI. Weinberg was "an unrepentant, cigar-chomping Runyonesque swindler from Long Island ... barely controlled by his FBI handlers, he helped orchestrate the sting operation," stated the NJ.com article.

A lifelong confidence artist, Weinberg ran an "advance fee" scam on Long Island. He claimed to head an international investment and banking firm that could secure loans from offshore sources for businesses with bad credit. Needless to say, none of these loans ever materialized, even after Weinberg's clients paid him substantial "advance fees."

In 1977, a Pittsburgh real estate figure whom Weinberg ripped off went to the FBI. A federal grand jury was convened and indicted Weinberg for mail fraud, wire fraud, and conspiracy. Instead of going to jail, Weinberg was recruited by the FBI to assist them with an investigation that eventually became Abscam.

Weinberg's role was to portray the president of Abdul Enterprises Ltd., a company that supposedly promoted the interests of a rich Arab client. Needless to say, the Arab client and the company Weinberg represented were all phony. Abscam was real enough, however, to fool a slew of political figures who accepted bribes for various favors, as hidden cameras recorded all.

"The undercover probe, which came to light in February 1980, ultimately led to the convictions of Sen. Harrison A. Williams (D-N.J.), Camden Democratic Mayor Angelo Errichetti, New Jersey Democratic Congressman Frank Thompson Jr., and other lawmakers, who were caught on secretly recorded surveillance video accepting tens of thousands of dollars in bribes," stated NJ.com.

Abscam remains controversial; critics say it amounted to entrapment. To catch their prey, the FBI deliberately engineered the crimes for which the defendants were charged. Controversial as Abscam might still be, *American Hustle* was generally well received by critics and the public. The film won kudos for its portrayal of disco-era police/criminal shenanigans and rapid-fire dialogue.

Argo (2012)

Ben Affleck stars and directs in this political thriller about a con job pulled by the CIA and Canadian officials to sneak six U.S. embassy staffers out of post-revolutionary Iran. The con involved a phony science fiction film and fake government documents to make it appear that the embassy workers were part of a Canadian production crew.

The film is set in Iran in late 1979. The country is undergoing a revolution. Militants overthrow the repressive Shah and establish a revolutionary government. Hardline Islam is in, while the United States is mostly definitely out. Militants seize the U.S. embassy in Tehran, taking 52 Americans hostage. Half a dozen additional staffers manage to escape and hide out in the home of Ken Taylor, the Canadian ambassador to Iran. The six employees can't leave the house for fear of being arrested, and live in dread of a police raid.

A CIA operative named Tony Mendez comes up with a plan to get the embassy staffers out of Ambassador Taylor's residence and out of the country. Mendez pretended to be "Kevin Costa Harkins," an Irish film producer leading a preproduction crew around Iran to scout locations for a possible film shoot. It was a good cover, as Mendez had contacts in the movie world from past initiatives.

Mendez would try to pass off the six staffers as Canadian film company employees. The ruse made sense, given that the staffers were with the Canadian ambassador, who could help with fake documents. The Iranian revolutionaries had no particular animus against Canada, reserving their scorn for "the Great Satan," as they called the United States.

Mendez brought his friend John Chambers (a makeup artist who had worked on *Planet of the Apes*) into the scam. Chambers brought in a friend of his named Bob Sidell, who did special effects. In only a few days, the three men created a phony Hollywood film production company. As part of the sham, fake business cards were made and identities concocted for the six members of the alleged location-scouting crew. The faux film company's offices were based in a suite at Sunset Gower Studios.

The office had real phone lines and an actual script to work from. The script was for a movie Chambers had been tentatively involved in called *Lord of Light*. It was based on a science-fiction novel. Sci-fi was all the rage at the time, with the release of *Star Wars*. Mendez changed the name of the script to *Argo*, and the film company placed fake ads for the movie in Hollywood trade journals.

In late January 1980, Mendez traveled to Iran. At the same time, a series of supplies were sent via diplomatic pouch to the Canadian Embassy in Tehran. The supplies included health cards, driver's licenses, passports, and other Canadian government documents for the six American embassy staffers, plus restaurant receipts from Montreal and Toronto, film company business cards, and more. All of these fakes were designed to look as real as possible.

Mendez met with the six U.S. embassy workers at Taylor's residence and explained the game plan. The workers were fitted out with their phony Canadian documents and film production gear; then the group went off to Mehrabad Airport. The film depicts a harrowing but eventually successful escape via plane.

Argo was a big hit and won the Academy Award for Best Picture. The movie was based on an April 24, 2007, *Wired* magazine article and a book by Mendez called *The Master of Disguise*.

Elmer Gantry (1960)

The titular character of Elmer Gantry is a hard-living former seminary student (who was kicked out of school for various debauches) turned salesman. Sensing an opportunity for financial and possibly romantic gain, Gantry, played by Burt Lancaster, joins a female evangelist, Sister Sharon Falconer (played by Jean Simmons), on a religious crusade.

At tent revival meetings, Gantry is portrayed as a salesman who found God. A charismatic, fiery speaker, Gantry is used to "warm up" the crowds. He rants and raves at audiences about sin and burning in hell—conveniently overlooking his own problems with alcohol and womanizing. Then Sister Falconer comes out to preach salvation and mercy.

Gantry has an affair with Sister Falconer, who loses her virginity to him. Gantry leads a religious procession into a brothel as part of an anti-vice campaign and is confronted by an ex-girlfriend turned prostitute (Shirley Jones). Gantry had previously seduced and abandoned the girl, whose father was a minister. Her reputation shattered, the girl turned to prostitution to earn a living. There is an attempt at blackmailing Gantry. The attempt fails, and newspapers reveal Gantry's relationship with the prostitute. He is mocked and egged by angry crowds at Sister Falconer's next tent revival.

At the end of the movie, Sister Falconer triumphantly opens a new tabernacle (house of worship). A fire breaks out, and the crowd panics. Sister Falconer refuses to leave, saying God will protect her and anyone who stays. Gantry, who has genuine feelings for Sister Falconer, tries to rescue her but is forced back by the mob rushing out. Sister Falconer dies, and Gantry is left to contemplate his next step.

The film *Elmer Gantry* is based on a celebrated and controversial novel by Sinclair Lewis, published in 1927. The character of Sister Falconer is based on real-life female evangelist Aimee Semple McPherson. It is the Gantry character, however, who has become something of an archetype for hypocritical religious leaders who preach against the kinds of sins they practice in private. These fallen, real-world preachers include both Jim Bakker and Jimmy Swaggart, 1980s-era religious-TV superstars who became embroiled in sex scandals.

Elmer Gantry was very well received and earned several Academy Award nominations. Lancaster won for Best Actor, while Jones won Best Supporting Actress.

The Hustler (1961)

"Fast Eddie" Felson (played by Paul Newman) is a pool hustler. The film starts with Eddie and his manager pulling a small-time con in a pool hall. Eddie pretends to be very drunk, making huge, foolish bets on his pool playing ability. The suckers in the pool hall assume he's an easy mark and take him on. Eddie easily beats them and returns to his manager with a handful of cash.

The movie concerns Eddie's obsession with beating top-ranked pool player "Minnesota Fats," memorably played by Jackie Gleason. A cold-hearted, big-time gambler named Bert Gordon (George S. Scott) watches from the sidelines to see if Eddie has the "character"—that is, the ruthless drive—to win, so he can use him for betting purposes.

Although the movie is ostensibly about pool, it is actually a character study, contrasting aggressive, self-defeating petty hustler Eddie against serenely confident Minnesota Fats. In an essay on the film posted online, movie critic Roger Ebert discussed Gleason's performance: "He gives the impression of a man purified by pool, who has moved through all the sad compromises and crooked bets and hustling moves and emerged as a man who simply, elegantly plays the game. He has long ago given up hustling; unlike Eddie, he makes his living by dependably being the best, time after time, so that others can test themselves against him."

Hardly an uplifting story, *The Hustler* was a critical and commercial hit, earning several Academy Award nominations.

The Sting (1973)

Set in Chicago in 1936, *The Sting* follows a complicated scheme by two con artists (Robert Redford and Paul Newman) to rip off a mob boss, played by Robert Shaw. The movie was inspired by David Maurer's book *The Big Con: The Story of the Confidence Man*.

Redford plays Johnny Hooker, a small-time con man in Joliet, Illinois. With the connivance of his African American associate Luther (James Earl Jones), Hooker uses the "Pigeon Drop" scam (described in the section on Classic Cons) to steal $11,000 from a dupe. Luther is delighted and announces plans to retire. He urges Hooker to meet up with an old pal, Henry Gondorff, in Chicago to do big-time cons.

It is soon revealed that Luther and Hooker's victim was a "numbers runner" for Chicago organized crime boss Doyle Lonnegan (Shaw). A corrupt cop confronts Hooker with this news, and demands a cut of the robbery. Hooker has spent it already, so he pays the policeman off with counterfeit bills. Lonnegan's gang murders Luther, and Hooker flees for his life to Chicago.

Hooker connects with Henry Gondorff (Newman), a once-brilliant confidence man now keeping a very low profile. Hooker wants to work with Gondorff to rip off Lonnegan and avenge Luther's death. Gondorff decides to revive an old scam called "The Wire" (also explained in the section on Classic Cons). Gondorff will construct a fake off-track betting parlor and staff it with various criminal associates posing as wealthy bettors and bustling clerks. It seems many underworld figures have a score to settle with Lonnegan and are eager to take part in this deception.

The con is put into play. Gondorff, pretending to be an obnoxious bookie named Shaw, horns in on a private high-stakes poker game run by Lonnegan. Gondorff acts boorishly, then blatantly cheats to win $15,000 from Lonnegan. Pretending to be a Shaw employee, Hooker goes to collect the $15,000 from Lonnegan. While speaking to Lonnegan, Hooker complains of ill-treatment and how he's itching to get back at his boss. Hooker tells Lonnegan about the off-track betting parlor, then reveals that he has an inside contact at Western Union who can feed him horse racing results before they're publicly released. Thus, bettors in the know can put their money on a sure thing. Hooker suggests that Lonnegan could make a huge bet, based on this inside information, that would result in such a big payout that it would bankrupt Shaw.

Hooker's Western Union "contact" tells Lonnegan to "place it all on Lucky Dan." Lonnegan enters the off-track betting parlor and puts down $500,000 on Lucky Dan. When the Western Union contact arrives at the parlor, he is aghast. He thought Lonnegan understood that Lucky Dan would "place"—that is, come in second. Lonnegan has bet on the horse to "win," come in first.

Lonnegan tries to change his bet just as a clutch of police and FBI agents burst into the parlor. One of the agents implies that Hooker is an informer who tipped the Bureau off about the parlor. Outraged, Gondorff shoots Hooker. The FBI agent, in turn, shoots Gondorff. Two men are now on the floor, bleeding. The FBI agents order a policeman to hustle Lonnegan away from the scene so he's not mixed up in a murder rap.

Lonnegan is forced out, and Gondorff and Hooker rise from the dead. Everything was a scam. Blanks were fired and props used to simulate bleeding. The fake off-track betting parlor is dismantled as Gondorff and Hooker leave together.

The Sting was a huge hit, and won the Best Picture Academy Award and Best Director. The film was notable for its performances, costumes, sets, and use of Scott Joplin ragtime music to set the mood.

Further Reading

Noah Adams, "Elmer Gantry, a Flawed Preacher for the Ages," NPR.org, February 22, 2008, http://www.npr.org/templates/story/story.php?storyId=19288767.

Joshuah Bearman, "How the CIA Used a Fake Sci-Fi Flick to Rescue Americans from Tehran," *Wired*, April, 24, 2007.

Vincent Canby, "The Sting (1973)," *New York Times*, December 26, 1973.

Manohla Dargisdec, "Big Hair, Bad Scams, Motormouths," *New York Times*, December 12, 2013.

Roger Ebert, "John Cusack Interview for *The Grifters*," *Chicago Sun-Times*, January 20, 1991.

Roger Ebert, "The Grifters," *Chicago Sun-Times*, January 25, 1991.

Roger Ebert, "The Hustler," Roger Ebert website, June 23, 2002, http://www.rogerebert.com/reviews/great-movie-the-hustler-1961.

Brian D. Johnson, "Ben Affleck Rewrites History," *Maclean's Magazine*, September 12, 2012.

David Maurer, *The Big Con: The Story of the Confidence Man*, 1940.

Ted Sherman, "Jersey Hustle: The Real-Life Story of Abscam," NJ.com, November 25, 2013, http://www.nj.com/inside-jersey/index.ssf/2013/11/jersey_hustle_the_real-life_story_of_abscam.html.

THE 1919 WORLD SERIES

In 1919, the Chicago White Sox were a powerhouse professional baseball team destined for the World Series. As great as they were on the field, the Sox were poorly paid by their stingy owner, Charles Comiskey. Professional baseball players lacked a union at the time, so there was little they could do to protest low salaries and unfair contracts.

A few weeks before the World Series commenced, first baseman Chick Gandil approached an acquaintance of his, a small-time gambler named Joseph Sullivan, with a proposal. Gandil said he could arrange for the heavily favored White Sox to lose the Series, in exchange for $100,000. Sullivan agreed to this plot, and both men began recruiting more people to their side.

Gandil couldn't throw all the games himself, so he had to convince some of his teammates to join in the scam. Sullivan, meanwhile, didn't have $100,000 on hand and needed co-investors. Sullivan got Abe Attell, a former boxing champion; William "Sleepy Bill" Burns, ex-White Sox pitcher; and Hall Chase, a New York Giants first baseman, to chip in. All three men were confirmed gamblers. Arnold Rothstein, New York City–based financier of the underworld, also made an investment in the scam.

Rothstein was famous for being the power behind the throne, a money man who was more venture capitalist than mob boss. He helped set up trans-Atlantic alcohol shipping routes during Prohibition, funded drug-smuggling operations, and mentored a slew of up-and-coming gangsters.

Some accounts say all Rothstein did was to provide a share of the $100,000 bribe. Other crime historians suggest Rothstein had a more direct hand in the scam, sending a thug to visit White Sox pitcher Claude "Lefty" Williams before the eighth game of the Series. This thug allegedly ordered Williams to lose the game or face violent repercussions. The threat extended to Williams' family. Rothstein had bet on the opposing Cincinnati Reds and didn't want the White Sox to win. With Williams pitching, the White Sox ended up losing the eighth game in the series 10–5, thus handing the World Series to the Reds.

Rumors abounded in Chicago sporting and press circles about a possible "fix." In September 1920, a grand jury in Cook County, Illinois, was convened to examine allegations of rigged professional baseball games. Soon, the grand jury was taking a close look at the 1919 World Series. Players, writers, gamblers, owners, and managers alike were called to testify before the grand jury. Rothstein's name came up on more than one occasion. Rothstein himself received a subpoena and appeared before the grand jury on October 27, 1920. He evidently made a good impression; after he spoke, the State's Attorney's office announced that Rothstein's testimony exonerated him "from complicity in the 1919 World Series" according to the *New York Times*.

In the end, criminal indictments were handed down to eight White Sox players, plus Hal Chase, Abe Attell, Joe Sullivan, Bill Burns, and a handful of others. Rothstein was not indicted, which was either an indication of his political pull or a reflection of his limited role.

The trial began in June 1921. On July 23, Rothstein huffily issued a statement to the press from his home on West 84th Street. While he admitted William Burns had approached him with a view to joining the scam, Rothstein angrily denied having anything to do with the man: "When Burns, with whom I had no previous acquaintance, sought me out in this city and advanced to me his proposition to enter into a scheme to fix the World Series, not only did I most emphatically refuse to have anything to do with him or his proposition, but I told him that I regarded his proposition as an insult and him as a blackguard, with whom I wanted no dealing whatsoever and warned him not to come near or speak to me on any pretext whatsoever," read Rothstein's statement.

The eight players were acquitted, but all ended up being banned for life from professional baseball. Rothstein managed to escape any indictment, much less conviction, but was known forever afterward as "the man who fixed the World Series."

Rothstein's fame was such that he entered pop culture consciousness. His persona formed the basis of the character Meyer Wolfsheim in F. Scott Fitzgerald's 1925 masterpiece *The Great Gatsby*. Described as the gambler who fixed the World Series, Wolfsheim is a shadowy bootlegger who provided the mysterious nouveau riche Gatsby with his income. Rothstein was also depicted as the character Nathan Detroit in the short stories by Damon Runyon that would form the basis of the musical *Guys and Dolls*.

The real-life Arnold Rothstein was shot and critically wounded in New York City on November 4, 1928, after welshing on a $250,000 gambling debt. He died two days later.

Further Reading

Chicago Historical Society, The Black Sox, http://www.chicagohs.org/history/blacksox .html.

Rich Cohen, *Tough Jews: Fathers, Sons, and Gangster Dreams*, 1998.

"Rothstein Quotes Burns in Defense," *New York Times*, July 24, 1921.

Paul Sann, *The Lawless Decade*, 1957.

DAMON RUNYON, CHRONICLER OF THE UNDERWORLD

Damon Runyon was a prolific writer who memorably chronicled New York life and the American underworld in a series of stories written from the 1910s to the 1940s. His accounts of colorful characters such as Nathan Detroit, Harry the Horse, and Good Time Charley delighted readers and inspired several popular films and plays, including the hit musical *Guys and Dolls*. Runyon was also a highly regarded sports and news reporter.

Runyon remains primarily known for his fiction. He generally wrote in the present-tense and used a great deal of underworld vernacular. His "hardboiled" style and use of shady characters with odd nicknames have become known as "Runyonesque."

During his career, Runyon interviewed or mingled with a large cast of figures, from petty criminals to leading mobsters, as well as actors, showgirls, gamblers, athletes, bookies, and others. He had no compunctions about befriending people on the wrong side of the law. Runyon "ate at some of the great dinner tables of the country, but he hated legitimate people and loved thieves," wrote New York columnist Jimmy Breslin in his biography, *Damon Runyon*.

Runyon was born October 4, 1880, in Manhattan, Kansas. His childhood name was Alfred Damon Runyan (spelled with an "a"). Runyon's grandfather had been an editor and journalist who ran a newspaper called the *Manhattan Independent*.

When Runyon was a boy, his father moved the family to Pueblo, Colorado, where he worked as a printer for a newspaper called the *Chieftain*. As a young teenager, Runyon took a job as a reporter at a paper called the *Pueblo Evening Press*. An editor apparently misspelled his last name on some copy (calling the boy "Runyon" instead of "Runyan"); not wanting to irritate his boss, Runyon adopted the new spelling himself and used it for the rest of his life, wrote Breslin.

In 1898, with the outbreak of the Spanish-American War, Runyon tried to join in the army, although he was a few months shy of 18, the minimum age for enlistment. Runyon was eventually accepted into the army and served as a soldier in the Philippines.

After leaving the armed forces, Runyon went back to writing for local newspapers in Colorado. He moved to New York City in 1910 and was soon working at the William Randolph Hearst–owned *New York American* newspaper. At the time, Runyon used all three of his names: Alfred Damon Runyon. According to Breslin, a newspaper editor at the *New York American* shortened his name to "Damon Runyon" for publishing purposes. The editor thought using three names was pretentious and that "Damon Runyon" made for a snappier byline, explained Breslin.

Runyon wrote sports and news. He married in 1911 and began a family. In addition to earning a reputation as a skilled journalist, Runyon became known for the company he kept. He interviewed or mingled with the likes of English-American gang leader Owney Madden, boxer Jack Dempsey, mob financier Arnold Rothstein, Chicago crime czar Al Capone, Mexican revolutionary Pancho Villa, and Otto Berman, accountant for Jewish gangster Dutch Schultz, among others.

After spending years writing newspaper copy, Runyon started turning out short stories, most of them centered on less-than-reputable characters embroiled in criminal or seedy acts. His stories became hugely popular, and Runyon began commanding high fees for his fiction—upwards of $1,000 a story, at a time when some people worked all year to earn as much, noted Breslin.

When writing fiction, Runyon generally stuck to the populist, slang-heavy style that had endeared him to the public. He based characters and plots on real people and real incidents he had encountered during his newspaper days. Far from trying to impress critics, Runyon was primarily interested in telling entertaining stories in a colorful manner. "Runyon knew he would please none of the literary judges because he was mostly writing about small thieves and other minor criminals and he made them humorous, even romantic," wrote Breslin.

Runyon's stories had names such as "Tobias the Terrible," "The Snatching of Bookie Bob," "The Lemon Drop Kid," and "Cemetery Bait." His work was soon embraced by movie studios. Runyon's story "Madame La Gimp" became a well-regarded 1933 film called *Lady For a Day*, while the film adaptation of his story "Little Miss Marker" helped bring child actress Shirley Temple to mainstream acclaim.

Here is an example of Runyon's work, from the story "Romance in the Roaring Forties":

> Only a rank sucker will think of taking two peeks at Dave the Dude's doll, because while Dave may stand for the first peek, figuring it is a mistake, it is a sure thing he will get sored up at the second peek, and Dave the Dude is certainly not a man to have sored up at you.
>
> But this Waldo Winchester is one hundred per cent sucker, which is why he takes quite a number of peeks at Dave's doll. And what is more, she takes quite a number of peeks right back at him. And there you are. When a guy and a doll get to taking peeks back and forth at each other, why, there you are indeed.

While his characters might have been on the seedy side, Runyon himself "always dressed and acted like a gentleman. He never swore in front of a woman, nor permitted others to do so," noted Breslin.

Runyon died of throat cancer, on December 10, 1946, in his adopted hometown of New York City. His work continues to delight and inspire after his death. Two of Runyon's stories formed the basis of the hit Broadway musical *Guys and Dolls*. This later became a popular film of the same title, starring Marlon Brando and Jean Simmons.

In all his fictional work, Runyon showed a distinct appreciation for the darker side of New York life. "He lived during Prohibition and the Depression and came from the West and understood his city better than anybody of his time," stated Breslin.

Further Reading

Jimmy Breslin, *Damon Runyon*, 1991.
Damon Runyon, *The Damon Runyon Omnibus*, 1944.

SUBLIMINAL MESSAGING

In December 1985, two very intoxicated teenage boys in Sparks, Nevada, decided to kill themselves. Hyped up on alcohol, drugs, and repeated listening of heavy metal music, particularly the British band Judas Priest, Ray Belknap and James Vance staggered to a children's playground armed with a 12-gauge shotgun.

Belknap aimed the weapon at himself, pulled the trigger, and died on the spot. His friend Vance retrieved the shotgun to do the same, but through a combination of nerves and extreme intoxication, only managed to injure himself, mutilating his face.

Disfigured, but alive, Vance endured countless plastic surgeries to restore his damaged facial features, before dying of drug complications three years after the shooting. He also became the subject of a sensational lawsuit. According to Vance's parents, Judas Priest had put hidden messages in their music that encouraged their son and his friend to attempt suicide. Allegedly, these phrases could be detected by discerning listeners, triggering all manner of mayhem. Vance's mother and father sued Judas Priest and CBS records.

The lawsuit focused on one of the boys' favorite Judas Priest songs, "Better By You, Better Than Me." The song, actually a cover version of a number written by the band Spooky Tooth, allegedly contained the words "Do it."

The Vance parents didn't deny that their son and his friend were troubled. When the trial opened in the summer of 1990, a clinical psychologist testifying for the defense said both Belknap and Vance were depressed, impulsive, and sometimes violent. Both teenagers had problems with drug abuse, unemployment, failure at school, and petty crime. It was acknowledged that Belknap and Vance had suicidal inclinations. The lawsuit, however, claimed that the supposedly buried phrase "Do it" served a subconscious trigger, so to speak, for a suicide pact. Vance himself testified to this on a video made before his death.

While they had suffered a terrible tragedy, did Vance's parents have a point? Do rock bands ever put so-called secret messages in their songs?

Such messages, believers claim, are either recorded backwards (as in the allegations against Judas Priest) or buried deep in a song's mix. The messages can't be detected on a conscious level but are instead discerned subconsciously. "Subliminal messaging" is the term for this kind of discreet communication, explained an article in the November/December 1996 *Skeptical Inquirer* about the Judas Priest trial.

The notion of "subliminal messages" in music can be traced in part to a strange controversy about the Beatles. In the fall of 1969, rumors began to emerge that Paul McCartney had been killed in a car accident three years prior. He had allegedly been replaced by a lookalike with a similar voice, so the Beatles could continue to cash in on their enormous success. It was claimed that the band planted overt and covert messages hinting at McCartney's demise in their music. The song "A Day in the Life," for example, details a fatal car accident, while the mumbled phrase "I buried Paul" can allegedly be heard at the end of the song "I am the Walrus."

Subliminal Messaging in Advertising

In 1974, writer Wilson Bryan Key published a controversial book called *Subliminal Seduction*. Described in an article in the November/December 1996 edition of *Skeptical Inquirer* magazine as, "the man who pretty much single-handedly popularized the myth of subliminal advertising," Key claimed he could spot all manner of semi-hidden, vulgar messaging in ads.

The subtitle of *Subliminal Seduction* asked, "Are you being sexually aroused by this picture?" and showed a photograph of a cocktail glass containing ice cubes. Photos like this, along with various other pictures published in the book, were riddled with erotic imagery designed to make consumers rush out and purchase products, claimed Key. Even magazine ads of innocent pleasures such as Ritz crackers, said Key, were covered with deliberately placed words such as "SEX."

Key was highly popular on the lecture circuit and published several other books in the same vein throughout the 1970s and 1980s.

Key testified for the plaintiffs in the James Vance/Judas Priest case. By all accounts, he didn't do a rousing job on the witness stand. It was pointed out that Key offered minimal scientific evidence in his books and lectures for the whole theory of subliminal seduction. Indeed, advertisers scoff at the notion that they add hidden images or text referring to fornication to inspire consumers.

"Key's books constitute quintessential pseudoscience; they contain no citations, no references and no documentation for any of his proclamations," stated the November/December 1996 *Skeptical Inquirer*.

The Beatles, the 1968 release best known as "The White Album," was said to contain backwards subliminal messages. "Spookiest of all were the clues embedded in songs played backwards. On a cheap turntable, I moved the speed switch midway between 33 1/3 and 45 to disengage the motor drive, then manually turned the [The White Album] backwards and listened in wide-eared wonder," stated an April 25, 2005, article in *Scientific American* by noted writer and skeptic Michael Shermer.

The song pondered by Shermer was "Revolution 9," a bit of experimental music and random phrases put together by John Lennon and his partner Yoko Ono. Played forward, a flat male speaker can be heard repeating the phrase "number nine … number nine" over and over. Supposedly, if you played the song backward, the phrase becomes, "turn me on, dead man … turn me on, dead man"—allegedly a reference to McCartney.

Bolstering the case for secret messages was the Fab Four's deliberate use of backwards music on some of their songs. The tunes, "Rain," "Tomorrow Never Knows," and "I'm Only Sleeping," for example, all contain guitar riffs that had been recorded normally, then played backward and rerecorded for an interesting sonic effect. If the Beatles were capable of putting backwards music on their songs, wouldn't they also be capable of inserting backwards phrases in their tunes?

The Beatles always denied putting such messages in their music. The members of Judas Priest said the same at the Vance trial.

Even if musicians do put "subliminal" messages in their songs, however, it is unclear what, if any, impact such messages would have on a listener. As the November/December 1996 *Skeptical Inquirer* pointed out, "sounds that are not consciously discernible are not necessarily unconsciously discernible either." In addition, "there is no evidence whatsoever that subliminal directives can compel compliance," noted the *Inquirer*.

Justice Jerry Carr Whitehead came to the same conclusion when he dismissed the James Vance lawsuit against CBS Records and Judas Priest. "The scientific research presented does not establish that subliminal stimuli, even if perceived, may precipitate conduct of this magnitude," stated the judge, in reference to Vance and Belknap's suicide pact.

Subliminal Messaging in the Movies

One of the most famous examples demonstrating the supposed power of subliminal messaging happened in September 1957 at a movie theatre in Fort Lee, New Jersey. James Vicary claimed to have inserted extremely brief text messages on a few frames of film. These messages, reading, "Eat popcorn" and "Drink Coke," appeared so quickly onscreen that they couldn't be registered on a conscious level by moviegoers. Vicary claimed, however, that such brief messaging triggered a stampede at the concessions stand, boosting sales enormously.

It turned out, however, that Vicary greatly exaggerated the number of people exposed to the messaging and the impact it had. While initial press accounts said 45,000 people had seen the messages and sales exploded, Vicary eventually admitted this wasn't the case. Only a handful of people had actually seen the messages. There had been no surge at the concessions stand, and the data from the experiment was "too small to be meaningful," reported the November/December 1996 *Skeptical Inquirer*.

"At best this so-called study was a shallow and meaningless empirical exercise. At worst, it was a complete fabrication," stated the *Inquirer*.

"[T]he strongest evidence presented at the trial showed no behavioral effects other than anxiety, distress or tension," added the judge, as noted in the November/December 1996 *Skeptical Inquirer*. The phrase "Do it" in "Better By You, Better Than Me" was most likely the result of coincidence, a guitar chord mingling with singer Rob Halford's taking a breath, said the judge.

But what about all those "subliminal messages" in songs by the Beatles? Such messages are actually the product of a trait called "pattern recognition," stated Shermer in *Scientific American*.

Put simply, the human brain has evolved to be able to find patterns. In order to survive, humans had to be able to quickly detect and interpret aural or visual cues that indicated danger. Such cues first had to be filtered through all kinds of noise and visual distractions.

According to the theory of pattern recognition, humans never lost this trait—which means that if you listen to a song played backward, or listen to static over the radio, you will almost certainly make out some kind of pattern after a while. Meaningless mutterings or sonic gibberish will be misinterpreted as specific phrases or words. In other words, "If you scan enough noise, you will eventually find a signal, whether it is there or not," as *Scientific American* put it.

Further Reading

Kory Grow, "Judas Priest's Subliminal Message Trial: Rob Halford Looks Back," *Rolling Stone*, August 24, 2015.

Wilson Bryan Key, *Subliminal Seduction*, 1974.

Timothy E. Moore, "Scientific Consensus and Expert Testimony: Lessons from the Judas Priest Trial," *Skeptical Inquirer*, November/December 1996.

Timothy E. Moore, "Subliminal Perception: Facts and Fallacies," *Skeptical Inquirer*, Spring 1992.

Michael Shermer, "Turn Me On, Dead Man," *Scientific American*, April 25, 2005.

POLITICS

The 1876 Presidential Election

The presidential election of 1876 between Republican Rutherford Hayes and Democrat Samuel Tilden was one of the most controversial political battles in American history.

Hayes was a decorated Civil War veteran who fought for the North. After hostilities ended, Hayes served as a Congressman and then governor of Ohio. He was widely respected for his integrity and his support of voting and civil rights for African Americans.

The Democrat, Samuel Tilden, had been governor of New York state. As governor, Tilden earned a reputation as a reformer, breaking up the so-called "Tweed Ring"—a group of corrupt Democrats who dominated politics in New York City.

Going into the presidential election, Tilden was widely perceived as the front-runner. The economy was in rough shape, and people were getting tired of Republican rule. (Republicans had dominated the White House since Abraham Lincoln took office in 1861.)

"In addition, Tilden was a superb political organizer and the Democrats in the South were certain to use violence to keep black and white Republicans from voting," noted "The Campaign and Election of 1876," an essay published by the Miller Center, a non-partisan University of Virginia affiliate dedicated to political history.

At the time, presidential candidates weren't supposed to do much campaigning. Such candidates were ideally seen as being "above the fray." National party committees had little say in the campaign either. Thanks to these factors, state and local party organizations welded a huge amount of influence when it came to presidential elections.

Rather than make stump speeches, candidates for president typically wrote a letter of acceptance after receiving their party's nomination. In his acceptance letter, Hayes called for civil service reform and a return to the gold standard. He also pledged to serve only one term and expressed support for "honest and capable local government in the South, as long as it respected the constitutional rights of all citizens," stated "The Campaign and Election of 1876" essay.

The ensuing election was a closely fought battle. On election night, returns from Ohio and New York, submitted by telegraph, indicated Tilden was leading. Hayes went to bed believing he had lost the election.

When the results were tallied, it was determined that Tilden had bested Hayes by 250,000 popular votes (out of 8.3 million cast). Tilden won 184 electoral votes, while Hayes had 166. Tilden only needed one more electoral vote to win the majority required to become president. However, there were complications: both parties, citing fraud on the part of their opponents, claimed they had won Florida, Louisiana, and South Carolina. There was an additional controversy in Oregon: while Hayes had won the state, he had lost one of his Oregon electors. (The person in question held federal office and was therefore not supposed to be an elector. The Democratic Governor of Oregon replaced this elector with one from his own party.) Thanks to this move, Hayes's electoral vote total slipped to 165.

All told, there were 19 disputed electoral votes in Florida, Louisiana, and South Carolina, plus one from Oregon. Tilden needed only one of these 20 electoral votes to win, while Hayes would require all 20.

Republicans accused the Democrats of violently preventing African Americans from voting in the three contested Southern states. Popular votes in these states would be reviewed by Republican-controlled returning or canvassing boards. Claiming voter intimidation and fraud on the part of the Democrats, these returning boards invalidated thousands of votes for Tilden.

Electors from both parties convened in Florida, Louisiana, South Carolina, and Oregon on December 6, 1876. Republicans and Democrats both declared victory in the three Southern states. All electoral votes, including the contentious votes from Florida, Louisiana, South Carolina, and Oregon, were sent to Washington DC to be tabulated. There was disagreement between Republicans and Democrats over the vital issue of which electoral votes would be counted. Depending on how electoral votes were tabulated, either Hayes or Tilden could be awarded the presidency.

A commission was struck in early 1877 to sort things out. The Electoral Commission consisted of five Senators (three Republicans, two Democrats), five representatives (three Democrats, two Republicans), and five Supreme Court Justices (two Republicans, two Democrats, and one independent). Thanks to the presence of the independent justice, the Commission was evenly divided, 7 to 7, between Republicans and Democrats.

The independent justice in question was named David Davis, and he would play a huge role in what happened next.

"Davis ... disqualified himself after a monumental miscalculation by Tilden's corrupt nephew, Colonel William T. Pelton, who assumed that electing Davis as senator from Illinois with Democratic votes would purchase his support for Tilden on the Electoral Commission," reported "The Campaign and Election of 1876" essay.

Justice Davis resented this implication and resigned. He was replaced by a Republican named Joseph P. Bradley, thus changing the balance of power on the Electoral Commission in favor of the Republicans.

In a series of state-by-state votes carried by Republicans 8–7, the Electoral Commission awarded all 20 disputed electoral votes to Hayes. Democrats were outraged. Although they couldn't stop the Commission from awarding the contested votes to Hayes, they could slow down the proceedings. Democrats in Congress filibustered and repeatedly adjourned, thus delaying official certification of the electoral vote count. There were so many delays that a frightening prospect loomed: there might not be a president of the United States on March 4, 1877, the day the new head of state was supposed to take office.

Intense negotiations ensued. Democrats were willing to concede defeat if Republicans promised to withdraw the remaining federal troops from the South, where their presence served as a crucial bulwark for enforcing federal civil rights legislation. The Democrats also wanted Hayes to appoint a Southerner to his cabinet. Republican negotiators were amendable to these proposals, as long as the civil and voting rights of white and black Southern Republicans were respected. Their Democratic counterparts assured them this would be the case.

With this informal agreement, Democrats ceased their protests, and Hayes was declared the winner on March 2, 1877. The final tally was 185 electoral votes for Hayes to 184 for Tilden. Hayes was sworn in as the nineteenth president of the United States.

True to his word, Hayes withdrew federal troops from the South. This move marked the end of "Reconstruction"—the refiguring of Southern politics to give rights to former slaves. State and local governments in the South quickly reasserted the pre-Civil War order, in which whites dominated and African Americans had little freedom.

"Hayes's ending of Reconstruction came at a cost. Pledges he had received from Southern Democrats to protect the rights of black citizens proved worthless and the civil rights revolution that Hayes had inherited would be stalled until the twentieth century," stated *The American President*, a companion book to a PBS TV series of the same title.

Although he won the White House, the new president was sneeringly referred to as "Rutherfraud" Hayes by opponents during his single term in office.

The 1948 Texas Democratic Primary

In 1948, Texas legislator Lyndon Baines Johnson set his sights on a new office. While he had served a Congressman representing the 10th District of Texas for over a decade, Johnson wanted to become a Senator. Johnson had unsuccessfully vied for the Senate in 1941. That defeat left him determined to win the next time he ran for the office.

In the 1940s, the Democratic Party totally dominated Texas politics. Whoever won the Democratic Senate primary would be almost guaranteed to win the actual Senatorial election against weak Republican opposition.

Johnson's main competitor in the 1948 Democratic primary was Coke Stevenson, a former governor of Texas. Stevenson was well regarded as a tough legislator who was tight-fisted with the budget.

Johnson worked incredibly hard during the primary. He used a helicopter to visit small towns, making hundreds of landings and doing countless speeches. The helicopter attracted huge crowds, particularly in rural parts of the state, where most people had never seen such an aircraft before. Johnson's public appearances also involved barbeque, beer, music, and an overall festive atmosphere.

Until the 1948 primary, Johnson had positioned himself as a New Deal liberal, in favor of Democratic president Franklin Roosevelt's progressive agenda. By the late 1940s, with the mood of the country growing more conservative, Johnson refashioned himself as a more right-wing candidate.

The initial primary election round was held July 24, 1948. Stevenson received 40 percent of the vote, while Johnson received 34 percent. A third candidate, George Peddy, garnered 20 percent. Since no one had received a definitive majority, a runoff election would be held. This rematch would be between Stevenson and Johnson (as the lowest finisher, Peddy was dropped from the primary).

The primary runoff election was scheduled for August 28, 1948. Once again, Johnson threw himself into the campaign, working ceaselessly to win the run-off election.

"The overall result, as one opinion poll earlier in the week had forecast, was so close that no one could be sure who won. The initial returns on election day, Saturday, August 28, favored Stevenson," states *Lone Star Rising*, the first volume of an exhaustive LBJ biography by Robert Dallek.

As ballots were carefully counted, the lead went back and forth. In pre-computer days, vote counting was a laborious process. By September 2, the unofficial tally had Stevenson leading by 362 votes. One day later, results changed: Stevenson's vote total was reduced by 205 votes, while Johnson's total increased by 174, giving him a lead of 17 votes.

"The biggest single shift in votes came from the town of Alice in south Texas … where Johnson received an additional 202 votes and Stevenson, one. Other 'corrections' from around the state boosted Johnson's lead to 162 votes," wrote Dallek.

The 202 Johnson votes came from Precinct Box 13. When examined more closely, officials discovered that signatures for the 203 new votes were written in the same ink and listed neatly in alphabetical order.

At the time, the territory around Alice was controlled by a political operator named George Parr. There were whispers that Parr had worked with Johnson supporters to fabricate additional votes for their candidate. Citing such rumors, Stevenson refused to concede. He challenged the election results at the Texas State Democratic Convention, held September 14 in Fort Worth. Johnson proved to be the cannier operator, however. Following intense political infighting and a court challenge, Johnson was declared winner of the primary by a mere 87 votes. The additional votes from Precinct Box 13 made the difference.

It is unclear how much direct involvement Johnson might have had in the backroom machinations surrounding Precinct Box 13. Nonetheless, the suspicious results tainted Johnson for the rest of his career.

LBJ "easily defeated his Republican opponent in the general election and won the Senate seat, but the cost to his credibility was steep. Everyone knew the election had been rife with fraud and his slim, questionable margin of victory was certainly no popular mandate. Critics began calling him 'Landslide Lyndon' and the new Senator found their disdain hard to shake for a long time," states "Lyndon B. Johnson: Life Before the Presidency," an essay published by the Miller Center, a non-partisan University of Virginia affiliate dedicated to political history.

Further Reading

Joseph Cummins, *Anything for a Vote*, 2007.
Robert Dallek, *Lone Star Rising*, 1991.

Kent Germany, ed., "Lyndon B. Johnson: Life Before the Presidency," Miller Center, University of Virginia, http://millercenter.org/president/biography/lbjohnson-life-before-the-presidency.

Ari Hoogenboom, ed., "The Campaign and Election of 1876," Miller Center, University of Virginia.

Philip B. Kunhardt Jr., Philip B. Kunhardt III, Peter W. Kunhardt, *The American President*, 1999.

Teapot Dome

Warren G. Harding presided over one of the most corrupt administrations in American history. Elected president in 1920, Republican Harding was "an obliging, generous-spirited, amiable man who could not bear to offend anyone," noted *The American President*, the companion book to a PBS TV series of the same title.

Prior to taking over the White House, Harding had been a state senator and lieutenant governor of Ohio, then a member of the U.S. Senate. He was noted for being handsome and friendly. "He had striking good looks and a faculty for pleasing people," stated *The American President*.

Though affable, Harding was a weak politician who make poor choices for his cabinet. According to the essay "Warren G. Harding: Domestic Affairs," published by the Miller Center, a non-partisan University of Virginia affiliate dedicated to political history, "As president, Warren G. Harding often seemed overwhelmed by the burdens of his administration. He frequently confided to friends that the job was beyond him … Harding also surrounded himself with an unpleasant group of dishonest cheats known as 'the Ohio gang.' Many of them were later charged with defrauding the government and a few of them went to jail."

Albert Fall, Secretary of the Interior, was arguably Harding's most notorious appointee. Fall had been one of New Mexico's first two Senators. As Secretary of the Interior, Fall accepted $300,000 in bribes to secretly allow private oil companies to tap oil reserves set aside by previous administrations to supply the Navy. These reserves were located in Elk Hills, California, and Teapot Dome, Wyoming. When it was revealed, the ensuing scandal became known as "Teapot Dome." Fall retired in 1923 but couldn't evade punishment.

"Fall's backroom deal later became a byword for government corruption and in 1931, the former Interior Secretary left his home by ambulance to serve a one-year prison term—the first cabinet member ever convicted and imprisoned for a major crime committed while in office," reported a *TIME* magazine article published November 12, 2008.

The Teapot Dome affair was only one of several scandals that occurred during the Harding presidency. The "Warren G. Harding: Domestic Affairs" essay notes, "[Harding's] close friend and political manager, Harry Daugherty, whom he named attorney general … survived impeachment attempts by Congress and two indictments for defrauding the government in the disposal of alien property confiscated by his office from German nationals … Charles Forbes, director of the Veterans Bureau, diverted alcohol and drugs from Veterans hospitals to bootleggers and narcotics dealers and took payoffs from contractors building the hospitals. He went to jail for two years."

Harding himself remained well liked by the public throughout his short term in office. Although Harding did not personally enrich himself through corruption, he did little to address the venality of his associates. President Harding died abruptly of a heart attack on August 2, 1923, before completing his first term.

"[Harding] was one of the most popular presidents in the history of the country, until after his death, when the scandals began to surface … Harding's chief presidential failure was his unwillingness to root out the corruption, or to offer his country any true moral leadership. Inhabiting an increasingly complex presidency with enormous responsibilities, Harding found himself unable to rise to the challenge. And the man who always so needed to be adored, the dark horse who could never say no, ended up one of the most vilified presidents in American history," stated *The American President*.

Further Reading

William Grimes, "There Will Be Scandal: An Oil Stain on the Jazz Age," *New York Times*, February 13, 2008.

Philip B. Kunhardt Jr., Philip B. Kunhardt III, Peter W. Kunhardt, *The American President*, 1999.

"Top 10 Worst Cabinet Members," *TIME* magazine, November 12, 2008.

Eugene Trani, consulting editor, "Warren G. Harding: Domestic Affairs," Miller Center, University of Virginia, http://millercenter.org/president/biography/harding-domestic-affairs.

William "Big Bill" Thompson

In the early 1990s, a group of historians, writers, and academics took part in a survey to determine the best and worst mayors in American history. The survey was conducted by Melvin Holli, a professor of history at the University of Illinois at Chicago and prolific academic author, who tabulated the results and wrote a book titled *The American Mayor: The Best & Worst Big-City Leaders*.

"Taking the first worst-prize," wrote Holli, "is Chicago's Mayor William H. 'Big Bill' Thompson (1915–1923, 1927–1931), one of the most colorful if not corrupt mayors in the city's history. Big Bill, who received campaign funds from gangsters like Al Capone, won the sobriquet 'Kaiser Bill' during World War One for his pro-German stand and earned more notoriety in the 1920s for his 'America First' program, his campaign to censor school textbooks and his threat to punch King George 'in the snoot.'"

The competition for worst mayor wasn't even close, noted Holli: "The experts ranked Big Bill a solid and undisputed first place; he led the pack … in the number of experts who put his leadership in the mayoral hall of shame."

Thompson earned this title through a combination of indifferent leadership, incompetence, and corruption. He presided over Prohibition-era Chicago, a period that featured open warfare between different groups of entrenched mobsters. Not only did Thompson fail to stem the bloodshed, he enjoyed the support of some of the gangsters battling for control of the city's rackets, including Capone. He had a flamboyant personality and frequently engaged in outlandish rhetoric, slamming British royalty for various woes and boasting about his disregard for the national Prohibition law.

Thompson was born in 1867 in Boston to a wealthy family with a New England pedigree, but was raised in Chicago, where his father had grown rich in real estate. As a youth, Thompson attended prep school in Chicago during winter months and spent the rest of the year out West. According to biographers, Thompson was particularly taken by the cowboy lifestyle. Thompson gave up his Western dreams, however, when his father died in 1891. Thompson dutifully returned to Chicago to run the family real estate business.

As a young man, Thompson earned a reputation as a convivial bon vivant, more interested in athletics than in economic or intellectual pursuits. "It was during his leisure hours—actually, most of the day—that [Thompson] distinguished himself as an all-star athlete, the idol of Chicago youth," wrote crime author John Kobler in his book *Capone: The Life and World of Al Capone*.

Thompson was induced to enter Chicago politics by his wealthy peers. He was elected an alderman in 1900, then two years later won election as Cook County Commissioner. He acquired the nickname "Big Bill" thanks to his six-foot-plus height, rapidly expanding girth (he would eventually weigh over 300 pounds), and exuberant persona.

Thompson rose slowly through the ranks of municipal government. Running as a Republican, he won the 1915 Chicago mayoral election. He made little attempt to suppress rampant vice and in fact counted criminals among his supporters.

Thompson allies ran something called "The Sportsmen's Club": "a Republican organization, used as a collection agency for graft. Not only gamblers, but saloon and brothel keepers received solicitations for $100 'life memberships' on club letterheads, bearing the mayor's name," reported Kobler.

Members of the Sportsmen's Club included "Big Jim" Colosimo, one of the top gangsters in Chicago during Thompson's first term. Along with his wife, Colosimo presided over a vast prostitution empire—a kingdom largely unaffected by Thompson's ascendancy to the mayor's office.

In addition to being friendly to criminals, Thompson held xenophobic tendencies. When the United States entered the First World War in 1917, Thompson called for isolationism and accused the British of dragging the United States into war. He became known as "Kaiser Bill" for his pro-German outbursts.

Thompson "developed a natural gift for campaign tent oratory. He knew instinctively how to tickle the prejudices of ethnic and national groups. Though his bull-roaring platform speeches ranged in content from the banal to the inane, Chicago's Irish and Italian voters responded enthusiastically when he vilified the British, calling them 'seedy and untrustworthy,'" wrote Kobler.

Thompson was re-elected in 1919. A year later, on May 11, 1920, "Big Jim" Colosimo was shot dead by an assassin. The killing was almost certainly orchestrated by Johnny Torrio, one of Colosimo's most able lieutenants. After Colosimo was shot, Torrio seized his crime domain and expanded into bootlegging, an activity "Big Jim" had been hesitant to enter. Torrio also encouraged a then-obscure young man named Al Capone to move from New York to Chicago, to work for him. Torrio had known Capone as a youth, in New York City.

Torrio was one of several street-level criminals who were fantastically enriched by the advent of Prohibition, the national law banning the sale and manufacture of alcohol. Canny criminals realized that enormous public demand for liquor still existed and rushed to make or sell "bootleg" (i.e., illicit) spirits. Wealthy crime bosses such as Torrio hired hundreds of thugs to round out their gangs and armed them with military-grade weapons. Chicago gangsters were soon attacking each other with rapid-fire machine guns and bombs.

As crime rose, public confidence in Thompson fell. "The abuses of the Thompson regime became so flagrant as to preclude Big Bill's chances of re-election. His campaign manager, the ex-medicine man Fred Lundin, was indicted with 23 co-conspirators for misappropriating more than $1 million of school funds … Thompson, knowing he was defeated in advance, withdrew his candidacy from the 1923 primary," wrote Kobler.

The new mayor, William Dever, was committed to cleaning up the city. His presence induced Torrio and his right-hand man, Capone, to flee. With Dever as mayor, Torrio moved his headquarters to the nearby city of Cicero, Illinois. In 1925, Torrio was almost gunned down by a rival gang and voluntarily handed his empire of vice over to his protégé, Capone.

Despite being out of the mayor's office, Thompson was determined to remain in the news. He earned headlines after announcing an expedition to the South Seas to photograph mudskippers—fish that could live on land for short periods of time. Thompson's yacht never actually made it to the South Seas, but the stunt generated a windfall of publicity. Thompson eyed a comeback. Mayor Dever had proven to be well-meaning but not entirely effective. Capone had moved his headquarters back to Chicago after Torrio's resignation. Capone and other mob leaders still dominated Chicago's underworld.

Thompson entered the 1926 Republican mayoral primary. During the election, he struck familiar themes. Thompson complained that public school textbooks in Chicago were biased in favor of the British and ranted about King George V, threatening to punch the monarch in the face. Thompson cagily portrayed himself as an opponent of Prohibition. He declared himself "wetter than the middle of the Atlantic Ocean" and promised to flout federal Prohibition laws, wrote Kobler. This resonated with Chicago voters who, like their counterparts in other big cities such as New York, opposed the U.S. government's attempt to ban liquor.

Naturally, Chicago gangsters were delighted by Thompson's rhetoric and his support for "speakeasies" (illegal drinking establishments). The prospect of getting "Big Bill" back in office "was so attractive to Capone he contributed $260,000 to Thompson's campaign chest and applied every technique of bribery and terrorism on his behalf," noted Kobler.

For his part, Dever was derided as a "dry"—that is, someone who supported enforcement of the Prohibition law. On Election Day, April 5, 1927, Thompson easily won over the hapless Dever, by 83,000 votes.

The re-elected mayor did, occasionally, pretend to be tough on crime. In the fall of 1927, for example, Thompson briefly entertained thoughts of running for the White House after President Calvin Coolidge decided not to seek another term in office. Thompson briefly cut his ties with Capone as he toured the country, making bombastic, isolationist speeches, promoting a jingoistic "America First" platform. Thompson soon concluded he couldn't win and gave up on the presidency, resuming his friendly relationships with gangsters.

Thompson's return to power did not proceed smoothly. Although he still retained a degree of personal popularity with voters, as evidenced by his 1927 comeback, that popularity didn't extend to his acolytes.

On April 10, 1928, Republican primary elections for state and county offices were held. Thompson wasn't running but had selected a slate of candidates who were loyal to him. In spite of intimidation efforts by Capone's gang, the electorate soundly rejected Thompson's picks for office.

"Although Thompson himself had three more years to serve as mayor, his political career had been shattered beyond repair. The rebuff, together with a judicial inquiry into his conduct and the whiplashes of a hostile press, left him with little zest for further combat as his party prepared to confront the Democrats in the fall elections. Physically and mentally deteriorated, drinking heavily, he retreated for the summer to a country hideaway, abandoning City Hall to Acting Mayor Samuel Ettelson," noted Kobler.

As Thompson grew listless, gangsters continue to run wild in the city. In the summer of 1928, Capone established a headquarters in Chicago's luxurious Lexington Hotel. When Frank Loesch, a founder of the Chicago Crime Commission visited Capone to beg him not to interfere with an upcoming election, the anti-vice crusader was chagrined to see portraits of three political leaders in Capone's office. The paintings depicted George Washington, Abraham Lincoln, and William Thompson.

The inclusion of Thompson's likeness was appropriate, given the extent to which Capone had infiltrated the Chicago power structure. By the late 1920s, "Capone estimated the total payoff to police from all sources at $30 million a year. His own payroll listed roughly half the entire Chicago police force," wrote Kobler.

Two climatic events in 1929 further eroded public trust in Thompson. First, on February 14, 1929, gunmen murdered six members of the George "Bugs" Moran gang, plus one civilian in a cold Chicago garage. Capone denied complicity but is regarded by crime historians as the most likely figure to have ordered the "hit" against the Moran gang.

The St. Valentine's Day Massacre, as it became known, made headlines across the country. The public was jarred by the level of violence involved and the sheer brazenness of a mass murder carried out in broad daylight. Since Mayor Thompson seemed incapable of or uninterested in dealing with organized crime, the Chicago Crime Commission and other civic groups pleaded with federal authorities to get involved. Newly elected President Herbert Hoover pledged to do just that. Under Hoover's prodding, federal officials built a two-pronged case against Capone, for violating Prohibition statutes and failing to pay his income tax.

Second, in the fall of 1929, the New York Stock Exchange crashed, triggering the period of massive economic malaise known as the Great Depression. Chicago was battered by the force of the Depression. "No major American city suffered more," wrote Kobler, "for the nationwide economic disaster was here compounded by the prodigality of the third Thompson administration. That year, it squandered $23 million above what it could collect in taxes. Outraged citizens organized a tax strike."

Thompson won the next Republican primary for mayor but lost to Democrat Anton Cermak in the general election on April 8, 1931. The *Chicago Tribune* rejoiced in Thompson's defeat with a searing editorial printed the day after the election: "For Chicago, Thompson has meant filth, corruption, idiocy and bankruptcy. He has given our city an international reputation for moronic buffoonery, barbaric crime, triumphant hoodlumism, unchecked graft and a dejected citizenship. He has ruined the property and completely destroyed the pride of the city. He made Chicago a byword for the collapse of American civilization."

The same year Thompson lost, Capone was found guilty of tax evasion in federal court and handed a stiff jail sentence. Thompson never regained the mayor's office in Chicago. He died March 19, 1944, of pneumonia in Chicago.

"At the time of [Thompson's] death, it was revealed that this dedicated public servant, who had never earned more than $22,500 a year as mayor of Chicago, had left an estate worth nearly $2 million, most of it in banknotes and gold certificates crammed into strongboxes," wrote author Laurence Bergreen, in his book *Capone: The Man and the Era*.

Bergreen added, "As a public servant, Thompson was a fraud and everyone knew it, even his backers, who supported him just for that reason. And to his opponents, he was scandal incarnate ... Thompson was a political cartoon satirizing corruption come to life ... Every racketeer in town, Torrio and Colosimo included, considered Thompson one of their own ... Here was a man the racketeers could understand; here was a politician they could work with. They bribed him and on election night, they delivered the votes, whatever it took to keep such a valuable man in office."

Further Reading

Laurence Bergreen, *Capone: The Man and the Era*, 1994.
"For Chicago Thompson," *Chicago Tribune*, April 9, 1931.
Nate Hendley, *American Gangsters Then and Now*, 2010.
Melvin Holli, *The American Mayor: The Best and Worst Big-City Leaders*, 1999.
Joel Hood, "Al Capone, Chicago Mayor 'Big Bill' Thompson Shown Together in Photo," *Chicago Tribune*, June 2, 2009.
John Kobler, *Capone: The Life and World of Al Capone*, 1971.

SECTION TEN

A GALLERY OF ROGUES
(AND ONE HERO)

INTRODUCTION

This section profiles a collection of rogues and one hero. The rogues in question gained their notoriety by enriching themselves at the expense of others. Some, like master showman P. T. Barnum, did this in a lighthearted fashion, charging admission to bogus exhibits. Others were more heavy-handed and ruthless. Rogues such as con woman Linda Taylor took from the government, while investor Bernie Madoff took from the rich or from those trying to be rich.

The one hero is magician and escape artist Harry Houdini. In his spare time, Houdini exposed phony "mediums"—charlatans who used magic and stagecraft to convince people they had the power to commune with the dead.

Like the mediums exposed by Houdini, all the rogues in this section relied on fakery and lies to achieve their ends, namely, taking money from the gullible.

P. T. BARNUM, SHOWMAN EXTRAORDINAIRE

Phineas Taylor Barnum was the king of hype, a master hoaxer, and the greatest American showman of the nineteenth century. Barnum was born in Bethel, Connecticut, in 1810. His father ran an inn and a store. As a young man, Barnum dabbled in various enterprises, running a newspaper for a time in Danbury, Connecticut.

Barnum had his eye on bigger things, however, and moved to New York City in 1834. He began his lengthy career as a showman a year later when he acquired the slave contract of an elderly, black woman named Joice Heth. Barnum claimed she was 161 years old and a former nurse of Founding Father George Washington. Barnum toured extensively with Heth, showing off his human exhibit. After Heth died in 1836, an autopsy revealed that she was probably no older than 80. No matter; Barnum had found his life calling as a huckster.

In 1841, Barnum purchased a facility called the American Museum, a popular New York attraction that offered a collection of stuffed animals and various curiosities, such as the remains of a two-headed sheep. Barnum's version of the American Museum was soon exhibiting the likes of "General Tom Thumb" (a dwarf named Charles Stratton) and the "FeJee Mermaid." The latter was actually a patched-together hybrid creature consisting of the top half of a dead monkey and the bottom half of a dead fish. This exhibit was wildly hyped by Barnum, who planted fake stories in newspapers about his astonishing find.

Such exhibits epitomized Barnum's love of "humbug." A "humbug" can be defined as a silly practical joke, intended to provoke laughter rather than anger. Barnum's "most famous humbug was the FeJee Mermaid," stated a write-up on the website of the Barnum Museum, a center devoted to the showman's life, based in Bridgeport, Connecticut.

The mermaid, purportedly from the Fiji islands in the Pacific, was depicted in advertisements as a beautiful young woman. When people saw the exhibit, they realized they'd been had. Museumgoers were more amused than offended: "They were so enthralled and unwilling to be seen as gullible that they encouraged friends to attend the exhibit and share in the wonder. The FeJee Mermaid is an excellent example of Barnum's ability to turn an obvious hoax or humbug into a believable curiosity," stated the Barnum Museum website.

Barnum pulled off a similar bit of hokum with a lady called "Zalumma Agra—Star of the East." According to Barnum, Ms. Agra was the daughter of a prince from Circassia (a region in the Caucasus Mountains on the Black Sea), who had been rescued from the slave markets of Constantinople. At the time, there was a widespread belief that the Caucasian race emerged from the Caucasus region. As "pure white people," Circassian women were understood to be stunningly beautiful and much prized by sultans seeking to expand their harems. Or so went the folklore of the day.

In truth, Ms. Agra looked like an ordinary white woman with a fair complexion and a strange hairstyle: she was decked out in thick, afro-style locks for the duration of her exhibition. "Surprisingly proficient in English and mysteriously deficient in her knowledge of 'Circassia,' Zalumma Agra was nonetheless a highly popular attraction at the American Museum. 'Circassian Beauties' were a mainstay of dime museums and sideshows until the end of the nineteenth century," according to the Lost Museum, a website devoted to Barnum's American Museum, created by staff and students at City University of New York and George Mason University.

On occasion, Barnum did actually promote genuine talent. He organized a tour of the United States for singer Jenny Lind, known as "The Swedish Nightingale," in 1850. Barnum agreed to pay Lind the then-astronomical sum of $1,000 per night for 150 nights. Thanks in large part to hype from Barnum, Lind was greeted by 40,000 people at New York Harbor upon her arrival, September 1, 1850.

"From her opening concert in New York City's Castle Garden to subsequent performances in cities and towns across the country, Barnum fueled public fascination with Lind by orchestrating events and negotiating Lind-endorsed products (including Jenny Lind songs, chairs, and pianos) ... Barnum shrewdly promoted Lind's character—her modesty, benevolence and selflessness—as much as her artistry," explains the Lost Museum.

The same year Lind hit the United States, Barnum opened a "Lecture Room" at the American Museum. The room was devoted to what were then called "moral dramas." The first production was a play entitled *The Drunkard*. In 1853, Barnum presented a watered-down, theatrical version of *Uncle Tom's Cabin* in the Lecture Room. This bowdlerized interpretation downplayed the anti-slavery sentiments of the book. Barnum would later host a more accurate rendering of the same novel-turned-play.

The Lecture Room was quite the spectacle: "Decades before the advent of motion pictures or even electricity, showmen like P. T. Barnum used all manner of technology to dazzle nineteenth-century audiences. The American Museum's Lecture Room employed the latest stagecraft—including lavishly painted backdrops and mechanical and pyrotechnic displays onstage—to add spectacle to its moral dramas," according to the Lost Museum.

The public loved Barnum's productions and exhibits, and in 1854, exhibition space in the American Museum was doubled. A year later, Barnum hosted an inaugural Baby Show. The show attracted 143 contestants and 60,000 spectators in total. Some critics complained that the show was degrading for mothers, but Barnum had clearly tapped a popular vein.

1855 marked Barnum's retirement from show business. It was a short-lived retirement, however, as financial problems pushed him back into the limelight. The American Museum continued to host spectacles that drew huge crowds.

In 1860, Barnum exhibited Chang and Eng Bunker, a pair of conjoined twins linked at the stomach who hailed from Siam (today, Thailand). It is the Bunkers to whom we owe the notion of "Siamese Twins." The pair were put on display for a six-week run.

In the early 1860s, Barnum exhibited a pair of big, white Beluga whales. To accommodate them, he installed a huge water tank in the basement of the American Museum. The whales measured some 23 and 18 feet respectively. By showing them off, Barnum arguably created the first large-sized aquarium in the United States.

"Professor" Livingston was another popular draw at the museum. The professor was an expert on phrenology—an example of nineteenth-century pseudo-science, based on the notion that bumps and marks on the head were indicative of certain personality traits. For a small fee, Professor Livingston would examine the heads of museumgoers and pronounce on their personalities and abilities.

In 1862, Barnum exhibited Anna Swan, a 17-year-old girl from Nova Scotia who was seven feet tall. Barnum had her lecture to museum attendees on the role of giants throughout history.

The end of the Civil War in 1865 marked another exhibition milestone. As the war wound down, Confederate President Jefferson Davis supposedly tried to avoid capture by putting on a dress that belonged to his wife. He was taken prisoner anyway. Barnum attempted to secure the garment worn by Davis but was unsuccessful. So Barnum had a wax figure made of the Confederate leader and outfitted it with a dress. Barnum called this exhibit "The Belle of Richmond."

In the early 1870s, Barnum focused his attention on a new endeavor. Barnum's "Grand Traveling Museum, Menagerie, Caravan, and Circus" offered clowns, acrobats, sideshow freaks, and performances by animals. This traveling show took up five acres of performance space and could house 10,000 seated patrons in total.

Barnum transported his circus around the country via rail—an expedient move, given the primitive state of roads outside major cities at the time. In the early 1880s, Barnum teamed up with James Bailey and James Hutchinson. One of the major attractions of this new entertainment juggernaut was Jumbo the elephant, a king-size pachyderm who delighted crowds. Barnum's merger with Bailey and Hutchinson eventually led to what is now Ringling Brothers and Barnum & Bailey circus.

In addition to being an impresario, Barnum was an author and elected politician. His books included titles such as *The Humbugs of the World* (1865), *Struggles and Triumphs* (1869), and his autobiography in 1854. Barnum was also politically involved, serving four terms as a Connecticut state legislator and briefly as Mayor of Bridgeport.

Interestingly enough, it's unlikely Barnum ever said or wrote, "There's a sucker born every minute"—the quote in praise of human gullibility that's been famously attributed to him. A search through Barnum's letters, notes, and other memorabilia turned up no trace of this comment, reported the October 3, 1982, *New York Times*.

The *Times* article concerned the efforts of Arthur H. Saxon, described by the paper as "a noted circus historian," to put together an edited collection of Barnum's letters. Saxon was eager to rehabilitate Barnum's image, presenting him as a canny promoter who offered the public interesting amusements for mere pennies, rather than a cold-hearted con artist. "There is not a whit of evidence … that Barnum ever said anything as callous as 'There's a sucker born every minute' … Barnum was just not the type to disparage his patrons … he loved a good show; a hoax. But the whole idea was that the audience would get a laugh out of being taken in and consider it part of the entertainment, rather than feel cheated," Saxon told the *Times*. It remains unclear where the "sucker" quote originated, if not from P. T. Barnum.

Barnum died April 7, 1891, in Bridgeport, Connecticut. "Mr. Barnum had natural genius as an advertiser. No man knew better than he the value of printer's ink. He made it part of his business to be talked about. The more attention he got in that way the better he liked it … nothing was too ambitious for him," noted his obituary in the *New York Times*.

Further Reading

American Social History/Center for Media and Learning, The Graduate Center, City University of New York and Center for History and New Media, George Mason University, The Lost Museum, http://www.lostmuseum.cuny.edu/.

Barnum Museum website, http://barnum-museum.org/.

"Barnum, Phineas Taylor," *Encyclopedia Britannica Eleventh Edition*, 1911.

Andree Brooks, "Debunking the Myth of P. T. Barnum," *New York Times*, October 3, 1982.

James I. Glasser and Benjamin M. Daniels, "P. T. Barnum, Justice Harlan, and Connecticut's Role in the Development of the Right to Privacy," *Federal Bar Council Quarterly*, December 13, 2004, http://federalbarcouncilquarterly.org/?p=396.

"The Great Showman Dead," *New York Times*, April 8, 1891.

Ringling Brothers and Barnum & Bailey Circus website, http://www.ringling.com /ContentPage.aspx?id=45832&section=45825.

JORDAN BELFORT, "THE WOLF OF WALL STREET"

He's been a hugely successful stock swindler, the inspiration for a blockbuster movie, a prison inmate, and now a highly-paid motivational/financial advice speaker. Along the way, Jordan Belfort crashed a helicopter and a Mercedes while stoned on Quaaludes, became addicted to cocaine, and nearly drowned his friends during an ill-conceived boat cruise.

Known as "The Wolf of Wall Street," Belfort ripped off stock investors to the tune of $200 million. The ripoff came in the form of a "pump and dump" scam, in which investors were induced to purchase "penny stock" that Belfort secretly held in abundance.

The Wolf was born in 1962 in the Bronx, to a middle-class Jewish family. Belfort himself has stressed the normalcy of his upbringing. Although Belfort earned a degree in biology from American University, his found his life calling in the financial sector. He took a sales job with venerable Wall Street firm L. F. Rothschild, but his timing was bad: Belfort started work on "Black Monday," October 19, 1987—the day the stock market crashed. Needless to say, Belfort was soon laid off.

In the late 1980s, Belfort took a job at an obscure financial firm on Long Island called Investors Center. The firm specialized in penny stock—low-value stocks sold for as little as a few dollars. Belfort had an aggressive sales manager and soon became highly successful.

A year after starting work with Investors Center, Belfort launched a franchise of Stratton Securities (a small-time broker/dealer) in the showroom of a former car dealership in Queens. Belfort and his partner, Danny Porush, bought out Stratton and formed a brokerage firm called Stratton Oakmont. Porush lived in the same building as Belfort and began his career as a trainee to the Wolf.

At its peak, Stratton Oakmont had 1,000 salespeople and took in millions of dollars a day. The company oversaw the initial public offering for women's shoe company Steve Madden Shoes, but was primarily famous for peddling penny stock.

"Stratton Oakmont would accumulate shares of so-called penny stocks, which tend to be thinly traded, stashing them in secret accounts ... the army of sales guys would feverishly work the phones, making cold calls like characters in a David Mamet play. As the price of a stock gradually rose, Belfort and his partners would dump their own shares at a profit then step out of the way as the thing crashed," explained a November 7, 2013, article in *Bloomberg Business Week* magazine. The colloquial term for this kind of swindle is "pump and dump." Belfort preferred to call it "stock manipulation."

Semantics aside, Belfort soon became enormously rich. "I was 24 years old and making more than $50 million, but something had changed. I was taking people with little or no selling skills and turning them into stock rock stars, but I began doing whatever it took to make money. I was partying hard, but I began manipulating stocks. I was a greed-fueled animal with sharp teeth and a feral growl that made people tremble," Belfort recounted, on JordanBelfort. com, a website that he currently hosts.

As Belfort later conceded, the good times couldn't last. "You can't take advantage of people and break all the rules without paying the price," he admitted on his website.

In 1994, Stratton Oakmont settled a civil securities fraud lawsuit with the Securities Exchange Commission (SEC). The company paid a $2.5 million fine, while Belfort, Porush, and another top Stratton Oakmont figure paid individual fines of $100,000 each. Two years later, Stratton Oakmont was closed by the SEC. In January 1997, the once high-living firm filed for bankruptcy protection.

This was just the start of Belfort's woes. In 1998, he was indicted for fraud and money laundering. More specifically, he was accused of swindling 1,513 people through "stock manipulation." A year after the indictment, Belfort pled guilty to the fraud and money laundering charges.

Belfort agreed to cooperate with authorities and provide details about criminal actions taken by Porush and other close associates. "Addicted to cocaine and facing a jail time, I made a deal to cooperate with the FBI," wrote Belfort on his website.

On July 18, 2003, Belfort was sentenced in Federal District Court in Brooklyn, New York. He was given four years in prison and ordered to pay $110 million in restitution to investors. To force payment, Belfort was ordered to divert half of any future gross monthly revenues into a fund that would offer payouts to some of his victims. The 50 percent revenue diversion was supposed to start a month after Belfort got out of jail. Belfort was also banned from ever working in the securities industry again.

Because of his help to the feds, Belfort only served 22 months of his sentence. Porush, interestingly enough, served almost double this time for his involvement in Stratton Oakmont crimes.

Belfort began working on his memoirs after getting out of prison. The result of his labors was a 2007 bestseller called *The Wolf of Wall Street*. The book detailed Belfort's meteoric rise and fall and predilection for wild partying.

"The book is peppered with contrition, but Belfort remains enamored of his crimes, of what he got away with and the lifestyle he used to lead with multiple mansions, disposable helicopters (he crashed one into his own front lawn) and disposable yachts (he ordered the captain to steer his chartered pleasure boat into a storm, destroying the vessel but somehow not getting anyone killed)," stated a December 23, 2013, feature on Jordan in *Esquire* magazine. Though Belfort was relatively open about his misdeeds, he stated that he only ripped off rich people who could afford to be scammed.

On December 25, 2013, the Martin Scorsese film version of *The Wolf of Wall Street* was released. Belfort was portrayed by Leonardo DiCaprio. Danny Porush was portrayed by Jonah Hill; his character was named "Danny Azoff," to avoid legal trouble. Both men received Academy Award nominations for their efforts.

Scorsese's movie was exceptionally well done and a big hit, but it was criticized for glorifying its subject, who was at heart a liar and a con man. A December 26, 2013, feature in *TIME* magazine assessed the accuracy of the movie. According to *TIME*, accounts of Belfort crashing a Mercedes while stoned, the presence of prostitutes at Stratton Oakmont parties, as well as an office "midget-tossing competition" were all true. Not true, however, was the notion that Belfort only robbed the rich. "Though Belfort claims in his book and in the film that he only took from the wealthy, the *New York Times* reports that many small business owners are still trying to recover financially from Belfort's scheme," stated *TIME*.

By the time the film came out, Belfort had created a new gig for himself as a highly paid motivational and financial advice speaker. In seminars, workshops, and DVDs, Belfort peddles something called the "Straight Line System"—a method of building wealth and success for individuals or businesses "without sacrificing integrity or ethics," as his website puts it. Central to the Straight Line System is a concept Belfort terms "ethical persuasion," which basically means convincing someone to buy something without lying to them. The website also contains a video testimonial from DiCaprio, praising Belfort for "honesty" in discussing his criminal past.

Indeed, Belfort's website is appropriately confessional: "In the '90s and early 2000s I was making millions of dollars on the market, but I was corrupt and ruthless … the problem was that as my success grew, so did my greed, and I began to play loose with my ethics. Let's face it, I pretty much threw them out with the morning trash," he wrote on JordanBelfort.com.

Further Reading

Susan Antilla, "Investors' Story Left Out of Wall Street 'Wolf' Movie," *New York Times*, December 19, 2013.

Jordan Belfort website, http://jordanbelfort.com/.

Nancy Dillon, John Marzulli and Larry McShane, "Real 'Wolf of Wall Street' Jordan Belfort Still Owes Millions to Victims: Prosecutors," *New York Daily News*, October 19, 2013.

Eliana Dockterman, "The Wolf of Wall Street: The True Story," *TIME*, December 26, 2013.

"Exclusive—A New $7.5M Miami Home and a $250,000 Rolls Royce: The Luxurious Life of Real-Life Wolf of Wall Street's Partner in Crime—And There's Nothing His Victims Owed $200M Can Do About It," Georgia News Day website, January 18, 2014, http://www.georgianewsday.com/news/regional/207484-exclusive-a-new-7-5m-miami-home-and-a-250-000-rolls-royce-the-luxurious-life-of-real-life-wolf-of-wall-street-s-partner-in-crime-and-there-s-nothing-his-victims-owed-200m-can-do-about-it.html.

David Haglund, "How Accurate Is The Wolf of Wall Street?" *The Toronto Star*, January 3, 2014.

Darah Hansen, "Wolf of Wall Street Jordan Belfort Back Making Millions Again," Yahoo.com, May 20, 2014, https://ca.finance.yahoo.com/blogs/insight/wolf-wall-street-back-sales-game-155916856.html.

Sheelah Kolhatkar, "Jordan Belfort, The Real Wolf of Wall Street," *Bloomberg Business Week*, November 7, 2013.

Michael Maiello, "The Wolf of Wall Street Is Real, and I've Been Reporting on Him for Years," *Esquire Magazine* blog, December 23, 2013, http://www.esquire.com /entertainment/news/a26702/real-wolf-of-wall-street/.

John Marzulli, "Feds Withdraw 'Deadbeat' Claim Against Jordan Belfort to Review Case Against 'The Wolf of Wall Street,'" *New York Daily News*, October 25, 2013.

STEVE BRODIE, THE BRIDGE JUMPER

On the afternoon of July 23, 1886, a "tall, slim man, who looked very much like an overgrown street boy," in the words of a *New York Times* story published the following day, bade an animated farewell to his wife at an entrance to the Brooklyn Bridge. The man was 23-year-old Steve Brodie—a professional gambler, footracer and "well-known Bowery character," as the February 7, 1901, *New York Times* put it.

To win a $200 bet, Brodie was about to leap from the Brooklyn Bridge into the East River, a jump of over 130 feet. Hitting water at such a height generally results in instant death. Indeed, a few weeks earlier, a fellow daredevil named Robert Odlum made the same leap and died.

If Brodie was concerned about Odlum's fate, he didn't show it. "Good-bye Steve; take care of yourself and may you be successful and scoop in dose $200, so we kin have a good time," stated Brodie's wife, according to the July 24, 1886, *Times*.

With that tender farewell, Brodie climbed aboard a lumber wagon that meandered onto the bridge. In the river below, a boatload of Brodie cronies rowed in the water, awaiting the leap.

Brodie got off the wagon and stepped to the bridge railing. Members of the public feared a suicide was in progress and began shouting an alarm. Police allegedly tried to intercept Brodie, but he was too fast for them.

"Brodie swung to and fro in the breeze and steadied himself as well as he could. When he hung perpendicularly over the river, he let go of his hold and shot down like an arrow. He was but a few seconds before he struck the water," reported the *Times*. Brodie disappeared underwater, then bobbed to the surface, to be fished out by his confederates in a boat.

Brodie found himself under arrest upon reaching the shore, for attempted suicide. Not that this outcome particularly bothered him: "All right, I'll go wid you, but I guess I'll get the $200. I kin jump off de highest bridge in de world now," Brodie told the arresting officer, according to the July 24 *Times*.

Brodie was taken to a police station, where his wet clothes were removed. He was toweled off, then given whisky and a change of dry clothing. Newspaper accounts indicate that Brody began complaining of intense pains from his right side, though a doctor could find little wrong with him.

The *New York Times* claimed a reporter interviewed Brodie after he was released, on $1,000 bail. Brodie allegedly told the reporter he had trained for two years prior to his leap, steeling himself mentally and physically by jumping off lower-hanging bridges and ship masts. He repeated the claim that he had leapt from the Brooklyn Bridge to win a $200 bet.

Needless to say, Brodie's daring made him an instant celebrity. He opened a tavern in the Bowery that was devoted to memorabilia about his jump. His feat was even commemorated in a 1933 movie called *The Bowery*, in which he was portrayed by actor George Raft. In the movie, the fictionalized Brodie schemes to toss a dummy off the Brooklyn Bridge but can't find the prop at the last minute. Reluctantly, the Brodie character decides to make the leap for real and jumps off the bridge into the water.

The movie hinted at one of the main issues with the Brodie story: detailed media coverage aside, it's unclear whether anyone actually witnessed his leap of faith. The July 24, 1886, *New York Times* article, for example, doesn't appear to be based on an eyewitness account from an objective journalist. Rather, it seems like a colorful recollection, with most of the details filled in by Brodie himself.

It has long been speculated that Brodie arranged for someone to toss a dummy off the bridge, while he waded into the river from the shoreline and swam out to the rescue boat. The fact that only a tiny handful of people who jumped from the bridge in the decades following Brodie survived lends credence to this theory. It's also been established that Brodie was broke before his brush with fame and thus had a financial motive to fool the public.

Brodie himself certainly never admitted to any fakery. In addition to running a bar, he took time to appear in vaudeville musicals called *Mad Money* and *On the Bowery*, which recounted his alleged jump.

Later in life, Brodie moved to Buffalo, launched another tavern, and toyed with the idea of leaping from Niagara Falls. He never actually made the jump. Instead, Brodie moved to San Antonio, Texas, where he died at the young age of 38, in 1901. The cause of death was either tuberculosis or diabetes. His funeral in New York City attracted seven coachloads of mourners and hundreds of curious onlookers, said the February 7, 1901, article in the *New York Times*.

Whether he was a true daredevil or a big faker, Brodie's feat has become legendary. His name has become a byword for recklessness. The expression "to pull a Brodie" has come to signify a feat of suicidal derring-do.

Further Reading

"A Leap From the Bridge," *New York Times*, July 24, 1886.
"Steve Brodie's Funeral," *New York Times*, February 7, 1901.
Jasmin K. Williams, "Steve Brodie—Daredevil or Hoaxer?" *New York Post*, November 5, 2007.

RITA CRUNDWELL, MUNICIPAL MENACE

On November 14, 2012, Rita Crundwell, the former city comptroller of Dixon, Illinois, entered a guilty plea in an astonishing case of embezzlement. Dixon is a small, nondescript Midwestern city with a population of 15,733 people. For decades, Crundwell controlled the city's finances, all the while siphoning off municipal funds for her own gain.

In federal court, Crundwell admitted that "she stole more than $53 million from [Dixon] since 1990 and used the proceeds to finance her quarter horse farming business and lavish lifestyle," stated a November 14, 2012, press release from the U.S. Attorney's Office, Northern District of Illinois. "Authorities have called her massive theft perhaps the largest municipal fraud in U.S. history," noted the February 15, 2013, *Chicago Tribune*.

Crundwell began working for the Dixon Finance Department in 1970, while still in high school. By 1983, Crundwell had worked her way up to being Dixon's comptroller/treasurer—guardian of the city's cash, in other words.

At her trial, Crundwell said she didn't start stealing money until 1990. On December 18 of that year, Crundwell opened a bank account in the name of the Reserve Sewer Capital Development Account (RSCDA). She was sole signatory and the only municipal employee who wrote checks for the account.

Crundwell began transferring city funds into the RSCDA account. Transfers were made in the form of checks from the city's Capital Development Fund. As far as the bank knew, the transfers were for city services or projects. In fact, the money was going into Crundwell's purse "to pay for her personal and private business expenses, including horse farming operations, personal credit card payments, real estate, and vehicles," stated the U.S. Attorney's Office press release.

At first, Crundwell only stole relatively small sums (in 1991, her total theft from the Capital Development Fund and other accounts came to $181,000). She soon started moving far larger amounts. In the year 2008 alone, she took nearly $6 million, according to a February 14, 2013, feature in *Forbes* magazine.

Crundwell became very adept at covering her traces. She would create invoices supposedly from the state of Illinois that she would show to auditors as proof that money going into the RSCDA account was being used for legitimate purposes. She also made sure to gather the city's mail, which would include statements from the bank with the RSCDA account. Needless to say, the mayor and other Dixon officials never saw these statements. If Crundwell was ill or on holiday, she would have a trusted employee or a relative take in the mail and separate anything directed to her.

As she siphoned off money, Crundwell made excuses for tight city budgets. "In budget meetings for the city with other City Council members, she voiced a need for Dixon to make spending cuts due to lack of sufficient funds," reported the February 14, 2013, article in *Forbes*.

Among other lies, she told beleaguered local officials that Dixon wasn't getting timely payment of tax revenue from the state of Illinois. Crundwell developed a reputation as a parsimonious bureaucrat, constantly harping on the need to cut expenses. According to the February 15, 2013, story in the *Chicago Tribune*, Crundwell would send memos to department heads with cartoons on them depicting a drowning victim or scissors slicing through a dollar sign, all designed to drive home her tight-fisted approach to city finances.

Her deception finally came to light in the fall of 2011. Crundwell was off on an unpaid vacation with her racehorses. In her absence, another city employee was brought in to handle Crundwell's duties. This employee asked to see all bank statements for the city, a routine request. When the statements came in, the bureaucrat discovered the existence of the RSCDA account and told the mayor, who knew nothing about it. Dixon authorities soon discovered that their trusted comptroller had been bleeding the city dry for years. On April 17, 2012, Crundwell was arrested by the FBI. She quickly confessed to stealing staggering amounts of municipal money.

Crundwell pled guilty on November 14, 2012, in federal court in Rockford, Illinois, to one count of wire fraud. As part of a plea deal with federal authorities, she also admitted to having engaged in illegal money laundering. Crundwell acknowledged that she owed the city of Dixon some $53,740,394 in restitution.

Crundwell's arrest and trial brought the stunning details of her decades-long deception to light. It was revealed she owned 400 racehorses, two residences and a horse farm in Dixon, a home in Englewood, Florida, a luxury motor home, a dozen trucks, trailers, and farm vehicles, a 2005 Ford Thunderbird convertible, a 1967 Chevrolet Corvette, a pontoon boat, jewels, and more.

And her motive for such thievery? At her sentencing hearing in February 2013, Dixon mayor James Burke got downright poetic when offering his take on what drove Crundwell. As reported in the February 15, 2013, *Chicago Tribune*, while on the stand Burke cited Shakespeare's *Richard III* and the famous line, "A horse! A horse! My kingdom for a horse!"

Other city bureaucrats spoke at the hearing of how tight the Dixon budget had been for years. "Several Dixon city officials—including the police chief and a city commissioner—were called to the witness stand, to detail how Crundwell's thefts crippled the city budget, delaying projects like repaving streets and replacing police radios and led to fears of layoffs," continued the *Tribune*.

The stoic resolve that Crundwell had shown throughout her arrest and trial crumbled at her sentencing hearing. "I'm truly sorry to the City of Dixon, my family and friends," she told the court, according to the February 14, 2013, feature in *Forbes* magazine.

U.S. District Judge Philip Reinhard wasn't impressed: "You showed much greater passion for the welfare of your horses than the people of Dixon you represented," he said, as quoted in the *Tribune*.

On Valentine's Day 2013, Judge Reinhard sentenced Crundwell to 19 years and 7 months in prison. Under federal sentencing regulations, she has to serve at least 17 of those years before being released.

That wasn't all the former trusted comptroller had to ponder. Throughout the courtroom drama, authorities were busy liquidating her assets. By the time Crundwell entered her guilty plea, the federal government had generated millions from the liquidation of her assets.

According to the press release from the U.S. Attorney's Office for the Northern District of Illinois, "To date, the United States Marshal Service has recovered approximately $7.4 million from the online and live auctions of approximately 400 quarter horses, vehicles, trailers, tack and a luxury motor home, with additional auctions of personal belongings and real property in Illinois and Florida still pending. The net proceeds from the forfeited property will be held in escrow pending further proceedings on restitution to the victim of the offence."

Further Reading

Melissa Jenco, "Ex-Dixon Comptroller Gets Nearly 20 Years for Theft," *Chicago Tribune*, February 15, 2013.

Walter Pavlo, "Former Dixon, IL, Comptroller, Rita Crundwell, Sentenced to 19½ Years in Prison," *Forbes*, February 14, 2013.

U.S. Attorney's Office, Northern District of Illinois, "Former Dixon Comptroller Rita Crundwell Pleads Guilty to Federal Fraud Charge, Admits Stealing $53 Million from City," November 14, 2012.

THE LONELY HEARTS KILLERS

Martha Beck and her paramour Raymond Fernandez robbed and murdered a series of women. As a duo, Beck and Fernandez made an extremely unlikely pair of killers. She was fat, dumpy, and prone to flights of fantasy, while he was handsome and charming, in a low-rent, sleazy manner—"a third-rate gigolo and his tubby tootsie," as the February 27, 2011, *New York Daily News* memorably phrased it. The strange relationship and murderous habits of the conniving couple were front-page news in the late 1940s. Together, the two conned, swindled, and killed.

Martha Seabrook, as she was known at her birth in 1920, had a rough childhood in Milton, Florida. Martha had an overbearing mother and a glandular condition that caused her to become obese. She claimed that her brother sexually abused her. When Beck told her mother, she was beaten. Starved for affection, Beck was picked on by her peers. As a young girl, she became withdrawn, indulging in a vivid inner fantasy life.

After high school, Martha studied nursing. She excelled in her studies, but upon graduation in 1942, she had trouble finding work because of her appearance. By this point, Martha weighed over 200 pounds. Eventually, she landed a job in a funeral home, prepping female bodies for burial.

Martha fled to California, where she took a job in an army hospital and trolled bars for men, looking or love and affection. After being impregnated and abandoned by one of her lovers, she went back to Florida with a tall tale about a make-believe husband who had died in the Pacific War. In Florida, she got pregnant again, only this time the father of the child—a bus driver named Alfred Beck—agreed to marry her. Martha became Mrs. Beck in the fall of 1944, but the marriage lasted only a few months.

Left with two small children and no male partner, Beck fell back into the dreamland reverie that had sustained her throughout her youth. She took a job at the Pensacola Hospital for Children in 1946 as a nurse. She proved to be a good worker, rising to the position of superintendent.

Beck connected with Fernandez through a "lonely hearts" club. Such clubs offered the pre-Internet equivalent of online dating. People wrote profiles, which were circulated among fellow club members. If someone felt a spark, they wrote that person a letter. Beck's profile was published, and her plea for love was answered by one Raymond Fernandez.

Fernandez was born in Hawaii to Spanish parents, in 1914. His family later moved to Connecticut. Fernandez himself moved to Spain in 1932, where he worked on a farm owned by a family member. He married and was well regarded, as a handsome, affable young man.

Following the Second World War, Fernandez took a ship to the Dutch West Indies. On board, a steel hatch fell open, fracturing his skull. Released after weeks in hospital, Fernandez drifted into a life of crime. He stole clothes from a ship, was arrested by U.S. Customs, and spent time in a Florida prison.

Released in 1946, Fernandez moved to Brooklyn, where he lived with his sister. He wrote letters to women in lonely hearts clubs, looking for gullible victims to charm and con. With his Latin good looks and courteous manner, he had no problem finding admirers. He typically seduced his prey, then robbed them of money, jewels, and other valuables. Just before Christmas 1947, Fernandez began communicating with Beck. He told her he was a rich Spanish businessman searching for a mate in America.

Beck fell instantly in love and eagerly agreed when Fernandez proposed a visit to Pensacola. The pair entered into a fiery affair. After days of passion, Fernandez moved back to New York and sent Beck a letter breaking off the relationship.

Fired from her hospital job (likely because of her affair with Fernandez), Beck took her two small children to New York City. In early January 1948, the trio showed up at the doorstep of Fernandez's apartment (which he had swindled from a previous lover and moved into after leaving his sister's place). The pair resumed their relationship. Fernandez was impressed by Beck's docility and loyalty, even when he admitted to being a con artist. Beck agreed to abandon her children with the Salvation Army when Fernandez complained about their presence.

Beck was so consumed with passion that she agreed to assist Fernandez with his deceptions. They selected a new potential victim: Esther Henne, a single woman living in southern Pennsylvania. Beck and Fernandez travelled to Pennsylvania to meet Henne. He was his usual charming self, introducing Beck as a family relative. Fernandez easily seduced the woman and married her on February 28, 1948, in Fairfax, Virginia. The trio returned to Fernandez's stolen apartment in New York. After only a few days, Henne departed, minus her car and the money Fernandez swindled from her.

More victims followed. On August 14, 1948, Fernandez married Myrtle Young of Greene Forest, Arkansas. Beck claimed to be Fernandez's sister. She couldn't let her feelings about Fernandez go, however, and prevented the newlyweds from consummating their marriage. Young erupted in anger, and Fernandez did his best to calm her, drugging her with sleeping pills. With Beck's help, Fernandez hustled the semiconscious Young onto a bus back to Arkansas. The woman had to be helped off the bus by police when she reached her home state. Young died in hospital one day later. Fernandez seemed unconcerned; he had stolen thousands of dollars from her and was momentarily flush.

Fernandez and Beck continued to con other lonely women, including Janet Fay, a 66-year-old widow in Albany, New York. Fay was a devout Catholic, so Fernandez (writing under the alias "Charles Martin") sprinkled his love letters with religious commentary. On December 30, 1948, Fernandez and Beck arrived in Albany and booked into a hotel. The following day, Fernandez met Fay, with Beck in tow, claiming to be his sister.

Fernandez soon proposed to Fay, and she accepted. The pair planned to move to Long Island, where Beck had rented an apartment. In early 1949, Fay withdrew several thousand dollars from her various back accounts and traveled with her new husband and his "sister" to Long Island.

Fay soon tired of having Fernandez's "sister" around all the time. Beck, for her part, was insanely jealous and again did her best to prevent the pair from making love. An argument in the Long Island apartment on January 4, 1949, soon turned into a bloodbath. Fay's head was caved in with a ball-peen hammer; then she was strangled with a scarf. It's unclear whether Beck or Fernandez was the killer. Regardless, they worked together to clean up the crime scene. Fay's bloody corpse was wrapped in sheets and towels, and placed in the closet. Then Fernandez and Beck went to bed, unmoved by the presence of a dead woman close by.

Fernandez acquired a trunk, into which he and Beck dumped Fay's body. The pair drove the trunk to a home belonging to a relative of Fernandez, who was cajoled into storing it in the basement. On January 15, 1949, Fernandez retrieved the trunk and buried it in the cellar of a rented home, then poured cement over the grave.

Fay's family grew suspicious when they started receiving typed letters, allegedly from Fay but actually written by Fernandez, detailing her life as a new bride. Fay didn't own a typewriter, nor could she type. Her family contacted police.

Fernandez and Beck had already moved on to a new victim. At 41 years old, Delphine Downing of Grand Rapids, Michigan, was younger than most of Fernandez's conquests. She was a widow with a two-year-old daughter. Fernandez charmed his way into Downing's life. Claiming again to be a wealthy businessman, Fernandez causally mentioned that he would be passing through Grand Rapids with his sister. Would Downing be interested in a visit? Downing eagerly agreed. With Beck by his side, Fernandez traveled to Grand Rapids.

Fernandez and Downing started a love affair, which infuriated Beck (pretending, once again, to be a relative of Fernandez). Downing, for her part, came to suspect her paramour's intentions. When she angrily accused Fernandez of trying to con her, he gave her sleeping pills, which made her pass out.

At this point, Downing's two-year-old daughter began to cry. Beck choked the child until she too passed out. Fernandez took a pistol and killed his new lover. He and Beck wrapped Downing's body in sheets and took her to the basement. Fernandez dug a hole for Downing's body, then covered the burial spot with cement. Beck, meanwhile, tidied up the murder scene.

The pair remained in Downing's house for two days. Her daughter wouldn't stop crying, however, so, at Fernandez's urging, Beck drowned her in a tub of dirty water. Fernandez dug another hole and tossed the dead toddler in.

Instead of fleeing, Beck and Fernandez went to the movies. Once the film was over, they returned to Downing's residence and began packing to leave. They were interrupted by the arrival of police, who had been summoned by Downing's neighbors. On February 28, 1949, Beck and Fernandez were taken into custody.

Fernandez quickly admitted to committing murder and signed a lengthy confession. By this point, the media had latched onto the story and wrote extensively about the unlikely pair of killers. Beck was greatly annoyed at being described as fat and homely.

Authorities made arrangements to ship Beck and Fernandez from Michigan (which had no death penalty) to New York state, which did. Charges against Fernandez and Beck for the murder of Downing and her daughter were waived, and the couple were extradited to New York. Once in the Empire State, the pair stood trial for the murder of Janet Fay.

The trial commenced June 28, 1949, in the Bronx Supreme Court. The public and press were fascinated by the pair and packed the courtroom. The duo were dubbed "the honeymoon killers" or the "lonely hearts killers" by the newspapers.

On the stand in July 1949, Fernandez retracted his earlier confession. He claimed he had confessed only to save Beck. He praised her virtues and said he was deeply in love with her. Fernandez admitted to being involved with the murder of Downing and her daughter, but denied killing Janet Fay.

In her testimony, Beck spoke of her unhappy childhood and poor luck with men. She acknowledged scheming with Fernandez to rip off lonely women. As for the Fay murder, Beck said she was in a trance state and uncertain of her actions.

The case went to the jury on August 18, 1949. The jury debated through the night and announced the verdict early the next morning. They found Fernandez and Beck both guilty of first-degree murder. The pair were sentenced to death.

While imprisoned at Sing Sing penitentiary in New York state, Fernandez and Beck maintained their strange relationship. One day the couple—who were kept in separate cells—would profess their profound love for each other. The next day, they were cold and indifferent.

On March 8, 1951, the pair were executed in the electric chair. Fernandez went first, followed by his lover and accomplice. It's unclear exactly how many women were victims to their duplicitous scamming. Some accounts say that as many as 17 people might have died at their hands.

In 1969, a movie based on Fernandez and Beck's exploits, called *The Honeymoon Killers*, was released. Their murderous relationship was also used as the basis of an episode of the popular TV show *Cold Case*. Even in death, the story of the Spanish lover and murderous nurse continued to fascinate the public.

Further Reading

Mark Gado, "The Lonely Hearts Killers," Crime Library.com (website no longer online).

William Grimes, "Behind the Filming of 'The Honeymoon Killers,'" *New York Times*, October 20, 1992.

David Krajicek, "60 Years Ago, Sing Sing's Electric Chair Had One Busy Night," *New York Daily News*, February 27, 2011.

BERNIE MADOFF

On March 12, 2009, Bernard L. Madoff pled guilty in Manhattan federal court to 11 criminal charges. These consisted of securities fraud, investment adviser fraud, mail fraud, wire fraud, three counts of money laundering, false statements, perjury, false filings with the U.S. Securities and Exchange Commission (SEC), and theft from an employee benefit program. He was 70 years old at the time. The one-time master investor was accused of running "a massive Ponzi scheme," as a March 12, 2009, press release from the U.S. Attorney's Office for the Southern District of New York put it.

As explained in the entry on crooked investor Charles Ponzi, in the chapter on Business Fraud, a Ponzi scheme is an illegal arrangement in which a firm entices investors with promises of high, consistent returns. The firm doesn't actually invest in anything tangible, however, but merely circulates clients' cash. Money from new investors goes to pay off old investors. Once new investors stop coming in and old investors want to pull out, the whole rickety edifice comes crashing down.

Madoff "engaged in wholesale fraud for more than a generation; his so-called 'investment advisory' business was a fraud; his frauds affected thousands of investors in the United States and worldwide; and he repeatedly lied under oath and filed false documents to conceal his fraud," stated a sentencing memorandum issued by Lev L. Dassin, Acting United States Attorney for the Southern District of New York, from June 26, 2009.

The scope of Madoff's fraud was almost unimaginable, running into tens of billions of dollars. A story published June 30, 2009, in *The Wall Street Journal* described Madoff as "the self-confessed author of the biggest financial swindle in history."

Bernard L. Madoff Investment Securities (BLMIS) occupied two and a half floors of a building in mid-Manhattan. The trading floor was on nineteen, while software programmers toiled on eighteen. On the seventeenth floor, Madoff operated a secretive inner trading office. A special pass was required to access this sanctum. This was where Madoff supposedly did his real magic, running a mysterious hedge fund that produced great returns for investors.

The seventeenth floor featured an ancient IBM computer server that Madoff insisted on keeping, along with a small collection of clerks and other officials. "This machine—which has been autopsied by the government—was the nerve center of the fraud. The thousands of pages of statements printed out from it showed trades that were never made," stated an April 24, 2009, investigative report in *Fortune* magazine.

The seventeenth floor was run by Frank DiPascali, chief deputy to Madoff. He worked with Madoff for decades and boasted a tough-guy aura and thick Queens accent. His stern presence was an indication of the importance the Madoff operation placed on their seventeenth-floor machinations.

Madoff also worked closely with his brother, Peter Madoff, head of compliance and de facto CEO of the firm's legitimate trading operations. Madoff also had two sons, Mark and Andy Madoff, on the payroll.

The Madoff clan first arrived in the United States in the early twentieth century, from various locales in Poland, Romania, and Austria. Bernie and Peter Madoff were raised in a middle-class section of Queens in New York City. His parents were not rich, but the family was comfortable.

Madoff apparently had a reputation as a hustler, even in high school. He attended one semester at the University of Alabama but soon returned home and started commuting to Hofstra College on Long Island. By all accounts, he was more focused on work and family than school. He married his high school sweetheart, Ruth Alpern, one day before Thanksgiving in late 1959. Just two days later, he filled out an SEC application to register a broker-dealer firm he named after himself. A financial statement attached to the application pegged Madoff's monetary assets at $200.

Young Madoff focused on over-the-counter stocks from small companies. He worked as a wholesaler, meaning he bought and sold small company stocks to various brokers. The over-the-counter stock world was somewhat rough and tumble, with no centralized exchange, much less computerized results. Regardless, Madoff thrived, and his capital expanded exponentially, from roughly $125,000 in 1967 to over half a million dollars two years later. By the early 1970s, he was reporting over $1 million a year in capital to SEC.

In addition to handling over-the-counter stocks, Madoff had begun to manage people's money, though this went unmentioned on his SEC forms. Initial investors in the early 1960s consisted of friends and family. Saul Alpern, father of Madoff's wife Ruth, "let his son-in-law share a desk at his accounting firm [and] began gathering smaller investors together and creating a fund that invested with Madoff as a single account. This was among the first of what came to be called feeder funds," stated the April 24, 2009, feature in *Fortune*.

Madoff was something of a pioneer in electronic trading, though he would later significantly exaggerate his role in this field. He claimed he helped start NASDAQ (National Association of Securities Dealers Automated Quotations) in 1971. In its embryonic version, this computerized trading system only showed stock bids and offers.

Within two decades of the founding of NASDAQ, Madoff's company was handling nearly 10 percent of the daily trading volume of stocks listed on the New York Stock Exchange. Madoff specialized in a concept called "payment for order flow."

The April 24, 2009, *Fortune* article explained, "Rather than taking a fee for trading stocks as NYSE specialists did, Madoff paid firms like Charles Schwab and Fidelity a penny or two a share for their orders; a practice known as 'payment for order flow.' In those days, there was a prevailing spread of at least 12.5 cents between the prices that a 'market maker' like Madoff's firm paid to buy shares and the price at which it would sell the same shares. Using its own software, Madoff's firm was adept at hedging the risk that buy-and-sell orders would be out of balance, preserving its profit."

Some stockbroker elites turned their noses up at payment for order flow, which they likened to a form of legalized kickbacks. Madoff was seen as an upstart, making profits in a legal but shady manner.

Madoff continued his upwards trajectory. In 1990, Madoff was made chairman of NASDAQ. One year later, a panel on which Madoff sat endorsed the concept of payment for order flow. Then, in 1997, "the rules governing trading spreads changed. They were slashed from 12.5 cents a share to 6.25 cents that year and then dropped to a penny in 2001. Madoff's firm, which had eschewed traditional commissions and made its money on the spread, watched its profit margins evaporate. Madoff's market-making operation would never again be the prodigious cash generator it had been," stated the April 24, 2009, issue of *Fortune*.

By this point, however, Madoff's more secretive seventeenth-floor operations appeared to be rolling in cash. He offered steady 12 to 15 percent returns for his investors and didn't strain himself to find new clients. In fact, it was difficult to become part of Madoff's golden circle of investors. Madoff ran his hedge fund like a private club and was picky about whom he let inside. This, of course, enhanced the appeal of the hedge fund for those whose money was accepted. Investors understood that it was a privilege to be part of the fund and kept their investments a secret.

Madoff became adept at side-stepping investigations. Two magazines—a trade publication called *Mar/Hedge* and the popular business publication *Barron's*—ran articles in 2001 questioning Madoff's financial machinations. For such a successful hedge fund (reporters pegged its value around $6–7 billion), it was curious that Madoff was so secretive about it. The articles also questioned Madoff's ability to offer consistent 15 percent annual returns.

For years, a whistleblower named Harry Markopolos had been warning the SEC about Madoff. According to Markopolos, Madoff's hedge fund had exploded in value, rising to almost $50 billion by late 2005, and was worldwide in scope. Investors included huge international concerns, such as the Abu Dhabi Investment Authority, which handed over millions to Madoff. Markopolos claimed that the hedge fund was simply a really big Ponzi scheme. Finally, the SEC responded and launched a probe in 2006.

To clients and anyone else who asked, Madoff claimed that his investing strategy was based on something called "split-strike conversion." In a March 12, 2009, plea allocution at his trial, Madoff stated, "Through the split-strike conversion strategy, I promised to clients and prospective clients that client funds would be invested in a basket of common stocks within the Standard & Poor's 100 Index, a collection of the 100 largest publicly traded companies in terms of their market capitalization. I promised that I would select a basket of stocks that would closely mimic the price movements of the Standard & Poor's 100 Index. I promised that I would opportunistically time these purchases and would be out of the market intermittently, investing client funds through these periods in United States government–issued securities such as United States Treasury Bills. In addition, I promised that as part of the split-strike conversion strategy, I would hedge the investments I made in the basket of common stocks by using client funds to buy and sell option contracts related to those stocks, thereby limited potential client losses caused by unpredictable changes in stock prices."

In reality, Madoff wasn't investing in anything other than himself. During his plea allocution he revealed that money earmarked for investments in his hedge fund was actually deposited in an account he controlled at Chase Manhattan Bank. Madoff used this account to pay returns and redeem clients' principal, if they so asked. In the meantime, Madoff and Co. came up with phony account statements for clients and issued false and/or misleading audit reports and financial statements to the SEC.

Everything worked fine as long as the economy kept buzzing along. The massive economic downturn of 2008, however, turned out also to be Madoff's downfall. As markets declined precipitously, clients began withdrawing money from Madoff's fund. As of early 2008, investors were demanding the return of roughly $7 billion—far more money than Madoff had on hand. Madoff was desperate to shore up the hedge fund to pay back money owed and began soliciting wealthy individuals for new investments.

Everything came to an abrupt end on December 10, 2008. Madoff confessed to his sons that the hedge fund had been one massive fraud. Madoff attended a company holiday party in a restaurant, where by all accounts he showed no signs of stress. Then, on December 11, he was arrested. On December 15, 2008, a federal judge ordered the American operations of Madoff's company to be liquidated.

Prosecutors at Madoff's ensuing trial stated that BLMIS had 4,900 client accounts, with a total balance of nearly $65 billion, as of late 2008. "In fact, BLMIS only held a small fraction of that balance on behalf of its client," stated the June 26, 2009, government sentencing memorandum.

Prosecutors were correct in that Madoff had nowhere near enough cash on hand to pay back his clients. However, the estimation of BLMIS's worth was exaggerated, representing the total amount of every investment with Madoff. "According to experts, the actual amount investors gave to Madoff over the years is probably closer to $20 billion," stated April 24, 2009, *Fortune* magazine article.

No matter; the Madoff coffers were bare. The $20 billion "will never be found; it was chipped away year after year after year. That, after all, is the definition of a Ponzi scheme: most of the cash put up by new investors went to pay the old ones … the collapse of a Ponzi scheme means there is no money left. In the end, victims will likely collect only a tiny fraction of what they lost," continued the April 24, 2009, *Fortune* story.

In court, Madoff was forthcoming about his illegal activities. "As I engaged in my fraud, I knew what I was doing was wrong, indeed criminal. When I began the Ponzi scheme, I believed it would end shortly and I would be able to extricate myself and my clients from the scheme. However, this proved difficult and ultimately impossible, and as the years went by, I realized that my arrest and this day would inevitably come," stated Madoff, in his plea allocution, on March 12, 2009.

Madoff confessed that he had lied to clients about the nature of their investments. He said his fraud began "in the early 1990s" during the recession of that period. Despite the economic downturn, Madoff's clients still expected healthy returns. So Madoff invented the tale of the "split-strike conversion strategy" while using money from new investors in his secret hedge fund to pay off old investors. In his plea allocution, Madoff admitted to lying under oath to the SEC and confessed to wiring money between the U.S. and United Kingdom "to make it appear as though there were actual securities transactions executed on behalf of my investment advisory clients."

The prosecution wasn't impressed by Madoff's show of penitence. They pointed to the thousands of clients who would never see any of the money they had invested with Madoff and the fact that he had perpetuated his fraud for decades.

"His crimes were not a one-time event arising, for example, from a split-second decision made under financial duress," stated the June 26, 2009, government sentencing memorandum. "Rather, Madoff's crimes were the product of a series of decisions made over the course of years, and it was within his power to stop his crimes at any point in time. Madoff first generated and then sent investors millions of pages of false documents 'confirming' securities transactions that had not taken place and 'confirming' account balances that amounted to IOUs not worth the paper on which they were printed."

As reported in the *New York Times* on June 30, 2009, Madoff told the court, "I am responsible for a great deal of suffering and pain. I understand that. I live in a tormented state now, knowing all of the pain and suffering that I have created."

U.S. District Court Judge Denny Chin took a dim view, and on June 29, 2009, he sentenced Madoff to 150 years in jail. The announcement of Madoff's penalty "sparked a burst of applause in a courtroom packed with victims of the fraud," reported a June 30, 2009, article in *The Wall Street Journal*.

Further Reading

James Bandler and Nicholas Varchaver, "How Bernie Did It," *Fortune*, April 24, 2009.

Lev L. Dassin, Acting United States Attorney for the Southern District of New York, "Government's Sentencing Memorandum," United States District Court, Southern District of New York, Filed June 26, 2009.

Amir Efrati and Robert Frank, "'Evil' Madoff Gets 150 Years in Epic Fraud," *Wall Street Journal*, June 30, 2009.

Martha Graybow and Grant McCool, "Madoff Pleads Guilty, Is Jailed for $65 Million Fraud," Reuters, March 13, 2009.

Tom Hays and Larry Neumeister, "J. P. Morgan to Settle Madoff Fraud Claims for $1.7B," The Associated Press, January 8, 2014.

Diana B. Henriques, "Madoff Is Sentenced to 150 Years for Ponzi Scheme," *New York Times*, June 30, 2009.

Bernard L. Madoff, "Plea Allocution of Bernard L. Madoff," United States District Court, Southern District of New York, March 12, 2009.

"The Madoff Case: A Timeline," *Wall Street Journal*, March 12, 2009.

U.S. Attorney's Office, Southern District of New York, "Bernard L. Madoff Pleads Guilty to 11-Count Criminal Information and Is Remanded into Custody," March 12, 2009.

OLD-SCHOOL SWINDLERS

William Thompson

Like Charles Ponzi, whose name is now forever associated with financial scams, William Thompson's exploits have been immortalized in the English language. Thompson was a criminal who operated in New York City in the late 1840s. He would dress in expensive clothes and saunter about in wealthy neighborhoods. Thompson would then approach total strangers and pretend they were vague acquaintances. The stranger, bound by strict rules of Victorian etiquette, usually played along, making small talk with Thompson.

At some point in the conversation, Thompson would make an odd request: "Have you confidence in me to trust me with your watch until tomorrow?" he would ask, according to a July 8, 1849, article in the *New York Herald*. Usually, the stranger complied. He never saw his watch again.

Thompson was eventually arrested for his misdeeds in the summer of 1849. In coverage of his arrest, the *New York Herald* referred to Thompson as the "Confidence Man." In this manner, the term "con man" entered the popular lexicon.

The term was further popularized by author Herman Melville, whose novel *The Confidence-Man* was released in 1857. It is that believed Melville's book was inspired by Thompson's exploits among the upper crust in New York City.

George C. Parker

George C. Parker was a master of fake real estate transactions. Born in 1870, Parker used phony deeds and documents to "sell" the Brooklyn Bridge, sometimes on a weekly basis. In a similar fashion, he sold several other famous New York City landmarks to wide-eyed buyers.

Parker wasn't the only con artist to "sell" the bridge (which was completed in 1883), but he was the most high-profile. The fraudulent realtor possessed "astounding chutzpah … no flim-flam man was a greater scoundrel than George C. Parker," stated a November 27, 2007, feature in the *New York Post*.

Parker and other turn-of-the-twentieth-century con men played upon the naivety of newcomers who were entering America by the millions at the time. Parker would approach people practically the moment they stepped off Ellis Island—the disembarkation point for immigrants who crossed the Atlantic Ocean. America, in the eyes of many immigrants, was a booming land of opportunity. They jumped at the chance to own a piece of public property.

In the early 1900s, the Brooklyn Bridge and the Statue of Liberty were two of the best-known symbols of the United States. The vast size of the Brooklyn Bridge made it highly visible and allowed Parker to show it off to prospective buyers while avoiding policemen who patrolled the span.

Parker's pitch was simple: whoever owned the bridge could make a fortune in tolls, he claimed. Indeed, some of his "marks" were so convinced of their good fortune that they had to be dissuaded by police from setting up toll barriers at the bridge entrances.

The bridge wasn't the only public landmark Parker "sold." At different times throughout his career, he also sold off the Statue of Liberty, the old Madison Square Garden, the Metropolitan Museum of Art, and Grant's Tomb. The latter contained the remains of the famous American Civil War general and president, Ulysses S. Grant. To pull off this particular con, Parker pretended to be Grant's grandson.

Eventually, newcomers and immigrant officials wised up to Parker's scams. Ellis Island authorities began handing out pamphlets that warned immigrants about con artists and made clear that public buildings were not for sale in America. By the 1920s or so, the Brooklyn Bridge scam had largely run its course.

Parker himself did not enjoy a trouble-free life. He was convicted three times of fraud and died in Sing Sing Prison in 1936. His audacity has been immortalized in the slang expression, "If you believe that, then I have a bridge to sell you"—derisively used to describe someone who is extremely gullible.

Joseph Weil, "The Yellow Kid"

If there ever was a King of the Con Artists, Joseph Weil would be a leading contender for the throne. Nicknamed the "Yellow Kid", after a comic strip character, Weil swindled over $8 million in his lifetime, worth several times that that today. Weil was also unusually self-reflective for a con artist, putting together an astonishing autobiography in which he gleefully explained his scams while waxing philosophic about human nature.

Weil was born in 1875, in Chicago, where his parents ran a small grocery store. He left school at age 17, and became a very efficient collector for Chicago loan sharks—criminals who loan money to desperate customers at huge rates of interest, payable on threat of injury or death to the borrower or their family. Weil noticed that his fellow collectors, cashiers, and bookkeepers always pocketed a small portion of the proceeds they gathered. Weil threatened his peers with exposure, blackmailing them into handing over some of their ill-gotten gains in exchange for his silence.

Weil had already decided not to follow in his parents footsteps and work as an honest merchant. "Having seen my parents struggle for their existence—my mother got up at five in the morning to open the store—I knew that such a life was not for me. Further, I had seen how much more money was being made by skullduggery than by honest toil," he related in his memoir.

The youthful Weil fell in with one "Doc Meriwether," who was something of a Chicago legend. "Doc Meriwether was one of the most picturesque characters in the Middle West. He was tall, broad-shouldered and gaunt. He wore a Van Dyke beard and pince-nez glasses. He usually dressed in black—black trousers and black frock coat with extra-long tails. He wore a flowing black cravat that covered half his shirt front," recalled Weil.

Meriwether peddled "medicine," of a sort. His specialty was a pleasant-tasting concoction called "Meriwether's Elixir." According to Weil, the main ingredient in said elixir was rainwater. The "Doc" would load up a cart filled with bottles of "Meriwether's Elixir" and hit the road. He was particularly effective in rural districts, where he peddled his potion as a sure-fire cure for tapeworms—a common parasite, blamed at the time for all manner of physical ailments, including malnutrition, exhaustion, and overall ill health.

Meriwether ran a so-called "medicine show"—a popular phenomenon in rural nineteenth-century America that mixed entertainment with medicinal pitches. (Further details about medicine shows can be found in the entry on patent medicine in the chapter on "Dubious Remedies.") Doc Meriwether's show offered dancing girls, solemn Indians, and his own dazzling spiel to get the audience's attention. The main product for sale was Meriwether's Elixir, available at a dollar a bottle.

Weil's job varied from community to community. In some locales, he served as a barker, bellowing out enticements to rural folks to come and see Doc Meriwether and his crew. In other communities, Weil would take the role of a "shill." He would pretend to be a farmer who had been cured of tapeworms thanks to the powerful potion. Weil would recount how sick he'd been and how the Elixir had eliminated his tapeworms and made him a new man.

For the price of $10, Doc Meriwether offered private consultations for patients in hotel suites. Meriwether would induce the client to guzzle his medicine, plus Epsom salts. The mark was then led into a darkened room, where he was led to believe his tapeworm would be eliminated via natural means. Weil's job was to show the client a water basin, allegedly containing the tapeworm the patient had just excreted. The parasite was actually a long potato peeling at the bottom of the basin.

Weil eventually parted ways with Doc Meriwether, but remained a con man at heart. Among other scams, Weil and a confederate would sell multi-year magazine subscriptions to farmers. To entice the farmers or their wives to hand over the fee, Weil would proffer a free set of silver spoons, supposedly a gift from the magazine publisher. The spoons looked real but were actually cheap knockoffs that Weil had acquired for pennies each. Weil also sold fake gold watches, worth about $2 each, for $50 apiece. "This desire to get something for nothing has been very costly to many people who have dealt with me and other con men," Weil recalled in his autobiography.

Weil married a young lady named Jessie, who was under the impression her husband was a traveling salesman peddling legitimate products. She regularly attended services of the Sacramento Congregational Church in Chicago. When he was home, Weil attended church as well. In his memoir, he recalled being mightily impressed by the florid delivery of the minister. He noted the ease and skill with which the minister used words to move the audience.

"This set me to thinking. I said to myself, 'Joe, you are not capable of hard physical work. You're too frail. Whatever you accomplish in life must be done through words. You have that ability. You can make words beautiful and scenic. What marble is to sculpture, what canvas is to painting, words can be to you. You can use them to influence others. You can make them earn their living for you,'" Weil revealed in his memoir.

Weil also made some powerful ethical insights: "I arrived at these conclusions: man has all the bestiality of the animal, but is cloaked with a thin veneer of civilization; he is inherently dishonest and selfish; the honest man is a rare specimen indeed," he recalled.

Shortly after the turn of the twentieth century, Weil acquired the nickname "Yellow Kid," which would follow him for life. The nickname came courtesy of notorious Chicago alderman "Bathhouse John" Coughlin. A hugely corrupt politician, Coughlin was an acquaintance of Weil and other criminals. Around 1903, Weil was working with a fellow con artist named Hogan. At the time, there was a highly popular newspaper comic strip called "Hogan's Alley and the Yellow Kid." Coughlin was amused by the similarity in names and began referring to Hogan and Weil as "Hogan and the Yellow Kid." In this manner, a moniker was born.

Over the next few decades, "Yellow Kid" Weil and trusted companions ran innumerable scams to separate "marks" from their money. Weil set up fake sports betting parlors, complete with cashiers, a telegraph operator, and well-heeled gamblers—all actors or confidents of Weil. This setup was used to deceive people into laying huge bets on "sure things"—only to lose their cash by means of trickery. In a variation on this scheme, Weil would set up fake brokerage houses, using props and furniture borrowed or purchased from banks and companies going out of business. (Both of these scams are described in the section on "Big Cons," in the chapter on "Classic Cons.")

Weil also helped run something called the Elysium Development Company. Said company specialized in selling "almost worthless Michigan swamp land [to] unsuspecting people," as Weil put it in his memoirs. At the time, Chicago residents regarded Michigan as a rustic vacation destination, filled with cottages, lakes, and lodges for fishermen and hunters. Thus, the notion of acquiring inexpensive Michigan land was highly appealing. Weil's trick was to hand over plots of Michigan turf for free. The catch was, the lots had to be "registered" (with a Weil confederate), at a cost of $30. Landowners grumbled but usually paid, pleased as they were with getting a "free" gift of land. Other "fees" typically followed.

Another Weil specialty was the fixed boxing match. Although boxing was enormously popular, prize fights were illegal in most states. Weil would set up a fake "private" boxing facility and once again populate it with fellow con artists and other rabble. Weil would induce marks to lay huge bets on the boxers. Before the sixth round of the fight, one of the boxers would be secretly "fed" a ball made from fish skin. Said ball was filled with chicken blood and hot water. During the sixth round, the boxer would take a savage punch, then bite down on the blood ball. The result would be torrents of very realistic blood.

Bloodied in this manner, the boxer would collapse on the canvas and lie there, prostrate. A fake ringside "doctor" would examine the man and solemnly declare he was dead. This would trigger a stampede for the exits. The marks who bet on the match would be urged to flee before police arrived, sacrificing their money in the process but ensuring their liberty. Few people wanted to be caught up with a shady murder in an illegal boxing match. (This scam is discussed at length in the section on "Short Cons" in the "Classic Cons" chapter.)

In the late 1940s, Weil collaborated with a writer to produce an autobiography. Besides offering an insider's look at various cons, the book provided valuable insights into the psychology of con artists. "All the people I swindled had one thing in common—greed, the desire to acquire money," stated Weil.

Interestingly, Weil claimed that con artists needed to possess certain positive traits in order to succeed: "One thing is very important to the successful con man: honor. That may sound strange, but it's true. I don't know how much truth there is to the old saying about honor among thieves, but it is an absolute necessity among con men. Though a con man may conspire to fleece others, he must always be on the level with his associates. The victim's cash is usually taken by one man, who disappears. And it would be a sorry day indeed if this man, who had taken the money, didn't meet later with his associates to divide the spoils," noted Weil.

Weil claimed he had grossed about $8 million through various scams over the years, but denied that he was victimizing people. "I am not talking about small swindles, where an honest person loses his money. I have never been a party to such schemes. I have never taken a dime from honest, hard-working people who could not afford to lose. But the victims of confidence games are usually people who are wealthy and can afford to pay the con man's price for the lesson," he stated.

Weil did serve time during his career but lived long enough to see his autobiography in print and his name become synonymous with con artist mastery. He died in Chicago in 1976, a centenarian and a brilliant schemer.

Further Reading

"Arrest of the Confidence Man," *New York Herald*, 1849.

W. T. Brannon, *The Autobiography of America's Master Swindler*, 1948.

Gabriel Cohen, "For You, Half Price," *New York Times*, November 27, 2005.

"Meet the King of NY Con Men," *New York Post*, November 25, 2007.

LINDA TAYLOR, THE WELFARE QUEEN

Linda Taylor was a con artist who used dozens of names, addresses, and phone numbers to fraudulently collect social assistance for decades. At her peak, Taylor's income was estimated at roughly $150,000 a year.

"If Taylor was a character in a movie, people would dismiss her as an implausibility. She really did bilk various government programs of hundreds of thousands of dollars. She also burned through husbands, sometimes more than one at a time. She was a master of disguise, armed with dozens of wigs. She flipped through assumed and fake identities and employed 33 known aliases," read an account of her life posted on the website of National Public Radio (NPR) on December 20, 2013.

Taylor was profiled at great length in a December 19, 2013, feature story by online magazine, Slate. According to Slate, Taylor's descent into national notoriety began on August 8, 1974, when she filed a report with Chicago police claiming to have been the victim of a robbery. Taylor told police that burglars had absconded with $14,000 of her cash and jewelry. Detective Jack Sherwin recognized her name from a previous instance when the same woman filed a similar robbery report two years earlier.

Det. Sherwin suspected Taylor was trying to pull off an insurance scam. The detective looked into her background a little more closely, and discovered she was wanted on felony charges of welfare fraud in Michigan.

Taylor remained oblivious. As Det. Sherwin investigated her case, Taylor showered money and gifts on her new boyfriend, a 21-year-old sailor named Lamar Jones. The pair were soon married

In late August 1974, Taylor was arrested on charges of welfare fraud. Jones gallantly paid her bond, to free his wife from jail. She repaid his kindness by stealing his color TV and fleeing the state. Jones, who was already getting suspicious about his new wife (he thought it odd how she received mail under five different names at her residence) would later testify against her before a grand jury.

A month after Taylor's arrest, the *Chicago Tribune* went to print with details about her parasitic existence. The *Tribune* said she drove three cars (a Cadillac, a Lincoln, and a Chevrolet station wagon), all the while ripping off the Illinois welfare system. The paper also said Taylor had three Social Security cards and multiple names, addresses, and phone numbers. The *Tribune* invented the moniker "welfare queen" to describe her. A subsequent Associated Press article noted her ability to take on different racial identities when it was convenient for her.

A fugitive, Taylor was caught in Tucson, Arizona, on October 9, 1974. Shipped to Illinois, Taylor was indicted on November 13, 1974, for theft, perjury, and bigamy. She was accused of using 80 aliases to illegally obtain $150,000 in fraudulent social assistance payments.

As the media soon discovered, Taylor's backstory was murky: "In court records listing the counts of the indictment, the defendant's name is recorded as Connie Walker, aka Linda Bennett, aka Linda Taylor, aka Linda Jones, aka Connie Jarvis. She was either 35, 39, 40, or 47 years-old, depending on whose story you believed," stated the December 19, 2013, story in Slate.

Even today, details of her family life are unclear. As far as anyone can tell, Taylor's real name was either Martha Miller or Martha Louise White. She was born in Alabama in 1926 or in Tennessee sometime between 1925 and 1927. Her parents were listed as a cotton farmer named Joe Miller and his wife, Lidy (alternately spelled Lyde or Lydie) Miller.

While young, Linda Taylor was listed as white in a 1940 census; she had dark hair and a dark complexion. Her biological father might have been African American, although this was never confirmed.

By all accounts, Taylor was a headstrong child, with a disobedient streak. After hitting puberty, Taylor became promiscuous, producing four children by the early 1950s. Taylor traveled around the United States with her brood, living like a gypsy. She had a habit of dumping her kids with friends, relatives, and vague acquaintances for unspecified periods of time. Her second son, Paul, had notably darker skin than his siblings, which made him the subject of much unwanted attention, particularly in the Deep South. In the mid-1950s, Taylor dropped Paul off with a family in Chicago, then essentially abandoned him.

Taylor and her remaining three children eventually drifted back to Chicago themselves. There, she struck up a relationship with an older African American criminal named Lawrence Wakefield. Wakefield, who ran a "policy" racket (essentially an illegal lottery), doted on Taylor's children, supplying them with cash, food, and presents.

On February 18, 1964, based on a report that he was ill, Chicago police entered Wakefield's residence. Police founded betting slips, coin wrappers, and huge amounts of hidden cash—over $750,000 worth in total. Wakefield, who was 60 years old, died in hospital of an intracranial hemorrhage within hours of the police raid.

Taylor (going under the name Constance Wakefield) told authorities she was Wakefield's daughter. She showed reporters a birth certificate that allegedly listed Lawrence Wakefield and Edith Jarvis as her parents. Taylor also produced a will showing she was supposed to inherit Lawrence Wakefield's wealth.

In November 1964, a witness named Hubert Mooney testified in Probate Court that Constance Wakefield was really Martha Louise White. Mooney said White was born in Summit, Alabama, in 1926 and that the girl was the daughter of his sister Lydie and a male partner named Marvin White. Mooney said his niece grew up in Arkansas. Mooney wasn't motivated to testify out of a concern for justice. Apparently, he was furious that a relative he assumed to be white would pretend to be African American for financial gain.

Mooney might have gotten a few facts wrong in his account, but he did shed light on Taylor's strange background. The Probate judge slapped Taylor with a six-month sentence for contempt of court and refused to give her any part of Lawrence Wakefield's estate.

Taylor soon found a new mark, in the form of a Chicago schoolteacher named Patricia Parks. Parks was in her thirties and had three children, a girl and two boys. Parks, who hailed from Trinidad, hired Taylor, out on bail from her welfare fraud trial, to watch her house and babysit her kids. "Taylor took up residence with the Parks family in 1974. At that point, Patricia Parks was a healthy woman with three young children. Less than a year later, she was dead," reported the December 19, 2013, Slate feature.

Parks died on June 15, 1975. Taylor came forward as the supposed beneficiary to various life insurance policies drawn up in Parks' name. Taylor also claimed Parks had willed her property and guardianship of her children.

Taylor informed the funeral home that Parks had suffered from cervical cancer. Officials at the funeral home checked Parks's blood and discovered the presence of barbiturates. A coroner declared Parks had died from an overdose of various drugs, not cancer. Police investigated and discovered that Taylor had put all kinds of voodoo and witchcraft paraphernalia in the Parks residence (possibly to spook Parks). A credit card belonging to Parks was later found in Taylor's possession.

For various reasons, Taylor was never charged with Parks's death. Authorities said they couldn't get samples of Parks's blood from the hospital where she died, which would make it difficult to prove she had drugs in her system. Officials decided there wasn't sufficient evidence to charge Taylor. Taylor did not, however, get custody of Parks's children or ownership of her house.

Against this backdrop, Taylor's trial for welfare fraud finally began, in early 1977. By this point, some charges (such as bigamy) had been dropped, while others were reduced due to lack of firm evidence. Taylor was officially accused of obtaining $8,000 under four fake names.

"Rather than trying to win sympathy, Taylor seemed to enjoy playing the scofflaw. As witnesses described her brazen pilfering from public coffers, she remained impassive, an unrepentant defendant bedecked in expensive clothes and oversize hats," reported the December 19, 2013, Slate story. Perhaps because of this total lack of remorse, the jury took a mere seven hours to come to a guilty verdict on March 17, 1977. Taylor received a sentence of two to six years for welfare fraud and one year for perjury, lying to a grand jury. She entered the Dwight Correctional Center on February 16, 1978.

Taylor served her time at the Dwight Correctional Center and was released in the early 1980s. (Records concerning her release have apparently been lost.) Upon getting out, Taylor reconnected with a beau named Sherman Ray, whom she married.

On August 25, 1983, Ray, who was 35, was shot and killed by a 63-year-old man named Willtrue Loyd in Momence, Illinois, a small town south of Chicago. Loyd told police it was an accident: he had been hunting a snake with his shotgun when Ray appeared unexpectedly and tried to grab his gun. Startled, Loyd tussled with Ray, and in the course of their maneuvers, the shotgun discharged. Police took Loyd into custody but later released him, for lack of firm evidence. It was whispered that Taylor had set the two men up. While this was never proven, Taylor did collect money from Ray's life insurance policy.

In the early 1980s, Taylor also befriended an elderly black woman in Chicago named Mildred Markham. Markham's deceased husband had been a Pullman porter on a railway and earned a decent salary. Taylor told Markham she was her husband's long-lost daughter.

Markham's friends and family tried to convince her that Linda Taylor was a con artist, but she wouldn't hear of it. Following Ray's death, Markham found herself living in Florida with Taylor and her new man, Willtrue Loyd. In the Sunshine State, Taylor soon reverted to form, inventing aliases to collect multiple Social Security checks. Taylor also drained Markham's bank account and stole her furniture, jewels, and furs. In 1985, Markham deeded 185 acres of family land in Mississippi to Taylor.

In March 1986, Markham married Loyd. Seven months later, she was dead, supposedly of natural causes. After Markham died, Taylor came forward with a series of insurance policies her elderly friend had allegedly taken out, naming her as the beneficiary. Taylor told officials she was Markham's daughter.

In May 1987, a doctor sent a note to the local medical examiner, suggesting Mildred Markham had actually died from falling and hitting her head. While Markham's death was reclassified as an accident, Taylor was never charged with her death.

Six years after Markham passed away, Loyd died in Florida, at age 72. The medical examiner cited heart disease as cause of death. Taylor claimed she was Loyd's granddaughter and was therefore entitled to his veteran's benefits.

Taylor's family eventually reconnected with her. They discovered that their mother was in bad shape, possibly going senile. Her son Johnnie took Taylor back to his home in Chicago. Taylor later lived with her daughter Sandra. Taylor became increasingly eccentric and erratic. She was admitted to a Chicago hospital, where she died of a heart attack, on April 18, 2002. It was unclear how old she really was.

The December 19, 2013, story in Slate suggested that Taylor's causal use of people, superficial charm, chameleon-like ability to change identities, total lack of empathy, constant churn of husbands and partners, and supreme manipulativeness pointed to a diagnosis of psychopathy. Taylor did achieve one positive thing in life. After her story went public, authorities began treating welfare fraud much more seriously.

Taylor also set a precedent for welfare-bashing. Conservative politicians such as Ronald Reagan picked up on her story. While running for the Republican presidential nomination in 1976 Reagan horrified audiences with accounts of the Chicago "welfare queen" who drove a Cadillac to pick up her checks. To Reagan and conservative audiences, Taylor's incredible story confirmed their worst fears about welfare "moochers" and government inefficiency.

Further Reading

Gene Demby, "The Truth Behind the Lies of the Original 'Welfare Queen,'" NPR.org, December 20, 2013, http://www.npr.org/sections/codeswitch/2013/12/20/255819681 /the-truth-behind-the-lies-of-the-original-welfare-queen.

Josh Levin, "The Welfare Queen," Slate.com, December 19, 2013, http://www.slate.com /articles/news_and_politics/history/2013/12/linda_taylor_welfare_queen_ronald _reagan_made_her_a_notorious_american_villain.html.

KEVIN TRUDEAU, TV PITCHMAN

Kevin Trudeau earned millions of dollars selling a wide array of books, products, and services, often through "infomercials"—lengthy television advertisements that aired late at night. Described in a July 29, 2005, article in online magazine Salon as a "master huckster," Trudeau sold everything from alleged cancer cures to financial schemes, treatments for male pattern baldness, and programs to boost reading comprehension.

Trudeau has had repeated run-ins with the Federal Trade Commission (FTC) and other authorities. These resulted in huge fines for making false or misleading claims. Since spring 2014, Trudeau has been an inmate at the Federal Prison Camp in Montgomery, Alabama. He will be staying there into the foreseeable future on criminal contempt charges for ignoring a steep fine. Seemingly unrepentant, Trudeau continues to post upbeat updates about his new life on his Facebook page.

While Trudeau likes to present himself as a crusader offering new or suppressed products to the public, his critics have other thoughts. "Throughout his career, [the] defendant has been motivated by simple greed and he has funded and protected a lavish lifestyle by bilking consumers and defying court orders," read a sentencing memo from U.S. Attorney Zachary Fardon, United States District Court, Northern District of Illinois, Eastern Division, issued March 17, 2014.

The memo continued: "[The] defendant's misrepresentations in the infomercials were not little fibs—they were bald-faced lies that were at the heart of the [the] defendant's scheme to defraud everyone who was listening ... [the] defendant preys upon the sick who want to be made healthy, the poor who want to become rich, and the insecure who want to feel better about themselves."

The man who earned this derision was born in 1963 and grew up in the Boston area. He has stated that his father was a welder and his mother a housewife. At the age of fifteen, Trudeau attended a meeting of Amway (a multilevel marketing company that sells health and beauty products, jewelry, electronic items, etc.) that changed his life. Inspired by the Amway gathering, Trudeau launched his own mail-order business. He claimed to have earned $1 million in profit before turning eighteen.

Once Trudeau graduated from high school, he started doing regular seminars on topics such as memory improvement. He also earned a criminal record. He first appeared on the police blotter after trying to scam a bank.

"In 1990 [Trudeau] was convicted of seven counts of larceny, after he posed as a doctor, opened a checking account using a false Social Security number, deposited over $80,000 worth of bad checks into the account, and withdrew over $27,000," stated U.S. Attorney Zachary Fardon's March 17, 2014, sentencing memorandum.

Trudeau pled guilty in a Cambridge, Massachusetts, state court. He received a two-year sentence, to be served in federal lockup, but said he served a far shorter time.

One year later, Trudeau "was convicted of credit card fraud in the United States District Court for the District of Massachusetts, after he racked up over $100,000 in fraudulent credit card bills. According to the presentence report, [Trudeau] attempted to pay a $5,000 bribe to get a witness, one of defendant's employees, to recant his statement implicating defendant in the crime," noted U.S. Attorney Zachary Fardon's March 17, 2014, sentencing memorandum.

As an October 23, 2005, story in *The Washington Post* states, "In prison on the West Coast, Trudeau hooked up with a fellow inmate named Jules Leib, who was in for attempted distribution of cocaine. He gave Leib some self-help books. When they got out, they went into business together, making infomercials and selling health products as distributors for an Amway-type multilevel marketing companied called Nutrition for Life."

Nutrition for Life International (NFLI) sold hundreds of goods to distributors, including cookies, nutritional supplements, and shark-cartilage capsules (a quack remedy with supposed medicinal qualities). NFLI was based in

Houston and had been around for a decade when Trudeau and Leib came on board in 1995.

Trudeau quickly became a master recruiter for Nutrition for Life, signing up thousands of new distributors. Most paid $1,000 for products to sell and agreed to purchase an additional $100 a month minimum worth of goods from NFLI. Distributors had to give back a portion of their earnings to Trudeau. They were also encouraged to bring other new distributors into the fold.

The media began taking notice of the rising sales star: "In less than 10 months, Kevin Trudeau and his marketing organization have persuaded some 15,000 people to plunk down more than $1,000 apiece for a highly touted opportunity to sell products," read a *Wall Street Journal* profile published January 19, 1996.

The piece revealed Trudeau's criminal past and underscored how much money he was bringing in. "For the fiscal year ended September 30, [NFLI] reported a ninefold jump in earnings from $2.2 million or 65 cents a share, on sales of $32.3 million. Its stock has soared more than ninefold since July," stated the January 19, 1996 *Wall Street Journal* article.

David Bertrand, the former president of NFLI, became concerned that Trudeau was overselling the company, promising distributors profits far in excess of what they could realistically earn. "We had a number of conferences where we asked him to cool it," Bernard is quoted as saying in the October 23, 2005, *Washington Post* article.

In 1996, the Illinois attorney general accused Trudeau and Leib "of running a pyramid scheme" under the guise of recruiting new NFLI distributors, as the July 29, 2005, Salon story reported. Trudeau and Leib ended up settling for $185,000, paid out to Illinois and seven other states. The pair split up, but Trudeau was just getting started.

After leaving NFLI, Trudeau continued to hawk a variety of products, including systems to improve memory and reading ability, baldness cures, real estate schemes, and more. The television infomercial was his marketing vehicle of choice.

In 1998, Trudeau ran afoul of the FTC. He was accused of making false or unsubstantiated claims in radio and television ads for weight-loss products and supposed remedies for drug, alcohol, and tobacco addiction.

"The FTC filed its first lawsuit against Trudeau in 1998, charging him with making false and misleading claims in infomercials for products he claimed could cause significant weight loss and cure addiction to heroin, alcohol, and cigarettes, and enable users to achieve a photographic memory. A stipulated court order resolving that case barred Trudeau from making false claims for products in the future, ordered him to pay $500,000 on consumer redress, and established a $500,000 performance bond to ensure compliance," stated an FTC press release from October 6, 2008.

This was just the start of years of trouble with federal regulators. The October 6, 2008, FTC press release continued: "In 2003, the Commission charged Trudeau with violating the 1998 order by falsely claiming in infomercials that a product, Coral Calcium Supreme, could cure cancer. The court subsequently entered a preliminary injunction that ordered him not to make such claims."

By this point, Trudeau had become a fierce promoter of supposedly "natural" health products—as opposed to lab-made pharmaceutical drugs. While the latter have been thoroughly tested and evaluated, the contents—much less the benefits—of unregulated "natural health" products are considerably murkier. It is extremely dangerous for seriously-ill patients to replace tested medicines of proven efficaciousness with "natural" remedies of dubious worth.

In September 2004, Trudeau found himself in trouble from the FTC once again for coral calcium. He was ordered to adhere to an FTC consent agreement and fined $2 million. Under the terms of the agreement, Trudeau promised not to participate in, produce, or disseminate any infomercials that advertised products, services, or programs to the public. There was a loophole: Trudeau could tout any books he wrote, as long as he didn't misrepresent their contents.

"By shifting his business model from selling supposed cure-all products to peddling books, which are protected by the First Amendment, Trudeau has been able to slip past federal regulators and continue to sell snake oil to the masses—first through his infomercials and now via mainstream book retailers like Amazon.com and Barnes & Noble," stated the July 29, 2005, feature in Salon.

In 2005, Trudeau wrote and self-published a best-seller called *Natural Cures "They" Don't Want You to Know About*. In July of that year, he paid for a full-page advertisement for the book in *Newsweek* magazine. Needless to say, Trudeau also produced a new infomercial to tout the contents of the book.

In the end, what brought down the infomercial king was a diet book he wrote, called *The Weight Loss Cure "They" Don't Want You to Know About*. Published in 2007, Trudeau's promotional spots promised that his weight-loss program was easy and that people on it could eat what they wanted. As it turned out, these two statements were blatantly false.

"The actual book contains a grueling diet and a labyrinth of often confusing, sometimes contradictory do's and don'ts … [it] requires a lifetime ban on foods that most Americans eat every day. If [the] defendant had described his book accurately in the infomercials, book sales would have been close to zero," noted the March 17, 2014, sentencing memo from U.S. Attorney Fardon.

Skeptical Inquirer investigated the diet protocol outlined in the book and published their findings in in the magazine's April 18, 2014, issue: "You, the dieter, will be doing the treatment for approximately 96 days, then following a maintenance routine. The plan itself is divided into four stages," noted the *Inquirer*.

During a 30-day preparatory phase, dieters are supposed to, among other things, drink a gallon of coral calcium-infused water each day, eat only organic food, get frequent colonic irrigation treatments (that is, enemas), take large amounts of supplements, sprinkle hot peppers and cinnamon on their meals, avoid fast food, carbonated drinks, and cold drinks, and not use a cell phone, television, or prescription drugs.

"And that's just the beginning ... the 45-day second phase is when the real treatment begins," noted the *Skeptical Inquirer*. In phase two, dieters are supposed to get injections of human chorionic gonadotrophin (hCG), a hormone given off by pregnant women in their urine, and restrict themselves to 500 calories a day.

In phase three, dieters are told not to eat anything with starch (no more potatoes, rice, bread, or pasta), fast food, cold drinks, trans fats, and others.

The final phase of the diet calls for more medical procedures—a liver cleanse, a colon cleanse, chelation therapy (a medical regime to remove heavy metals from a patient's body)—and a strict adherence to organic food. "And how long does phase four last? ... The rest of your life," noted the April 18, 2014, *Inquirer*.

The *Skeptical Inquirer* tallied up all the vitamins, supplements, special food items, procedures, and cleanses involved in the diet, and calculated they cost a total of $18,000. After finishing the diet, a maintenance plan involving yoga, pure organic food, infrared sauna treatments, and further supplements cost an addition $1,700 a month.

In addition to being extremely tough and costly, Trudeau's diet plan could also be deadly, given that he instructed followers to stop using pharmaceutical drugs—including insulin and HIV medications.

However, it was the clear misrepresentation of the diet as easy and flexible that got Trudeau into trouble. On November 16, 2007, U.S. District Court judge Robert Gettleman found Trudeau in contempt of court for violating the 2004 injunction, which prohibited him from misrepresenting the content of books he wrote.

The 2004 injunction "contained a narrow exemption for infomercials for books and other publications, but specifically required that Trudeau not misrepresent the content of the books. Judge Gettleman ruled that Trudeau "has misrepresented the contents of his book by stating in his infomercials that his diet protocol was 'easy' and that it allowed dieters to 'eat whatever they want,' and he has misled thousands of consumers," stated a November 21, 2007, press release from the FTC. In further rulings, Trudeau was ordered to pay a penalty of $5.1 million—later increased to $37.6 million.

Despite court orders to pay up, Trudeau wasn't forthcoming with any money. In July 2012, when the FTC moved to hold him in contempt for not paying his $37.6 million fine, Trudeau claimed to be broke—a claim easily disputed, given his lavish lifestyle.

In November 2013, Trudeau was found guilty in federal court of criminal contempt for violating the 2004 injunction on misrepresenting the content of his books. Trudeau was jailed. The pitchman remained defiant, refusing to disclose hidden assets that might have gone toward his multi-million-dollar fine. In a post made to his Facebook page in late 2013, Trudeau compared himself with Jesus, Nelson Mandela, Gandhi, and Cesar Chavez.

Trudeau's "lack of remorse is part of a pattern: he has never shown genuine remorse in his long history of frauds," stated U.S. Attorney Zachary Fardon's March 17, 2014, sentencing memorandum. The same day the sentencing memorandum was released, Trudeau was given a 10-year sentence on the contempt charge.

Further Reading

Dr. Stephen Barrett, "What 'They' Don't Want You to Know: An Analysis of Kevin Trudeau's Natural Cures, *Skeptical Inquirer*, January/February 2006.

Libby Copeland, "Wait, There's More," *The Washington Post*, October 23, 2005.

Christopher Dreher, "What Kevin Trudeau Doesn't Want You to Know," Salon.com, July 29, 2005, http://www.salon.com/2005/07/29/trudeau_4/.

John R. Emshwiller, "Nutrition for Life's Top Recruiter Has a Criminal Past—Despite Convictions, Trudeau Gets New Distributors to Fork Out the Cash," *Wall Street Journal*, January 19, 1996.

Zachary T. Fardon, United States Attorney, April M. Perry, Assistant United States Attorney, Marc Krickbaum, Assistant United States Attorney, "Government's Sentencing Memorandum," United States District Court, Northern District of Illinois, Eastern Division, March 17, 2014.

Federal Trade Commission, "Federal Court Finds Kevin Trudeau in Civil Contempt," November 21, 2007.

Federal Trade Commission, "Kevin Trudeau Banned from Infomercials for Three Years, Ordered to Pay More Than $5 Million for False Claims About Weight-Loss Book," October 6, 2008.

MyFox 8.com, "TV Infomercial Star Kevin Trudeau Gets 10 Years in Prison," March 17, 2014, http://myfox8.com/2014/03/17/kevin-trudeau-sent-to-prison/.

Carrie Poppy, "Kevin Trudeau's $18,000 Weight Loss Plan: A Book Review," *Skeptical Inquirer*, April 18, 2014.

Kevin Trudeau, Facebook postings, May 3, 28, 29, 2014, https://www.facebook.com/pages/Kevin-Trudeau/106186792746742?fref=ts#.

HARRY HOUDINI, GHOST BUSTER

Harry Houdini was a brilliant magician and escape artist, who amazed early twentieth-century audiences with series of elaborate stunts. Whether it was handcuffs, a straitjacket, a locked trunk, a milk jug, or a jail cell, Houdini proved able to escape them all. No chains could hold him or locks contain him. His talents made him a rich, much-admired figure on the vaudeville circuit.

What is less known is that Houdini also had a second career as a "ghost buster" and scourge of Spiritualists.

At the time, the Spiritualist movement was hugely popular in certain circles (the entry on the Fox Sisters in the "Para-Abnormal" chapter offers further details on Spiritualism). The basic notion was that some people possessed psychic powers that enabled them to communicate with the spirits of the dead. Typically, this communication was done by a so-called medium during a séance—a gathering, usually in the dark, during which a medium conjured up spirits on command for amazed guests. Séance attendees were often treated to a wide spectrum of visual and auditory effects, from ghostly trumpets floating across the room, to spectral apparitions (supposedly the returning spirits of loved ones), eerie voices, rapping and clanking sounds, music seemingly from nowhere, and other uncanny sights and sounds.

It has been suggested that Houdini became interested in Spiritualism following the death of his beloved mother, Cecilia, in 1913. Spiritualism had been around since the Victorian era but got a huge boost in popularity thanks to the First World War, which broke out a year after Houdini's mother passed away. Between 1914 and 1918, millions of young men were killed in terrible battles. Devastated parents turned to Spiritualism as a way of assuaging their guilt and communicating with their beloved sons.

Into this milieu, Houdini plunged. He might have initially hoped he could find a way to speak to his mother. What he found, however, was trickery and sleight of hand. Mediums were using stage magic to summon spirits and take money from gullible people. Houdini was outraged.

"My business has given me an intimate knowledge of stage illusions, together with many years of experience among show people of all types. My familiarity with the former and what I have learned of the psychology of the latter, has placed me at a certain advantage in uncovering the natural explanation of feats that to the ignorant, have seemed supernatural," wrote Houdini in a book called *Miracle Mongers and their Methods*, published in 1920.

At the time, Houdini was friends with Sir Arthur Conan Doyle, the hugely popular author of the Sherlock Holmes detective stories. Although these tales "celebrated the triumph of reason and logic over superstition and magical thinking" the same couldn't be said of their creator, as noted an article in the January 18, 2011, edition of *Scientific American* magazine. Doyle was a firm believer in the Spiritualist movement who regularly took part in séances to communicate with his son, Kingsley, who had been killed during the First World War.

Houdini and Doyle eventually had a falling out. When Doyle visited Houdini in New York City in spring 1922, the magician demonstrated how common Spiritualist practices such as "slate writing" (in which spirits allegedly wrote messages in chalk or white ink on a slate) were simply tricks of stagecraft. Doyle refused to believe Houdini's explanations and insisted that his friend possessed true psychic powers. This incident marked the end of the friendship between the two men.

Houdini continued his research into the Spiritualist world. He attended séances and observed mediums in action. Houdini continued to regularly do escape tricks on stage but now incorporated an expose of Spiritualism into his performances.

On November 25, 1925, *Liberty* magazine (then a hugely popular periodical) published an article written by Houdini entitled, "Inside the Icons: Tricks of Fake Mediums." In this piece, Houdini methodically deconstructed the séance experience to demonstrate that it was nothing more than a magic show that people took for real.

First off, Houdini pointed out that séances were almost always done in the dark—all the better to conceal trickery and heighten the spooky atmosphere—in a location chosen by the medium. Sometimes, the medium had confederates daubed in luminous paint enter the room or put their hands through the window, to give the appearance of visiting ghosts. Other assistants, dressed entirely in black, would secretly enter the séance room to make noises and wave trumpets or rods coated in glow-in-the-dark paint.

Prior to the start of many séances, the medium would ask guests to join hands. During the ensuing darkness, the medium would work to get one or both hands free, without the guests noticing. This allowed the medium to make all sorts of ruckus with ringing bells, blocks of wood, and other props.

Another popular séance trick involved the sudden appearance of a ghostly bird, who seemed to flutter around the room and brush up against startled guests. This was accomplished by having a confederate throw a feathered object on a string into the room, then pull it about. Another stunt involved levitation. The medium would announce that one of the séance guests would be lifted to the ceiling. A confederate would tilt one of the guest's chairs back and lift it a few inches off the ground with hand and foot. Then, the confederate would slap their free hand against the head of the sitter, who was convinced their cranium had come in contact with the ceiling.

The medium kept up a steady monologue during the séance, which distracted guests and intensified the ambiance. Often, the medium changed voices and would talk like a young child, supposedly channeling the youthful spirit voice of someone decreased.

"'Patter' is as necessary to a fake medium as it is to any charlatan. Hence, the solemn prayer, the working on the other's emotions with talk of the 'clean young soul' [of the deceased] and exhortations to the sitters," wrote Houdini in *Liberty* magazine.

"Of course, so long as mediums insist on working in darkness or semi-obscurity, adequate investigations will be almost impossible. In the dimness, it is easy for the spirit-invoker to lift a table by means of a piece of steel projecting from his sleeve or with a steel hook hidden in his vest," added Houdini.

Other tricks: mediums often put luminous-headed tacks in their shoes. No one would notice these tacks while the lights were on. When the séance room became dark, however, the tacks would glow. The medium simply moved their feet about, to simulate "spirit lights". When the medium had had enough, they would put their feet back under the table. Once the lights went on, no one would be the wiser. Other mediums secured blocks of wood beneath their dresses or pants. When the lights dimmed, the medium clapped these blocks together, to make it appear the dead were trying to communicate through a series of rapping sounds.

Of course, special effects were just part of the medium's arsenal of tricks. If a medium or Spiritualist came into a town they weren't familiar with to do a séance, they engaged in extensive research, explained Houdini. They might visit the local graveyard to take down people's names and the dates of their deaths and births. Or they might scan the local newspaper for details on births, dates, weddings, children, funerals, etc. The medium would cite bits of this information during the séance, to the amazement of attendees.

In February and May 1926, Houdini testified before Senate and House sub-committees about the dangers posed by fake mediums. On a professional level, Houdini—like all true magicians—was outraged to see simple magic tricks being fobbed off as evidence of psychic or spiritual power. On a personal level, he found it obscene to take money from gullible people by tapping into their emotions. "Fake mediums prey upon the unfortunate and the bereaved, taking their money, duping them with lies and often driving them to insanity," wrote Houdini, in *Liberty* magazine.

Unfortunately, Houdini's medium-busting crusade ended abruptly, on Halloween in 1926. A few days prior, Houdini had been visited by some college students in his dressing room. One of them asked if it was true that Houdini could withstand any blow to his stomach, no matter how hard. When Houdini indicated that yes, he could, the student punched him the in the gut. Houdini doubled over in pain. When Houdini recovered, he said the gut-punch stunt only worked when he was ready for the blow. To demonstrate, Houdini asked the student to hit him again. Only this time, Houdini properly flexed his stomach muscles first. The student struck a second time, and it was like hitting a brick wall.

Unfortunately, the first blow led to a burst appendix. Despite running a high temperature, Houdini insisted on continuing with some shows he had booked. He eventually collapsed, succumbing to the unexpected injury on All Hallow's Eve.

Many of Houdini's stage tricks and escapes still confound. How he pulled off some of his legendary stunts remains a mystery. On the other hand, Houdini also left behind a legacy of skepticism and rational investigation into the occult.

"Houdini's principle states that just because something is unexplained, this does not mean that it is paranormal, supernatural, extraterrestrial, or conspiratorial. Before you say something is out of this world, first make sure that it is not in this world, for science is grounded in naturalism, not supernaturalism, paranormalism, or any other unnecessarily complicated explanations," noted the January 18, 2011, issue of *Scientific American* magazine.

Further Reading

Harry Houdini, *A Magician Among the Spirits*, 1924.

Harry Houdini, "Inside the Icons: Tricks of Fake Mediums," *Liberty Magazine*, November 25, 1925.

Harry Houdini, *Miracle Mongers and Their Methods*, 1920.

Daniel Loxton, "Dark Secrets of the Oracle Monger," *Skeptic*, Volume 17, Number 4, 2012.

PBS.org, "Timeline of Houdini's Life," http://www.pbs.org/wgbh/amex/houdini/timeline/index.html.

Michael Shermer, "Houdini's Skeptical Advice: Just Because Something's Unexplained Doesn't Mean It's Supernatural," *Scientific American*, January 18, 2011.

SECTION ELEVEN

INTERVIEWS

INTERVIEW WITH ALAN ABEL

Alan Abel is a notorious hoaxer. His bizarre hoaxes—always presented with a straight face—include lobby groups such as The Society for Indecency to Naked Animals (SINA, whose motto was "a nude horse is a rude horse") and Citizens against Breastfeeding. He's also promoted a company called Euthanasia Cruises Ltd. (in which passengers enjoy cruise-ship luxury, then jump overboard to end their lives), a national "fat tax," and a symphony made up of Ku Klux Klan members (to mock the political aspirations of former Klansman David Duke). Abel faked his own death so believably, the New York Times ran his obituary—and then printed an unprecedented retraction when Abel revealed he was still very alive. Another Abel stunt, "Omar's School for Beggars," was taken seriously by the media, who ran bemused accounts of lectures on professional panhandling.

Abel created a fake presidential campaign around one "Yetta Bronstein," a Jewish mother running for president under the slogan, "Things will get betta with Yetta." He also once held a press conference in which he claimed he would reveal the erased minutes of the Watergate tapes. When the press conference took place, Abel acted appropriately shocked upon discovering his own tape has been erased too.

Abel's life was recounted in an award-winning documentary, Abel Raises Cain, which featured clips of some of his greatest hits. The documentary was made by Abel's daughter, Jenny Abel, and her partner, Jeff Hockett.

Abel currently lives with his wife in Connecticut, plotting new stunts in the Internet era.

(E-mail interview April 25, 2015, and phone interview April 30, 2015.)

I had a chance to see the documentary, *Abel Raises Cain*. What did you think of it?

It was a magnificent embarrassment. [My daughter] Jennifer did it. She and [her partner] Jeff, put it together.

One of the newspaper headlines in the movie described you as "the world's greatest hoaxer." What's your take? Do you consider yourself the world's greatest hoaxer?

No, no. I don't consider myself the greatest per se of anything. That's a bit too much vanity. I certainly like to think I have done a lot of hoaxes, probably more than many of the other so-called professional media pranksters … it's amazing to me when I look down to see all the different [hoaxes I've done] over the years. How did I ever get away with this? Nowadays, I'd probably be behind bars and incarcerated. Nowadays, everyone's so sensitive and litigious, suing everyone in sight. It's a whole different ball game these days, but I do have one hoax going on about banning bird watching, because I say bird watchers are voyeurs, interfering with the bird's right to consummate their [relationships in private]. They're defenseless little birds and they can't fight back. And we should stop it. In America, there's supposed to be 38 million people watching birds all the time. So I had that campaign going on. That hasn't been discovered as of yet or exposed.

Smoking Gun, Snopes.com, Slate.com—these Internet outfits go around spying and revealing the hoax … I have a series of blogs, called questionable commentaries, I'm up to 82 right now. Probably do another 20 or so and see what happens. It's a commentary on injustice and all these scams that I discovered … like that one where someone says they're stranded overseas, you've got to send money. So, I played with them. I sent two dollars through Western Union for them. Then I notify Interpol that they should set up a sting operation when the guy comes to Western Union for his money. He'll find the two dollars and handcuffs.

I enjoy playing with those things. Even the telemarketers who call. We used to have someone call, said I had free dancing lessons with the Arthur Murray Studio. I claimed I only had one leg. They apologized profusely. "What about pole dancing?" They hung up on that one. I'm off their list now.

What year were you born?
According to Wikipedia, I was born in 1930, August 2. But actually I was born in 1924, but I like the extra six years because it makes me a bit younger.

You've worked as a drummer. Any regrets you didn't become a full-time musician instead of doing hoaxes?
I could have [been a full-time musician]. I did sub at Radio City Music Hall and the Roxy Theatre Orchestra. Especially in the 1960s. They had big orchestras. Lew Walters, Latin Quarter. Lester Lanin. I did all that work and a lot of recordings. I could have stayed in the music industry. I avoided that, because I had already done that. I had already played. When I was in service [in World War II] I was with a group called Winged Victory … I spent almost two years touring the country with that group. It was an all-soldier cast. We had members who became famous later on, Karl Malden, the actor. John Forsyth, who was in *Dynasty*. They were in the company. Mario Lanza, the opera singer.

It was quite an experience for me. It whet my appetite to stay in show business if I could. I found pulling off a hoax was a means for getting on stage without auditioning.

[Doing hoaxes] was resourceful and fun. I was making a point. I tried to do satire almost all the time. The underlying theme [in my hoaxes] always had to be amusing. Nothing physical or criminal that would put me in jail or in trouble financially.

What do you make of people who take hoaxes very seriously—like the men landing on the moon was a hoax or the Protocols of the Elders of Zion hoax?

We're all very gullible. If someone was able to prove that it was a hoax—the landing on the moon—it was just a set-up by a movie studio, I would laugh and say, "Hey, good job. Nice going." That's it.

It's like the Loch Ness Monster. I was going to discover the Loch Ness Monster, but my backer at the time, which is going back into the mid-1970s, was Max Sackheim. He founded the Book of the Month club and made millions of dollars. And I met him accidentally on a subway train in New York. We had lunch. He said he was retiring the next day and had never ridden a subway until that day. And I thought, "My God. Here's a man in his late 70s. In the subway just one hour because his wife says you got to ride it once before you retire, and on that train, on that day, in the twelfth car, everybody standing up, there I was." And we became friends for a few years. He sent money when I needed it to stage a larger stunt.

But the Loch Ness Monster hoax never got off the ground, because he passed away. We had already got to the stage of building [a fake monster]. It was like a giant toy. We were going to secretly land it in Loch Ness in Scotland and then fly around in a helicopter and discover it, then put it on a flatbed truck and drive to the British Museum with a lot of fanfare … we never got off the ground. We got the monster built in three sections. It was a great-looking monster. I think there's one shot of it in the documentary. But [the hoax] was never fulfilled.

I've had that happen when I was trying to land an alien. I advertised for, and along with Robert Downey Sr.—Robert Downey Jr.'s father—we found a guy who seemed to be from another planet. And we asked him if he would appear an alien, just to see what would happen.

We painted him phosphorescent and had him on a beach opposite Asbury Park, New Jersey. People in a bar called the sheriff and the police when they saw this guy glowing in moonlight and babbling what seemed to be a foreign language. We had taught him a language that was pig Latin, and part Hebrew, and part Farsi. A mixture of all these languages. And the sheriff, two of them in a police car drove up on the boardwalk with a search light, and Bob Downey Sr. and I were under the boardwalk with a camera crew, filming all of this. Our alien standing there glowing in a pit that had been dug to resemble a spaceship that had taken off and dumped him. He had bruises on himself. Two fishermen ran into their trailer, locked the door, and turned out the lights. Because we had set up a weather balloon with a pencil light on it, a flashlight. Then we had a soundtrack of the *Twilight Zone*, Rod Serling's show, the music playing. And we set up this eight-foot weather balloon. It looked like a spaceship, filled with hydrogen. The sheriff puts his searchlight onto the guy glowing in the dark at midnight. There are all these people lining the boardwalk. We could hear [the sheriff] say, "Ah, it's probably just some drunken fairy." They got in their police cars and drove off and ignored it. We had all that on film, Bob Downey Sr. and I. We got together last August, I think it was, and had a dinner in New York for the first time in a few years. He was still laughing over how crazy that was.

What year was that, that you did that?
We did that in the early '80s. Probably '83, '84.

Do you think Omar the Beggar is your most celebrated hoax?
I think that, that was one of the big ones, along with clothing naked animals. The Society for Indecency to Naked Animals ran from 1955 until 1963. So about eight years, until *TIME* magazine finally brought down the curtain. But Omar the Beggar, there's a feature article in *New Times* magazine by this reporter from the *New York Times* … he did a full feature on Omar the Beggar's school of begging and came to one of my classes, where I had all these actor friends posing as beggars. This reporter sat there and took notes. Even after many years, I saw him on the street, he said he still believed I was teaching begging to people, that I did that for a living. He just couldn't overcome that seriousness of it.

How do you keep a straight face during these pranks?
That is the most difficult. I remember an interview I did [for the hoax on banning breast feeding], with radio station CHUM in Toronto, and gosh, there were so many people calling in who were outraged. Just absolutely outraged. I claimed that breast feeding was something women got off with … and oh, my goodness [listeners] went crazy. Absolutely mad. Fortunately, I was on the phone. I wasn't anywhere near where they could find me. Because they would absolutely chop me up into little pieces.

Do you consider yourself an anarchist? Is the purpose of the hoaxes to create mayhem?
At times, I guess so … my wife and I did a documentary on Watergate called *The Faking of the President*. We had our world premiere in Salt Lake City in

1976. There were 400 Mormons in the theatre who objected to the license we took in showing this fellow who looked like Richard Nixon stealing gasoline from Ted Kennedy's car, putting it in his own, stealing flowers [to put on his pet dog] Checkers' grave … doing all these nefarious activities. We had a really great Nixon lookalike. [Mayhem] erupted in the theatre.

I was across the street in a restaurant having dinner. Suddenly, 20 minutes into the documentary, these people came running out of the theatre. It was incredible … the people rioted. I'm sitting there having dinner on a Sunday night in Salt Lake City. These people had seen an advance screening of *The Faking of the President* … it was, like, 1976. Just soon after Nixon left office. And [the audience] didn't like anyone making fun or kicking when a guy was down. They rioted. They were breaking up the glass cases with the posters … turned the manager's car over. He had a sign on top. They destroyed that. One guy had a pipe wrench in his hand. They were looking for trouble. They closed down the theatre. It was an old-fashioned theatre with a stand-up box office. Special screening for the premiere. Then I heard the sirens, and the police came.

One of the sheriffs came over to me—this is about 9 o'clock Sunday night. Said, "We have serious concerns about your safety; we have to get you out of Salt Lake City." But the airport, no planes were going out. I know; I checked. "No, no. We have a friend with a plane, and he's waiting there for us. He'll fly you to Reno, and you can get out of Reno and go back to New York." I get into the sheriff car, on way to airport, and the plane belonged to John Wayne. He was standing there at the door of this private plane and waiting for me. They're going to Reno to gamble overnight. I sat next to him for 40 minutes during the plane ride, and he was laughing, with tears coming down his face, because I had told him what had happened with the movie. He had made like 300 movies and never, ever had anything [like this] happen. He couldn't stop laughing. So I got saved by John Wayne.

You had mentioned in the movie and e-mail, Universal was trying to do a movie about your life at one point?

Oh, yes. When I went out to the meetings in Hollywood and I went up the elevator on the first or second day. I was supposed to meet my lawyer. [The studio] lawyers were in the elevator, two of them, not aware I was there. One of them said, "Why don't we terminate these negotiations, because we don't want to spend any money for this property. We can wait until this guy dies and get the rights for peanuts." I heard that, and thought, "Oh, yeah? We'll see." So I never even got off the elevator. I stayed on. Went back down, checked out of the hotel. Went home. And I called my lawyer and told him and said, "Forget it. These guys are playing hardball." He said "Yeah. Agreed."

Then I came up with the idea of passing away. I got eight [column] inches the *New York Times*, two inches more than the guy who invented the six-pack, who died on the same day. I thought dying was a very good idea, to see what would happen. And of course, I was 100 percent wrong. The people I thought would care the most, cared the least, and vice-versa. There was an aunt in Indianapolis who rented a Ryder truck and drove all the way to Connecticut. At the time we lived in Westport, and she drove the truck up there. I had a guard in the house. And she claimed she was there to get all the furniture I always promised her. She couldn't get in the house. And she's still angry to this day. She's mad, thinking I played that joke just to embarrass her. She sent me the bill for the truck rental. I didn't pay that. People are crazy. There's a lot of madness out there. That's why Prozac is very popular.

What is your opinion of recent high-profile hoaxes you weren't involved in? Such as actor Joaquin Phoenix pretending to ditch his film career to become a spaced-out rapper?
I am not terribly impressed by the so called "celebrity hoaxes." They are all highly funded and obvious pranks.

Do you consider what you do "allegorical satire"? That was one of the terms used in the documentary.
Yes. I'm trying to do that. For example, with the Society for Indecency to Animals, my intent was to protest censorship of any kind. And that message was never seen. Even by esteemed reporters. Walter Cronkite, he did seven minutes on the CBS evening news talking about the campaign to clothe naked animals. My partner, Buck Henry, who was posing as G. Clifford Prout, president of SINA, was playing his ukulele and singing the SINA marching song.

Walter was so angry when he found out later that the guy doing the ukulele was a writer for the Gary Moore show, [which] was popular in the 1950s and 1960s. In fact, Walter, until he went to his grave, he carried that chip on his shoulder, according to a friend of a friend of Buck Henry. He had dinner with Buck Henry. [The friend said], "Walter is still angry at you. It's been years since you did that. He's not mad at Hitler or Mussolini. He's angry at you and this guy—Abel, his partner, because you fooled him."

Then a friend of mine in advertising tried to get a copy of that seven-minute segment on the evening news. All of the old tapes for CBS are stored in a warehouse in New Jersey. He got a friend to go over there, had permission to make a copy. They took the tape from that broadcast. There was one seven-minute segment that had been erased. That was when Buck was there, with his ukulele and singing. Someone had taken it out of the master tape.

Similar to you claiming to have the 18-minute gap of the Watergate tape.
Right, right. Where I pretended to find it. Mine had been erased too.

One thing that came up in the movie … It was said you were poking fun at something on the surface but underneath, there was real meaning [to the hoax]. Would you say that's for all of your hoaxes? Have you ever done a hoax just for the sake of a joke?

Well, not really. I don't think so. I never just liked to do it for fun or for somebody else, let's go pour cement on this guy. I don't do anything that crosses that line into what could be considered criminal or just so frivolous that it really annoys people.

Are you concerned at all with the public's gullibility?

The public continues to be gullible, and the Internet fuels far too many scams and hoaxes that are designed to defraud, rather than amuse.

Has the Internet been a boon or a hindrance for doing hoaxes?

It's like setting up a business in a foreign country. You have to suddenly become aware of the customs, the way they do business, and so on. Same with the Internet. There are people I know who claim they make 99 percent of their income on the Internet. I marvel at that, that they could earn a living just on the Internet. But for me, for my trade, quote unquote, it's difficult because you risk immediate disclosure. There's always someone there, a whistle-blower or a party pooper, that's ready to say, "I know you're pulling my leg." Discovery can be made in a matter of 2.1 seconds.

Are you planning on new hoaxes?

I am always planning, so to speak. I would like to plan something. Right now, what I'd really like to do, unload all my memorabilia. I'm looking to my left here, to what I call the box room, an empty bedroom with 100 storage boxes all stacked up. It's got all my memorabilia. And there's not room to turn around or do anything, because it's all boxes. I've got my letters, tapes, and photographs. Over 2,000 audio and videotapes and films on 16 mm and 35 mm. And it's a valuable collection. My alma mater would like me just donate it to the college. They would have a special collection in their library there just for my memorabilia. The collections curator called me once a few years ago, and said, "You can get a tax write-off." And I said, "What's that? I don't even know what this [is]."

Do you have a single hoax you're the most proud of?

Uh, I suppose the animal campaign and Omar the Beggar. And Citizens against Breast Feeding—saying it was ludicrous and incestuous to drink milk out of the breast. Mothers should pump it out. How do you explain to your three- or four-year-old child who comes into his mother's bedroom and sees his daddy still breast feeding? How do you ever explain that?

How do you want people to remember you?
I have three words on my tombstone: I had fun.

INTERVIEW WITH DR. STEPHEN BARRETT

Dr. Stephen Barrett has been battling quackery—that is, medical fraud—for decades. On the website Quackwatch, Dr. Barrett says his interest in the subject "began by accident ... during the mid-1960s I read two books that irritated me greatly. One was about the government's struggle to clean up the patent medicine fraud ... the other described how chiropractors had achieved legal recognition even though the theory behind their work was nonsense. When I voiced my concern to my local medical society president, he suggested that I organize a committee focused on quackery."

The result was the launch of an organization called the Lehigh Valley Committee Against Health Fraud in Allenton, Pennsylvania, in 1969. The Committee was the forerunner of Quackwatch, which Dr. Barrett launched in December 1996. The Quackwatch site contains voluminous essays and reports by Dr. Barrett and other writers, warning about medical scams. Quackwatch has expanded to include sister sites of a similar bent, focused on specific ailments.

A psychiatrist by profession, Dr. Barrett has written over 50 books and countless articles. He has appeared on Dateline, The Today Show, Good Morning America, *and* Donahue, *among other radio and television programs.*

While Dr. Barrett is no longer formally involved with Quackwatch, he remains an energetic foe of health quackery. He is currently retired and living in Chapel Hill, North Carolina.

(E-mail interviews March 29, 2015, and May 11, 2015.)

What is your current relationship with Quackwatch and all the additional websites that go with it? Do you still post regular updates?
Quackwatch is no longer a formal organization. It is an informal network of people who are interested in fighting or learning about health frauds and quackery.

In the mid-1980s you experienced a "Babe Ruth" moment, as you called it, when you submitted hair samples from two healthy girls to a series of labs that claimed they could determine a person's nutritional requirements by studying their hair. Can you tell me more about this incident?
Baseball lore has it that Babe Ruth pointed to the stands before he hit a certain home run. In 1983, when applying for a grant to cover the cost of an under-cover investigation of hair analysis laboratories, I predicted that the results would be sufficiently important that they would be published in an article in the *Journal of the American Medical Association* and would be reported as the lead item in the AMA's weekly press packet. That's exactly what happened. The

outcome of my study was reported in thousands of press outlets. During the next month I appeared twice on national television and was bombarded with questions from reporters.

In your opinion, who is the more dangerous quack: the overt con artist promoting an obviously ineffective treatment or service ("Heal cancer with magnetic therapy!") or the semi-respectable quack, such as the dentist who rails about the dangers of mercury fillings but otherwise provides mainstream dental services?

Danger can be quantified as the severity of harm, the number of people victimized, or both. The danger to specific individuals depends on how sick they are and how important it is for them to get effective treatment. There's also the danger of false beliefs and their cumulative danger to our society. Anti-vaccination and anti-fluoridation probably cause the greatest amount of aggregate harm.

You've spent decades fighting quackery. Do you get frustrated by the durability of certain medical falsehoods (such as the need for "colonic irrigation" to "detoxify" the body, or the notion that sharks can't get cancer, therefore consuming shark cartilage will make you cancer-immune)?

Of course. James Harvey Young, a leading medical historian, once said "Quacks never sleep." In order to prevent "burnout," it is necessary to understand that quackery will never disappear. Fighting quackery is somewhat analogous to the process of trash pickup. Trucks are needed to keep it from piling up too high. But there will always be trash.

We're seeing a lot of misinformation today about vaccines "causing" autism and other maladies. Does it frustrate you how the public seems more willing to listen to celebrities rather than informed doctors?

People tend to believe what they hear the most. Celebrities cause much trouble because they can reach large audiences. The primary goal of people who hold power in the media is to build audience share in order to increase advertising revenue. Most consider education less important. There's also the Internet, where messages can be spread very inexpensively.

How long have you been involved with the Committee for Skeptical Inquiry?

Since it began. The initial targets included astrology, UFOs, and other paranormal subjects. Involvement with health-related matters began much later and was probably accelerated by a talk I gave at a CSICOP meeting during the mid-1980s. During the talk, I asked the audience of hundreds of skeptics how many had been victimized by quackery. Almost nobody. Then I asked how many of them took vitamins. About 95% raised their hands. After determining what they took, I reviewed why nearly all of them were wasting money and said that the percentage of supplement victims was the highest of any audience I had ever met. One man made a classic comment, something like, "Wow. I'm a skeptic but I never considered questioning what I had heard about vitamins." I believe CSICOP's leads were startled by what they saw.

Some media accounts suggest skepticism is on the rise, as the public moves away from traditional religion. What are your thoughts? Are we becoming a more skeptical society?
False beliefs are rampant. I can't measure the trend.

What's the biggest danger associated with Chelation Therapy [a medical procedure that allegedly removes heavy metals from the body]?
Probably that the doctors who administer it are unlikely to help patients with what they actually need. Chelationists are also involved in spreading fear of vaccination.

I understand you've written over 50 books. Which book do you think has had the most impact, in terms of fighting quackery? Are you writing any new books?
Probably my college textbook (*Consumer Health: A Guide to Intelligent Decisions*). I'd like to write more books but have focused more on the Internet because it can reach a much wider audience.

In 1993, you inactivated your Pennsylvania medical license, to investigate and write about quackery full-time. What propelled you to take such a drastic step?
It wasn't drastic. During the previous 30 years, I gradually increased my journalistic activities and decreased my psychiatric activities. By age 60, I could afford to "retire" and did so.

What is the most dangerous "quack" treatment or service in common use today in the United States?
Cancer quackery that lures patients away from treatments that can cure them.

Quackwatch contains an article on "How to spot a 'Quacky' website." Do you make a distinction between a genuine quack site and, say, a yoga studio whose website might contain flowery descriptions of their services and photos of rainbows but doesn't make false medical claims?
I recommend learning how to spot misinformation and not relying on anyone who spreads it. Yoga can provide useful exercise, but the associated theories should be ignored.

In your article, "How Quackery Sells," on Quackwatch, you state, "another slick way for quackery to attract customers is the invented disease." Are there any modern-day "invented diseases" you are focused on?
An article on Quackwatch called "Index of Fad Diagnoses" contains a list:

> Candidiasis hypersensitivity ("yeast allergy")
> Cavitational osteopathosis: Also called neuralgia-inducing cavitational osteone-
>   crosis (NICO)
> Electrical hypersensitivity (also called electromagnetic hypersensitivity)
> Enzyme deficiency (generalized)
> Gulf War syndrome
> Leaky gut syndrome
> Mercury efflux disorder
> Morgellon's disease
> Multiple chemical sensitivity
> Reward Deficiency Syndrome (RDS)
> Sick building syndrome
> Vertebral subluxation complex
> Wilson's syndrome

The article also notes that there are also real diseases that are systematically over-diagnosed.

You sent me an article on chiropractic therapy that distinguishes between "straight" chiropractors, who focus on spinal manipulation, and those who embrace the notion of "subluxations" and other esoteric subjects. What's your take? Is chiropractic therapy a legitimate medical service when it focuses on fixing spines?
Spinal manipulation may be useful for appropriately selected patients with acute back pain, but most chiropractors offer inappropriate services in addition to or instead of appropriate ones.

In your opinion, has the Internet made the public more skeptical or more gullible when it comes to quackery?
Probably lots of each. On balance, I don't think anyone knows.

How do you combat the notion that organic food/natural herbal medicine = good, while processed food/pharmaceutical drugs = evil?
No specific way. I just publish the best information I can.

There seems to be a common misperception that the notion "everyone has the right to an opinion" is tantamount to "every opinion is equally valid." How do you combat this basic misunderstanding?

I liken people who say that to ships without rudders. I think that most people who say that are unlikely to acquire a rudder unless they experience a harmful event that shocks them into reality.

The article "How Quackery Harms Cancer Patients," on Quackwatch, points to two harms that most people wouldn't think of: misplaced trust (quack enthusiasts decide all "mainstream" medicine is a lie and government is all corrupt) and conversion to deviance (cancer patients or their family break the law by smuggling illegal drugs over the border for treatment). Are there any other, non-obvious, harms caused by quackery?

Passage of laws that make it difficult to remove incompetent practitioners and useless dietary supplements and herbs from the marketplace.

Some doctors connected to Columbia University are petitioning their school to remove TV celebrity doctor Mehmet Oz (aka "Dr. Oz") from his faculty position at this Ivy League School. What's your take?

A good idea, because his media behavior has been disgraceful. School officials claim that under the principle of academic freedom they should not intervene. However, I don't believe academic freedom should be applied to commercial speech.

You have written critically about dietary supplements and weight-loss herbs, comparing them to patent medicines from decades past. In your opinion, what is the best way to deal with the dietary supplement/herbal industry? Should the FDA criminally prosecute makers and promoters of such goods, or would you prefer to see a class-action lawsuit against makers and promoters?

I believe that the FDA should conduct enough criminal prosecutions (without warning letters) to make sellers afraid that making false claims could send them to jail. To achieve such an effect, it would need to figure out which actions would have the greatest impact on the marketplace. I have been unable to detect any evidence of such strategic thinking in choosing who should get regulatory attention.

INTERVIEW WITH DEAN JOBB

The book Empire of Deception *examines the life of con man extraordinaire Leo Koretz. A crooked Chicago lawyer, Koretz swindled millions from investors who believed his wild tales of timber operations and oil fields in Panama. Koretz mastered the same "robbing Peter to pay Paul" scheme used by his contemporary, Charles Ponzi. Oddly, Koretz has been largely forgotten, while Ponzi's name has become synonymous with financial skullduggery.*

Author Dean Jobb is a journalism professor at University of King's College in Nova Scotia, Canada. Empire of Deception *is the first book devoted to the enigma who was Leo Koretz.*

(Phone interview June 23, 2015.)

Had you heard of Leo Koretz before you started writing this book?

I had not. Years ago, by chance, I stumbled on a reference to him being arrested in Halifax in 1924. I was doing other research at the provincial archives in Halifax and found this reference and was intrigued. I did some research, checked to see what I could find. I discovered there were no books on him. He had been in a few anthologies of con men and prominent criminals but really had been forgotten. So it was really lucky to find this, what turned out to be this incredible story of this fellow who out-Ponzi'ed Charles Ponzi.

Why is it that we remember Charles Ponzi but not Leo Koretz?

Leo is a victim of his own success. By the time Charles Ponzi was exposed in 1920, Leo had been running some form of Ponzi scheme for 15 years and had really mastered it. Charles Ponzi's scheme in Boston lasted about nine months. Leo was so slick and so good that when Charles Ponzi's name got into the news, Leo's investors started jokingly calling him "our Ponzi"—teasing him about being such a great financial wizard.

So, in effect, the first guy caught, Charles Ponzi, becomes notorious. Once this rob-Peter-to-pay-Paul scheme [is established] and people are casting around for a name [for the scam], he seems to be the likely candidate. But if you can cheat a cheater … Leo Koretz got cheated out of the infamy of calling it a "Koretz scheme."

Some people suggest that anyone who fell for the Bayano River Syndicate and bought shares had really no one to blame but themselves for being swindled, for being so foolish about the whole endeavor. What are your thoughts?

There's two sides to every con. One is the skill of the conman, essentially, to sell trust. Leo was extremely sincere. He was a wonderful actor. He was generous to a fault—generous with other people's money. He played the part of a millionaire oil baron. He made his investors feel special. He made them feel he was doing them a favor by allowing them to invest. That was very seductive to investors.

We're talking about the 1920s. It's an era when the stock market is booming, heading towards the crash of 1929. You could sell Florida land. You could sell minute stakes in California oil wells. People were always looking for a big score and easy money. Not so much different from any era in history. But Leo did have timing on his side. All by way of saying, some blame does have to fall on the victims. For whatever reason, they fall for the con man. They do have to take some responsibility and say, "Was the investment too good to be true?" The idea that no one bothered to even see if Panama produced oil, even as Leo touted his massive syndicate and its huge oil holdings and production in Panama.

The red flags should have been the returns. He had been paying fairly modest returns for years. But when he claimed to strike oil, he started paying 5 percent a month or 60 percent a year. These were astronomical returns that should have made anyone dubious. But at the time they didn't raise eyebrows. So there is some gullibility, certainly, and greed by investors, but it's really a two-way street, because the con man preys on that, and unless he's good at preying on that and building trust, the investors won't be taken in.

When you look at people like Bernie Madoff, do you think we've learned anything from past examples like Leo Koretz?
Ponzi schemes persist today. One estimate I've seen by an academic, is something like $35 billion a year is lost in Ponzi schemes. They're huge overseas in India and Southeast Asia. Hardly a day goes by in the States or Canada that a Ponzi scheme isn't in the news or someone hasn't been exposed or is going to jail. People are continuing to fall for these schemes. I think it really is a testament that people are seduced by the idea of the inside track or hot tip. That they do believe there are people like Bernie Madoff, or Leo Koretz, or a Charles Ponzi out there, who have the edge or the secret, people who can beat the market or have the sure-fire route to easy money. It is amazing that people to this day are seduced by that. Not recognizing that stocks go up and down, returns will vary. And really, there is no quick route to riches. Investing is a long-term proposition.

Were a movie to be made, who would you like to play Leo?
I've thought of Kevin Spacey. Other people have been mentioned. Since Leo was such an obscure figure before this book came out, and few had seen his photo, people wouldn't look at a particular actor and say, "That doesn't ring true."

What are you working on now?
I'm working on a story of international intrigue and terrorism in the 1880s. It's about an Irish American extremist plot hatched in the United States, at a time when the U.S.—now a leader in the fight on global terrorism—was actually shirking its responsibilities. And Irish Americans were threatening

and bombing targets in England in this period, in their fight for Irish independence. And in the midst of this, they made an attempt to kill a member of the Royal Family, a future heir to the throne. It's a fascinating story, and timely, because some of the issues we're still talking about more than a century later: how do you deal with global terrorism? How do you deal with radicalized citizens who are trying to export terror and attacking other countries?

How long did it take you to write *Empire of Deception*?
The writing itself [was done] over the space of a few years. The research was longer because of other projects intervening. But suffice it to say, it took several years to put it all together and to see how the pieces fit together. Because on one level, obviously, the story is about Leo Koretz and this amazing swindle, but it's also a story about Chicago. About excess and the corruption of politics and justice in Chicago and the parallel character of the state's attorney Robert Crowe, who in an amazing coincidence, knew Leo and practiced law with him as a young man, who ultimately becomes the prosecutor who has to track him down when the swindle falls apart. All those elements came together and coalesced into this wider story of the times as well as the con.

Could this con have taken place in any other city besides Chicago?
I think so. Chicago was the epitome of the American Dream at the time. The city itself was as aggressive as any businessman or con artist. One writer called it a city on the make. Another writer said it was the sole place on earth where everyone [arrived] with the idea of making money. So there was an ethos, a get-ahead, bold brashness about the city that perhaps contributed to this. But I think every time and place can have someone like this, someone who is basically selling something that is too good to be true. That's why we're still seeing the Ponzi schemes today.

Something that really struck me when I read the book was how the world seems so different today with instant communications and the Internet. Would something like the Bayano River Syndicate even be possible today as a con, with people able to push a few buttons on their computer and look at satellite images of Panama?
I think the answer is no. A similar scheme might be possible, but Leo did really benefit from the remoteness. Panama was at once close and far away. It was only a few days by steamer. The Canal Zone and the construction of the Panama Canal in this period had put it on the map, brought it to the mind of Americans. But no one knew this particular region. And it was remote enough that he could take some comfort in the fact that no one would go there. But again, as I point out in the book, if you cracked the cover of one of the yearly

almanacs published by the *Chicago Daily News*, you would have seen that oil was nowhere mentioned as a Panamanian export. Some inquiries to people in the oil business would have quickly turned up the answer that no one produces oil in Panama. So it obviously would be more difficult in our age of Google and Google maps.

It also would have been tougher for Leo to hide out in Nova Scotia, where I ultimately found out about his story and his time on the lam. While there's an international manhunt going on in Chicago, he's living quite openly in Nova Scotia under a different name with a different persona. It was easier to hide even in plain sight in those days. On another level, even the news of this spectacular Bayano Swindle, when it finally breaks and Leo disappears and hides out in Nova Scotia, there were only a couple references to that in the Nova Scotia papers. He was in an age where he could stay ahead of the news.

You touch on the fact that not a huge amount is known about Koretz's initial motivations. He works as a lawyer and starts coming out with fake mortgages and stuff like this. Was there a pivotal moment that you discovered in his life where he went bad?
One of the interesting things about Leo, he goes on to be this amazingly successful, if unknown or forgotten until now conman, but he started out in a very mundane way. [He faced] the kind of temptation that lawyers and other professionals who handle money have had for eons. He needed some cash. He was dealing with a client who wanted to make an investment, so he simply forged a mortgage on a non-existing property. Used the proceeds to live on as well as pay the interest and kept redoing this scam, churning out more and more fake mortgages to keep the money flowing. In other words, in 1905, as a young lawyer, he started the genesis of a Ponzi scheme.

One thing I did have was Leo's ultimate confession, where he did try to account for how he got into this game. He obviously wanted to get ahead. I think he just realized that his legal career wasn't going to be the route to fast riches. He said he "dipped into dishonesty." He didn't set out to say, "Okay, I need some money, I'm going to invent the greatest swindle ever seen." He started very small, but it snowballed, and at some point it got out of control. That's another feature of the Ponzi scheme. Initially there might be a possibility of making it all right, if he had been able to score some legitimate money or enough money somewhere else, he could have topped it all up and stopped basically selling nothing. But very early on, he admitted there was no going back. And it snowballs, and what's remarkable is the extent to which those very small crimes turned into this huge fraud with all of its accoutrements of fake stock certificates, fake blueprints, and maps of company holdings. And inflated claims of this oil company that, in Leo's telling, was being actively sought for a buy-out by Standard Oil, which was the biggest petroleum firm in the world at the time.

He primarily did all this on his own. Did he forge the certificates himself? Did he have any confederates?

My research turns up no evidence, not a single reference to a confederate. This is another remarkable feature of Leo Koretz. He acted alone. He didn't have a company or a sales force like Charles Ponzi did. He didn't have a corporate reputation and a company like Bernie Madoff. He did all of this under the radar, in secret, except when he let his investors and friends in on the secret. For the better part of 20 years, he had to juggle this whole world of lies and exaggeration and phantom installations and oil fields and keep it all straight and never miss a dividend payment in all that time. If a Ponzi schemer doesn't deliver the profits he claims he can, that's when the questions get asked. This is how good Leo was. He fooled everybody he dealt with, even his closest friends and family … and did it all single-handedly. A remarkable performance, really, if you call it that, for a con man.

You mention at one point that Leo had an office with a staff of basically two people. Did anyone twig in and think, "Hey. He doesn't have a lot of support staff. Maybe this is a con?"

No. That's the thing. I found no references to that kind of suspicion being aroused. In retrospect people said, "Yeah we should have realized this was nuts," but he must have been so good, at the time, the red flags didn't mean anything to anyone. For instance, he had a secretary. Afterwards, when questioned, she says, "It's funny, I never did deal with anyone in Panama." It never twigged to her before this. She was actually a stockholder. She had a modest stake in the company, and she thought her boss Leo had done her a favor by letting her invest.

No one twigged to the fact he was doing it all alone. That was really what he was selling. He was selling this idea that he was plugged into this big syndicate. [People were] making all this money, and no one seemed to question the details. He did claim, as part of his elaborate scheme, that the Bayano Syndicate consisted of five millionaires. And these were shadowy figures. One guy's name was Fischer, and Leo would be talking about some aspect of the deal with an investor, and he would say, "Before I do this, I have to check with Mr. Fischer." He would talk about these people like they were real, like they were in the room. And investors never twigged to the fact this was all a product of his imagination. He spoke of his oil fields, he spoke of his syndicate in such a convincing way, people believed it was real.

After his scam is revealed, Koretz moves to Nova Scotia, where he throws money around and leads a flashy lifestyle. Was he incapable of keeping a low profile?

Well, he obviously was. When his scheme falls apart in 1923, he scrapes up as much money as he can and vanishes from Chicago. Within a few months, he turns up in Nova Scotia, where he heard there was a very secluded hunting lodge for sale. This would look like the perfect place for a swindler on the run to [lie] low. He develops this new persona as, of all things, as a book lover, literary figure, and writer. Sort of a self-made man who retired to enjoy books and write. And he has a new name, Lou Keyte.

When I was doing my research, the last thing I expected was to find references to Lou Keyte in the press. But that's exactly what I found. The newspapers even announced that this wealthy American writer of reputation in New York was buying a summer home in Nova Scotia. Which at the time wasn't that strange, because wealthy Americans were buying up property in Nova Scotia or spending their summers here. But to see him living that openly, turning his lodge into this backwoods mansion, throwing elaborate parties, hosting dinner dances for new circle of friends … He did make a spectacle of himself but felt secure under his assumed name. And he grew a beard so he didn't resemble his photo. His photo was not being circulated in Nova Scotia through the press anyway.

So, even though he was drawing attention to himself, he could be secure in the fact nobody knew who he really was. Why he did this, why he lived so large in Nova Scotia, might have been his health. He was very severely ill with diabetes at this point. It's almost like he was going to burn the candle at both ends and enjoy what time he had. Once he's tripped up and discovered and arrested, he doesn't fight extradition [from Canada]. He heads right back to Chicago to face justice. It's like he knew his time was limited, either by his health or just trying to stay ahead of the law. And he chose to enjoy himself while he could.

Do you have any opinion on whether diabetic Koretz committed suicide in jail by consuming a box of chocolates?

Well, the evidence I have, I presented in the book. It's clear there were reports he had candy smuggled in. There were reports he was consuming too much sugar. He was in the late stages of severe diabetes at this point. One of the elements of that is a hunger or desire for sugar. So, in a sense, you can kill yourself with too much sugar at this stage even if you don't mean to. Whether or not it was intentional by Leo or he simply craved sugar and it killed him is a question, but if the story is true that he arranged to have chocolate smuggled in, that would suggest a deliberate [attempt] from his part. It would be one of the more bizarre suicides.

We sometimes have a tendency to glamorize con artists. I'm thinking of movies like *The Sting*, where they're portrayed as loveable rogues. Do people forget that Leo left behind a devastated wife, children, and family, and ruined lives? Does that sometimes get forgotten in the narrative?

Well, I certainly did not forget. Through my research, I've been in contact with, and gotten to know, quite a few of Leo's descendants. [Koretz had a] devastating impact on his family, his wife and children and his immediate family, who lost tens of thousands of dollars in the collapse of the scam. They were all invested. They all thought they had it made.

When you talk about *The Sting*, it's a little different. Con men often draw their victims into shady dealings. So it'll be the way to beat the market, or the insider tip, or the tip-off before anyone else knows the outcome of a horse race, or perhaps it's a fixed fight. So in those cases, it's hard to feel any real remorse for the victims because what the con man is preying on is greed, to the point where the victim will commit a crime myself or be an accomplice in the fraud to make money. With Ponzi schemes, you can argue that the investor should know better, but people do believe they are dealing with a legitimate person and a legitimate investment. The investment might be ludicrous like this one was, the returns may be too good to believe, as they were in this case, but the investors don't believe that they are party to an offence or that they're somehow benefiting or profiting at someone else's expense. That's only clear when it falls apart …

Con men prey on the darker side of people's personalities, that desire to get ahead, and whether it's legitimate or not, I think we all sort of can feel in some ways [that] the victim is getting what they deserve. Sure the con man broke the law, and sure, they shouldn't have done this, but on some level, you have to almost admire the skill and bravado of people who can pull off such an elaborate scheme.

Using your amateur armchair psychology skills, was Leo a sociopath in your opinion?

I haven't really thought about that in actual forensic, psychological terms. I think the facts speak for themselves. I think there's plenty of material there if you want to play psychologist.

Is there any one lesson you would like readers to take away from your book?

Well, I suppose you could read *Empire of Deception* and come away and very understandably go, "What were those investors thinking? How could they be so stupid? So gullible?" But on the other hand, the persistence of Ponzi schemes means that 90 years later, it's not like we're much smarter. Maybe people are a little more sophisticated about their investments, but Ponzi schemers are still working out there, and I think we should remember, every time and place can have its Bayano swindle or its bubble. Maybe it's dot-com stocks, maybe it's the housing bubble, maybe it's whatever commodity comes along next that everyone thinks is the next big thing. I don't think fundamentally that human nature changes a lot, and I think there's still lots of room for someone like a Leo Koretz to operate and to sell what con men sell, which is trust. And make people trust them, as Leo was so brilliantly able to do—not worry about the details, just enjoy the profits as they're rolling in without giving any thought to, "How is he doing this?"

INTERVIEW WITH JAMES RANDI

James Randi is one of the leading figures in the skeptical community. Since retiring as a magician, he has devoted himself to the pursuit and exposure of "flimflam"—that is to say, confidence scams and magic tricks fobbed off as miracles by faith healers and psychics for a fee. In this, Randi resembles legendary escape-artist Harry Houdini, who exposed phony séances and mediums a century ago.

Randi famously proved Christian faith healer Peter Popoff to be a con artist and a fake on The Tonight Show, *with Johnny Carson hosting. He is also the instigator behind the Million-Dollar Challenge—in which psychics are dared to prove their paranormal abilities in an objective test, the rules of which have been agreed upon by all in advance. So far, no one has ever won.*

Author of 10 books and currently the subject of a hit documentary, An Honest Liar, *Randi was born in Toronto, Canada, in 1928. He currently lives with his partner, Deyvi Peña, in Plantation, Florida.*

(Phone interview April 7, 2015, and e-mail interview June 16, 2015.)

You've been compared to Harry Houdini. Do you feel that's an apt comparison? Do you feel you are continuing in his footsteps?
He was dead for two years before I was born. I had nothing to do with it, I swear. [Laughs.] In one way yes, but in another way, no. Houdini had no education in sciences or logic. He did very, very well and made quite a name for himself not only as an entertainer but certainly as a skeptic of the paranormal scene—though it was not called "paranormal" in those days. They hadn't come up with that terminology.

But I think I am sort of carrying on from where he might have carried on, had he lived longer. I take pride knowing this and following his lead in the matter, though frankly, I was not necessarily inspired by his record in the field, because ever since I was a boy I have always been skeptical of these things. I determined one day I would look into it. But I certainly rode on his coat-tails for a short distance.

Are people like Oprah Winfrey to blame for the spread of [flimflam] by putting people like John of God or Jenny McCarthy on their show?

Substantially, yes. I've had mild arguments with Oprah. Her last response to me on her TV program was, "Oh, Randi. Be kind." My response to her was, I'll be kind as soon as these people start to be kind to the people they are victimizing. The whole thing deteriorated after that moment, of course.

Oprah is a remarkable success, and I have great respect for her. But the problem with Oprah, in general, is that everything that seems attractive to her for a moment, she will accept without thinking very long about it … she accepts these people and promotes them heedlessly, and I think she's made some dreadful errors along the way. We don't hear her admitting them. I'm sure she recognizes some of those grievous errors.

Of all the people you've exposed, is there one take-down you are most proud of?

Because I had some very good help—namely Johnny Carson—the exposure of Peter Popoff. Although it didn't work for very long. He's back in business, and he's just as crazy and vicious as he ever was. But the exposure of Peter Popoff. I remember after Johnny's retirement, he used to call me about once every two weeks, always beginning with an apology, "Oh, I know you're busy." [Laughs.] If he realized how pleased I was to get a call from him in his retirement, he would not have said that, because I'd have stayed on the phone for hours had I been allowed to. He would do it for 15 minutes, reminding me of the fact Peter Popoff was still in business, and expressing his astonishment at that. I always told him, "John, this is an unsinkable rubber duck. They're all unsinkable rubber ducks. There's no way we're going to get rid of them, because people don't listen. People don't think about these things."

I've often heard the phrase, "People want to believe in this." No. They *need* to believe in it. They develop a need for that kind of support.

Have you ever spoken to Peter Popoff? Has he ever confronted you or tried to talk about your exposé?

Oh, no. He's a Man of God, and I'm an atheist. He wouldn't want to talk to me. That would be "impure." No, he stays to himself. He doesn't confront me directly … he won't come anywhere near me. He's avoided me as much as he possibly can, because he hasn't got an argument. He just has not got an argument that he can present that is in any way convincing. You know the piece in the movie [*An Honest Liar*], where he says, "But our ratings are up!" That's the bottom line, making money. So, everything's okay. He's making money. He's not worried.

With all the popular psychics today like Popoff and John Edward, do you ever want to give up, just throw up your hands and say, 'The public is so gullible, I can't keep doing this. I can't be a skeptic anymore"?

No. I can't do that. I get e-mail; it pours in. People are writing me all the time, saying, "I so much appreciate what you do." After showings of *An Honest Liar*, I've been traveling around this country, and I just came back from Finland and Italy. In a matter of a few days I'm leaving again for exactly the same purpose. During the Q&A period after the film, I get people coming up to me with tears in their eyes. This is difficult to tell you. Deyvi and I, wherever we're confronted by these people, they reach out to me, take me by the hand and say, "You made a big change in my life." I have a hard time saying that, because that's something you just can't buy. There's no price on a thing like that, someone saying that I made a change in their lives. It's an incredible feeling of responsibility. I'll go on until the moment I breathe my last—though I'm not encouraging that moment!

There's a lot of talk now in media circles that atheism and skepticism are becoming more popular with the public. I'm thinking of books by Christopher Hitchens and Richard Dawkins, even Penn and Teller with their TV show, *Bullsh*t!* What's your feeling? Is the public more skeptical than they were in decades past?

It's hard to tell. But from the reactions Deyvi and I are getting from the movie, I would say yes, that is true.

Many people say, "I've never stopped to think about this. This made *me* stop and think." What a wonderful declaration, that we made them stop and think somehow. If that made a change in their lives, I'm convinced that it's a change for the better. I've never had anybody back up on me and say, "No, I've decided I was right after all." That has never happened.

I get gratitude from a lot of people around the world. I can't tell you how affecting that is to me and to Deyvi. We're both so grateful for that expression of thanks. Again, you can't buy that. Yes, I think that maybe our efforts have been somewhat responsible for that change.

I've got to continue with it. I'm currently very much involved in getting the picture together on the anti-vaxxers—people who are going to lead us and the world back into enjoying such things as smallpox and measles and such. These semi-celebrities, people who are preaching that vaccines causes autism. Penn and Teller have a wonderful expression for that. It's short and quick: it's "Bullsh*t!" There is no sense in that argument whatsoever. The chemicals that were once used in vaccination materials as preservatives are no longer used and have not been used for a long time now. And these people ignore that fact.

They don't want to discuss the truth of it. They want to discuss the fiction. They get a certain amount of attention and I'm sure a great deal of delight of being represented in the media as fighters for truth and whatnot.

There's a statistic I heard, that in some wealthy neighborhoods in Los Angeles the vaccination rate for children is lower than it is in Bangladesh.

Can you imagine that? And these are supposed to be educated people. Our educational standards in certain respects are rather low. And I'm going to point out that I really fear for the standards of education in the United States of America, even among well-to-do people.

What about the Internet? Has it made people more ignorant or more skeptical?

I think it's equal in both ways. It brings us knowledge and it brings us nonsense as well, and we've got to be very careful. You've got to be able to sift these things out. You've got to be able to look up the right references—and people often don't bother to do that—because, as I said to Johnny Carson so many times, people don't just *want* to believe, they *need* to believe a lot of these things because they seem magical, they're often attractive, they're widely advertised … and the media embrace them, generally speaking. I think this is so damaging to our civilization and to our individual culture.

You came from Toronto originally. Are you an American citizen now?

Oh yes. For a long time. I came to a parting of the ways with Canadian citizenship when I was with the Alice Cooper group in the 1970s and did a tour with them, which was very, very educational in many ways, as you can imagine. When we got to Niagara Falls, Canada, we had a visit from the RCMP—the federal police in Canada—they trashed our dressing rooms and the lockers of the kids in the school where we were doing our show. We were appalled by that. They were looking for dope, and they didn't find any. They were so pissed off that they trashed the whole room and destroyed the kids' records and their books and whatnot. It was just vicious. And at that point I decided, "I don't know whether I'm all that satisfied being a Canadian citizen."

I'd been invited by many individuals and some rather important persons to accept American citizenship, and I accepted it with great gusto. I'm very proud to be American now, albeit, one inducted by a magistrate and not by a right of birth. I was just not geographically located correctly to be born an American citizen. I find that so strange. People believe that the geographical position of their mother at the moment they emerge from the womb determines their citizenship. But yes, that's the way it is.

What do you think about all these TV shows about mediums? You've got *Mom's a Medium*, *Long Island Medium*, **and there was a show a few years ago just called** *Medium*. **What's your take on this?**

TV mediums don't have to be right, they only have to be spectacular. It's like these ghost shows. The ghost shows are usually shot in infrared, so it looks green and black. People run around in the dark and they scream and they fall down. A chair creaks and everyone runs for the door and yells. Picture people in a dark room. It's never in a new house, because those walls and the floors don't creak. These shows love creaking floors. Anything that falls, even someone dropping a nickel on the floor, "Oh! That had to be a spirit!"

What's the focus right now at the James Randi Educational Foundation? Are you working on any specific projects?

Some of these things we can't talk about. But what I said earlier, the anti-vaxxer people … And Peter Popoff, he's still in business. He's still making millions. He's on BET, Black Entertainment Television. He's very big there. And he's still carrying on.

In spite of your exposé on Popoff, I'm sure he has followers who would just shrug and say, "I don't care if he's a total fake. I still love him." How do you deal with that?

I can't tell you the number of times we've encountered people exactly like that. Once I was with a CBS TV crew. We went to some place in New York, some large arena in New York City, and we had cameras with us. I went there in my usual disguise—red wig, beard dyed red, and brown contact lenses. We hung around and we saw a lady with two canes—very fragile—staggering into the auditorium. We stopped her and we asked her what it was all about. She said, "Oh, I'm going to be healed by Reverend Popoff." Oh, okay. Can we talk to you afterwards? "Oh, of course, of course." So we waited until the crowd left and we found her on her canes, still. She'd gone on the stage and Popoff had taken the canes away from her, thrown them on the floor. She tottered and almost fell. She sat down again.

I said to her quite frankly, that it seems the healing had failed. "No, no. I failed because I didn't have enough faith. I spoke with them afterwards, and they explained that if I didn't have the strength in my faith, God wouldn't give me the healing. So I'm going to ask for it again, and I'm sure it'll work the next time." She staggered off on her canes, then suddenly turned towards us, poor lady. She said, "Oh, but I still believe, I still believe." She clenched her fist and staggered off on her canes. We get that all the time. Nothing, nothing is going to discourage these people. They want the fantasy, they want the mythology. They really need it.

You started the Million-Dollar Challenge in the 1960s. It started off as a $1,000 challenge. Has anyone ever come close to winning the challenge? Has anyone ever accepted the challenge then done reasonably well?

[Chuckles.] Well, we've designed it in such a way that you can't just "do reasonably well." Either you do it, or you don't do it. It's like, "I can fly by flapping my arms." Okay, step over to the window here. Oops, you lose! We have to make it very obvious that there can't be any voting to make a decision. We make the rules in advance, and they have to agree to them. Most of them will agree. They'll sign the document saying that the rules are well within their purview, and then they do the test. Every year, at the Amazing Meeting, which we hold in Las Vegas, we attract a huge, huge crowd. At the end of it we have a special session where we invite the psychics up there to do their thing, and they seem to be the most astonished of all when they fail.

The reason is, they tend to make excuses for themselves. We see that all the time. I've seen them actually doing their own tests. What happens, they miss altogether, and they say, "I wasn't really feeling up to it at that moment. I've had this awful headache. I've taken some aspirins. Perhaps it'll be better. Let's try that again." They make excuses for themselves. They don't know how to properly test themselves, and when we show them how to do a really definitive test with numbers and such, they fall on their collective nose—all of them do, they fail—they seem puzzled by it.

We often get a response a month later, saying, "I figured what was wrong there. That colored drape. That was a nasty yellow color. I'm thrown off by yellow." Or something like that. Something absolutely ridiculous. But they offer it as an excuse, and I think they believe it's a legitimate reason.

That leads into my next question. Do you make a differentiation between people who genuinely think they have some paranormal power and people who are using the paranormal just to make money? Is there a distinction?

Oh, yes, of course. One of the groups are out-and-out crooks and liars and cheats, and the others are deluded. I have great sympathy for those who are deluded. I know our arguments don't convince them at all. They just smile, like the lady with the crutches; they turn and say, "I still believe."

Have you always been an atheist, or did you ever go through a period of religious belief?

[Laughs.] Well, briefly, when I was a kid, I think I was 11 or 12 or so, I had to go to Sunday School. My family was Anglican, which is sort of watered-down Catholic. They stayed in bed and sent me off with a quarter in my hand ... I was a terrible failure from the very moment that I stepped in there. Every time they read a quotation to me from something or other, I said, "How do you know that's true?" I was only a little kid, mind you, but I was rather adamant on that. They just tapped the Bible and said, "It's in the Holy Book!" Well, how do you know that holy book is right? "It is the word of God." Wait a minute, it says John and Peter here. Who are these people? "Oh, they spoke on behalf of God." So, God didn't do it directly then? "Yes, but they were godly people, you see." And then they gave up arguing with me and said I wasn't very welcome at Sunday school.

The next week, my parents gave me the quarter again and then I made a wonderful discovery. I found that at Purdy's Drug Store on Bayview Avenue in Leaside, outside Toronto where I was born and raised, Purdy's Drug Store offered a two-flavor ice cream sundae for 25 cents. For 20 cents, you only got one flavor. My friend Gary, he only got 20 cents as an allowance—and this coin for the plate became my allowance all of a sudden—but my parents never found out ... that I know of. Perhaps they did but never mentioned it to me. So for several months, I had good sundaes on Sunday.

Are you still involved with *Skeptical Inquirer* magazine?
Oh, yes. And I've been working hard on my eleventh book, which is *A Magician in the Laboratory*. I'm working on that currently, putting the finishing touches to it, so I haven't had a chance to contribute much to *Skeptical Inquirer*, but we're on very close terms. I was one of the founders of the Committee for Skeptical Inquiry and *Skeptical Inquirer*.

I had an argument with the chairman some years ago. He wanted me to stop my investigations of Uri Geller because Geller was suing them all the time. I said, I'm sorry I can't do that. Geller has never got a dime out of me—I should say a nickel, not even a nickel—but they were scared, they were worried. They were running for the woods, and I don't run for the woods.

Have you ever been worried about being assassinated?
Well, I answer my door very cautiously. I have a glass door, you see. I've had to take a certain amount of care. Every now and then some substantial damage is done to my property here in Plantation, Florida. We suspect there are disgruntled folks out there who have done this kind of thing. But we live in a good community here. When I say, a good community, a community that is well-protected by safeguards. I'm not too worried. But I travel a lot and I have good people around me, let's put it that way.

I've met or read about skeptics who are skeptical about paranormal stuff but believe in mainstream religion. They believe in God, they believe in Jesus. What's your take on that? Is that all just one part of the flimflam continuum?
Yes, I believe so. I have no problem with people who are religious, as long as they don't let it run their lives so completely that they can't doubt anything

that has the word God or Jesus in it … I can't see that logic because there is no evidence whatsoever for the existence of a deity, at least none that [has] ever satisfied me. All kinds of claims and writings from thousands of years back. Just because it's old and written by people who weren't as informed as we are today …

Of the books you've done, is there one you are most proud of?
I think *Flim-Flam!* is the one that sort of put me on the map, as far as books go. You'd be amazed—well, maybe "astonished" would be more like it—at the number of people who show up for the book signings and the showings of *An Honest Liar* … and we always get full houses … the number of people that have copies of *Flim-Flam!* What I'm overjoyed to see are very well-worn copies of *Flim-Flam!*

You're probably aware, after the First World War, of the big interest in séances and spiritualism in Europe …
Oh, yes.

…because of the devastation of the war. If families are getting comfort from this, what's the harm? Why is this a bad thing, in your view?
Well, if they can get some comfort out of it, I'm happy for them, of course. If it helps people in any way to handle a bad situation, I'm all for it. I'm much in favor. But I only hope that it doesn't change their thinking in such a way that they'll fall for one of the fakers out there who promises magic water from Chernobyl—which is what Popoff is offering now. I just fear, if they let it take over their lives and affect them adversely … they may surrender to some fancy talker—like the ones I've been fighting all these years. And I think that can be very, very, harmful.

You started your work as a skeptic when you were around 60, correct? When you retired from the magic business?
Oh, no, no, no. I was into skepticism when I was a kid—at that Sunday school meeting I told you about. All the way along I've always had in the back of my head that when I retired from the magic profession I would certainly become a full-time skeptic. I was into the skeptical mode and contributing to skeptical sites and whatnot, well before anything like that happened with my career. I've always been supportive of this sort of thing. I've always sought out other people like me, no matter where I went as a magician in the United States and around the world.

In different parts of the world, I have people coming to me saying "I enjoyed the show. Very entertaining, very entertaining. But when you told that lady her telephone number and you'd never met her before, that was ESP, right?" No, no, no. That was what we call in the magic trade, mentalism. It was a trick.

"Oh, no. I can tell the difference between a trick and something real. The telephone number—that was real!" They get angry. They think I'm lying to them. And that discombobulates me rather considerably, but I can't do much about it. They walk away shaking their head saying, "Oh, what a pity he had to lie to me about that trick."

From the start of your full-time work as a skeptic, have things changed? Have you seen any changes in the public, from the time you started doing full-time skeptical work?

I get more people coming to me saying they used to believe in it but then they read my book, or whatever. That's very encouraging and flattering. It makes me think very deeply about what I've done. But no, I don't notice that much difference, except for those people who tell me I made a difference in their lives.

We've run through all my questions. Is there anything you want to add or emphasize that we've already gone over?

I would say, certainly, read my books. I don't know if I have much more to say than that. I want to thank you for your questions. They were very penetrating.

Selected Bibliography

PUBLICATIONS — BOOKS

Abagnale, Frank W., and Redding, Stan. *Catch Me If You Can.* New York, NY: Broadway Books, 1980.

Adams, Samuel Hopkins. *The Great American Fraud* (collected articles on patent medicines reprinted from *Collier's Weekly*), 1906.

Anson, Jay. *The Amityville Horror.* New Jersey, NY: Prentice Hall, 1977.

Ashbury, Herbert. *The Gangs of New York.* New York: Thunder's Mouth Press, 1927.

"Barnum, Phineas Taylor." *Encyclopedia Britannica, Eleventh Edition,* 1911.

Baum, Dan. *Smoke and Mirrors.* New York: Little, Brown & Company, 1996.

Bergreen, Laurence. *Capone: The Man and the Era.* New York: Simon & Schuster, 1994.

Brannon, W. T. *The Autobiography of America's Master Swindler.* Chicago: Ziff-Davis Publishing Company, 1948.

Breslin, Jimmy. *Damon Runyon.* New York: Ticknor & Fields, 1991.

Carter, Forrest. *The Education of Little Tree.* Albuquerque: University of New Mexico Press, 1976.

Champlain, Pierre de. *Mobsters: Gangsters and Men of Honour.* Toronto, ON: HarperCollins Publishers, 2004.

Cody, Colonel William F. (Buffalo Bill). *The Adventures of Buffalo Bill.* New York, Evanston and London: Harper & Row, Publishers, 1904.

Cody, William F. (Buffalo Bill). *An Autobiography of Buffalo Bill (Colonel W. F. Cody).* Murray Hill, NY: Farrar & Rinehart Incorporated, 1920.

Cohen, Rich. *Tough Jews: Fathers, Sons, and Gangster Dreams.* New York: Random House, 1998.

Cummins, Joseph. *Anything for a Vote.* Philadelphia, PA: Quirk Books, 2007.

Dallek, Robert. *Lone Star Rising.* New York: Oxford University Press, 1991.

Dictionary of Canadian Biography. Toronto, ON: University of Toronto Press, 1966.

Frey, James. *A Million Little Pieces.* New York: New York: Nan A. Talese/Doubleday, 2003.

Gray, Mike. *Drug Crazy.* New York: Random House, 1998.

Hendley, Nate. *Al Capone: Chicago's King of Crime.* Neustadt, ON: Five Rivers Chapmanry, 2010.

Hendley, Nate. *American Gangsters, Then and Now.* Santa Barbara, CA: ABC-CLIO, 2010.

Hendley, Nate. *Dutch Schultz: The Brazen Beer Baron of New York.* Canmore, Alberta: Altitude Publishing, 2005.

Hendley, Nate. *The Mafia: A Guide to an American Subculture.* Santa Barbara, CA: ABC-CLIO, 2013.

Holli, Melvin. *The American Mayor: The Best and Worst Big-City Leaders.* University Park, PA: Pennsylvania State University Press, 1999.

Houdini, Harry. *A Magician Among the Spirits.* New York and London: Harper & Brothers, 1924.

Houdini, Harry. *Miracle Mongers and Their Methods.* E. P. Dutton & Company, 1920.

Jack, Albert. *Loch Ness Monsters and Raining Frogs.* London, UK: Penguin Books, 2007.

Jobb, Dean. *Empire of Deception.* Toronto, Canada: HarperCollins, 2015.

Key, Wilson Bryan. *Subliminal Seduction.* Signet, 1974.

Kobler, John. *Capone: The Life and World of Al Capone.* Cambridge, MA: Da Capo Press, 1971.

Kunhardt, Philip B. Jr., Kunhardt, Philip B. III, Kundhardt, Peter W. *The American President.* New York: Riverhead Books, 1999.

Laqueur, Walter. *Fascism: Past, Present, Future.* New York, NY: Oxford University Press, 1996.

Lee, Martin A. *The Beast Reawakens.* Little, Brown and Company, 1997.

Maurer, David W. *The Big Con: The Story of the Confidence Man.* New York: Anchor Books, 1940.

Mezrich, Ben. *Bringing Down the House.* New York: Free Press, 2002.

Monk, Maria. *Awful Disclosures of Maria Monk.* 1836.

Morgan, Hal, and Tucker, Kerry. *More Rumor!* New York: Penguin Books, 1987.

Pendergrast, Mike. *Victims of Memory: Sex Abuse Accusations and Shattered Lives.* Upper Access Books, 1996.

Pistone, Joseph, and Woodley, Richard. *Donnie Brasco: My Undercover Life in the Mafia.* New York: New American Library, 1987.

Pistone, Joseph. *The Way of the Wiseguy.* Philadelphia, PA: Running Press, 2004.

Ponzi, Charles. *The Rise of Mr. Ponzi.* Despair, Inc., 2009.

Randi, James. *James Randi: Psychic Investigator.* London: Boxtree Limited, 1991.

Reppetto, Thomas. *American Mafia: A History of Its Rise to Power.* New York: Henry Holt and Company, 2004.

Runyon, Damon. *The Damon Runyon Omnibus.* 1944.

Sann, Paul. *Kill the Dutchman!* New Rochelle, NY: Arlington House, 1971.

Sann, Paul. *The Lawless Decade.* New York: Bonanza Books, 1957.

Shermer, Michael. *Why People Believe Weird Things.* New York: W. H. Freeman and Company, 1997.

Showalter, Elaine. *Hystories: Hysterical Epidemics and Modern Media.* New York: Columbia University Press, 1997.

Southwell, David. *The History of Organized Crime: The True Story and Secrets of Global Gangland.* London: SevenOaks, 2006.

Turkus, Burton, and Sid Feder, *Murder, Inc.: The Story of the Syndicate.* Cambridge, MA: Da Capo Press, 1951.

Young, Dr. James Harvey. *The Medical Messiahs: A Social History of Health Quackery in Twentieth-Century America.* Princeton, NJ: Princeton Legacy Library, 1967.

PUBLICATIONS — PERIODICALS

"Abduction by Aliens or Sleep Paralysis?" *Skeptical Inquirer*, May/June 1998.

"The Abrams Cult Again." *Journal of the American Medical Association*, December 8, 1923.

"Academic Obfuscations." *Skeptic Magazine*, Volume 17, Number 4, 2012.

"After Seeking Money from Friends, Leone Pleaded Guilty to Felony Theft." *Baltimore Sun*, October 27, 2010.

"Albert Abrams—A Defense by Upton Sinclair." *Journal of the American Medical Association*, April 29, 1922.

"Al Capone, Chicago Mayor 'Big Bill' Thompson Shown Together in Photo." *Chicago Tribune*, June 2, 2009.

"Amityville: The Horror of It All." *Skeptical Inquirer*, January/February 2003.

"Arrest of the Confidence Man." *New York Herald*, 1849.

"The Art of Counterfeiting Money." *TIME*, June 15, 2009.

"Author Is Kicked Out of Oprah Winfrey's Book Club." *New York Times*, January 27, 2006.

"Behind the Filming of 'The Honeymoon Killers'." *New York Times*, October 20, 1992.

"Ben Affleck Rewrites History." *Maclean's Magazine*, September 12, 2012.

"The Bermuda Triangle and the 'Hutchinson Effect.'" *Skeptical Inquirer*, September, 2007.

"Big Hair, Bad Scams, Motormouths." *New York Times*, December 12, 2013.

"Big Run on Ponzi Company." *Wall Street Journal*, August 4, 1920.

"Births Up 9 Months After the Blackout." *New York Times*, August 10, 1966.

"CAM for Cancer: Preying on Desperate People." *Skeptic Magazine*, Volume 17, Number 4, 2012.

"Cancer Quackery: Past and Present." *FDA Consumer*, July/August 1977.

"Card Counting Gig Nets Students Millions." *The Tech*, October 25, 2002.

"Children of Cocaine." *Washington Post*, July 30, 1989.

"A Clinical Trial of Amygdalin (Laetrile) in the Treatment of Human Cancer." *The New England Journal of Medicine*, January 28, 1982.

"A Close Look at Therapeutic Touch." *Journal of the American Medical Association*, 1998.

"Cocaine Habit's Horrors." *New York Times*, April 30, 1905.

"The Consumers Union Report: Licit and Illicit Drugs." *Consumer Reports Magazine*, 1972.

"Cry and You Cry Alone? Not If You Write About It." *New York Times*, April 21, 2003.

"C. W. Barron Skeptical About 'Exchange Wizard.'" *Wall Street Journal*, July 30, 1920.

"Dark Secrets of the Oracle Monger." *Skeptic Magazine*, Volume 17, Number 4, 2012.

"Debunking the Myth of P. T. Barnum." *New York Times*, October 3, 1982.

"Disputed Book Pulled from Oprah Website," *Washington Post*, November 6, 2007.

"The Effect of the Great Blackout of 1965 on Births in New York City." J. Richard Udry, School of Public Health, University of North Carolina, Chapel Hill, *Demography*, August 1970.

"The Electronic Reactions of Albert Abrams." *American Artifacts*, No. 39.

"Emperor Norton, Zaniest S.F. Street Character." *San Francisco Chronicle*, September 17, 2009.

"End to a Twisted and False Episode in Psychiatry." *Skeptical Inquirer*, March/April 2012.

"Energy Medicine." *Skeptic Magazine*, Volume 11, Number 3, 2005.

"Ex-Dixon Comptroller Gets Nearly 20 Years for Theft." *Chicago Tribune*, February 15, 2013.

"'Evil' Madoff Gets 150 Years in Epic Fraud." *Wall Street Journal*, June 30, 2009.

"FDNY, NYPD Retirees Who 'Faked 9/11 Illness in Scam' Not Too Sick to Have Fun." *New York Post*, January 7, 2014.

"Feds Withdraw 'Deadbeat' Claim Against Jordan Belfort to Review Case Against 'The Wolf of Wall Street.'" *New York Daily News*, October 25, 2013.

"$50M 'Pump-and-Dump' Scam Nets 20 Arrests." *USA Today*, March 2, 2001.

"5 Questions: Interview with Bill Kaplan." *USA Today*, April 11, 2008.

"Florida Officials, Insurers Demonstrate Staged Car Crash." *SunSentinel*, September 25, 2011.

"Fooled by Ponzi." *Skeptic Magazine*, Volume 14, Number 4, 2009.

"For Chicago Thompson." *Chicago Tribune*, April 9, 1931.

"For You, Half Price." *New York Times*, November 27, 2005.

"Former Dixon, IL, Comptroller, Rita Crundwell, Sentenced to 19½ Years in Prison." *Forbes*, February 14, 2013.

"A Fortnight Under the Pure Food Law." *New York Times*, January 13, 1907.

"Gary Schwartz's Energy Healing Experiments: The Emperor's New Clothes?" *Skeptical Inquirer*, March/April 2008.

"A Girl Not Named Sybil." *New York Times*, October 14, 2011.

"Go Ask Alice Lit Crit: The House That Alice Built." *School Library Journal*, October 1979.

"The Great Paper Caper." *GQ*, October 28, 2014.

"The Great Radium Craze." *Skeptic Magazine*, Volume 18, Number 3, 2013.

"The Great Showman Deal." *New York Times*, April 8, 1891.

"The Grifters." *Chicago Sun-Times*, January 25, 1991.

"Hacking Las Vegas." *Wired*, September 2002.

"His Last Name Is Scheme." *New York Times*, April 10, 2005.

"Houdini's Skeptic Advice: Just Because Something's Unexplained Doesn't Mean It's Supernatural." *Scientific American*, February 2011.

"The House That Alice Built." *School Library Journal*, October 1979.

"How Accurate Is The Wolf of Wall Street?" *The Toronto Star*, January 3, 2014.

"How One Man's Invention Is Part of a Growing Worldwide Scam That Snares the Desperately Ill." *The Seattle Times*, November 18, 2007.

"How the CIA Used a Fake Sci-Fi Flick to Rescue Americans from Tehran." *Wired*, April, 24, 2007.

"How Bernie Did It." *Fortune*, April 30, 2009.

"How Oprahness Trumped Truthiness." *New York Times*, January 30, 2006.

"How to Be a Skeptical News Consumer." *Skeptic Magazine*, Volume 14, Number 4, 2012.

"In Ponzi We Trust." *Smithsonian Magazine*, December 1998.

"Inside the Icons: Tricks of Fake Mediums." *Liberty Magazine*, November 25, 1925.

"Iraq Swears by Bomb Detector U.S. Sees as Useless." *New York Times*, November 3, 2009.

"Is There a 100C Grain of Truth to Homeopathy?" *Skeptical Inquirer*, July/August 2011.

"Investors' Story Left Out of Wall Street 'Wolf' Movie." *New York Times*, December 19, 2013.

"John Brinkley, The Goat-Gland Quack." *The Telegraph*, April 18, 2008.

"John Cusack Interview for *The Grifters*." *Chicago Sun-Times*, January 20, 1991.

"The Jolly Millionaire." *Walrus*, May 27, 2015.

"Jordan Belfort, the Real Wolf of Wall Street." *Bloomberg Business Week*, November 7, 2013.

"JPMorgan to Settle Madoff Fraud Claims for $1.7B." The Associated Press, January 8, 2014.

"Just Say 'Uh-Oh.'" *New York Times*, November 15, 1998.

"Kevin Trudeau's $18,000 Weight Loss Plan: A Book Review." *Skeptical Inquirer*, April 18, 2014.

"Laetrile: A Lesson in Cancer Quackery." *CA—A Cancer Journal for Clinicians*, March/April 1981.

"A Leap from the Bridge." *New York Times*, July 24, 1886.

"Le Roi Est Mort." *San Francisco Chronicle*, January 11, 1880.

"A Little Poison Can Be Good for You: The Received Wisdom About Toxins and Radiation May Be All Wet." *Fortune*, June 9, 2003.

"The Lives They Lived: Peggy McMartin Buckey, b. 1926; The Devil in the Nursery." *New York Times* magazine, January 7, 2001.

"The Longest Trial—A Post-Mortem; Collapse of a Child-Abuse Case: So Much Agony for So Little." *New York Times*, January 24, 1990.

"Lost Manuscript Unmasks Details of Original Ponzi." *New York Times*, May 5, 2009.

"Luka Rocco Magnotta: Online Reaction to Video Reveals a Disturbing Appetite for Gore." *The Toronto Star*, May 31, 2012.

"Madoff and His Models." *The New Yorker*, March 23, 2009.

"The Madoff Case: A Timeline." *Wall Street Journal*, March 12, 2009.

"Madoff Is Sentenced to 150 Years for Ponzi Scheme." *New York Times*, June 30, 2009.

"Madoff Pleads Guilty, Is Jailed for $65 Million Fraud." Reuters, March 13, 2009.

"Magical Thinking in Complementary and Alternative Medicine." *Skeptical Inquirer*, November/December 2001.

"Magnetic Healing: An Old Scam That Never Dies." *Skeptical Inquirer*, January/February 2011.

"Meet the King of NY Con Men." *New York Post*, November 25, 2007.

"Mexico Is Warned on Drug Detector." *New York Times*, March 15, 2010.

"Mortuary Employee Convicted for Role in Fake Funeral Scam." The Associated Press, August 2, 2010.

"Multiple Personality Delusions." *Skeptic Magazine*, Volume 17, Number 3, 2012.

"Negro Cocaine 'Fiends' Are a New Southern Menace." *New York Times*, February 8, 1914.

"'Nigerian Scam' Lures Companies." *New York Times*, May 21, 1992.

"Nutrition for Life's Top Recruiter Has a Criminal Past—Despite Convictions, Trudeau Gets New Distributors to Fork Out the Cash." *Wall Street Journal*, January 19, 1996.

"Of Martians and Media." *Skeptic Magazine*, Volume 18, Number 3, 2013.

"Official Will Be Removed for LSD Blindness Hoax." *New York Times*, February 19, 1968.

"Officials Say Mob Stole $200 Million Using Phone Bills." *New York Times*, February 11, 2004.

"An Old Swindle Revived." *New York Times*, March 20, 1898.

"Online Dating Relationship Ends Badly, $1.3M Later." *Toronto Star*, November 30, 2013.

"Oprah vs. James Frey: The Sequel." *TIME*, July 30, 2007.

"Patent Medicine Bill to Curb Drug Users." *New York Times*, March 15, 1906.

"The Perfect Mark." *The New Yorker*, May 15, 2006.

"Phone Executive Admits Conspiracy in Mob Fraud." *New York Times*, January 9, 2005.

"A Physicist Experiments with Cultural Studies." *Lingua Franca*, May/June 1996.

"Ponzi Arrested by Federal Authorities." *Wall Street Journal*, August 13, 1920.

"Ponzi Creditors Get Final Payment." *Wall Street Journal*, December 24, 1930.

"Proof Lacking for Ritual Abuse by Satanists." *New York Times*, October 31, 1994.

"The 'Protocols' at 100: A Hoax of Hate Lives On." *New York Sun*, November 18, 2005.

"Psychic Detective: Sylvia Browne's History of Failure." *Skeptical Inquirer*, March/April 2010.

"P. T. Barnum, Justice Harlan, and Connecticut's Role in the Development of the Right to Privacy." *Federal Bar Council Quarterly*, December 13, 2004.

"Radio Listeners in Panic, Taking War Drama as Fact." *New York Times*, October 31, 1938.

"Real 'Wolf of Wall Street' Jordan Belfort Still Owes Millions to Victims: Prosecutors." *New York Daily News*, October 19, 2013.

"Reel or Real? The Truth Behind Two Hollywood Ghost Stories." *Skeptical Inquirer*, March 2005.

"Remotely Viewed? The Charlie Jordan Case." *Skeptical Inquirer*, March 2001.

"Report: Story of Girl Getting Tossed from KFC Hoax." *The Clarion Ledger*, June 23, 2014.

"Return to Roswell." *Skeptical Inquirer*, January/February 2009.

"Rio Journal; Live, in Brazil (Again): The Reincarnated Dr. Fritz." *New York Times*, January 12, 1996.

"The Ritual Sex Abuse Hoax." *The Village Voice*, January 12, 1990.

"The Roswellian Syndrome: How Some UFO Myths Develop." *Skeptical Inquirer*, May/June 2012.

"Rothstein Quotes Burns in Defense." *New York Times*, July 24, 1921.

"Saints, Sinners, and Reformers." *The Crooked Lake Review*, fall 2005.

"The Scam Artist Who Turned to a Life of Literary Lies." *The Toronto Star*, May 23, 2015.

"A Scheme with No Off Button." *New York Times*, December 21, 2008.

"Scientific Consensus and Expert Testimony: Lessons from the Judas Priest Trial." *Skeptical Inquirer*, November/December 1996.

"SEC Says Utah Family Used Mormon Ties for $220 Million Fraud." *Bloomberg BusinessWeek*, December 16, 2011.

"She Played on the Heartstrings." *Toronto Star*, May 25, 2013.

"Six College Men Take LSD, Blinded by Sun." *Los Angeles Times*, January 13, 1968.

"60 Years Ago, Sing Sing's Electric Chair Had One Busy Night." *New York Daily News*, February 27, 2011.

"A Skeleton's Tale: The Origins of Modern Spiritualism." *Skeptical Inquirer*, July/August 2008.

"Slaves to the Cocaine Habit." *New York Times*, May 26, 1886.

"Snake Oil: A Guide for Connoisseurs." *Skeptical Inquirer*, September 2006.

"Spread of Illegal Devices Causes Alarm." *The Seattle Times*, November 21, 2007.

"States of Mind: Some Perceived ET Encounters." *Skeptical Inquirer*, November/December 2012.

"Steve Brodie: Daredevil or Hoaxer?" *New York Post*, November 5, 2007.

"Steve Brodie's Funeral." *New York Times*, February 7, 1901.

"The Sting (1973)." *New York Times*, December 26, 1973.

"Subliminal Perception: Facts and Fallacies." *Skeptical Inquirer,* Spring 1992.

"Sybil: The Making of a Disease: An Interview with Dr. Herbert Spiegel." *New York Review of Books*, April 24, 1997.

"Sylvia Browne Takes the Case!" *Skeptic Magazine*, Volume 18, Number 3, 2013.

"Teens Still Falling Victim to Online 'Sextortion.'" *The Toronto Star*, September 5, 2014.

"10 Dead, 20 Hurt in a Race Riot—Drug-Crazed Negroes Start a Reign of Terror and Defy Whole Mississippi Town." *New York Times*, September 29, 1913.

"Testing Dowsing: The Failure of the Munich Experiments." *Skeptical Inquirer*, January/February 1999.

"Texas Pair Released After Serving 21 Years for 'Satanic Abuse.'" *The Guardian*, December 5, 2013.

"That's Where the Money Is." *The Economist,* May 21, 2014.

"There Will Be Scandal: An Oil Stain on the Jazz Age." *New York Times,* February 13, 2008.

"The Transformation of a Klansman," *New York Times*, October 4, 1991.

"The Truth? Just Catch It If You Can." *Los Angeles Times*, December 28, 2002.

"The Vision Thing." *TIME*, December 11, 1995.

"Top 10 Worst Cabinet Members." *TIME* magazine, November 12, 2008.

"Transgressing the Boundaries: Toward a Transformative Hermeneutics of Quantum Gravity." Alan Sokal, Department of Physics, New York University, *Social Text*, spring/summer 1996.

"Turn Me On, Dead Man." *Scientific American*, May 2005.

The $272 Billion Swindle." *The Economist*, May 31, 2014.

"Unmasking Sybil." *Newsweek*, January 24, 1999.

"Unproven Methods of Cancer Management: 'Psychic Surgery.'" *CA—A Cancer Journal for Clinicians*, May/June 1990.

"Wait, There's More," *Washington Post*, October 23, 2005.

"What Really Happened at Roswell." *Skeptical Inquirer*, July/August 1997.

"What 'They' Don't Want You to Know: An Analysis of Kevin Trudeau's Natural Cures." *Skeptical Inquirer*, January/February 2006.

"Who Abused Jane Doe? The Hazards of the Single Case History." *Skeptical Inquirer*, May/June 2002.

"The Wolf of Wall Street: The True Story." *TIME*, December 26, 2013.

"Vancouver Man Wanders Streets of Shenzhen, China, Looking for an Online Love He's Never Met." *National Post*, April 29, 2015.

"'Youngest African-American CEO' Pleads Guilty to $7M Fraud." *Kansas City Business Journal*, October 9, 2014.

DOCUMENTS, REPORTS, AND TESTIMONY

"Annual Report for Fiscal Year 2013." Department of Health and Human Services and Department of Justice, Health Care Fraud and Abuse Control Program, February 2014.

"Baby-Selling Ring Busted." Federal Bureau of Investigation, San Diego Division, August 9, 2011.

"Bernard L. Madoff Pleads Guilty to 11-Count Criminal Information and Is Remanded into Custody." U.S. Attorney's Office, Southern District of New York, March 12, 2009.

"Beware of Scams and Fraudulent Phone Calls." Federal Emergency Management Agency, October 10, 2014.

"Bulgarian Citizen Sentenced in Manhattan Federal Court to 21 Months in Prison for Stealing $1.8 Million from Banks Using ATM 'Skimming' Scheme." U.S. Attorney's Office, Southern District of New York, July 13, 2011.

"The Campaign and Election of 1876," Miller Center, University of Virginia.

"Cancer Facts and Figures 2015." American Cancer Society.

"CEO of Capitol Investments USA Charged in $880 Million Ponzi Scheme Based on Phony Grocery Business." U.S. Attorney's Office, District of New Jersey, April 21, 2010.

"CFO Jeff Atwater Announces Nine Miami PIP Fraud Arrests." Jeff Atwater, Chief Financial Officer, Florida Department of Financial Services, January 27, 2015.

"Child Predator Is Sentenced to 35 Years in Prison for His Massive Online Sextortion Scheme." U.S. Attorney's Office, Middle District of Alabama, January 23, 2013.

"Complementary, Alternative, or Integrative Health: What's In a Name?" U.S. Department of Health and Human Services, National Institutes of Health, National Center for Complementary and Alternative Medicine website, https://nccih.nih.gov/health/integrative-health.

"Crashing: A Serial Staged-Crash Artist Earns Colorado Attorney's Prosecutor of the Year Award." Coalition Against Insurance Fraud, January 5, 2015.

"Debit Card Skimming Group Arrested and Charged with Fraud and Identity Theft." U.S. Attorney's Office, Southern District of Florida, May 1, 2009.

"Department of Justice Disrupts International Cyber Crime Rings Distributing Scareware." June 22, 2011, U.S. Department of Justice.

"Ephren Taylor, II, Pleads Guilty to Conspiracy to Commit Fraud." U.S. Attorney's Office, Northern District of Georgia, October 8, 2014.

"An Evaluation of Remote Viewing: Research and Applications." Prepared by American Institutes for Research, September 29, 1995.

"FBI Alerts Public to Be Aware of Disaster Fraud in Aftermath of Recent Wildfires." Federal Bureau of Investigation, San Diego Division, May 16, 2014.

"Federal Court Finds Kevin Trudeau in Civil Contempt." Federal Trade Commission, November 21, 2007.

"Florida Man Pleads Guilty in Stock Scheme That Swindled Millions from Investors." U.S. Attorney's Office, District of New Jersey, January 21, 2010.

"Former Dixon Comptroller Rita Crundwell Pleads Guilty to Federal Fraud Charge, Admits Stealing $53 Million from City." U.S. Attorney's Office, Northern District of Illinois, November 14, 2012.

"FTC Halts Massive Tech Support Scams." Federal Trade Commission, October 3, 2012.

"Government's Sentencing Memorandum." Lev L. Dassin, Acting United States Attorney for the Southern District of New York, United States District Court, Southern District of New York, Filed June 26, 2009.

"Government's Sentencing Memorandum." Zachary T. Fardon, United States Attorney, April M. Perry, Assistant United States Attorney, Marc Krickbaum, Assistant United States Attorney, United States District Court, Northern District of Illinois, Eastern Division, March 17, 2014.

"Guidance for Industry on Complementary and Alternative Medicine Products and Their Regulation by the Food and Drug Administration." Draft guidance, U.S. Department of Health and Human Services, Food and Drug Administration, December 2006.

"Health Fraud." Statement of John M. Taylor, Director, Office of Enforcement, Office of Regulatory Affairs, Food and Drug Administration before the Senate Special Committee on Aging. September 10, 2001.

"Hey, Wanna Buy a Baseball Autographed by … Mother Teresa?" Federal Bureau of Investigation, press release, July 22, 2005.

"A Hoax of Hate: The Protocols of the Learned Elders of Zion." Anti-Defamation League.

"In the Matter of Travel King, Inc., et al." Federal Trade Commission, Docket 8949, Amended Complaint, May 17, 1974—Order, September 30, 1975.

"Investigator's Guide to Allegations of 'Ritual' Child Abuse." Behavioral Science Unit, National Center for the Analysis of Violent Crime, Federal Bureau of Investigation, 1992.

"Justice Department Officials Raise Awareness of Disaster Fraud Hotline Following Typhoon Haiyan." Department of Justice, November 14, 2013.

"Kevin Trudeau Banned from Infomercials for Three Years, Ordered to Pay More Than $5 Million for False Claims About Weight-Loss Book." Federal Trade Commission, October 6, 2008.

"Lyndon B. Johnson: Life before the Presidency." Miller Center, University of Virginia.

"Manhattan U.S. Attorney and FBI Assistant Director in Charge Announce Charges Against Seven Individuals for Conspiring to Commit Securities Fraud and Extortion: Defendants' 'Pump and Dump' Scheme Targeted 'Penny' Stocks." Federal Bureau of Investigation, New York Office, April 4, 2013.

"Manhattan U.S. Attorney Charges Bulgarian Man with Using Stolen Bank Account Information to Defraud Banks of Over $1 Million." U.S. Attorney's Office, Southern District of New York, September 23, 2010.

"Modesto Surrogate Parenting Agency Owner Indicted for $2 Million Fraud Scheme." Federal Bureau of Investigation, Sacramento Division, April 20, 2012.

"Modesto Surrogate Parenting Agency Owner Pleads Guilty in $2 Million Fraud Scheme." Federal Bureau of Investigation, Sacramento Division, February 19, 2013.

"More Than 900 Defendants Charged with Disaster-Related Fraud by Hurricane Katrina Fraud Task Force During Three Years in Operation." Federal Bureau of Investigation, National Press Office, October 1, 2008.

"MPs Urge Government to Withdraw NHS Funding and MHRA Licensing of Homeopathy." House of Commons, Science and Technology Committee, February 22, 2010.

"New York Man Sentenced to 63 Months for Selling Fake Cancer Cure." Food and Drug Administration, June 23, 2004.

Pistone, Joseph, Testimony before the U.S. Senate Permanent Subcommittee on Investigations of the Committee on Governmental Affairs, 1988.

"Plea Allocution of Bernard L. Madoff." United States District Court, Southern District of New York. March 12, 2009.

"Prepaid Funeral Scam: Fitting End to Multi-State Fraud Scheme." Federal Bureau of Investigation, January 17, 2014.

"Prominent Surrogacy Attorney Sentenced to Prison for Her Role in Baby-Selling Case." Federal Bureau of Investigation, San Diego Division, February 24, 2012.

"Protocols of the Elders of Zion." U.S. Holocaust Memorial Museum, last updated June 10, 2013.

"Public Beware! Warning Against the Hoxsey Cancer Treatment." Food and Drug Administration poster, April 1956.

"Scams Coming with Health Reform in October, Coalition Warns." Coalition Against Insurance Fraud, September 11, 2013.

"Science and Technology Committee—Fourth Report, Evidence Check 2: Homeopathy." House of Commons, Science and Technology Committee, fourth report of Session 2009-10, February 22, 2010.

"SEC Charges Ponzi Schemer Targeting Church Congregations." U.S. Securities and Exchange Commission, April 12, 2012.

"Seventeen Defendants Indicted in Chicago in International ATM Skimming and Money Laundering Scheme, Two Arrested in Bulgaria." Federal Bureau of Investigation, Chicago Office, March 26, 2014.

"Six Defendants Sentenced to a Total of 36 Years in Prison in National Prearranged Services Case." U.S. Attorney's Office, Eastern District of Missouri, November 14, 2013.

"Surrogate Parenting Agency Owner Ordered to Pay $1.7 Million to Victims." Federal Bureau of Investigation, Sacramento Division, September 10, 2013.

"Therapeutic Touch." American Cancer Society.

"2014 Internet Crime Report." Federal Bureau of Investigation and National White Collar Crime Center, The Internet Crime Complaint Center, http://www.ic3.gov/media/annualreport/2014_IC3Report.pdf.

"Unconventional Cancer Treatments." United States Congress, Office of Technology Assessment, 1990, United States Congress, Office of Technology Assessment, Unconventional Cancer Treatments, 1990, http://www.quackwatch.org/01QuackeryRelatedTopics/OTA/ota00.html.

"Unidentified Flying Objects—Project Blue Book." The National Archives, http://www.archives.gov/research/military/air-force/ufos.html#mj12.

"Warning: Bogus Phone Calls on Jury Service May Lead to Fraud." Administrative Office of the U.S. Courts.

"Warren G. Harding: Domestic Affairs." Miller Center, University of Virginia.

"Woman Who Staged Fake Funerals as Part of Life Insurance Scam Found Guilty of Federal Fraud Charges." U.S. Attorney's Office, Central District of California, August 2, 2010.

WEBSITES AND ONLINE ARTICLES

AARP blog, "Eight Scams That Take Aim at Veterans," June 11, 2015. http://blog.aarp.org/2015/11/06/veteransdayscams/.

AARP blog, "Inside the Grandparents Scam: A Con Artist Reveals All," April 21, 2014. http://blog.aarp.org/2014/04/21/inside-the-grandparents-scam-a-con-artist-reveals-all/.

AARP Bulletin, "Phony Phone Numbers Can Cost You Money," September 2015. http://www.aarp.org/money/scams-fraud/info-2015/avoid-scam-800-numbers.html.

ABCNews.com. "Are Cancer Fraudsters Desperate of Psychopathic?" August 12, 2010. http://abcnews.go.com/Health/MindMoodNews/ashley-kirilow-cancer-charity-fraudsters/story?id=11369697.

ABCnews.com. "Ephren Taylor Accused of $11 Million Christian Ponzi Scheme by SEC." August 21, 2013. http://abcnews.go.com/US/ephren-taylor-accused-11-million-christian-ponzi-scheme/story?id=20030745.

ABCNews.com. "Maryland Woman Allegedly Lies About Cancer, Bilks Friends for Thousands of Dollars." February 1, 2009. http://abcnews.go.com/Business/dina-leone-maryland-woman-accused-fraud-lying-cancer/story?id=9703436.

ABCNews.com. "New York Cops, Firefighters in Massive 9/11 Fraud, Indictment Says." January 7, 2014. http://abcnews.go.com/US/york-cops-firefighters-massive-911-fraud-indictment/story?id=21445783.

ABC30.com. "Surrogacy Scam." http://abc30.com/archive/6790514/.

About.com. "Spot the Frauds and Hoaxes and Deal with the Fakers." August 20, 2014. http://breastcancer.about.com/od/Caregiver_Support/a/How-To-Avoid-Cancer-Frauds.htm.

Allthingscrimeblog.com. "Their Satanic Majesty's Release: Child Sex Abuse Day Care Owner Released After 20 Years." December 8, 2013. (Article no longer online.)

An Almanac of California, Emperor Norton's Archives. http://www.notfrisco.com/nortoniana/.

American Cancer Society website. http://www.cancer.org/.

American Cancer Society website. Hoxsey Treatment. http://documents.cancer.org/acs/groups/cid/documents/webcontent/002420-pdf.pdf.

American Cancer Society website. Therapeutic Touch. http://www.cancer.org/treatment/treatmentsandsideeffects/complementaryandalternativemedicine/manualhealingandpsychicaltouch/therapeutic-touch. (Webpage no longer online.)

Barnum Museum website. http://barnum-museum.org/.

BBC News. "Fight Back on ID Theft." April 9, 2006, http://news.bbc.co.uk/2/hi/business/4754733.stm.

Better Business Bureau, Metropolitan New York, Long Island and the Mid-Hudson Region. "The Nigerian Prince: Old Scam, New Twist." http://www.bbb.org/new-york-city/get-consumer-help/articles/the-nigerian-prince-old-scam-new-twist/.

Blackjackinfo.com. "Interview with 'MIT Mike' Aponte." https://www.blackjackinfo.com/interviews/mit-mike-aponte/.

BoxOfficeMojo.com, "The Education of Little Tree." http://www.boxofficemojo.com/search/?q=the%20education%20of%20little%20tree.

Buffalo Bill Center of the West. http://centerofthewest.org/.

Casewatch.org. "Sylvia Browne's Criminal Conviction." December 12, 2013, http://www.casewatch.org/crim/browne/complaint.shtml.

CBC News online. "Amanda Todd Case: RCMP Detail 5 Charges Against Dutch Citizen." April 17, 2014. http://www.cbc.ca/news/canada/british-columbia/amanda-todd-case-rcmp-detail-5-charges-against-dutch-citizen-1.2614034.

Center for Inquiry blog. "Another Sylvia Browne Failure." May 9, 2013. http://www.centerforinquiry.net/blogs/entry/another_sylvia_browne_failure/.

Center for Inquiry blog. "'Dr.' McLean's Nostrums." February 8, 2013. http://www .centerforinquiry.net/blogs/entry/dr._mcleans_nostrums/.

Center for Inquiry blog. "Dr. Porter and His Healing Oil." August 12, 2013. http:// www.centerforinquiry.net/blogs/entry/dr._porter_and_his_healing_oil/.

Center for Inquiry blog. "Horrors! Amityville Returns!" March 20, 2013. http://www .centerforinquiry.net/blogs/entry/horrors_amityville_returns/.

Center for Inquiry blog. "Old Anti-Catholic Hoax Continues." November 14, 2012. http://www.centerforinquiry.net/blogs/entry/old_anti-catholic_hoax_continues/.

Center for Inquiry blog. "The New Snake Oil." March 4, 2009. http://www.centerfor inquiry.net/blogs/entry/the_new_snake_oil/.

Chicago Historical Society. The Black Sox. http://www.chicagohs.org/history/black sox.html.

CNN.com. "Prosecutor: More than 100 NYC Police and Firefighters Indicted in PTSD Scam." January 7, 2014. http://www.cnn.com/2014/01/07/justice/new-york-ptsd -9-11-scam/index.html.

Coalition Against Health Fraud website. "Smelly Sinus Ploys Buy Nose Doc's Luxury Life." January 29, 2013. http://www.insurancefraud.org/article.htm?RecID=3239# .VZLaZtFRHIU.

Coalition Against Insurance Fraud website, Fraud Statistics. http://www.insurance fraud.org/statistics.htm#Health%20Insurance.

Coalition Against Insurance Fraud website. "The Impact of Insurance Fraud." http:// www.insurancefraud.org/the-impact-of-insurance-fraud.htm#.VZBfFNFRHIU.

Coalition Against Insurance Fraud website. "Impact of Insurance Fraud Statement by John Sargent at the Sentencing of Joseph Haddad." July 10, 2014. http://www .insurancefraud.org/IFNS-detail.htm?key=18967#.VZBgR9FRHIU.

Common Ground Foundation website. Biography, Ephren W. Taylor II. http://www .commongroundfoundation.org/ephren.html.

Crimes of Persuasion website. http://www.crimes-of-persuasion.com/.

Crime Library.com. "The Lonely Hearts Killers." (Website no longer online.)

Daily Mail online. "'I Was Conned into Smuggling Cocaine by a Voluptuous Bikini Model—Then Locked Up in an Argentinian Hellhole Where an Inmate Was Butch-ered in Front of Me': Incredible Tale of 'Naïve' Professor, 71." February 25, 2015. http://www.dailymail.co.uk/news/article-2968276/He-went-straight-neck-decap itated-Professor-fell-honeytrap-cocaine-sting-relives-horrifying-moment-prisoner -butchered-eyes-notorious-Argentinian-jail.html.

Department of Justice, Elder Justice website, http://www.justice.gov/elderjustice/.

Deseret News. "Did Con Man Teach at BYU?" December 26, 2002. http://www.deseret news.com/article/956024/Did-con-man-teach-at-BYU.html?pg=all.

DigitalHeritage.org. Dr. John Brinkley. http://digitalheritage.org/2010/08/dr-john -brinkly/.

Embassy of the United States Abidjan, Cote d'Ivoire. "419 Scams." http://abidjan.usembassy .gov/art_of_scam.html.

Encyclopedia.com. Contemporary Black Biography. Ephren W. Taylor, II. http://www .encyclopedia.com/doc/1G2-2694600054.html.

Ephren Taylor. "Create the Success" website. http://createthesuccess.com/index.html.

eSkeptic. "Charlatan: Quackery Then and Now." July 9, 2008. http://www.skeptic .com/eskeptic/08-07-09/.

eSkeptic. "Faith Healing." March 27, 2008. http://www.skeptic.com/eskeptic/08-03-27/.

Esquire.com, "Q&A with Alan Abel, Hoax Master," February 7, 2007. http://www .esquire.com/entertainment/interviews/a1960/esq0406-esq04006news-76-1/.

Esquire.com, "Ten Questions for the Best Prankster Ever," March 30, 2011. http:// www.esquire.com/entertainment/interviews/a5816/alan-abel-hoaxes-033109/.

Esquire Magazine blog. "The Wolf of Wall Street Is Real and I've Been Reporting on Him for Years." December 23, 2013. http://www.esquire.com/entertainment /news/a26702/real-wolf-of-wall-street/.

Examiner.com. "Heroin Addicts Pleads Guilty to Cancer Scam." December 12, 2013. http://www.examiner.com/article/heroin-addict-pleads-guilty-to-cancer-scam.

Facebook.com. Kevin Trudeau Facebook postings. May 3, 28, and 29, 2014. https:// www.facebook.com/pages/Kevin-Trudeau/106186792746742?fref=ts#.

Federal Bureau of Investigation. "FBI Records, The Vault: Majestic 12." https://vault .fbi.gov/Majestic%2012.

Federal Bureau of Investigation podcast. "Baby-Selling Ring." https://www.fbi.gov /news/podcasts/inside/baby-selling-ring.mp3/view.

Federal Bureau of Investigation, San Diego Division. "Looking for Love? Beware of Online Dating Scams." February 14, 2013. https://www.fbi.gov/sandiego /press-releases/2013/looking-for-love-beware-of-online-dating-scams.

Federal Bureau of Investigation, San Diego Division. "Operation Bullpen." April 2000. https://www.fbi.gov/sandiego/about-us/history/operation-bullpen.

Federal Bureau of Investigation website. "A Cautionary Tale—Staged Auto Accident Fraud: Don't Let It Happen to You," February 18, 2005. https://www.fbi.gov /news/stories/2005/february/staged_auto021805.

Federal Bureau of Investigation website. "A Case of 'Sextortion': Cons Like 'Bieber Ruse' Targeted Minor Girls." February 5, 2013. https://www.fbi.gov/news/news _blog/a-case-of-sextortion.

Federal Bureau of Investigation website. "Adoption Scams Bilk Victims, Break Hearts." August 28, 2006. https://www.fbi.gov/news/stories/2006/august/adoptscams_082806.

Federal Bureau of Investigation website. "America's National Pastime." October 15, 2003. https://www.fbi.gov/news/stories/2003/october/bullpen_101503.

Federal Bureau of Investigation website. "Another Ponzi Case and a Warning for Investors." 2010. https://www.fbi.gov/news/stories/2010/may/ponzi_050310.

Federal Bureau of Investigation website. "Common Fraud Schemes." https://www.fbi .gov/scams-safety/fraud.

Federal Bureau of Investigation website. "Consumer Alert, Online Rental Ads Could Be Phony." July 29, 2009. https://www.fbi.gov/news/stories/2009/july /housingscam_072909.

Federal Bureau of Investigation website. "Fake Funerals, Empty Caskets: A Different Kind of Scam." https://www.fbi.gov/news/stories/2010/september/funeral-scams /financial-fraud-and-funeral-scams.

Federal Bureau of Investigation website. "Fighting Fraud in the Wake of Natural Disasters." https://www.fbi.gov/news/stories/2008/october/disasterfraud_100808.

Federal Bureau of Investigation website. "Gone Phishing: Global Ring Gets Rather Slick." May 20, 2008. https://www.fbi.gov/news/stories/2008/may/phishing052008.

Federal Bureau of Investigation website. "Health Care Fraud." https://www.fbi.gov /about-us/investigate/white_collar/health-care-fraud.

Federal Bureau of Investigation website. "Malware Targets Bank Accounts: 'Gameover' Delivered via Phishing E-Mails." January 6, 2012. https://www.fbi.gov/news /stories/2012/january/malware_010612/malware_010612.

Federal Bureau of Investigation website. "New Internet Scam: 'Ransomware' Locks Computers, Demands Payment." August 9, 2012. https://www.fbi.gov/news/stories /2012/august/new-internet-scam.

Federal Bureau of Investigation website. "Nigerian Letter or '419' Fraud." https://www .fbi.gov/scams-safety/fraud.

Federal Bureau of Investigation website, "Operation Bullpen: Overview." July 2005. https://www.fbi.gov/news/stories/2005/july/operation-bullpen-overview.

Federal Bureau of Investigation website. "Organized Crime: Italian Organized Crime—Overview." http://www.fbi.gov/hq/cid/orgcrime/lcnindex.htm.

Federal Bureau of Investigation website. "'Scareware' Distributors Targeted: 12 Nations Coordinate Anti-Cyber Crime Effort." June 22, 2011. https://www.fbi.gov/news /stories/2011/june/cyber_062211/cyber_062211.

Federal Bureau of Investigation website. "Senior Citizen Fraud." https://www.fbi.gov /news/stories/2008/april/seniofraud_041008.

Federal Bureau of Investigation website. "Something Vishy: Be Aware of a New Online Scam." February 23, 2007. https://www.fbi.gov/news/stories/2007/february/vishing _022307/.

Federal Bureau of Investigation website. "Surrogacy Scam Played on Emotions of Vulnerable Victims." September 13, 2011. https://www.fbi.gov/news/stories/2011 /september/surrogacy_091311/surrogacy_091311.

Federal Bureau of Investigation website. "Taking a Trip to the ATM? Beware of 'Skimmers.'" https://www.fbi.gov/news/stories/2011/july/atm_071411.

Federal Bureau of Investigation website. "Telephone Fraud Involving Jury Duty." September 28, 2005. https://www.fbi.gov/news/pressrel/press-releases/telephone -fraud-involving-jury-duty.

Federal Bureau of Investigation website. "The Grandparent Scam: Don't Let It Happen to You." https://www.fbi.gov/news/stories/2012/april/grandparent_040212.

Federal Bureau of Investigation website. "The Latest Phone Scam Targets Your Bank Account." June 21, 2010. https://www.fbi.gov/news/stories/2010/june/phone -scam.

Federal Bureau of Investigation website. "The Verdict: Hang Up—Don't Fall for Jury Duty Scam." June 6, 2006. http://www.fbi.gov/news/stories/2006/june/jury_scam 060206.

Federal Trade Commission. "Consumer Information: Advance Fee Loans." http:// www.consumer.ftc.gov/articles/0078-advance-fee-loans.

Food and Drug Administration website. "Beware of Online Cancer Fraud." June 17, 2008. http://www.fda.gov/ForConsumers/ConsumerUpdates/ucm048383.htm.

FoxNews.com. "Report: Gotti Breast Cancer a Sham." August 24, 2005. http://www .foxnews.com/story/2005/08/24/report-gotti-breast-cancer-sham.html.

Frank Abagnale website. http://www.abagnale.com/.

Frank Bourassa website. http://www.frankbourassa.com/en/.

From the Heart Foundation. Father Joshua. http://www.psychicsurgeon.org/.

Georgia News Day website. "Exclusive—A New $7.5M Miami Home and a $250,000 Rolls Royce: The Luxurious Life of Real-Life Wolf of Wall Street's Partner in Crime—And There's Nothing His Victims Owed $200M Can Do About It." January 18, 2014. http://www.georgianewsday.com/news/regional/207484-exclusive-a -new-7-5m-miami-home-and-a-250-000-rolls-royce-the-luxurious-life-of-real-life -wolf-of-wall-street-s-partner-in-crime-and-there-s-nothing-his-victims-owed -200m-can-do-about-it.html.

Huffington Post. "Sylvia Browne: Dead Psychic's Legacy Riddled with Failed Predictions, Fraud." November 21, 2013. http://www.huffingtonpost.com/2013/11/21 /sylvia-browne_n_4317470.html.

Inc.com. "Luck Is for Losers." August 1, 2008. http://www.inc.com/magazine /20080801/luck-is-for-losers.html.

Internet Archive Wayback Machine. About Prof. C Nelson. http://web.archive.org/web /20070810183304/http:/pennyfox.com/nelson.htm.

James Randi Educational Foundation: An Encyclopedia of Claims, Frauds, and Hoaxes of the Occult and Supernatural. "Dowsing." https://web.archive.org/web /20140707120029/http://www.randi.org/encyclopedia/dowsing.html.

Jordan Belfort website. http://jordanbelfort.com/.

Kansas Historical Society, Kansapedia. John R. Brinkley. http://www.kshs.org/kansa pedia/john-r-brinkley/11988.

Kansas Historical Society, KansasMemory.org. *After Twenty-One Years: The Success Story of Dr. John R. Brinkley* (archived version of booklet originally published by the Brinkley Hospitals of Little Rock, Arkansas). http://www.kansasmemory.org /item/213226.

Keep American Beautiful, Public Service Television Announcement. "The Crying Indian." 1971. https://www.youtube.com/watch?v=j7OHG7tHrNM.

Lost Museum, American Social History/Center for Media and Learning, The Graduate Center, City University of New York and Center for History and New Media, George Mason University. http://www.lostmuseum.cuny.edu/.

Microsoft.com. "How to Recognize Phishing E-mail Messages, Links, or Phone Calls." http://www.microsoft.com/security/online-privacy/phishing-symptoms.aspx.

Museum of Hoaxes website. "The Cardiff Giant." http://hoaxes.org/archive/permalink /the_cardiff_giant/.

Museum of Hoaxes website. "The Great Chess Automaton." http://hoaxes.org/archive /permalink/the_great_chess_automaton.

Museum of Hoaxes website. "The Great Moon Hoax of 1835." http://hoaxes.org /archive/permalink/the_great_moon_hoax.

Museum of Hoaxes website. "The Protocols of the Elders of Zion, 1903." http://hoaxes .org/archive/permalink/the_protocols_of_the_elders_of_zion.

Museum of Quackery.com. Albert Abrams. http://www.museumofquackery.com/am quacks/abrams.htm

My Fox 8.com. "TV Infomercial Star Kevin Trudeau Gets 10 Years in Prison." March 17, 2014. http://myfox8.com/2014/03/17/kevin-trudeau-sent-to-prison/.

National Cancer Institute, "Gerson Therapy (PDQ)." http://www.cancer.gov/about-cancer/treatment/cam/patient/gerson-pdq.

National Cancer Institute. "Laetrile/Amygdalin (PDQ)—Patient Version." Last modified February 20, 2013. http://www.cancer.gov/about-cancer/treatment/cam/patient/laetrile-pdq/.

National Council Against Health Fraud. "NCAHF Consumer Information Statements on Faith Healing and Psychic Surgery (1987)." http://www.ncahf.org/pp/faith.html.

Naval History & Heritage Command website, "Exorcizing the Devil's Triangle," http://www.history.navy.mil/research/library/online-reading-room/title-list-alphabetically/e/exorcizing-the-devils-triangle.html.

News.com.au website. "KFC 'Hoax' Girl Victoria Wilcher Arrives for Surgery in Florida." July 8, 2014.

NJ.com. "Jersey Hustle: The Real-Life Story of Abscam." November 25, 2013. http://www.nj.com/inside-jersey/index.ssf/2013/11/jersey_hustle_the_real-life_story_of_abscam.html.

NPR.org. "Elmer Gantry, a Flawed Preacher for the Ages." February 22, 2008. http://www.npr.org/templates/story/story.php?storyId=19288767.

NPR.org. "The Truth Behind the Lies of the Original 'Welfare Queen.'" December 20, 2013. http://www.npr.org/sections/codeswitch/2013/12/20/255819681/the-truth-behind-the-lies-of-the-original-welfare-queen.

Oak Ridge Associated Universities, Health Psychics Historical Instrumental Collection website. "Radioactive Quack Cures." http://www.orau.org/ptp/collection/quackcures/quackcures.htm.

Officer Down Memorial Page—Joseph Petrosino. http://www.odmp.org/officer/10600-lieutenant-joseph-petrosino.

PBS.org. "Timeline of Houdini's Life." http://www.pbs.org/wgbh/amex/houdini/timeline/index.html.

Psychologytoday.com blog. "Cancer Fraud: People Who Fake Illness to Scam Others, Gain Sympathy, Get Rich and Avoid Other Problems." January 28, 2010. https://www.psychologytoday.com/blog/the-human-equation/201001/cancer-fraud-people-who-fake-illness-scam-others-gain-sympathy-get.

Quackwatch.org. "Homeopathy: The Ultimate Fake." http://www.quackwatch.org/01QuackeryRelatedTopics/homeo.html.

Quackwatch.org. "Questionable Cancer Therapies." http://www.quackwatch.org/01QuackeryRelatedTopics/cancer.html.

Quackwatch.org. "Some Notes on the Quantum Xrroid (QXCI) and William Nelson." http://www.quackwatch.org/01QuackeryRelatedTopics/Tests/xrroid.html.

Quackwatch.org. "Sylvia Browne: Psychic or Con Artist?" December 14, 2013, http://www.quackwatch.com/11Ind/browne.html.

Quackwatch.org. "The Goat Gland Doctor: The Story of John. R. Brinkley." http://www.quackwatch.org/11Ind/brinkley.html.

QX Conference website. http://www.qxconference.com/.

Randi.org, James Randi. "Message from James Randi on Sylvia Browne's Death." November 21, 2013. http://archive.randi.org/site/index.php/swift-blog/2273-message-from-james-randi-on-sylvia-brownes-death.html.

Ringling Brothers and Barnum & Bailey Circus website. http://www.ringling.com /ContentPage.aspx?id=45832&section=45825.

Roger Ebert website. "The Hustler." June 23, 2002. http://www.rogerebert.com /reviews/great-movie-the-hustler-1961.

Romance Scams website. http://www.romancescams.org/.

Royal Canadian Mounted Police. "E-mail Fraud/Phishing." http://www.rcmp-grc.gc .ca/scams-fraudes/phishing-eng.htm.

Salon.com. "The Education of Little Fraud." December 20, 2001. http://www.salon .com/2001/12/20/carter_6/

Salon.com. "What Kevin Trudeau Doesn't Want You to Know." July 29, 2005. http:// www.salon.com/2005/07/29/trudeau_4/.

San Francisco Museum and Historical Society, Encyclopedia of San Francisco web-site. "Emperor Norton." http://sfhistoryencyclopedia.com/articles/n/nortonJoshua .html.

Scambusters.org, Scambusters website. "What Everyone Ought to Know About Can-cer Fraud." http://www.scambusters.org/cancerfraud.html.

Skeptoid.com podcast, Skeptoid # 438. "The *War of the Worlds* Panic Broadcast." Octo-ber 28, 2014. http://skeptoid.com/episodes/4438.

Skeptoid.com podcast, Skeptoid #203. "Therapeutic Touch." April 27, 2010.

Slate.com. "'A Shocking Sabbath Carnival of Death.'" July 24, 2014. http://www.slate. com/articles/news_and_politics/history/2014/07/james_gordon_bennett_jr_s _new_york_herald_the_central_park_zoo_wild_animal.html.

Slate.com. "The Myth of the *War of the Worlds* Panic." October 28, 2013. http:// www.slate.com/articles/arts/history/2013/10/orson_welles_war_of_the_worlds _panic_myth_the_infamous_radio_broadcast_did.html.

Slate.com. "The Real Victims of Satanic Ritual Abuse." January 7, 2014. http://www .slate.com/articles/health_and_science/medical_examiner/2014/01/fran_and _dan_keller_freed_two_of_the_last_victims_of_satanic_ritual_abuse.single .html.

Slate.com. "The Welfare Queen." December 19, 2013. http://www.slate.com/articles /news_and_politics/history/2013/12/linda_taylor_welfare_queen_ronald_reagan _made_her_a_notorious_american_villain.html.

The Smoking Gun website. "A Million Little Lies." January 8, 2006. http://www.the smokinggun.com/documents/celebrity/million-little-lies.

The Smoking Gun website. "A Thousand Little Refunds." October 1, 2007. http:// www.thesmokinggun.com/documents/crime/thousand-little-refunds.

Snopes.com. "Blinded by the Light." http://www.snopes.com/horrors/drugs/lsdsun .asp.

Snopes.com. "From Here to Maternity." http://www.snopes.com/pregnant/blackout .asp.

Snopes.com. "Iron Eyes Cody." Updated August 9, 2007. http://www.snopes.com /movies/actors/ironeyes.asp.

Snopes.com. "Slice Appeal." http://www.snopes.com/horrors/drugs/facepeel.asp.

Snopes.com. "Wasted and Basted." http://snopes.com/horrors/drugs/babysitter.asp.

Society of Novus Spiritus website. http://novus.org/home/index.cfm.

The Straight Dope website. "Was the Indian Who Shed a Tear in That Anti-Pollution Commercial Really Indian?" August 30, 1999. http://www.straightdope.com /columns/read/1677/was-the-indian-who-shed-a-tear-in-that-anti-pollution-com mercial-really-italian.

Swift, the online newsletter of the James Randi Educational Foundation. "From the Archives: Randi's Inside Scoop into ABC News' 'John of God' Investigation." February 18, 2005. http://web.randi.org/home/from-the-archives-randis-inside -scoop-into-abc-news-john-of-god-investigation-2005.

Sylvia Browne website. http://sylviabrowne.com/.

United States Secret Service, "Criminal Investigations." http://www.secretservice.gov /criminal.shtml.

United States Secret Service. "Know Your Money." http://www.secretservice.gov /know_your_money.shtml.

University of Nebraska Lincoln, Buffalo Bill Center of the West, The William F. Cody Archive (scholarly digital archive). http://codyarchive.org/life/wfc.bio.00002.html.

U.S. Department of Health & Human Services. "Departments of Justice and Health and Human Services Announce Record-Breaking Recoveries Resulting from Joint Efforts to Combat Health Care Fraud." February 26, 2014.

U.S. Department of Health and Human Services and Department of Justice, Health Care Fraud and Abuse Control Program. "Annual Report for Fiscal Year 2013." February 2014.

U.S. Department of Homeland Security, United States Coast Guard website. "Frequently Asked Questions: Does the Bermuda Triangle Really Exist?" http://www .uscg.mil/history/faqs/triangle.asp.

U.S. Department of State, Bureau of Consular Affairs. "Alert: Adoption Scams and Frauds." April 7, 2014. http://travel.state.gov/content/adoptionsabroad/en/about -us/newsroom/alert-adoption-scams-and-fraud.html.

U.S. Department of State, Bureau of Consular Affairs. "Inheritance and Money Laundering Scams." http://travel.state.gov/content/passports/english/emergencies/scams /inheritances.html.

U.S. Department of State, Bureau of International Narcotics and Law Enforcement Affairs. "Nigerian Advance Fee Fraud." April, 1997. http://www.state.gov/documents /organization/2189.pdf.

U.S. News and World Report website. "How Frank Abagnale Would Swindle You." May 19, 2008, http://money.usnews.com/money/blogs/the-collar/2008/05/19/how -frank-abagnale-would-swindle-you.

U.S. Securities and Exchange Commission, "Affinity Fraud." http://www.sec.gov /investor/pubs/affinity.htm.

U.S. Securities and Exchange Commission. "Investor Alert: Beware of Pyramid Schemes Posing as Multi-Level Marketing Programs." http://www.sec.gov/investor /alerts/ia_pyramid.htm.

U.S. Securities and Exchange Commission. "Pump-and-Dumps and Market Manipulations." http://www.sec.gov/answers/pumpdump.htm.

U.S. Securities and Exchange Commission. "Pyramid Schemes." http://www.sec.gov /answers/pyramid.htm.

U.S. Securities and Exchange Commission. "SEC Enforcement Actions Against Ponzi Schemes." http://www.sec.gov/spotlight/enf-actions-ponzi.shtml.

Village of Amityville, Long Island, New York website. http://amityville.com/.

Watch for Scams website. "Adoption Scam." http://www.watchforscams.com/adoption_scam.html.

WTHR.com. "Woman Sentenced in Adoption Scheme." http://www.wthr.com/story/5453762/woman-sentenced-in-adoption-scheme.

Yahoo.com. "Man Who Chewed on Other's Face Not on 'Bath Salts.'" June 28, 2012. https://nz.finance.yahoo.com/news/man-chewed-others-face-not-bath-salts-084801314.html.

Yahoo.com. "Sharks Do Get Cancer: Tumor Found in Great White." December 5, 2013. https://ca.news.yahoo.com/sharks-cancer-tumor-found-great-white-142906847.html.

Yahoo.com. "Wolf of Wall Street Jordan Belfort Back Making Millions Again." May 20, 2014. https://ca.finance.yahoo.com/blogs/insight/wolf-wall-street-back-sales-game-155916856.html.

MOVIES AND TELEVISION SHOWS

Jenny Abel, Producer, Jeff Hockett, Director, *Abel Raises Cain*. 2005.

Eye Too Productions, History Channel, *Ripped Off: Madoff and the Scamming of America*, 2009.

Mercela Gaviria, Director, *Frontline*, Public Broadcasting Service, "The Madoff Affair," 2009.

Jeff Prosserman, Writer, Director, *Chasing Madoff*, 2011.

Index

About the Author

Nate Hendley is a Toronto-based journalist and author. His previous books for Greenwood/ABC-CLIO include *American Gangsters: Then and Now*, *The Mafia: A Guide to An American Subculture*, and *Bonnie and Clyde: A Biography*. Nate Hendley has a website at www.natehendley.com and can be reached at nhendley@sympatico.ca.